# Zits®

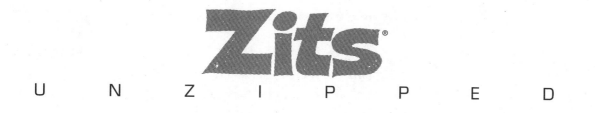

## U N Z I P P E D

**Also by Jerry Scott and Jim Borgman**

*Zits: Sketchbook 1*
*Growth Spurt: Zits Sketchbook 2*
*Don't Roll Your Eyes at Me, Young Man!: Zits Sketchbook 3*
*Are We an "Us?": Zits Sketchbook 4*


*Humongous Zits: A Zits Treasury*
*Big Honkin' Zits: A Zits Treasury*

# Zits®

## UNZIPPED

### SKETCHBOOK NUMBER 5

by JERRY SCOTT and JIM BORGMAN

**Andrews McMeel
Publishing**

Kansas City

**Zits**® is syndicated internationally by King Features Syndicate, Inc. For information, write King Features Syndicate, Inc., 888 Seventh Ave., New York, New York, 10019.

02 03 04 05 06  BAH  10 9 8 7 6 5 4 3 2 1

ISBN: 0-7407-2322-7

Library of Congress Control Number: 2001096507

**Zits**® may be viewed online at:
www.kingfeatures.com

━━━ **ATTENTION: SCHOOLS AND BUSINESSES** ━━━

Andrews McMeel books are available at quantity discounts with bulk purchase for educational, business, or sales promotional use. For information, please write to: Special Sales Department, Andrews McMeel Publishing, 4520 Main Street, Kansas City, Missouri 64111.

To Linda, Howard, and Josh Elson.
—J.B.


For Cady. Welcome to the world, sweetheart.
—J.S.

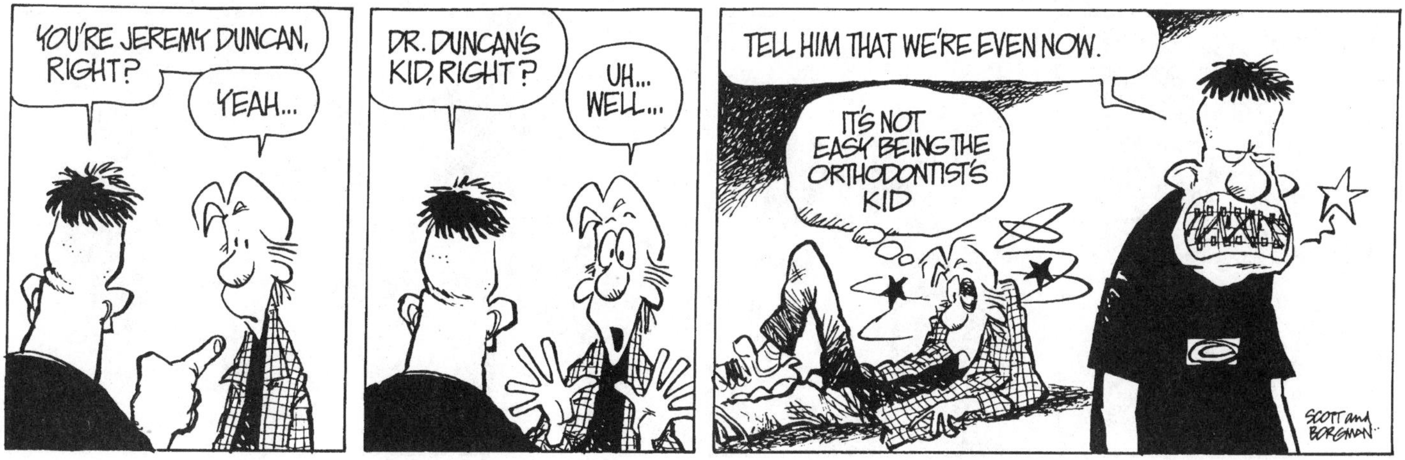
YOU'RE JEREMY DUNCAN, RIGHT?
YEAH...
DR. DUNCAN'S KID, RIGHT?
UH... WELL...
TELL HIM THAT WE'RE EVEN NOW.
IT'S NOT EASY BEING THE ORTHODONTIST'S KID
SCOTT and BORGMAN

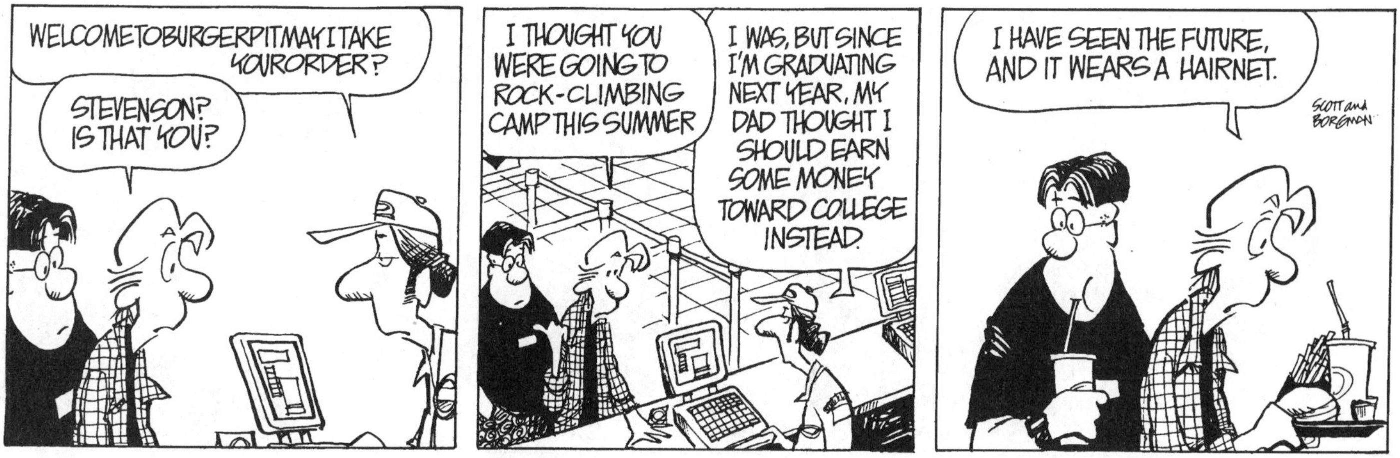
WELCOMETOBURGERPITMAYITAKE YOURORDER?
STEVENSON? IS THAT YOU?
I THOUGHT YOU WERE GOING TO ROCK-CLIMBING CAMP THIS SUMMER
I WAS, BUT SINCE I'M GRADUATING NEXT YEAR, MY DAD THOUGHT I SHOULD EARN SOME MONEY TOWARD COLLEGE INSTEAD.
I HAVE SEEN THE FUTURE, AND IT WEARS A HAIRNET.
SCOTT and BORGMAN

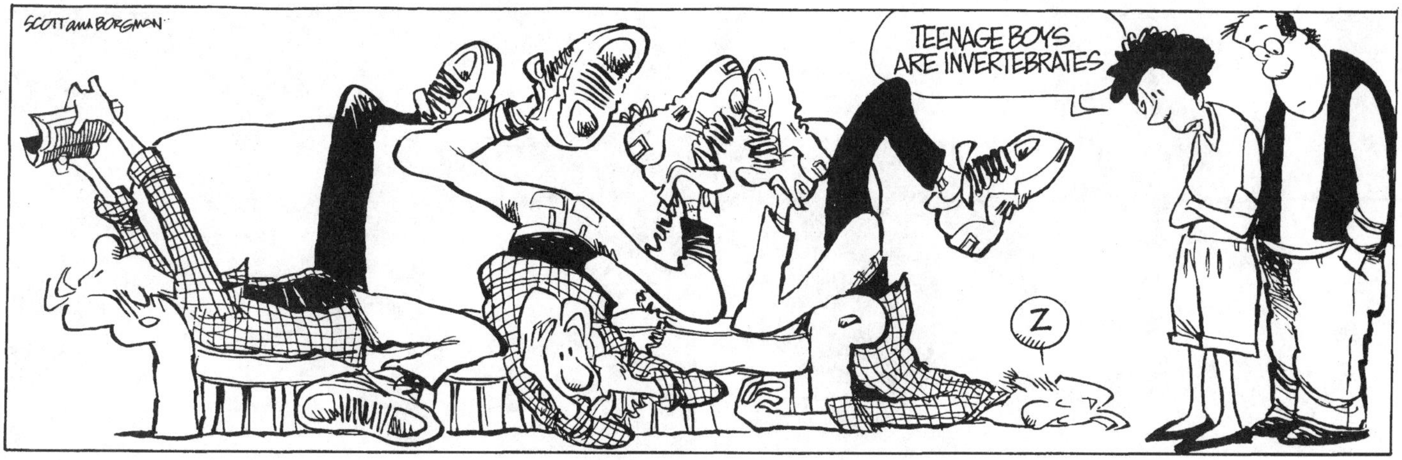
SCOTT and BORGMAN
TEENAGE BOYS ARE INVERTEBRATES
Z

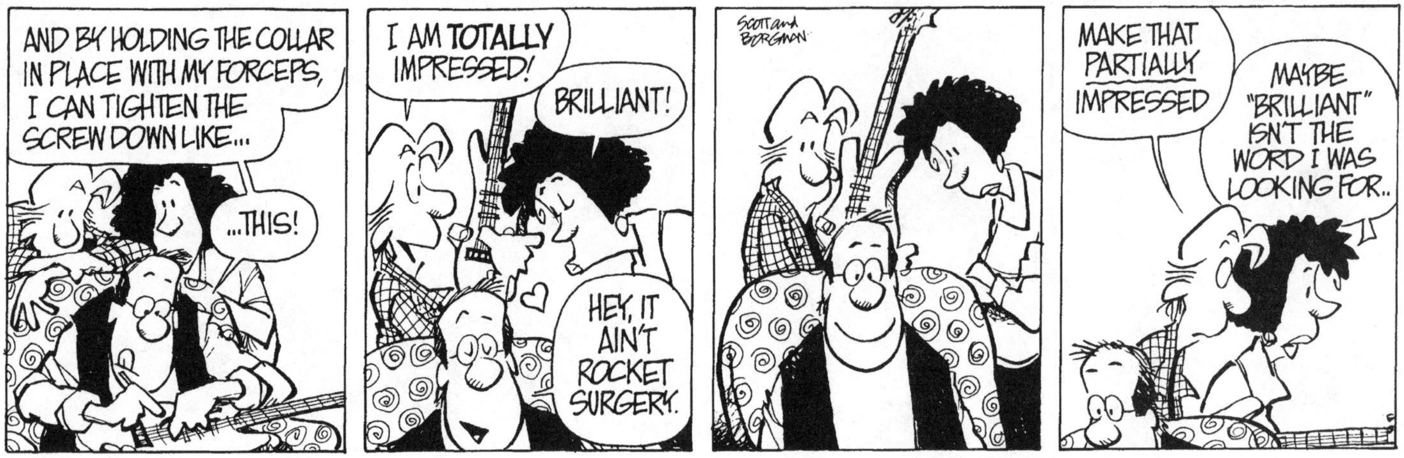
AND BY HOLDING THE COLLAR IN PLACE WITH MY FORCEPS, I CAN TIGHTEN THE SCREW DOWN LIKE...
...THIS!
I AM TOTALLY IMPRESSED!
BRILLIANT!
HEY, IT AIN'T ROCKET SURGERY.
SCOTT and BORGMAN
MAKE THAT PARTIALLY IMPRESSED
MAYBE "BRILLIANT" ISN'T THE WORD I WAS LOOKING FOR..

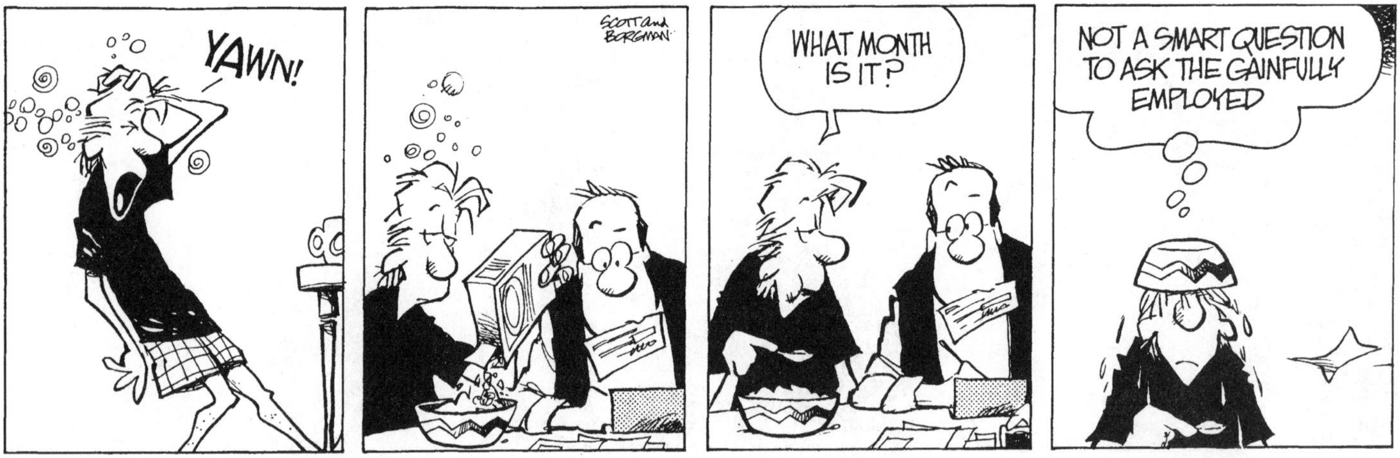
YAWN!
SCOTT and BORGMAN
WHAT MONTH IS IT?
NOT A SMART QUESTION TO ASK THE GAINFULLY EMPLOYED

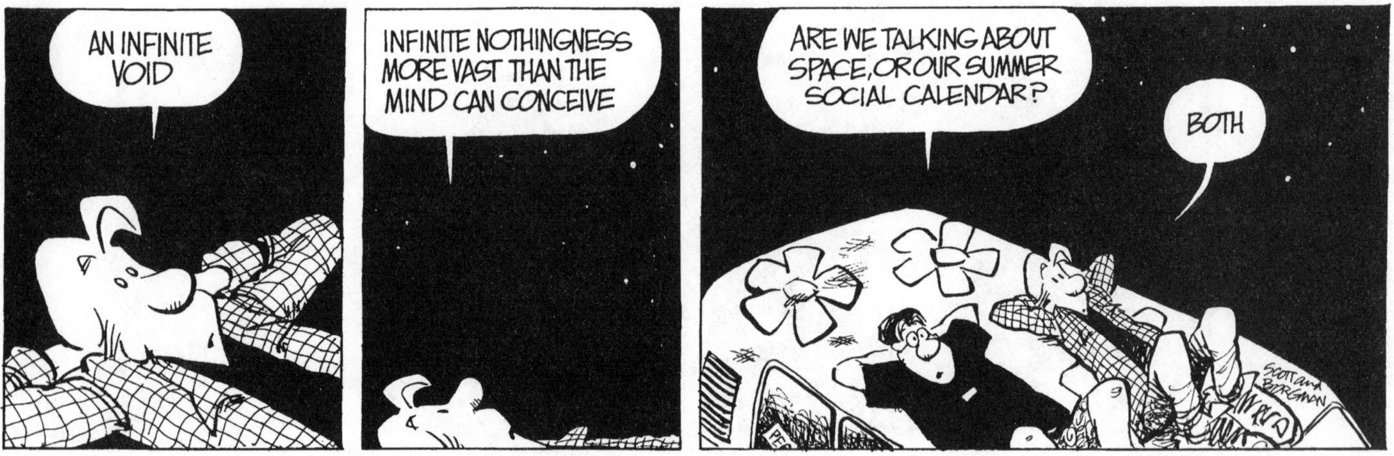
AN INFINITE VOID
INFINITE NOTHINGNESS MORE VAST THAN THE MIND CAN CONCEIVE
ARE WE TALKING ABOUT SPACE, OR OUR SUMMER SOCIAL CALENDAR?
BOTH
SCOTT and BORGMAN

Zits
by JERRY SCOTT and
JIM BORGMAN

PAT! PAT! PAT!
SCOTT and BORGMAN
WHEW!
THATWASGREATIGOTTAGOSEEYOULATER!

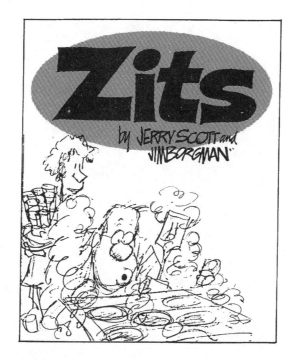

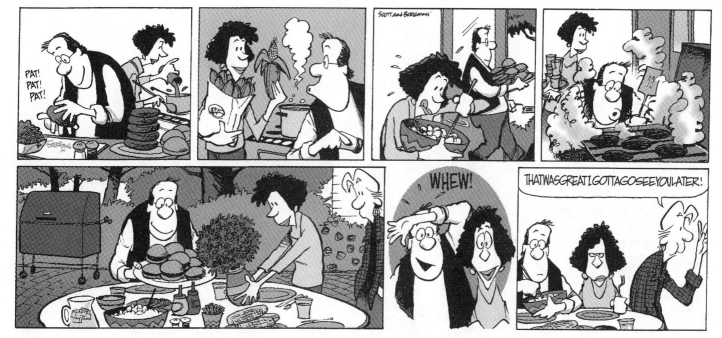

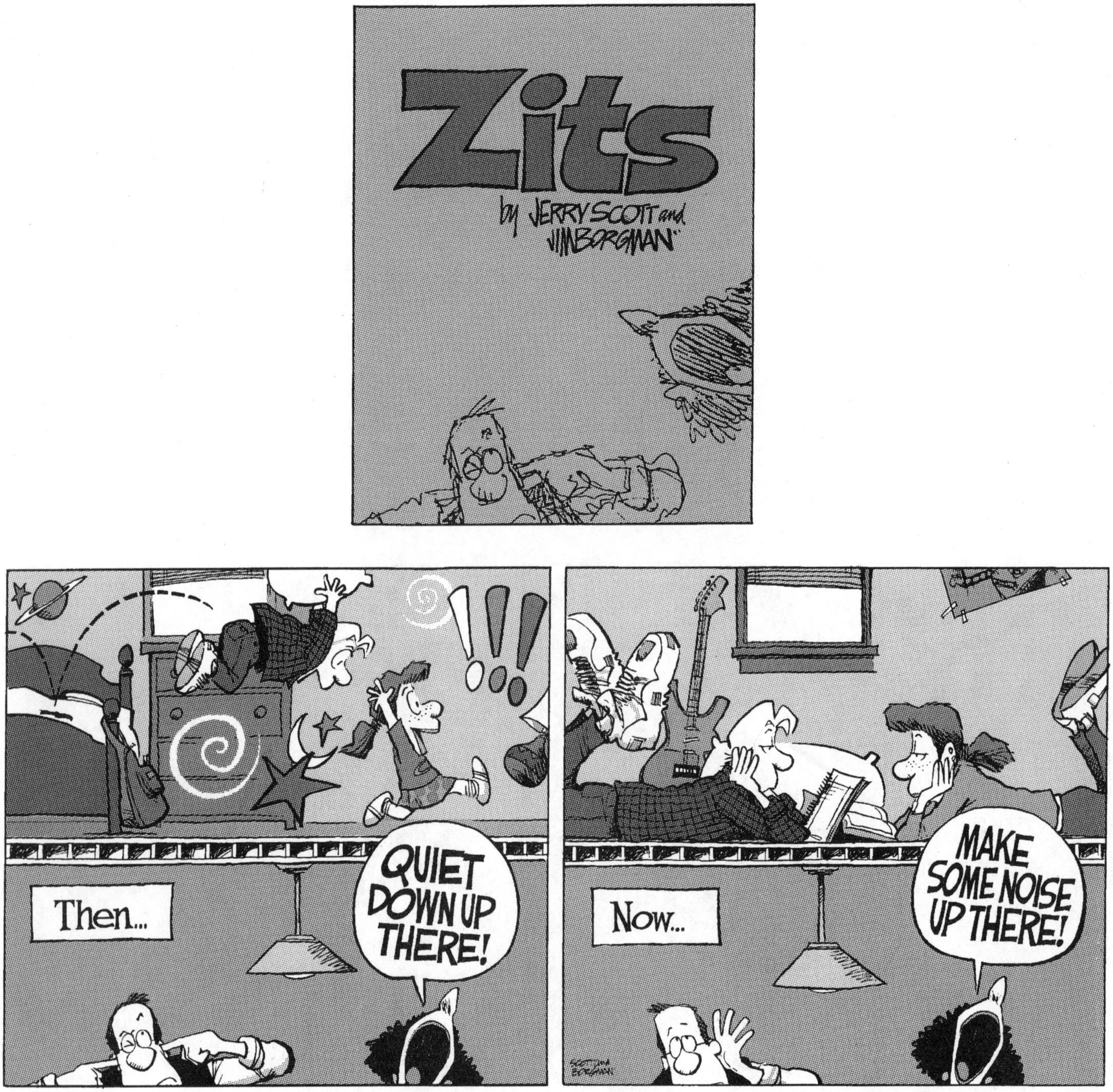
Zits
by JERRY SCOTT and JIM BORGMAN
Then...
QUIET DOWN UP THERE!
Now...
MAKE SOME NOISE UP THERE!

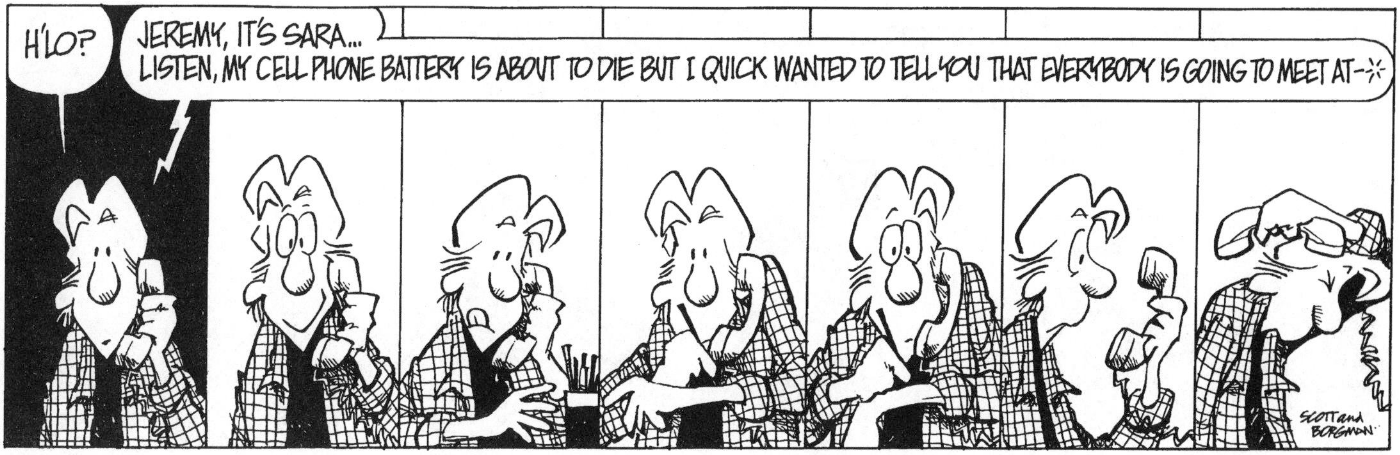
H'LO?
JEREMY, IT'S SARA... LISTEN, MY CELL PHONE BATTERY IS ABOUT TO DIE BUT I QUICK WANTED TO TELL YOU THAT EVERYBODY IS GOING TO MEET AT-
SCOTT and BORGMAN

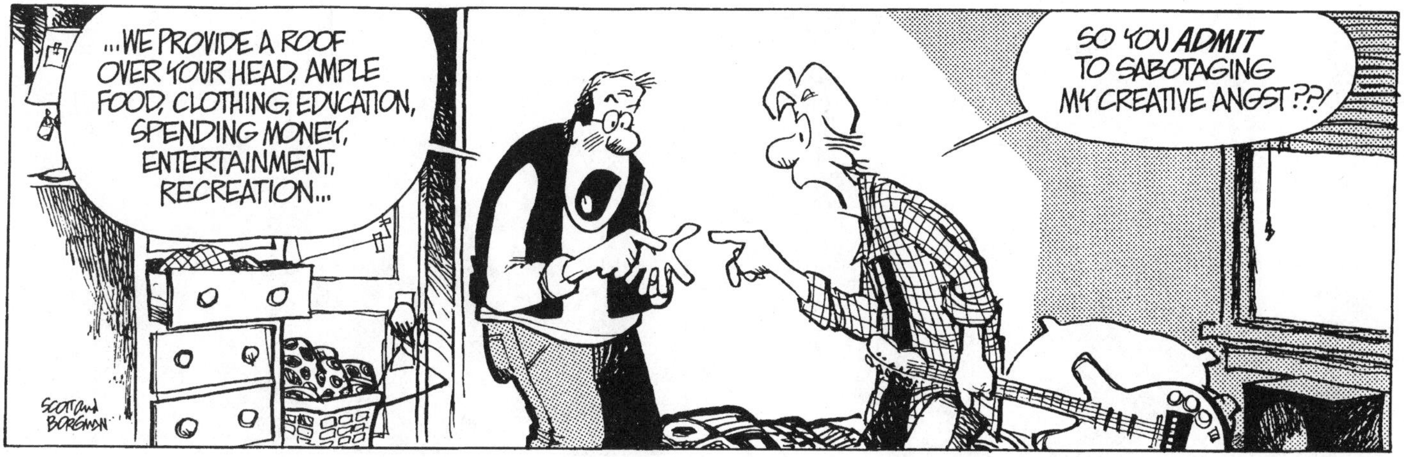
...WE PROVIDE A ROOF OVER YOUR HEAD, AMPLE FOOD, CLOTHING, EDUCATION, SPENDING MONEY, ENTERTAINMENT, RECREATION...
SO YOU ADMIT TO SABOTAGING MY CREATIVE ANGST ??!
SCOTT and BORGMAN

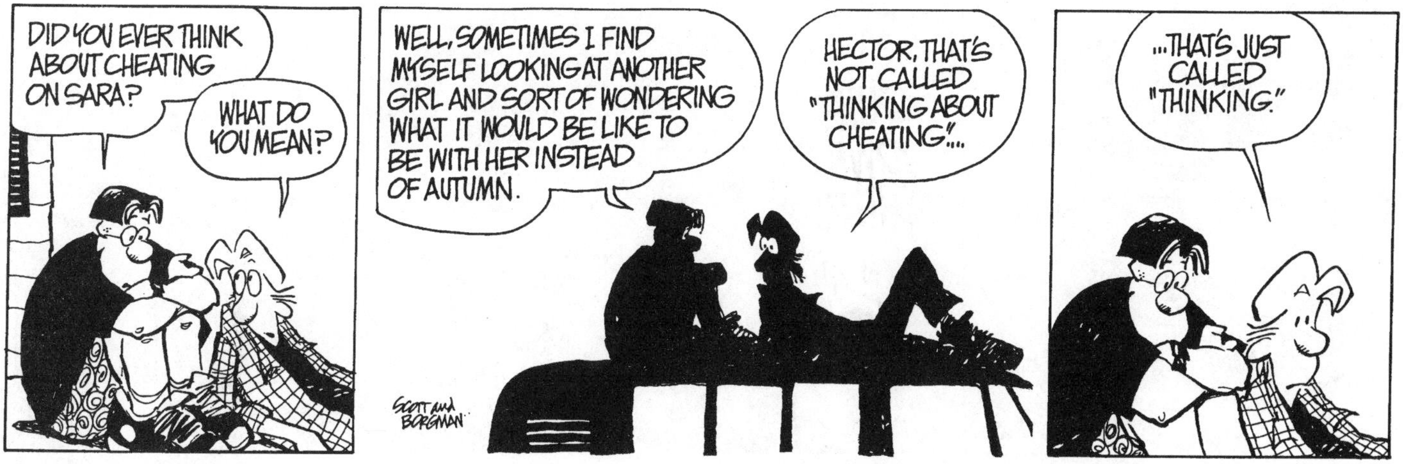
DID YOU EVER THINK ABOUT CHEATING ON SARA?
WHAT DO YOU MEAN?
WELL, SOMETIMES I FIND MYSELF LOOKING AT ANOTHER GIRL AND SORT OF WONDERING WHAT IT WOULD BE LIKE TO BE WITH HER INSTEAD OF AUTUMN.
HECTOR, THAT'S NOT CALLED "THINKING ABOUT CHEATING"...
...THAT'S JUST CALLED "THINKING."
SCOTT and BORGMAN

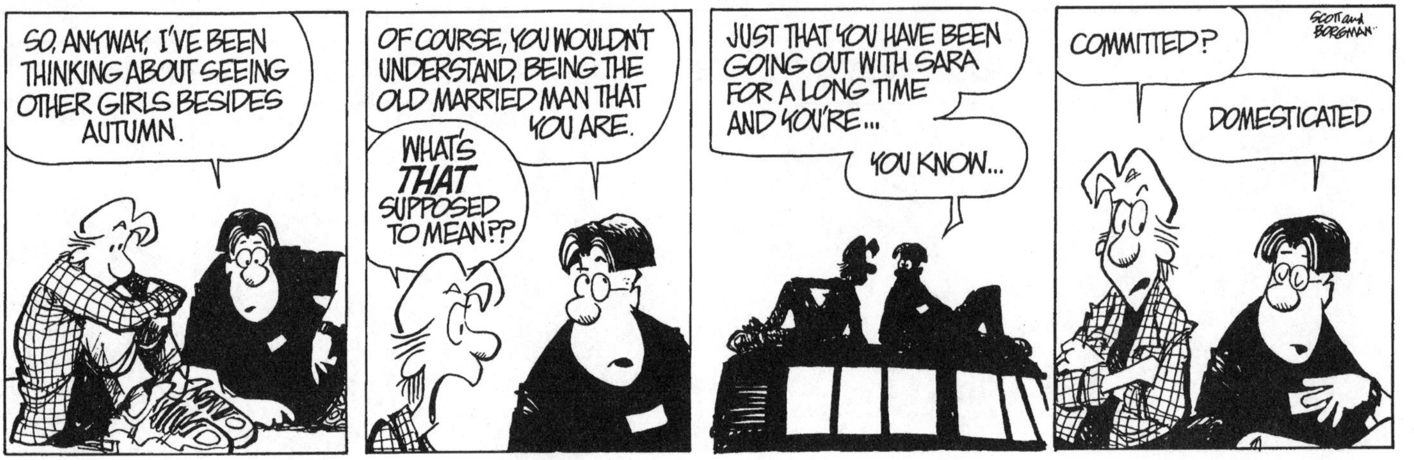
SO, ANYWAY, I'VE BEEN THINKING ABOUT SEEING OTHER GIRLS BESIDES AUTUMN.
OF COURSE, YOU WOULDN'T UNDERSTAND, BEING THE OLD MARRIED MAN THAT YOU ARE.
WHAT'S THAT SUPPOSED TO MEAN?!?
JUST THAT YOU HAVE BEEN GOING OUT WITH SARA FOR A LONG TIME AND YOU'RE...
YOU KNOW...
COMMITTED?
DOMESTICATED
SCOTT and BORGMAN

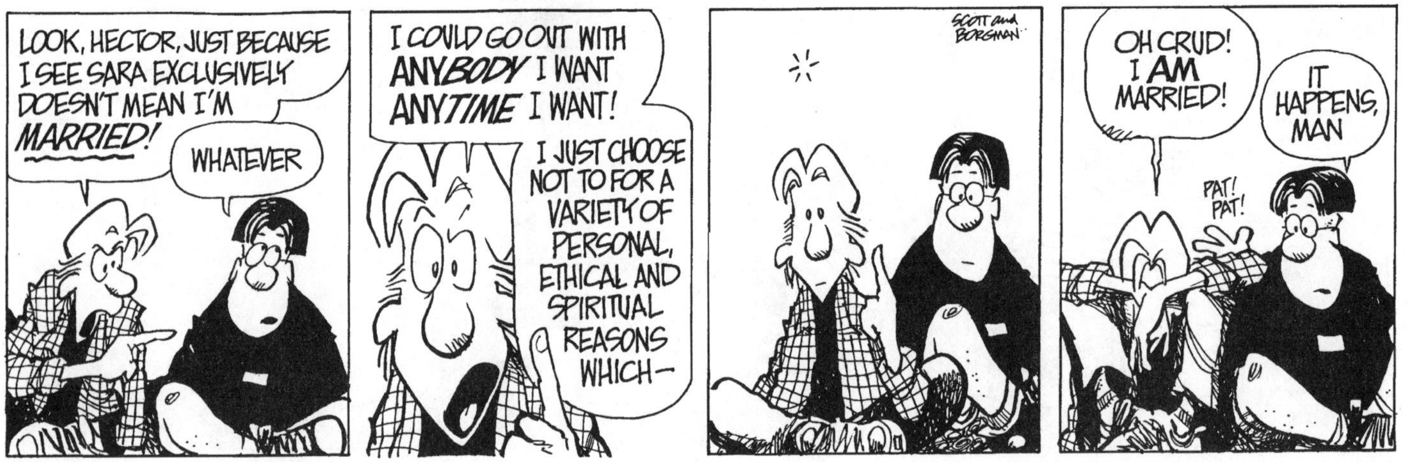
LOOK, HECTOR, JUST BECAUSE I SEE SARA EXCLUSIVELY DOESN'T MEAN I'M MARRIED!
WHATEVER
I COULD GO OUT WITH ANYBODY I WANT ANYTIME I WANT!
I JUST CHOOSE NOT TO FOR A VARIETY OF PERSONAL, ETHICAL AND SPIRITUAL REASONS WHICH—
SCOTT and BORGMAN
OH CRUD! I AM MARRIED!
IT HAPPENS, MAN
PAT! PAT!

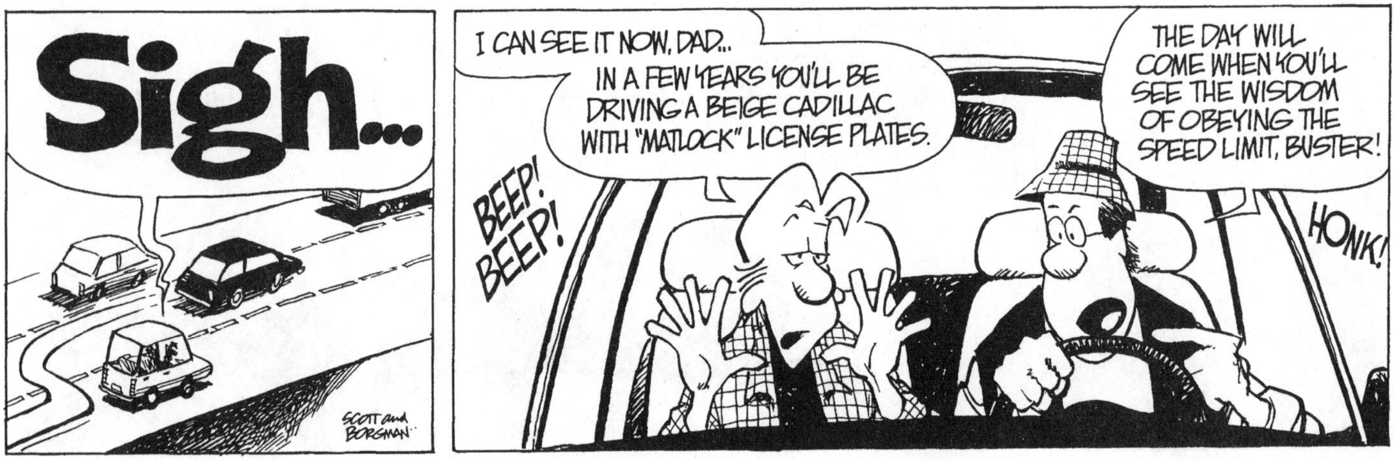
Sigh...
SCOTT and BORGMAN
I CAN SEE IT NOW, DAD...
IN A FEW YEARS YOU'LL BE DRIVING A BEIGE CADILLAC WITH "MATLOCK" LICENSE PLATES.
THE DAY WILL COME WHEN YOU'LL SEE THE WISDOM OF OBEYING THE SPEED LIMIT, BUSTER!
BEEP! BEEP!
HONK!

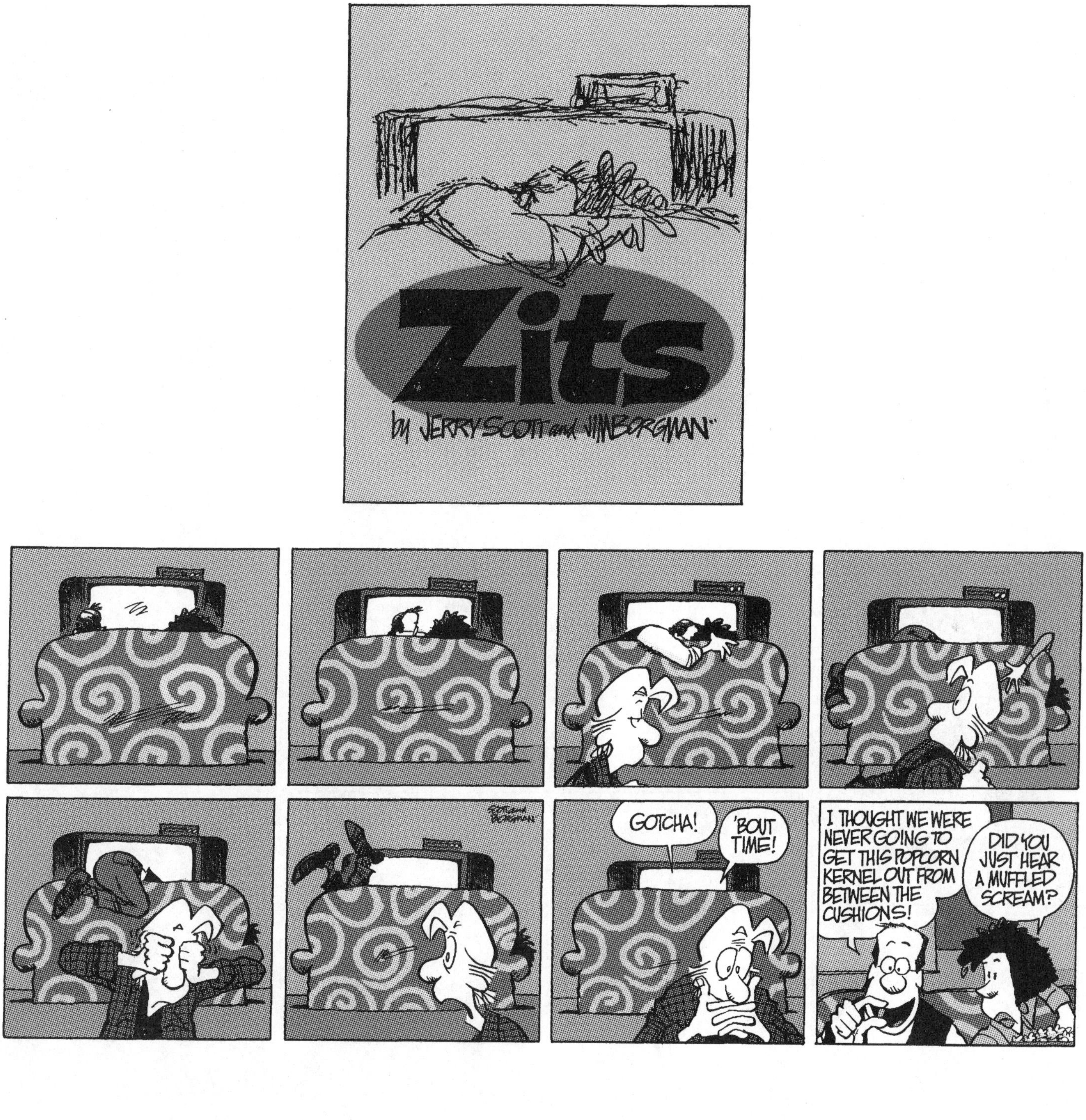
Zits
by JERRY SCOTT and JIM BORGMAN
GOTCHA!
'BOUT TIME!
I THOUGHT WE WERE NEVER GOING TO GET THIS POPCORN KERNEL OUT FROM BETWEEN THE CUSHIONS!
DID YOU JUST HEAR A MUFFLED SCREAM?

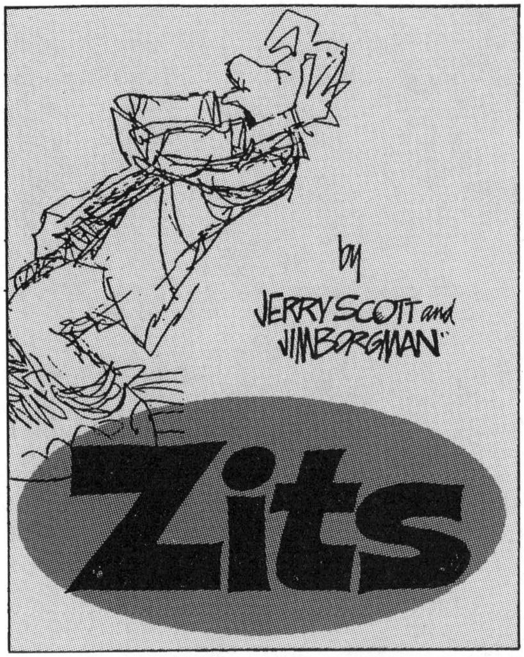
by
JERRY SCOTT and
JIM BORGMAN
Zits

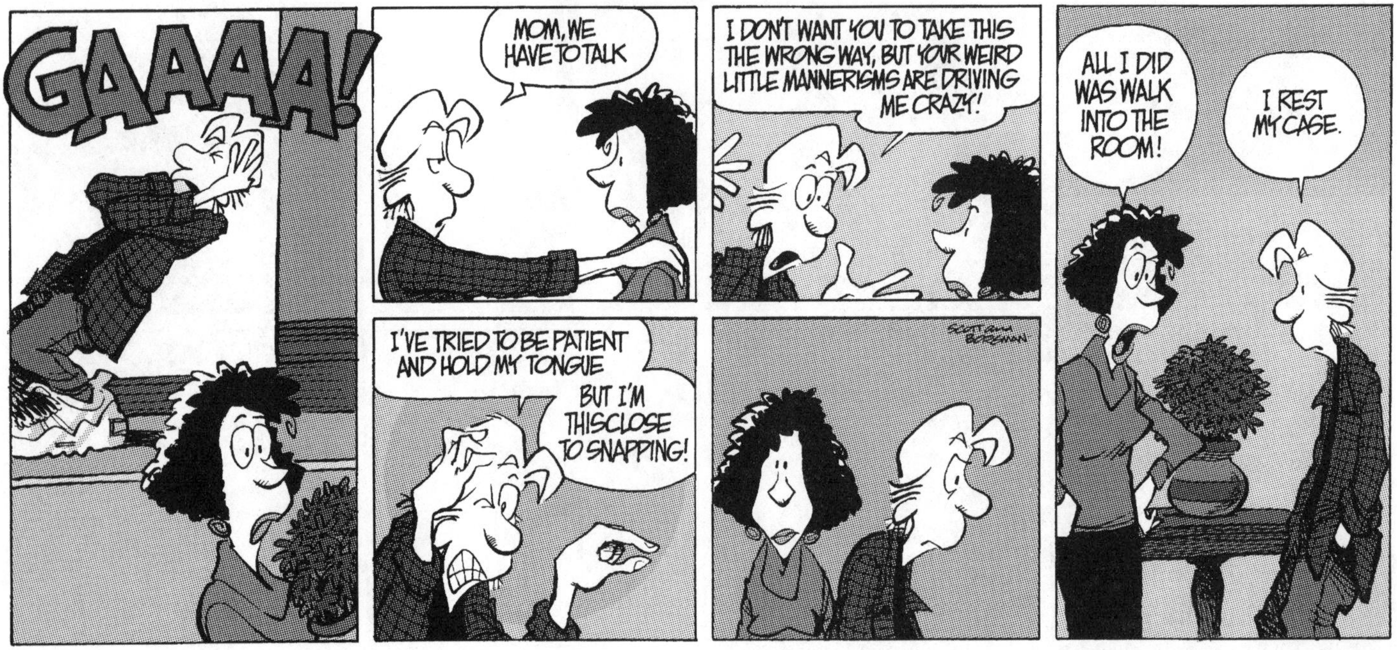
GAAAA!
MOM, WE HAVE TO TALK
I DON'T WANT YOU TO TAKE THIS THE WRONG WAY, BUT YOUR WEIRD LITTLE MANNERISMS ARE DRIVING ME CRAZY!
I'VE TRIED TO BE PATIENT AND HOLD MY TONGUE
BUT I'M THISCLOSE TO SNAPPING!
ALL I DID WAS WALK INTO THE ROOM!
I REST MY CASE.

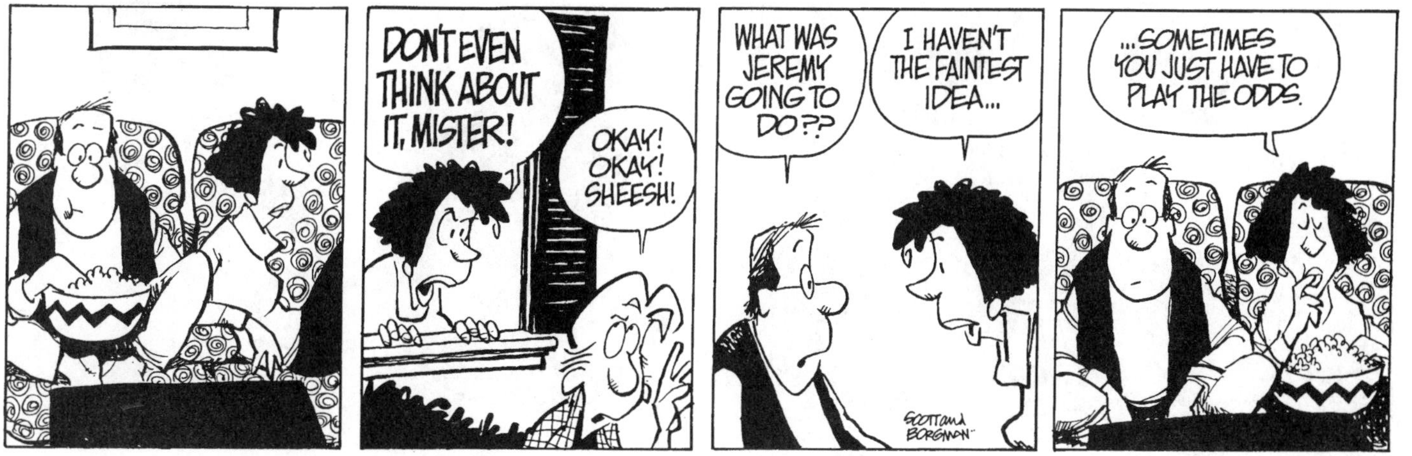

DON'T EVEN THINK ABOUT IT, MISTER!
OKAY! OKAY! SHEESH!
WHAT WAS JEREMY GOING TO DO??
I HAVEN'T THE FAINTEST IDEA...
SCOTT and BORGMAN
...SOMETIMES YOU JUST HAVE TO PLAY THE ODDS.


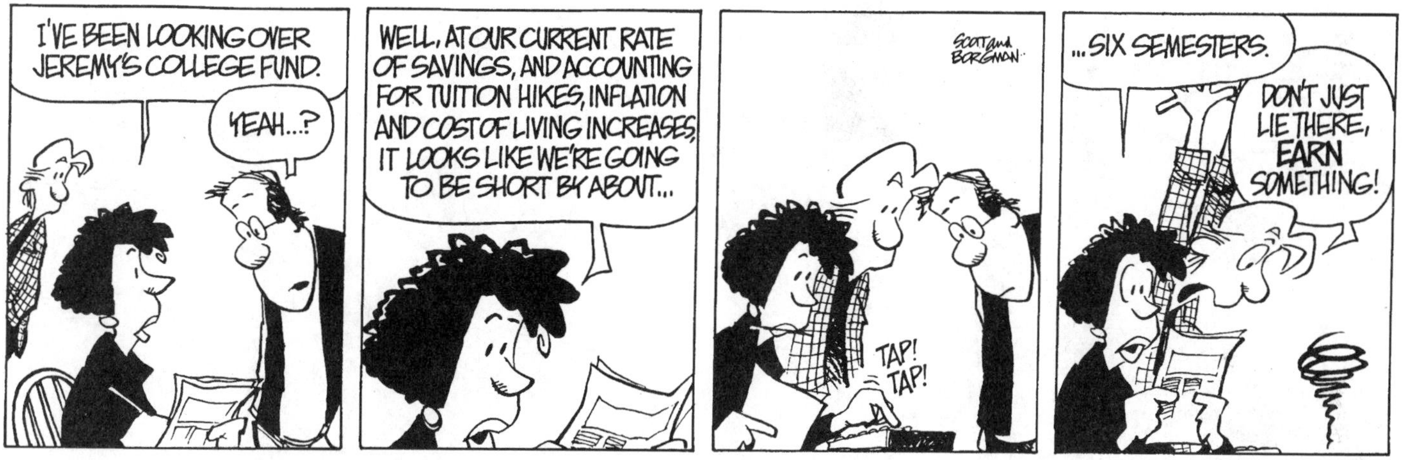

I'VE BEEN LOOKING OVER JEREMY'S COLLEGE FUND.
YEAH...?
WELL, AT OUR CURRENT RATE OF SAVINGS, AND ACCOUNTING FOR TUITION HIKES, INFLATION AND COST OF LIVING INCREASES, IT LOOKS LIKE WE'RE GOING TO BE SHORT BY ABOUT...
SCOTT and BORGMAN
TAP! TAP!
...SIX SEMESTERS.
DON'T JUST LIE THERE, EARN SOMETHING!


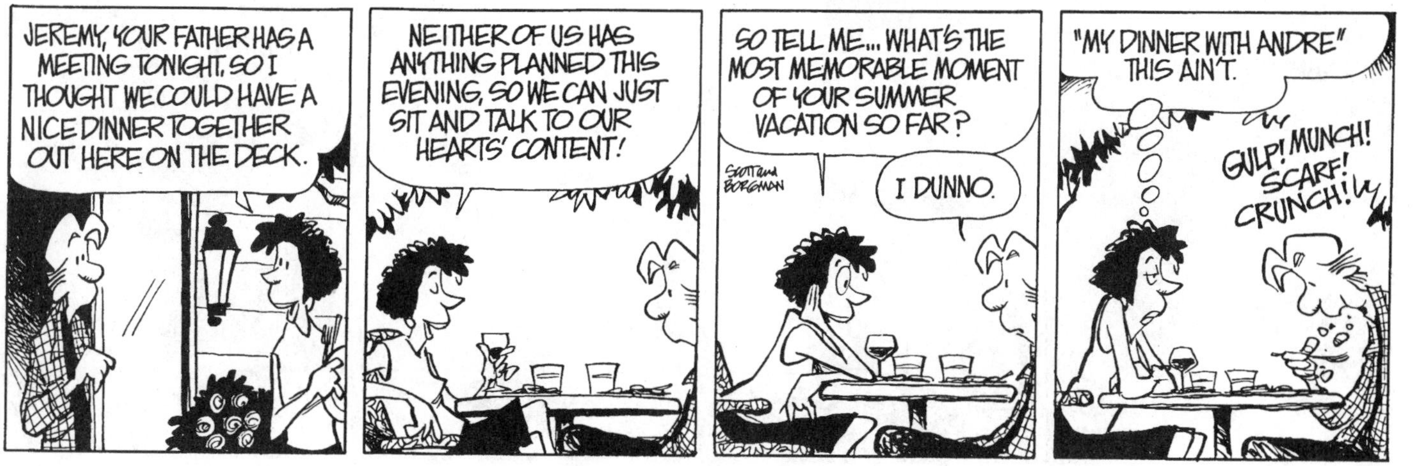

JEREMY, YOUR FATHER HAS A MEETING TONIGHT, SO I THOUGHT WE COULD HAVE A NICE DINNER TOGETHER OUT HERE ON THE DECK.
NEITHER OF US HAS ANYTHING PLANNED THIS EVENING, SO WE CAN JUST SIT AND TALK TO OUR HEARTS' CONTENT!
SO TELL ME... WHAT'S THE MOST MEMORABLE MOMENT OF YOUR SUMMER VACATION SO FAR?
SCOTT and BORGMAN
I DUNNO.
"MY DINNER WITH ANDRE" THIS AIN'T.
GULP! MUNCH! SCARF! CRUNCH!

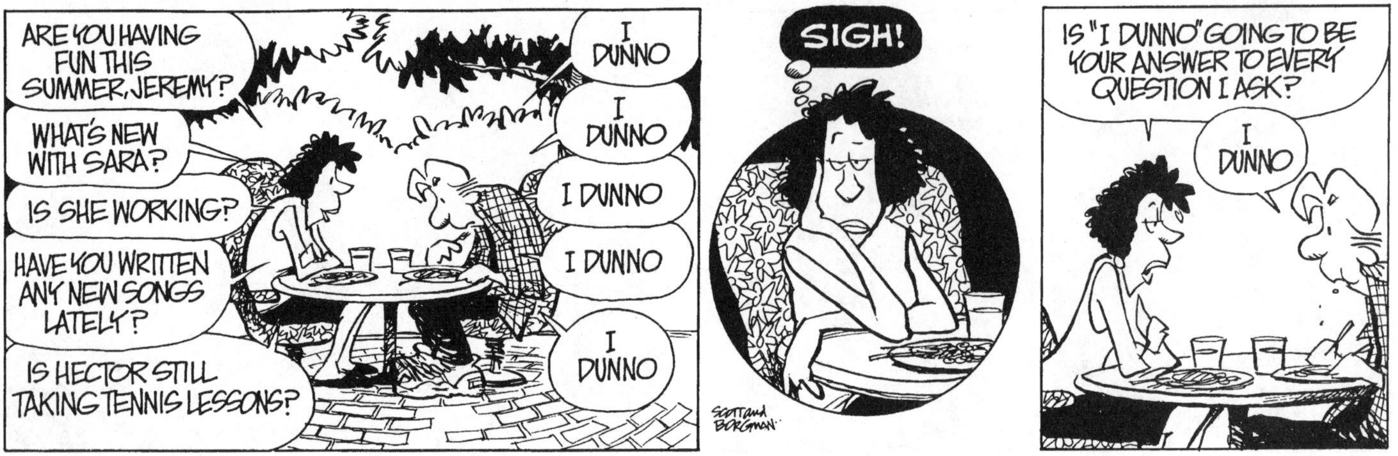
ARE YOU HAVING FUN THIS SUMMER, JEREMY?
I DUNNO
WHAT'S NEW WITH SARA?
I DUNNO
IS SHE WORKING?
I DUNNO
HAVE YOU WRITTEN ANY NEW SONGS LATELY?
I DUNNO
IS HECTOR STILL TAKING TENNIS LESSONS?
I DUNNO
SIGH!
SCOTT and BORGMAN
IS "I DUNNO" GOING TO BE YOUR ANSWER TO EVERY QUESTION I ASK?
I DUNNO

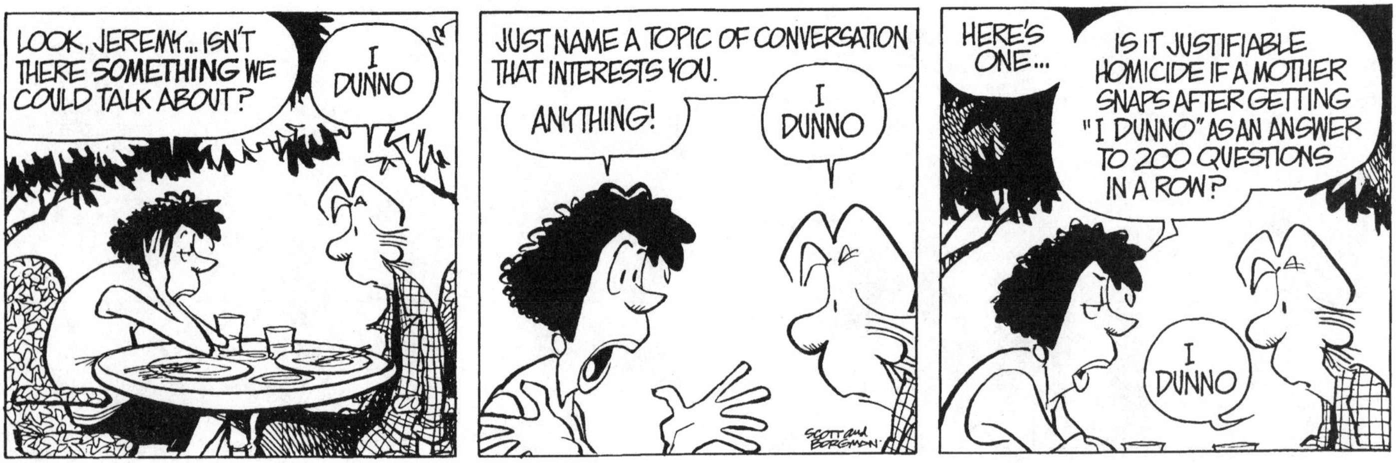
LOOK, JEREMY... ISN'T THERE SOMETHING WE COULD TALK ABOUT?
I DUNNO
JUST NAME A TOPIC OF CONVERSATION THAT INTERESTS YOU.
ANYTHING!
I DUNNO
SCOTT and BORGMAN
HERE'S ONE...
IS IT JUSTIFIABLE HOMICIDE IF A MOTHER SNAPS AFTER GETTING "I DUNNO" AS AN ANSWER TO 200 QUESTIONS IN A ROW?
I DUNNO

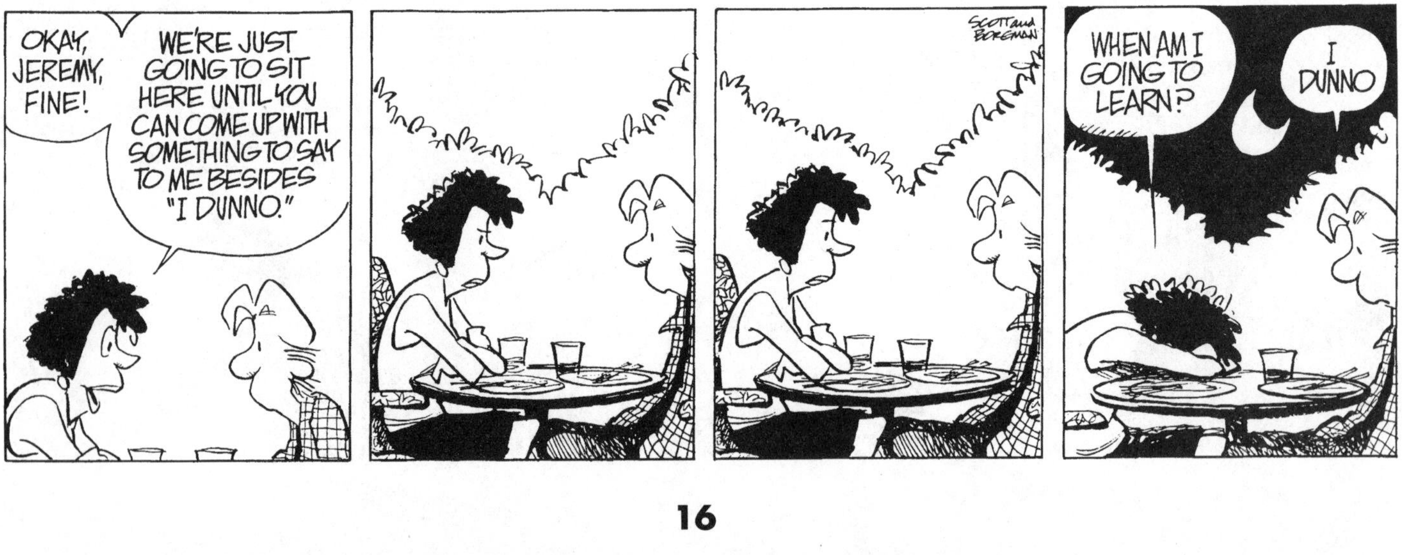
OKAY, JEREMY, FINE!
WE'RE JUST GOING TO SIT HERE UNTIL YOU CAN COME UP WITH SOMETHING TO SAY TO ME BESIDES "I DUNNO."
SCOTT and BORGMAN
WHEN AM I GOING TO LEARN?
I DUNNO

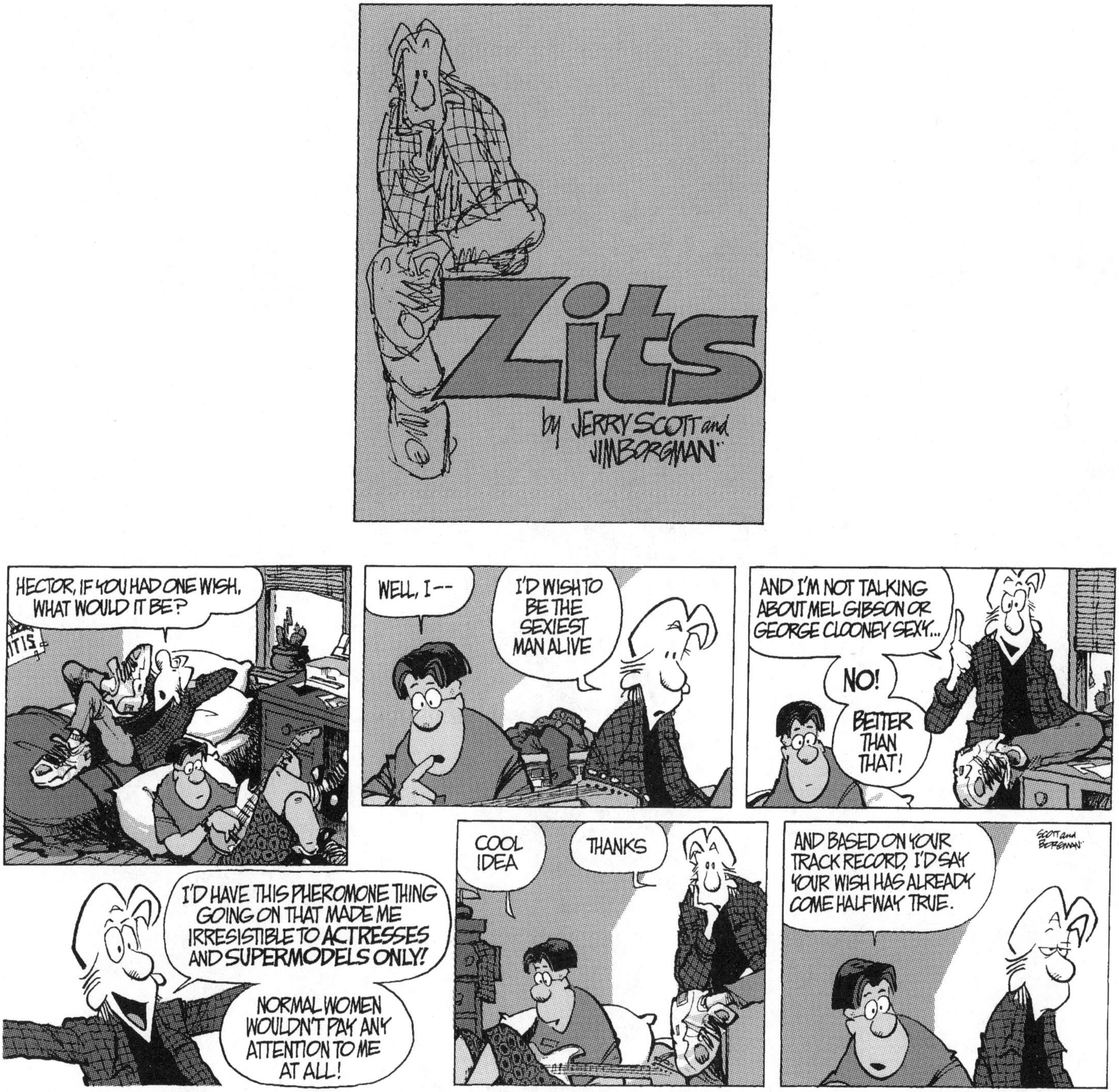
Zits
by JERRY SCOTT and JIM BORGMAN
HECTOR, IF YOU HAD ONE WISH, WHAT WOULD IT BE?
WELL, I--
I'D WISH TO BE THE SEXIEST MAN ALIVE
AND I'M NOT TALKING ABOUT MEL GIBSON OR GEORGE CLOONEY SEXY...
NO!
BETTER THAN THAT!
I'D HAVE THIS PHEROMONE THING GOING ON THAT MADE ME IRRESISTIBLE TO ACTRESSES AND SUPERMODELS ONLY!
NORMAL WOMEN WOULDN'T PAY ANY ATTENTION TO ME AT ALL!
COOL IDEA
THANKS
AND BASED ON YOUR TRACK RECORD, I'D SAY YOUR WISH HAS ALREADY COME HALFWAY TRUE.
SCOTT and BORGMAN

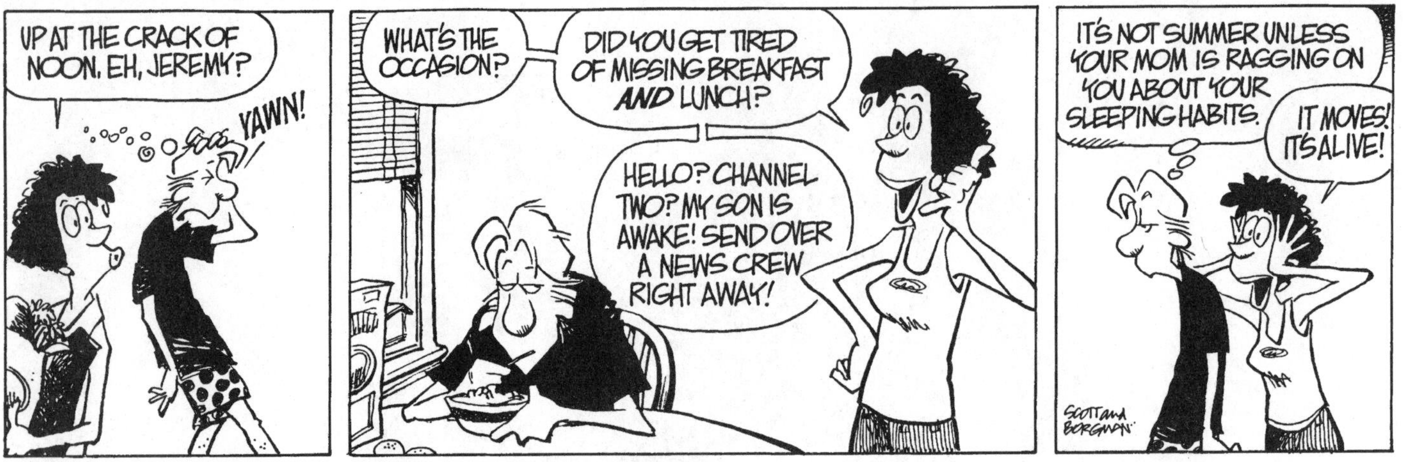
UP AT THE CRACK OF NOON, EH, JEREMY?
YAWN!
WHAT'S THE OCCASION?
DID YOU GET TIRED OF MISSING BREAKFAST **AND** LUNCH?
HELLO? CHANNEL TWO? MY SON IS AWAKE! SEND OVER A NEWS CREW RIGHT AWAY!
IT'S NOT SUMMER UNLESS YOUR MOM IS RAGGING ON YOU ABOUT YOUR SLEEPING HABITS.
IT MOVES! IT'S ALIVE!
SCOTT AND BORGMAN

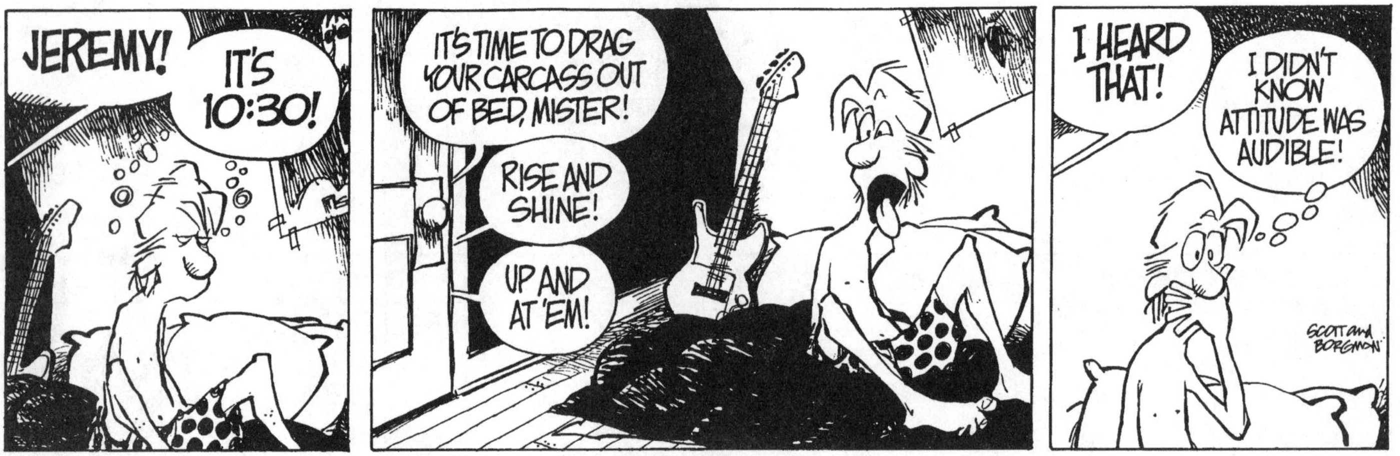
JEREMY!
IT'S 10:30!
IT'S TIME TO DRAG YOUR CARCASS OUT OF BED, MISTER!
RISE AND SHINE!
UP AND AT 'EM!
I HEARD THAT!
I DIDN'T KNOW ATTITUDE WAS AUDIBLE!
SCOTT AND BORGMAN

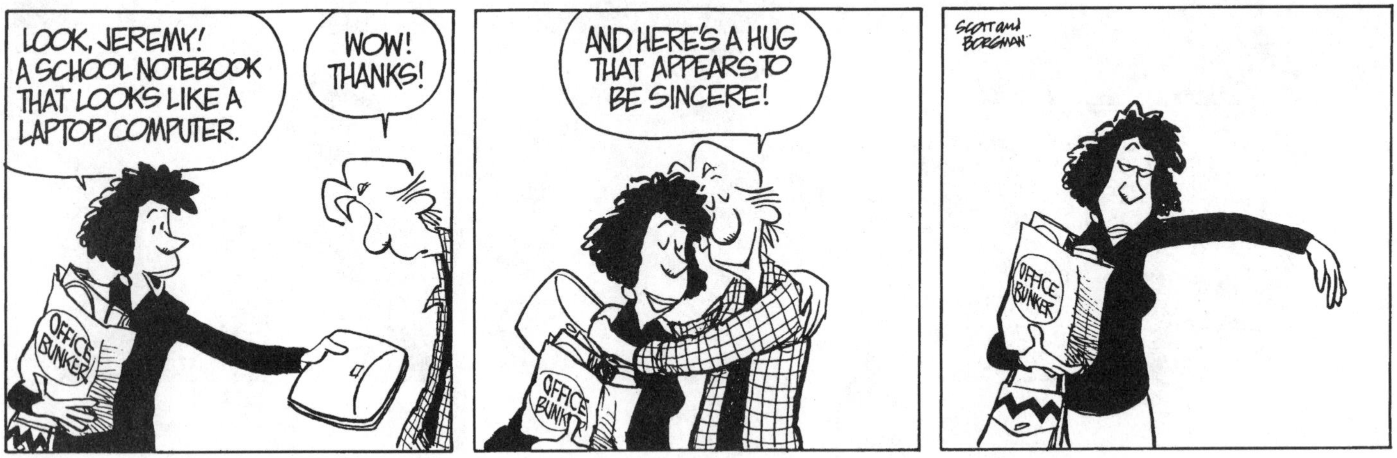
LOOK, JEREMY! A SCHOOL NOTEBOOK THAT LOOKS LIKE A LAPTOP COMPUTER.
WOW! THANKS!
OFFICE BUNKER
AND HERE'S A HUG THAT APPEARS TO BE SINCERE!
SCOTT AND BORGMAN

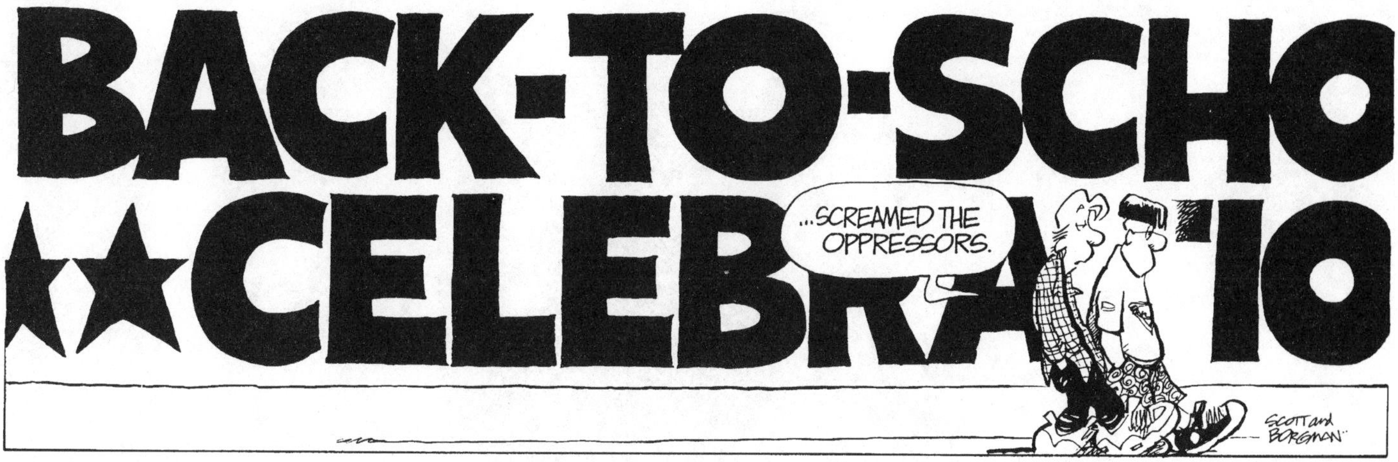
BACK-TO-SCHO
CELEBRA IO
...SCREAMED THE OPPRESSORS.
SCOTT and BORGMAN

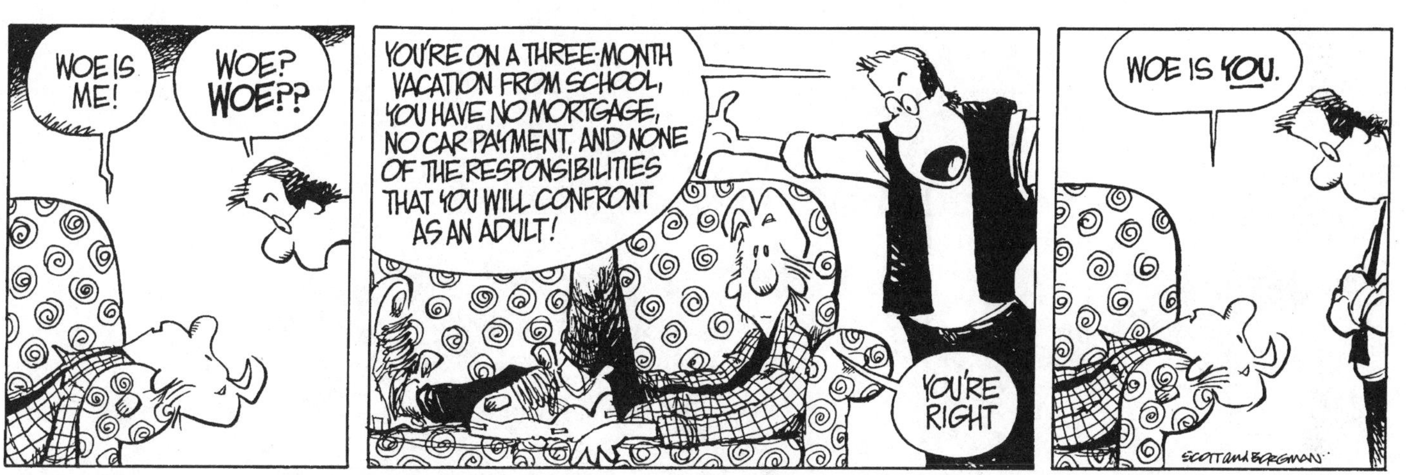
WOE IS ME!
WOE? WOE??
YOU'RE ON A THREE-MONTH VACATION FROM SCHOOL, YOU HAVE NO MORTGAGE, NO CAR PAYMENT, AND NONE OF THE RESPONSIBILITIES THAT YOU WILL CONFRONT AS AN ADULT!
YOU'RE RIGHT
WOE IS YOU.
SCOTT and BORGMAN

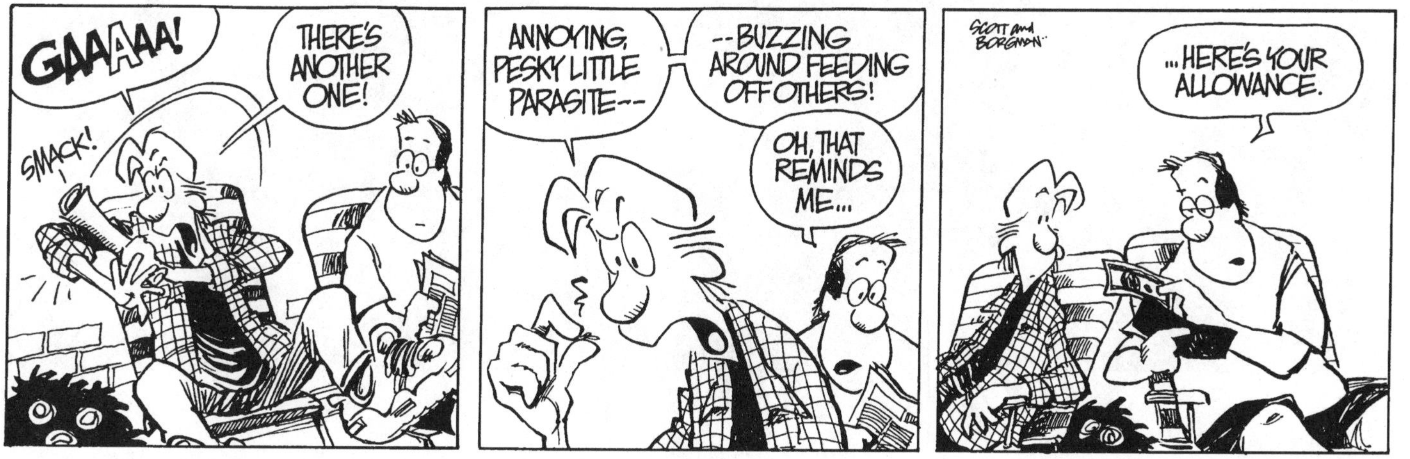
GAAAAA!
THERE'S ANOTHER ONE!
SMACK!
ANNOYING, PESKY LITTLE PARASITE--
--BUZZING AROUND FEEDING OFF OTHERS!
OH, THAT REMINDS ME...
SCOTT and BORGMAN
...HERE'S YOUR ALLOWANCE.

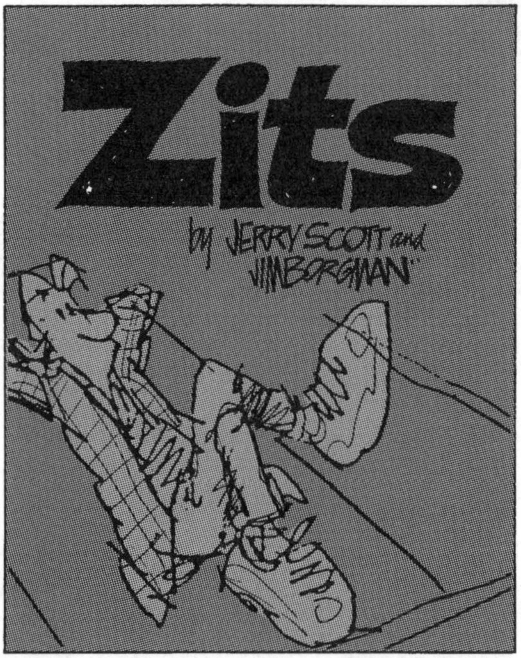
Zits
by JERRY SCOTT and JIM BORGMAN

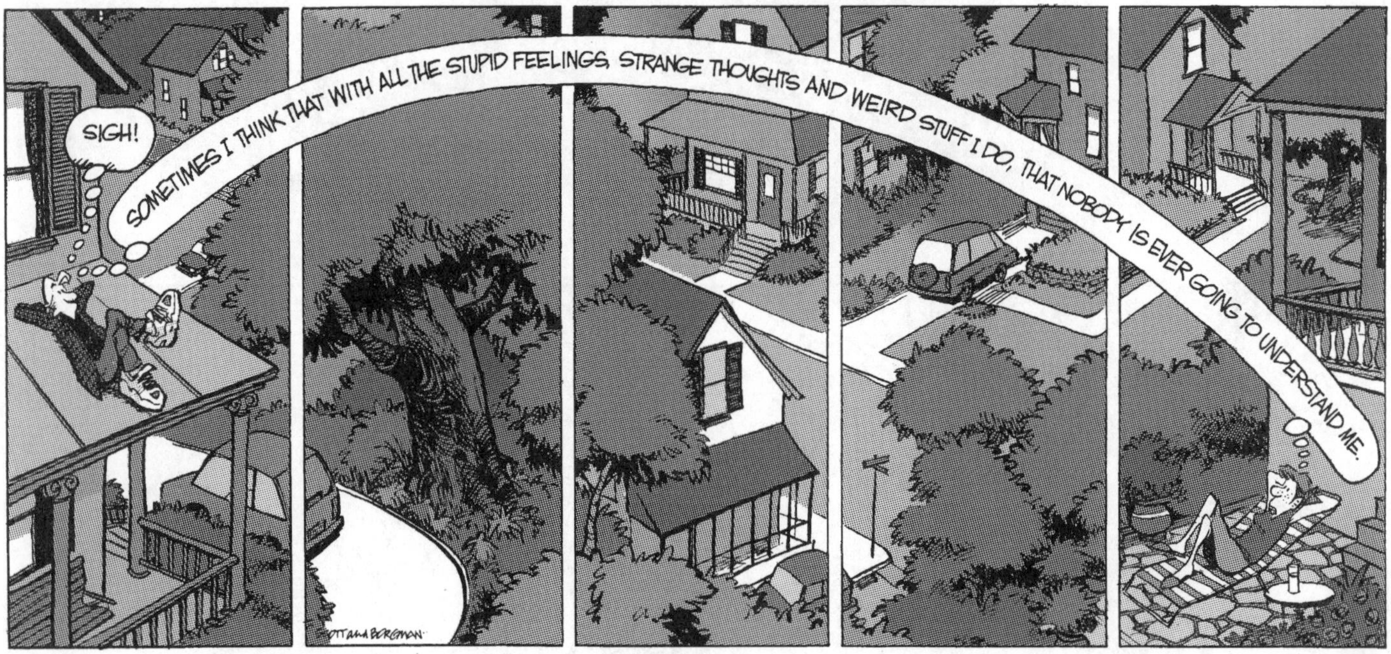
SIGH!
SOMETIMES I THINK THAT WITH ALL THE STUPID FEELINGS, STRANGE THOUGHTS AND WEIRD STUFF I DO, THAT NOBODY IS EVER GOING TO UNDERSTAND ME.

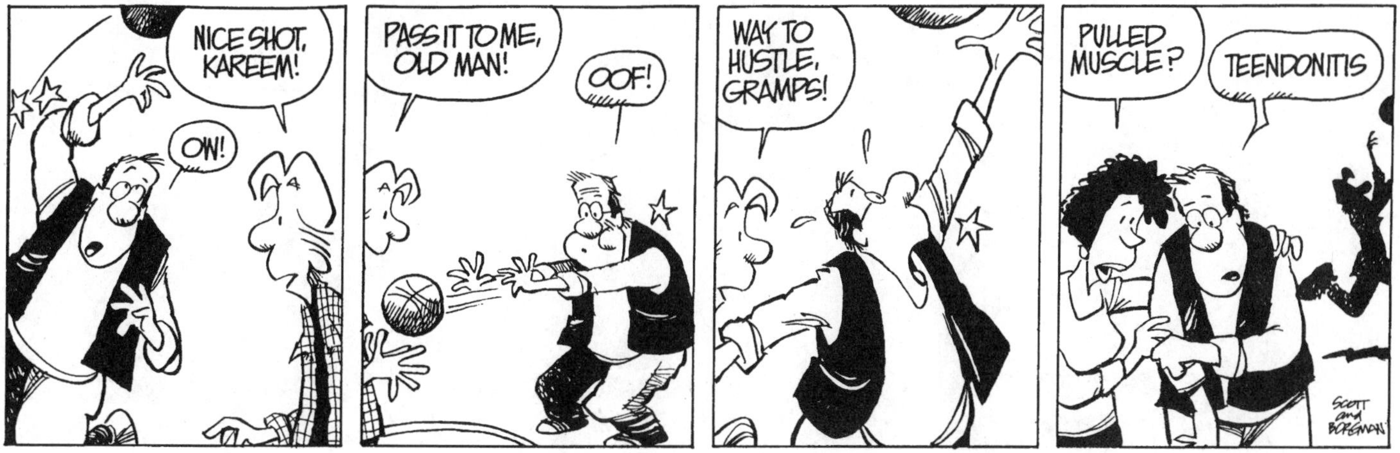
NICE SHOT, KAREEM!
OW!
PASS IT TO ME, OLD MAN!
OOF!
WAY TO HUSTLE, GRAMPS!
PULLED MUSCLE?
TEENDONITIS
SCOTT and BORGMAN

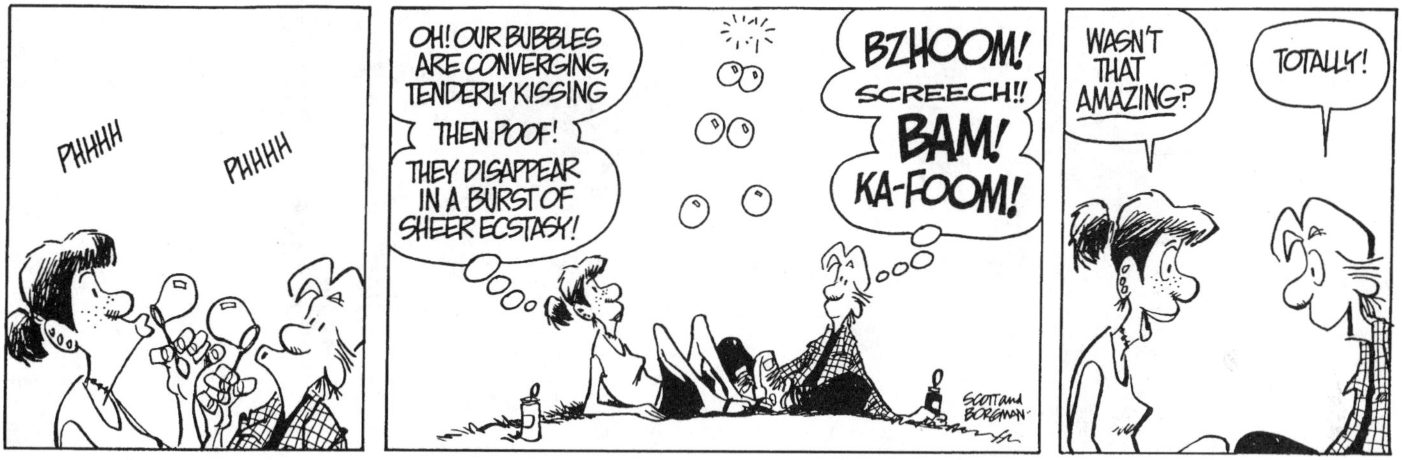
PHHHH
PHHHH
OH! OUR BUBBLES ARE CONVERGING, TENDERLY KISSING
THEN POOF!
THEY DISAPPEAR IN A BURST OF SHEER ECSTASY!
BZHOOM!
SCREECH!!
BAM!
KA-FOOM!
SCOTT and BORGMAN
WASN'T THAT AMAZING?
TOTALLY!

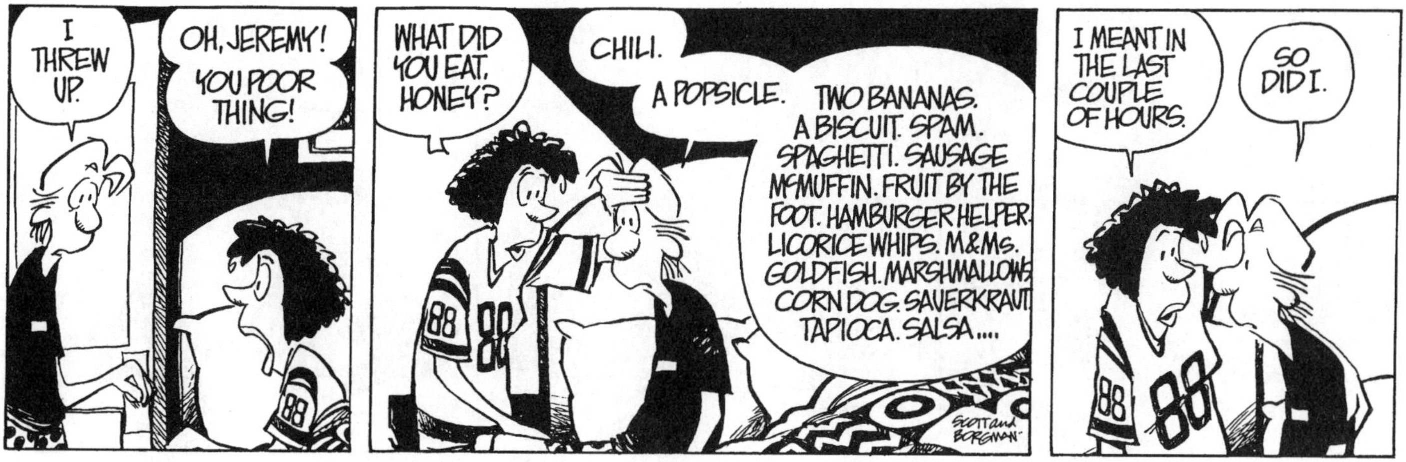
I THREW UP.
OH, JEREMY!
YOU POOR THING!
WHAT DID YOU EAT, HONEY?
CHILI.
A POPSICLE.
TWO BANANAS. A BISCUIT. SPAM. SPAGHETTI. SAUSAGE McMUFFIN. FRUIT BY THE FOOT. HAMBURGER HELPER. LICORICE WHIPS. M&Ms. GOLDFISH. MARSHMALLOWS. CORN DOG. SAUERKRAUT. TAPIOCA. SALSA....
SCOTT and BORGMAN
I MEANT IN THE LAST COUPLE OF HOURS.
SO DID I.

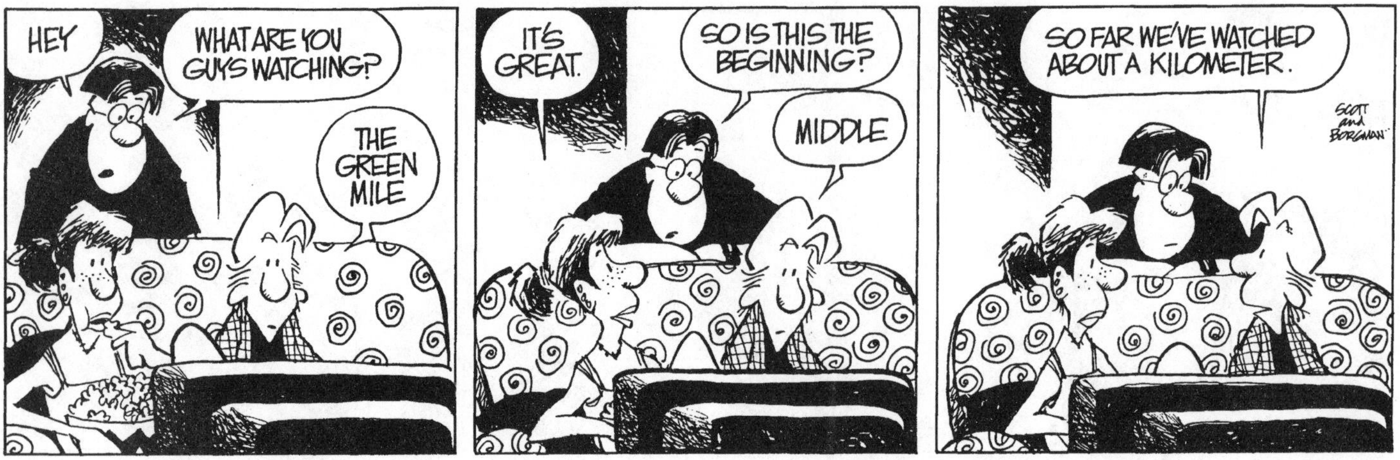
HEY
WHAT ARE YOU GUYS WATCHING?
THE GREEN MILE
IT'S GREAT.
SO IS THIS THE BEGINNING?
MIDDLE
SO FAR WE'VE WATCHED ABOUT A KILOMETER.
SCOTT and BORGMAN

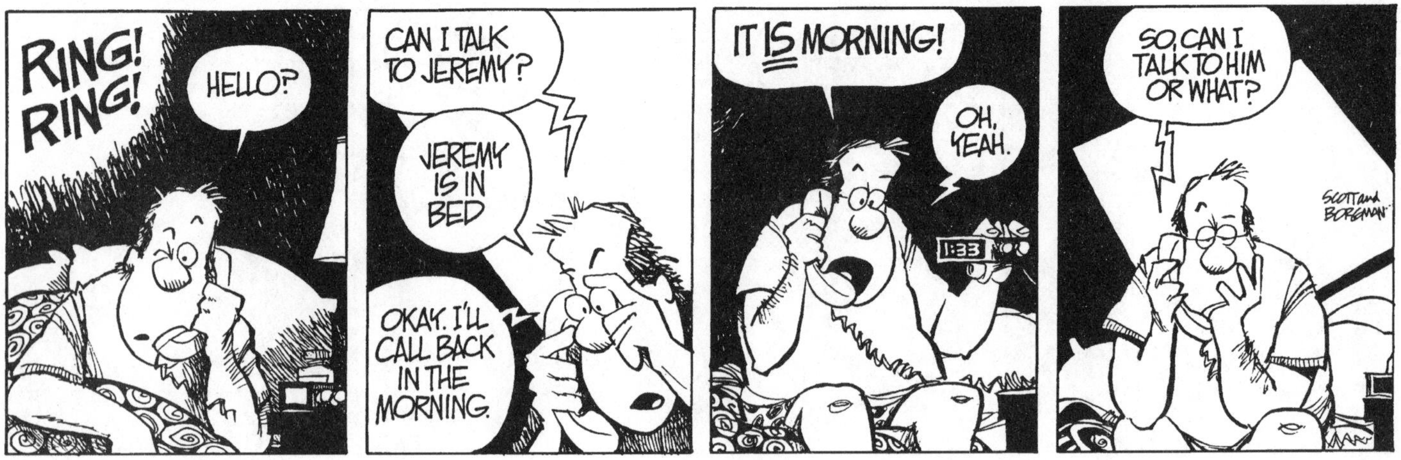
RING! RING!
HELLO?
CAN I TALK TO JEREMY?
JEREMY IS IN BED
OKAY. I'LL CALL BACK IN THE MORNING.
IT IS MORNING!
OH, YEAH.
1:33
SO, CAN I TALK TO HIM OR WHAT?
SCOTT and BORGMAN

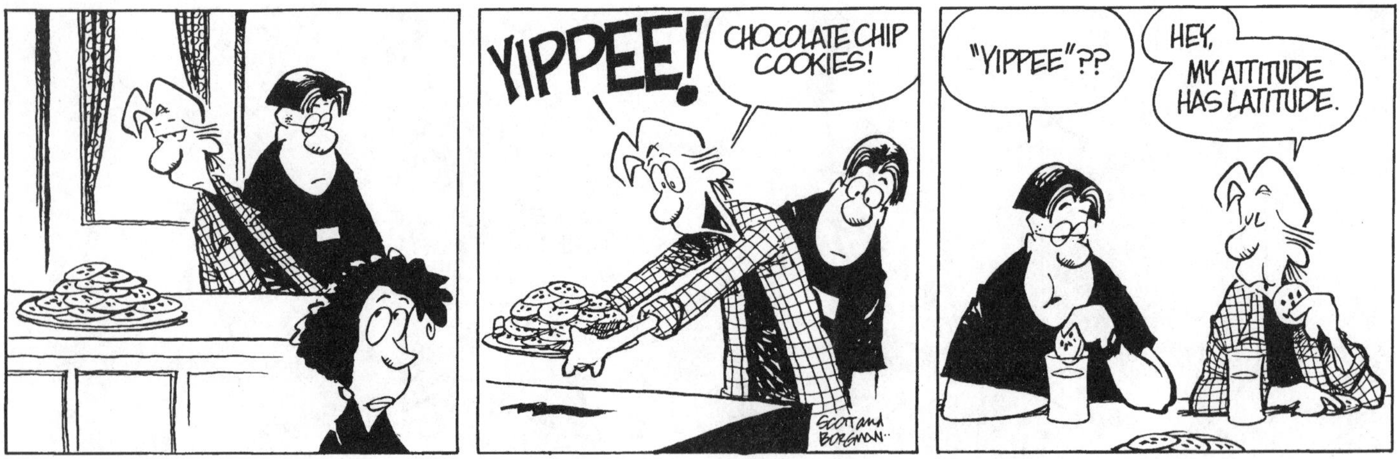
YIPPEE!
CHOCOLATE CHIP COOKIES!
SCOTT and BORGMAN
"YIPPEE"??
HEY, MY ATTITUDE HAS LATITUDE.

Zits
by
JERRY SCOTT and
JIM BORGMAN

JEREMY, CAN YOU COME IN HERE FOR A MINUTE?
YOUR DAD AND I NEED TO GO OUT OF TOWN NEXT WEEKEND.
THE PROBLEM IS THAT THERE WON'T BE ANYTHING FOR YOU TO DO IF YOU COME ALONG WITH US.
SO WE WERE JUST DISCUSSING THE POSSIBILITY OF LETTING YOU STAY HERE BY YOURSELF...
WITH US OUT OF TOWN...
HOURS AWAY, WHERE WE COULDN'T POSSIBLY MONITOR YOUR WHEREABOUTS OR ACTIVITIES FOR
TWO
WHOLE
DAYS.
SURE. I'LL BE FINE.
FORGET IT. HE'S SALIVATING.
TOLD YA

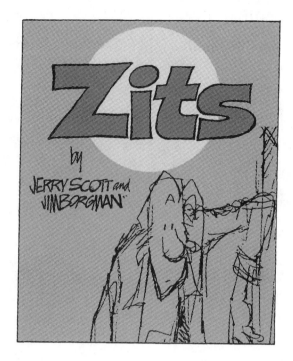

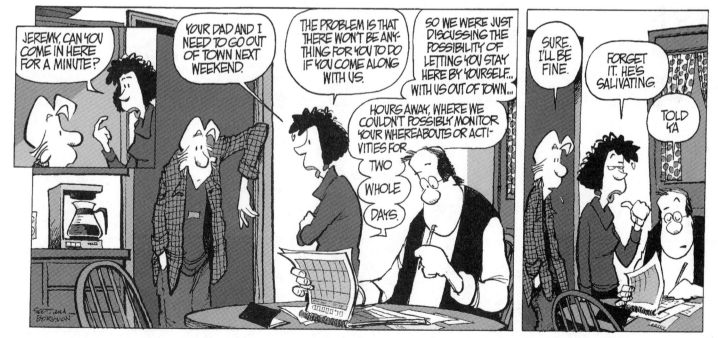

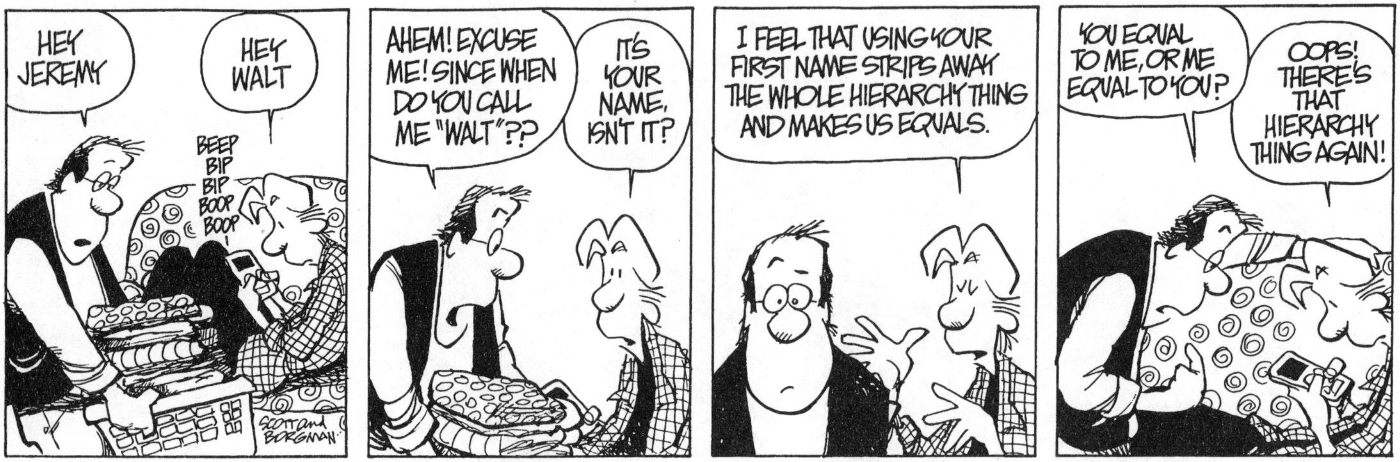
HEY JEREMY
HEY WALT
BEEP BIP BIP BOOP BOOP
SCOTT and BORGMAN
AHEM! EXCUSE ME! SINCE WHEN DO YOU CALL ME "WALT"?!?
IT'S YOUR NAME, ISN'T IT?
I FEEL THAT USING YOUR FIRST NAME STRIPS AWAY THE WHOLE HIERARCHY THING AND MAKES US EQUALS.
YOU EQUAL TO ME, OR ME EQUAL TO YOU?
OOPS! THERE'S THAT HIERARCHY THING AGAIN!

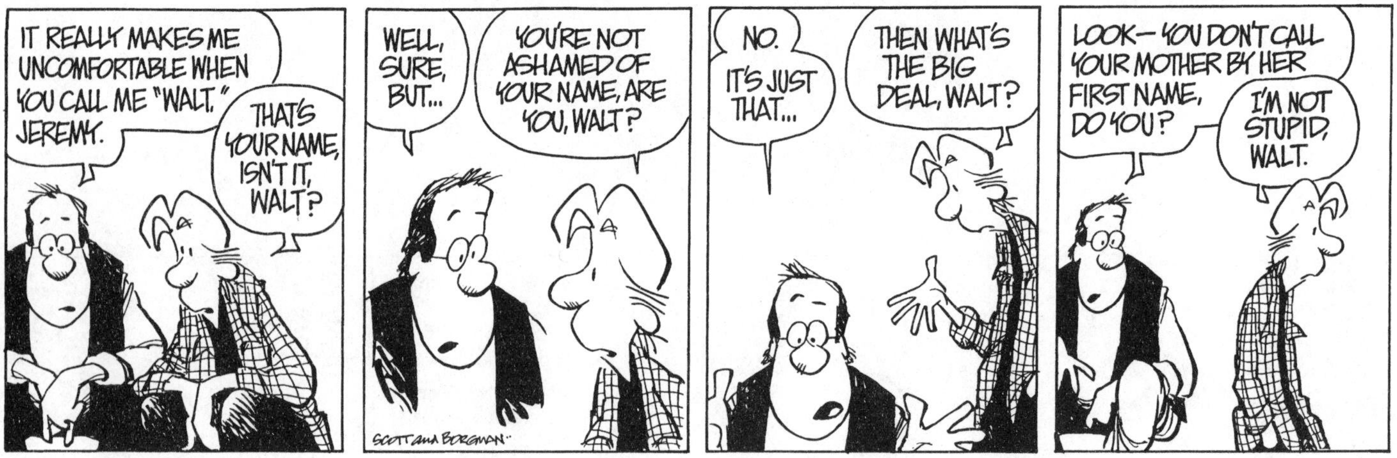
IT REALLY MAKES ME UNCOMFORTABLE WHEN YOU CALL ME "WALT," JEREMY.
THAT'S YOUR NAME, ISN'T IT, WALT?
WELL, SURE, BUT...
YOU'RE NOT ASHAMED OF YOUR NAME, ARE YOU, WALT?
SCOTT and BORGMAN
NO. IT'S JUST THAT...
THEN WHAT'S THE BIG DEAL, WALT?
LOOK— YOU DON'T CALL YOUR MOTHER BY HER FIRST NAME, DO YOU?
I'M NOT STUPID, WALT.

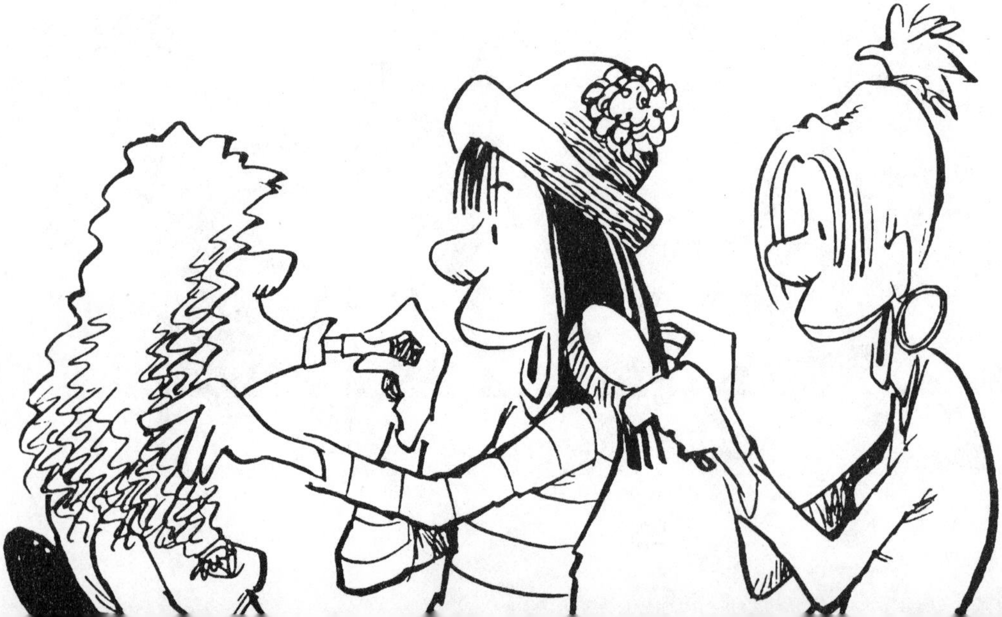

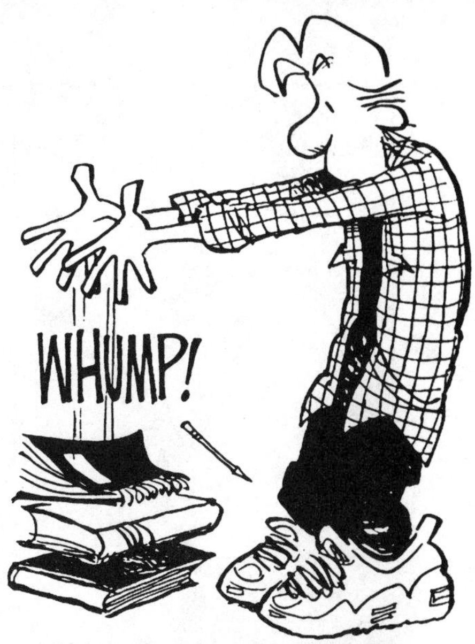
WHUMP!

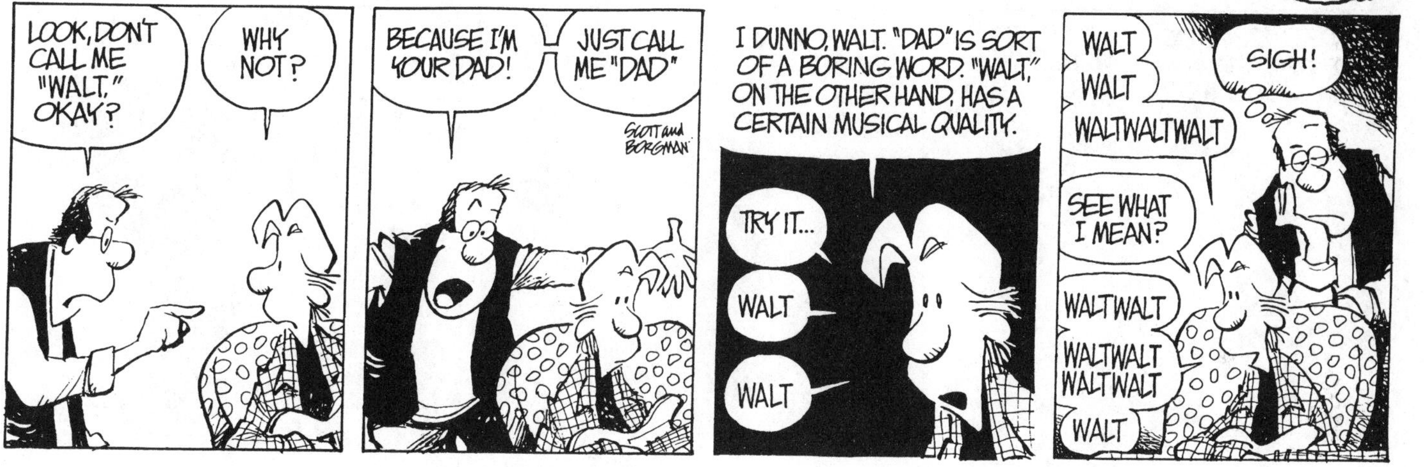
LOOK, DON'T CALL ME "WALT," OKAY?
WHY NOT?
BECAUSE I'M YOUR DAD!
JUST CALL ME "DAD"
SCOTT and BORGMAN
I DUNNO, WALT. "DAD" IS SORT OF A BORING WORD. "WALT," ON THE OTHER HAND, HAS A CERTAIN MUSICAL QUALITY.
TRY IT...
WALT
WALT
WALT
WALT
WALTWALTWALT
SIGH!
SEE WHAT I MEAN?
WALTWALT
WALTWALT WALTWALT WALTWALT
WALT

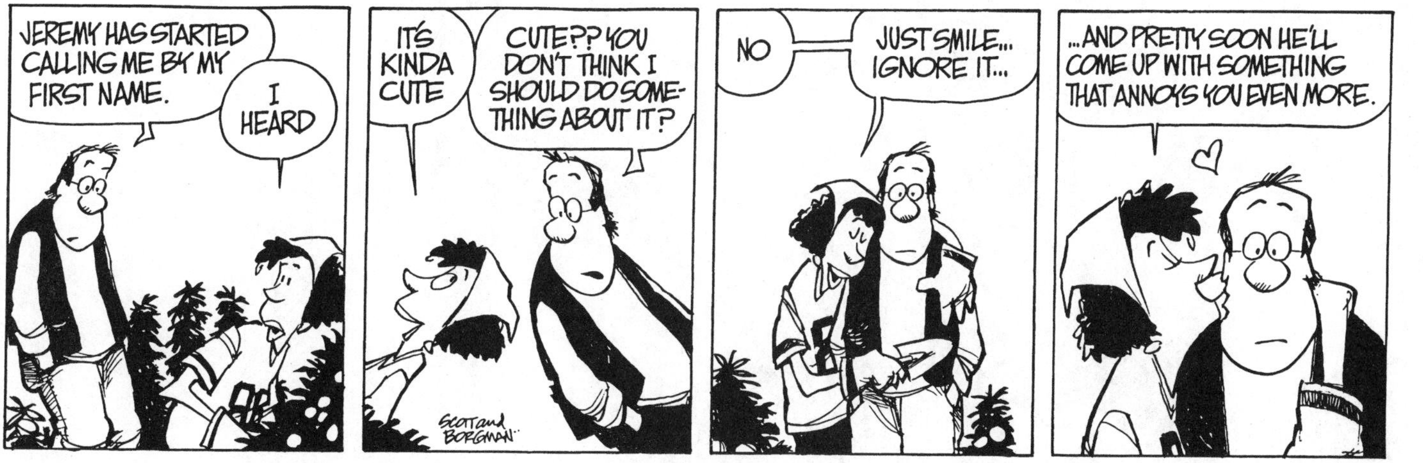
JEREMY HAS STARTED CALLING ME BY MY FIRST NAME.
I HEARD
IT'S KINDA CUTE
CUTE?? YOU DON'T THINK I SHOULD DO SOMETHING ABOUT IT?
SCOTT and BORGMAN
NO
JUST SMILE... IGNORE IT...
...AND PRETTY SOON HE'LL COME UP WITH SOMETHING THAT ANNOYS YOU EVEN MORE.

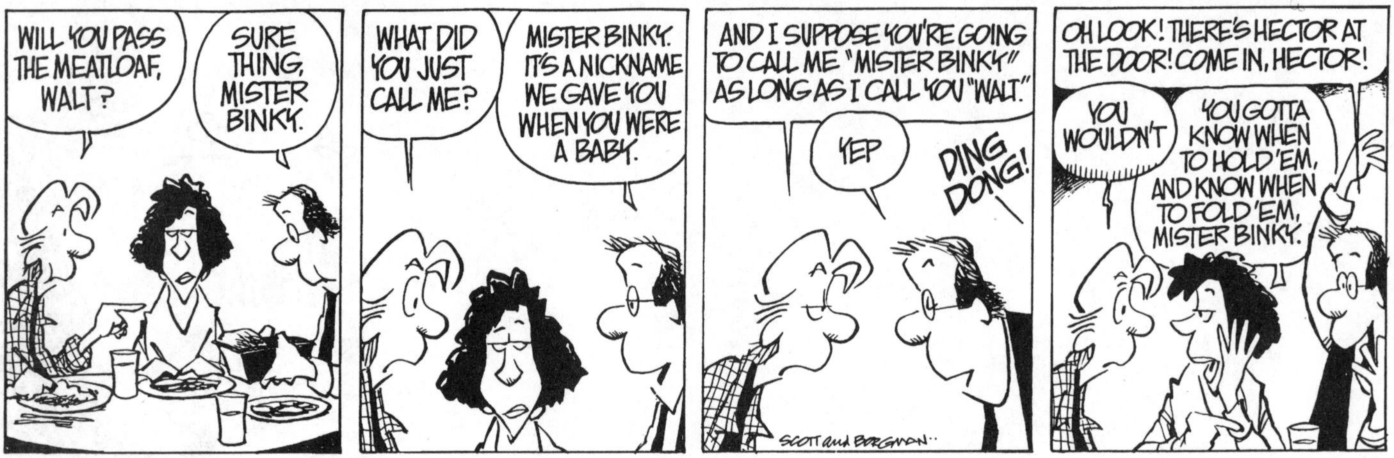
WILL YOU PASS THE MEATLOAF, WALT?
SURE THING, MISTER BINKY.
WHAT DID YOU JUST CALL ME?
MISTER BINKY. IT'S A NICKNAME WE GAVE YOU WHEN YOU WERE A BABY.
AND I SUPPOSE YOU'RE GOING TO CALL ME "MISTER BINKY" AS LONG AS I CALL YOU "WALT."
YEP
DING DONG!
SCOTT and BORGMAN
OH LOOK! THERE'S HECTOR AT THE DOOR! COME IN, HECTOR!
YOU WOULDN'T
YOU GOTTA KNOW WHEN TO HOLD 'EM, AND KNOW WHEN TO FOLD 'EM, MISTER BINKY.

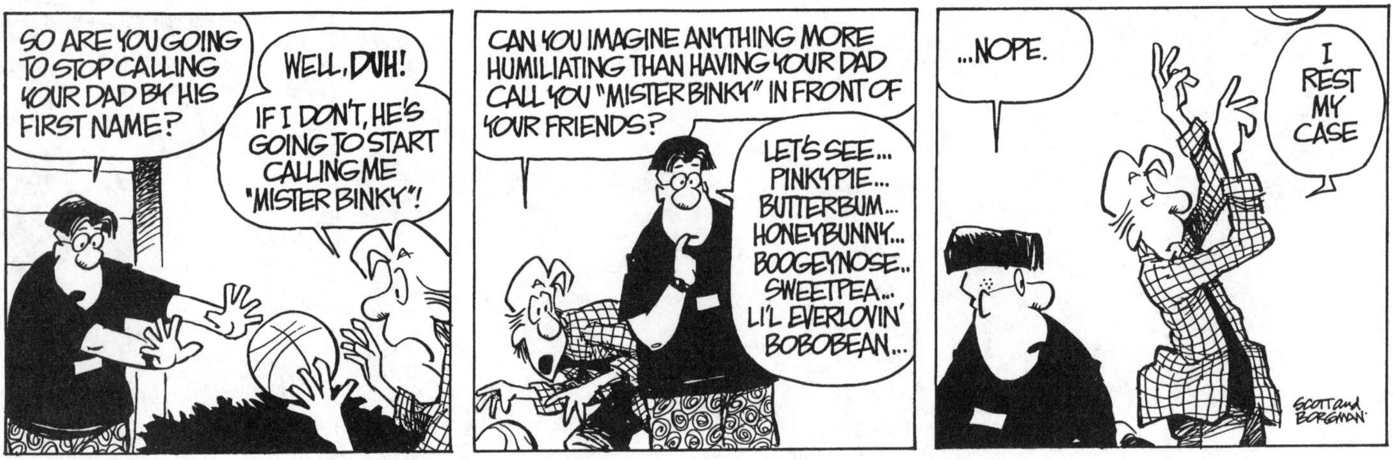
SO ARE YOU GOING TO STOP CALLING YOUR DAD BY HIS FIRST NAME?
WELL, DUH!
IF I DON'T, HE'S GOING TO START CALLING ME "MISTER BINKY"!
CAN YOU IMAGINE ANYTHING MORE HUMILIATING THAN HAVING YOUR DAD CALL YOU "MISTER BINKY" IN FRONT OF YOUR FRIENDS?
LET'S SEE... PINKYPIE... BUTTERBUM... HONEYBUNNY... BOOGEYNOSE... SWEETPEA... LI'L EVERLOVIN' BOBOBEAN...
...NOPE.
I REST MY CASE
SCOTT and BORGMAN

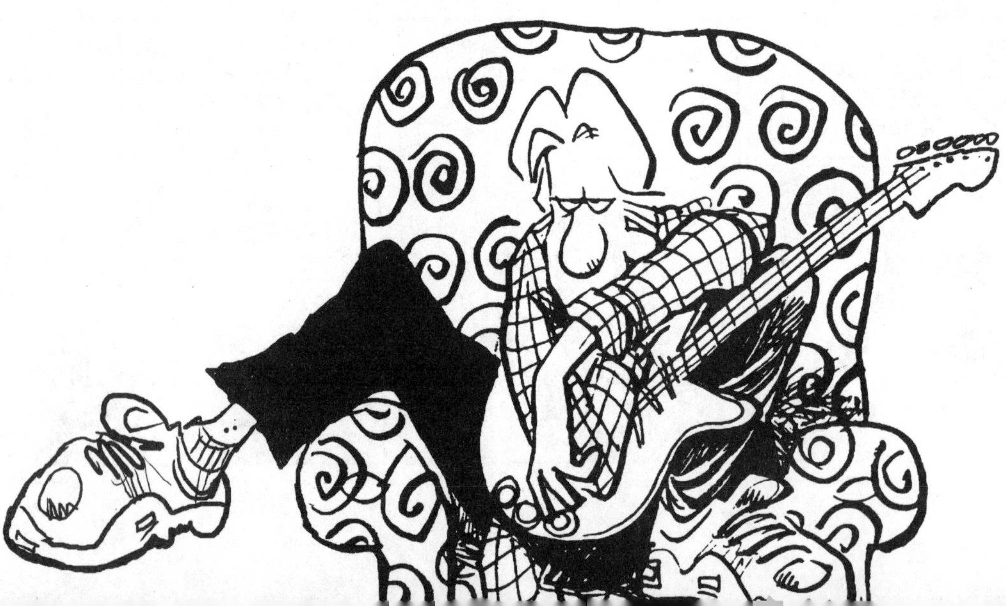

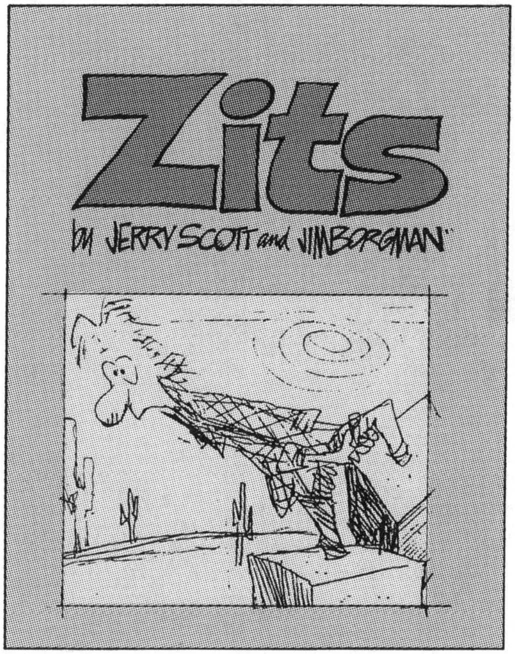
Zits
by JERRY SCOTT and JIM BORGMAN

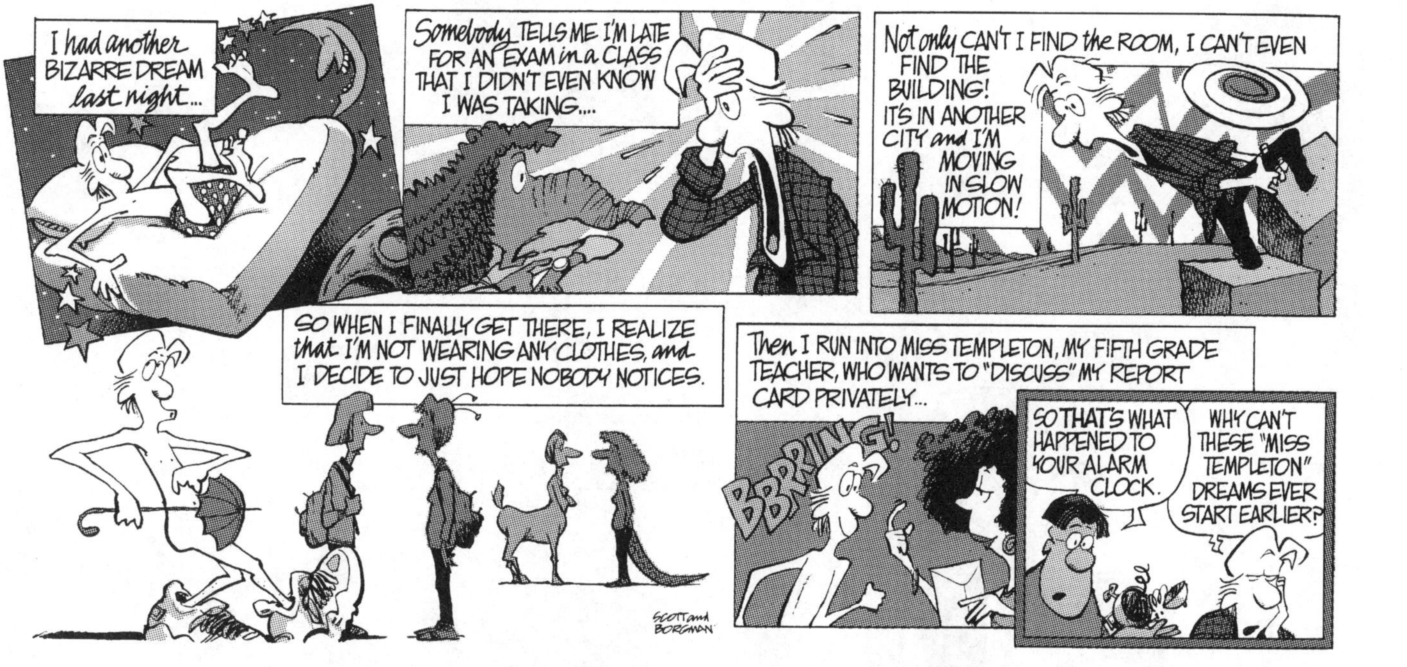
I had another BIZARRE DREAM last night...
Somebody TELLS ME I'M LATE FOR AN EXAM in a CLASS THAT I DIDN'T EVEN KNOW I WAS TAKING....
Not only CAN'T I FIND the ROOM, I CAN'T EVEN FIND THE BUILDING! IT'S IN ANOTHER CITY and I'M MOVING IN SLOW MOTION!
SO WHEN I FINALLY GET THERE, I REALIZE that I'M NOT WEARING ANY CLOTHES, and I DECIDE TO JUST HOPE NOBODY NOTICES.
SCOTT and BORGMAN
Then I RUN INTO MISS TEMPLETON, MY FIFTH GRADE TEACHER, WHO WANTS TO "DISCUSS" MY REPORT CARD PRIVATELY...
BBRRING!
SO THAT'S WHAT HAPPENED TO YOUR ALARM CLOCK.
WHY CAN'T THESE "MISS TEMPLETON" DREAMS EVER START EARLIER?

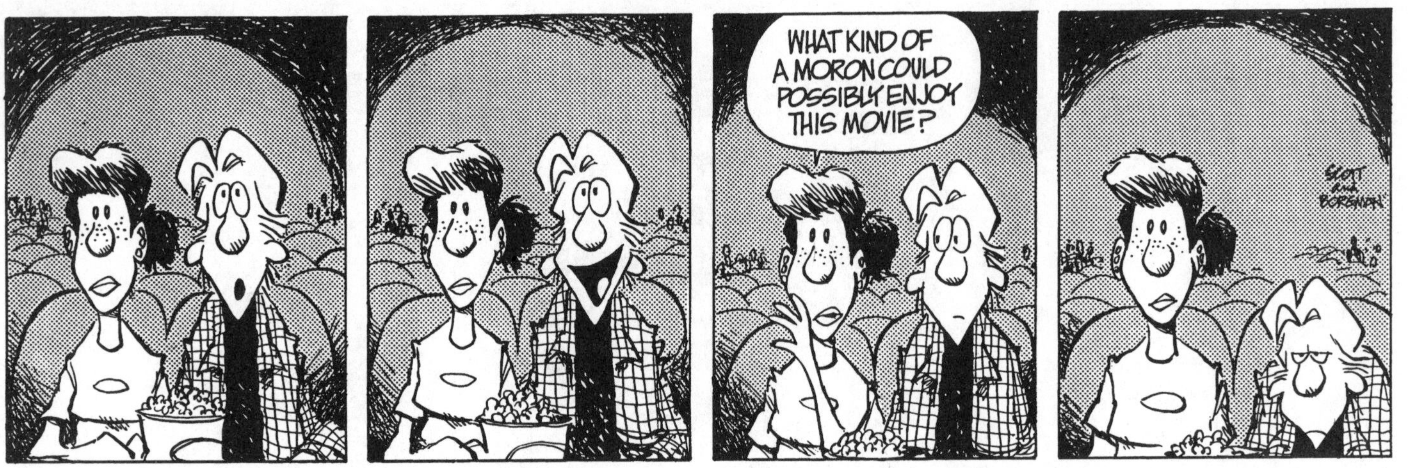
WHAT KIND OF A MORON COULD POSSIBLY ENJOY THIS MOVIE?
SCOTT AND BORGMAN

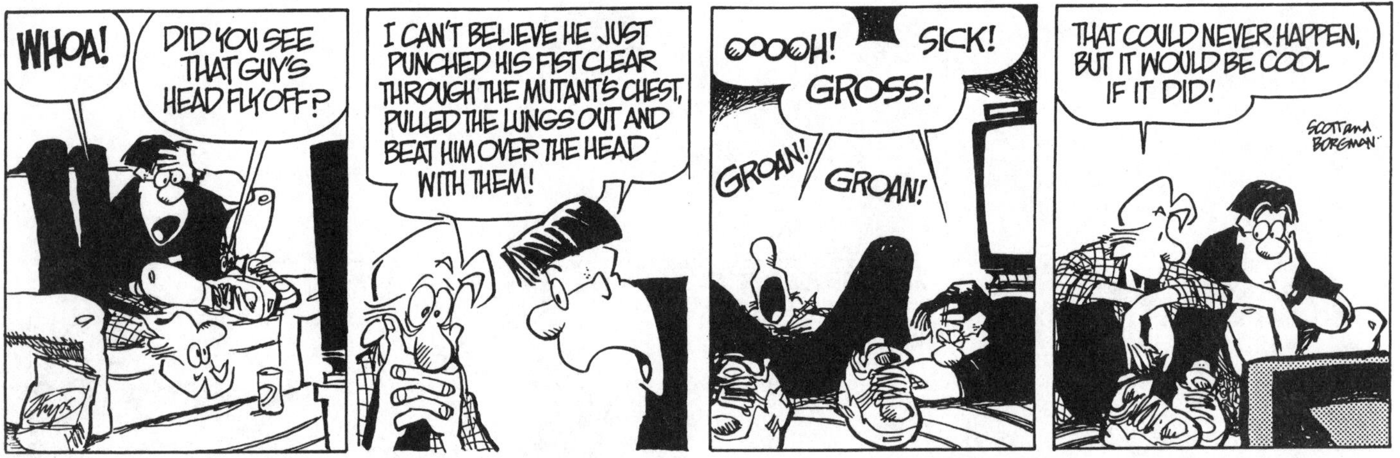
WHOA!
DID YOU SEE THAT GUY'S HEAD FLY OFF?
I CAN'T BELIEVE HE JUST PUNCHED HIS FIST CLEAR THROUGH THE MUTANT'S CHEST, PULLED THE LUNGS OUT AND BEAT HIM OVER THE HEAD WITH THEM!
OOOOH!
SICK!
GROSS!
GROAN!
GROAN!
THAT COULD NEVER HAPPEN, BUT IT WOULD BE COOL IF IT DID!
SCOTT AND BORGMAN

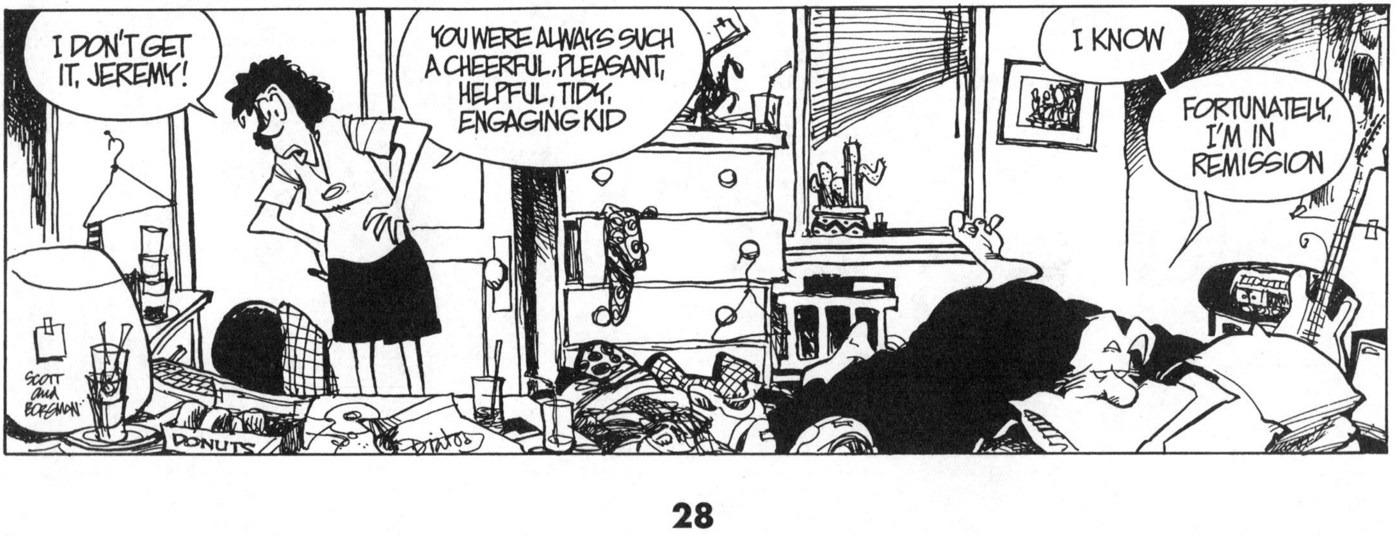
I DON'T GET IT, JEREMY!
YOU WERE ALWAYS SUCH A CHEERFUL, PLEASANT, HELPFUL, TIDY, ENGAGING KID
I KNOW
FORTUNATELY, I'M IN REMISSION
SCOTT AND BORGMAN
DONUTS

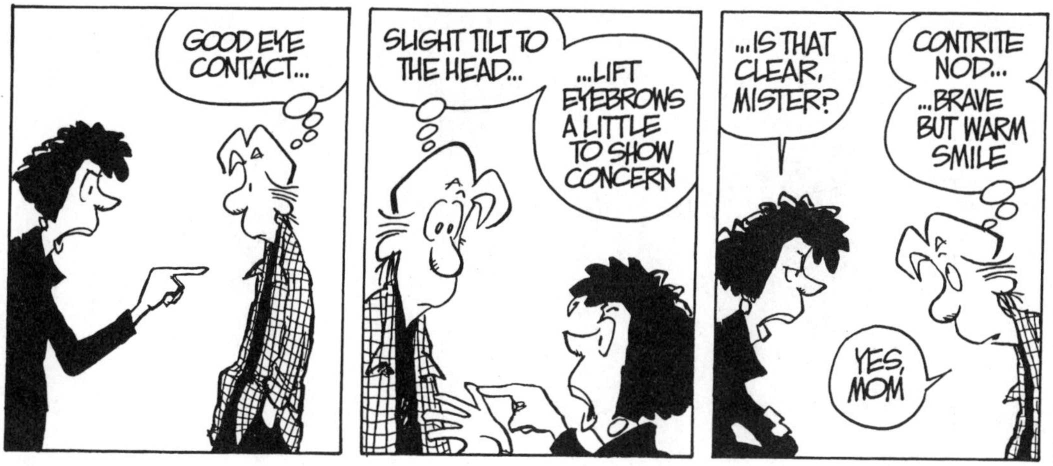
GOOD EYE CONTACT...
SLIGHT TILT TO THE HEAD...
...LIFT EYEBROWS A LITTLE TO SHOW CONCERN
...IS THAT CLEAR, MISTER?
CONTRITE NOD... ...BRAVE BUT WARM SMILE
YES, MOM
I MAY NOT LISTEN WELL, BUT I'M AN ATTENTIVE IGNORER.

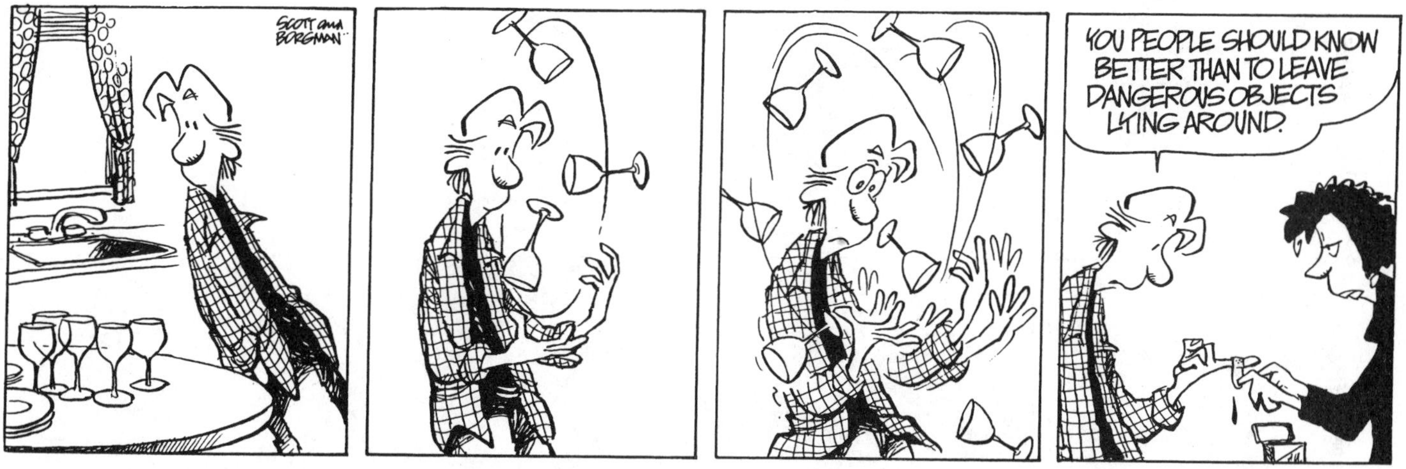
YOU PEOPLE SHOULD KNOW BETTER THAN TO LEAVE DANGEROUS OBJECTS LYING AROUND.

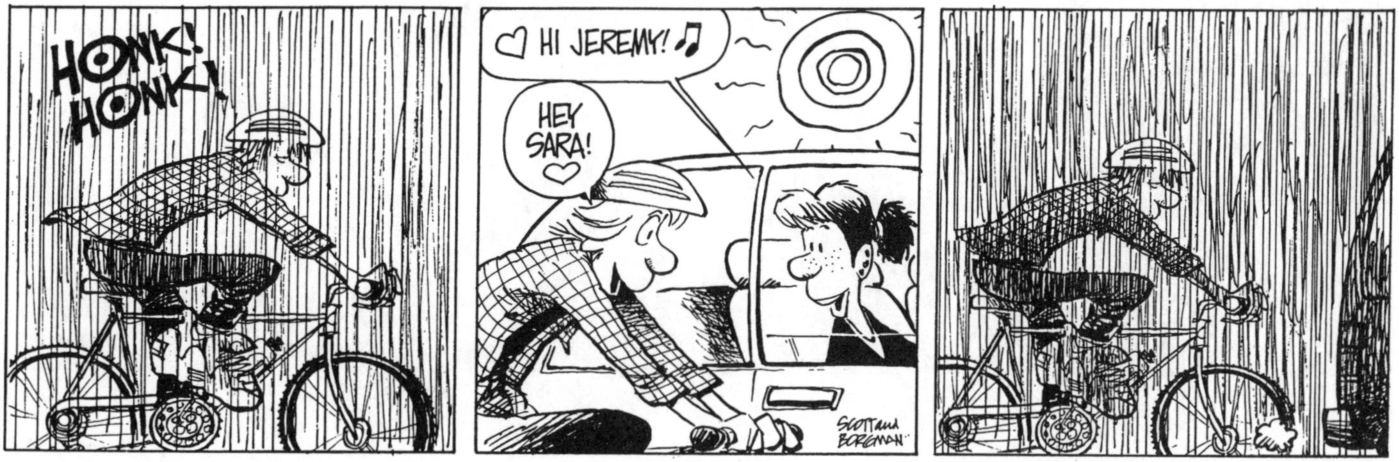
HONK! HONK!
HI JEREMY!
HEY SARA!

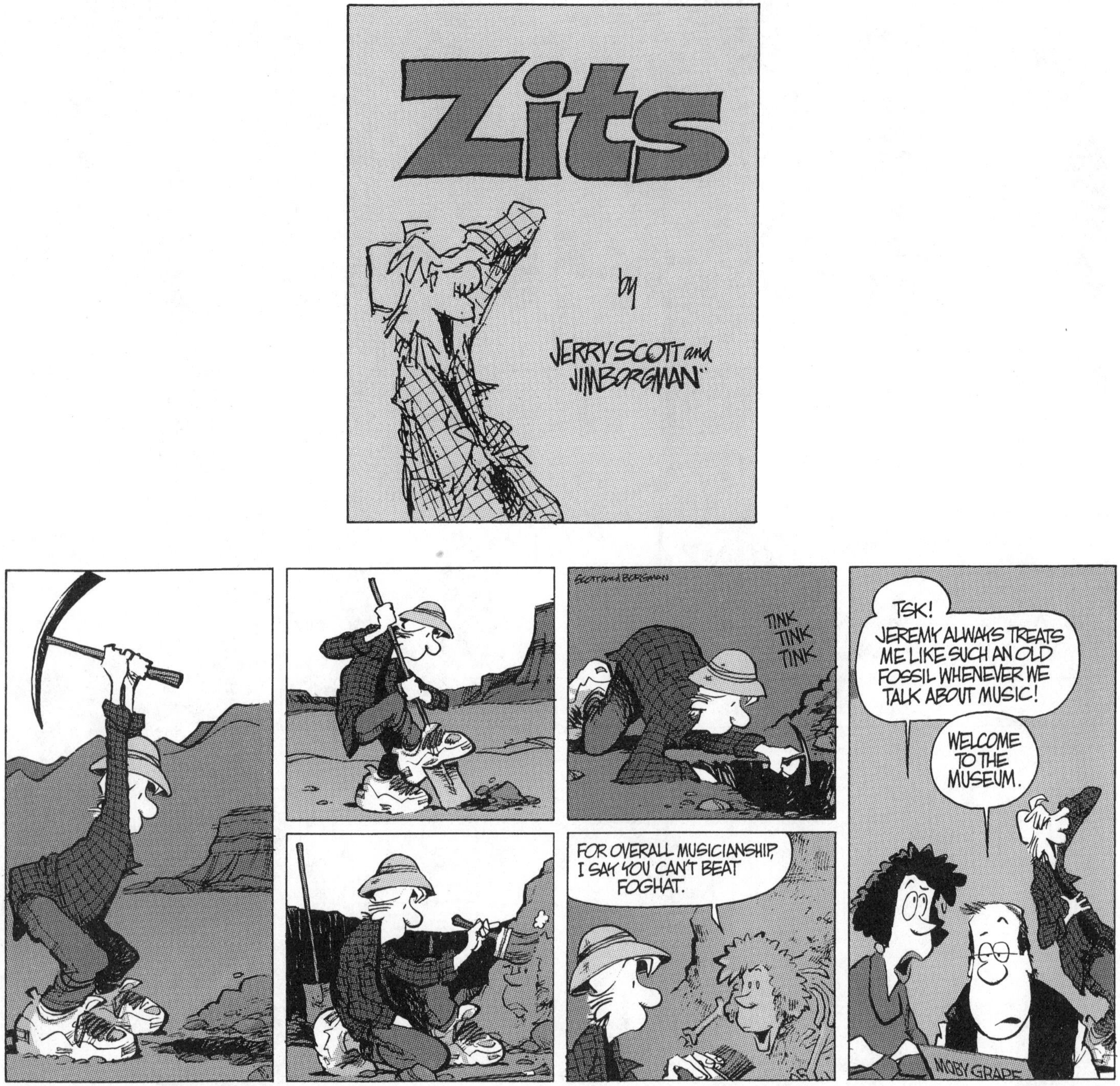
Zits
by
JERRY SCOTT and
JIM BORGMAN
SCOTT and BORGMAN
TINK
TINK
TINK
FOR OVERALL MUSICIANSHIP, I SAY YOU CAN'T BEAT FOGHAT.
TSK! JEREMY ALWAYS TREATS ME LIKE SUCH AN OLD FOSSIL WHENEVER WE TALK ABOUT MUSIC!
WELCOME TO THE MUSEUM.
MOBY GRAPE

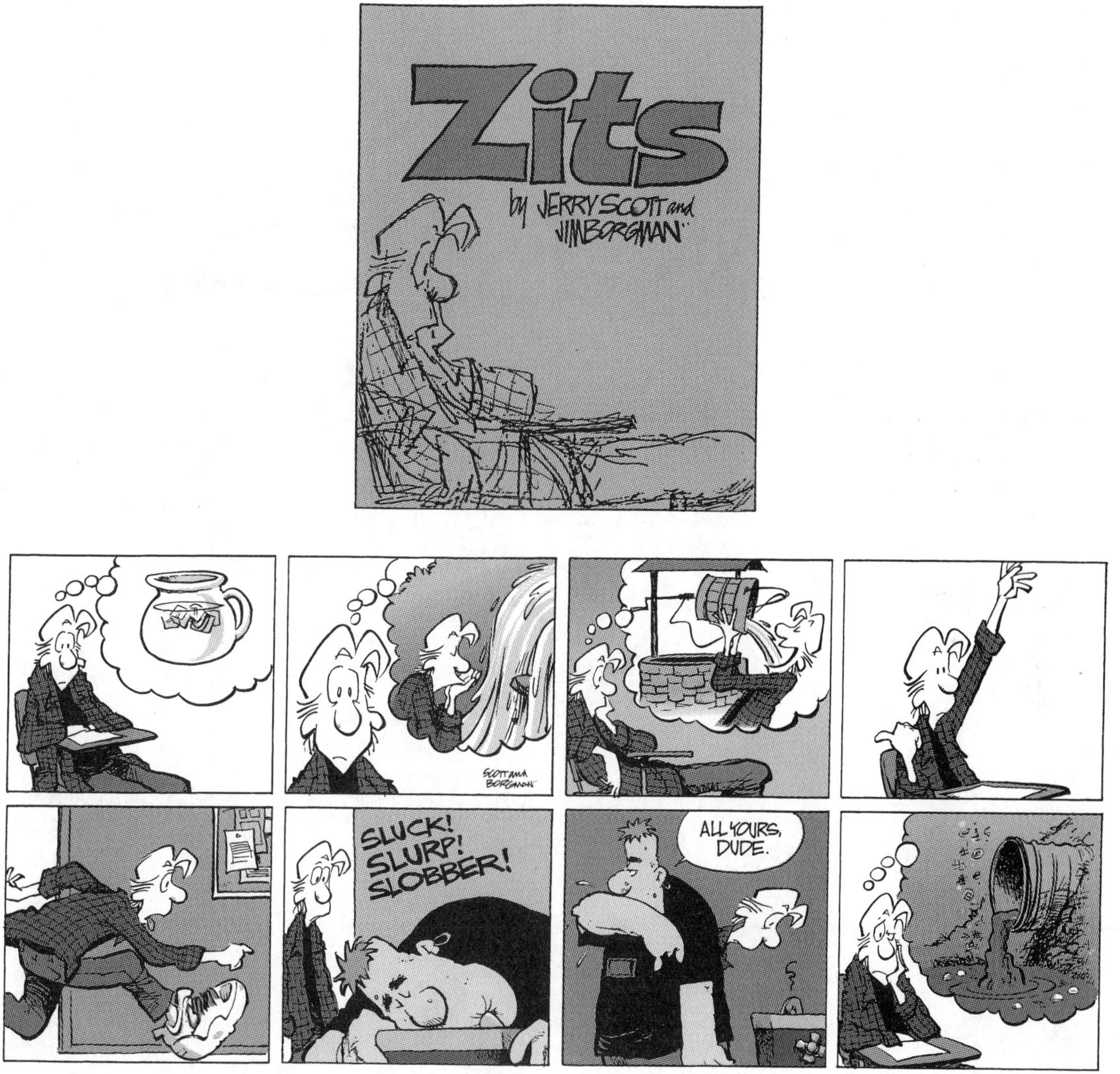
Zits
by JERRY SCOTT and JIM BORGMAN
SLUCK!
SLURP!
SLOBBER!
ALL YOURS, DUDE.

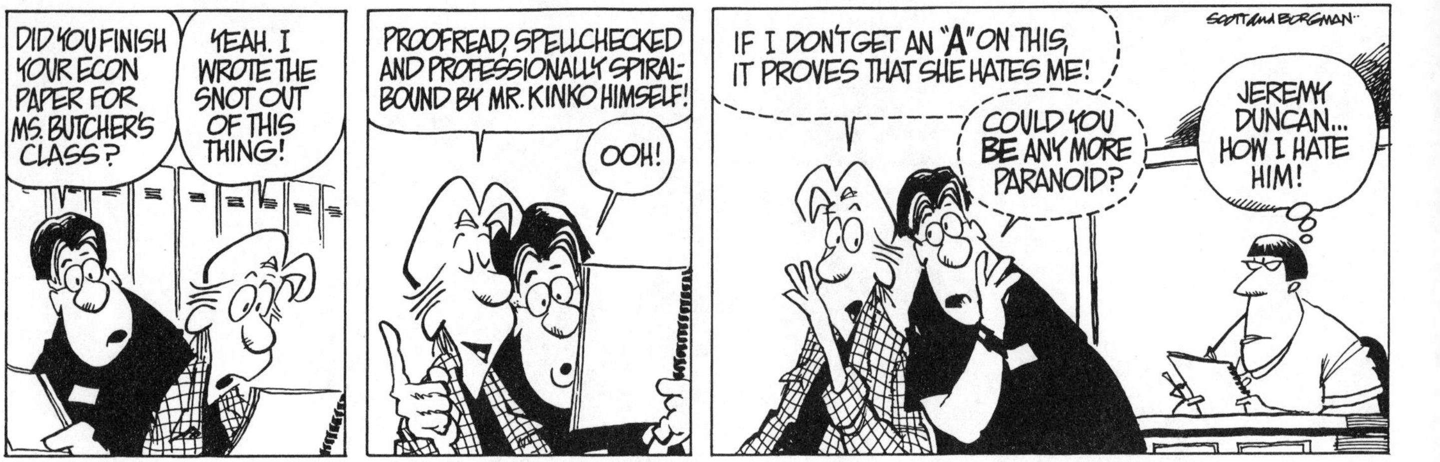
DID YOU FINISH YOUR ECON PAPER FOR MS. BUTCHER'S CLASS?
YEAH. I WROTE THE SNOT OUT OF THIS THING!
PROOFREAD, SPELLCHECKED AND PROFESSIONALLY SPIRAL-BOUND BY MR. KINKO HIMSELF!
OOH!
SCOTT AND BORGMAN
IF I DON'T GET AN "A" ON THIS, IT PROVES THAT SHE HATES ME!
COULD YOU BE ANY MORE PARANOID?
JEREMY DUNCAN... HOW I HATE HIM!

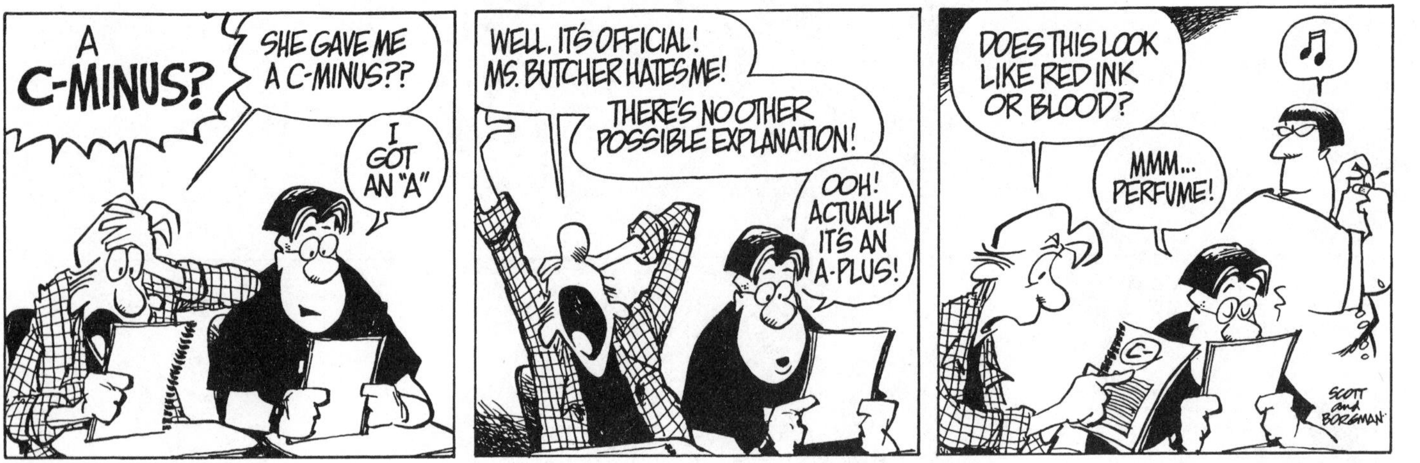
A C-MINUS?
SHE GAVE ME A C-MINUS??
I GOT AN "A"
WELL, IT'S OFFICIAL! MS. BUTCHER HATES ME!
THERE'S NO OTHER POSSIBLE EXPLANATION!
OOH! ACTUALLY IT'S AN A-PLUS!
DOES THIS LOOK LIKE RED INK OR BLOOD?
MMM... PERFUME!
SCOTT and BORGMAN

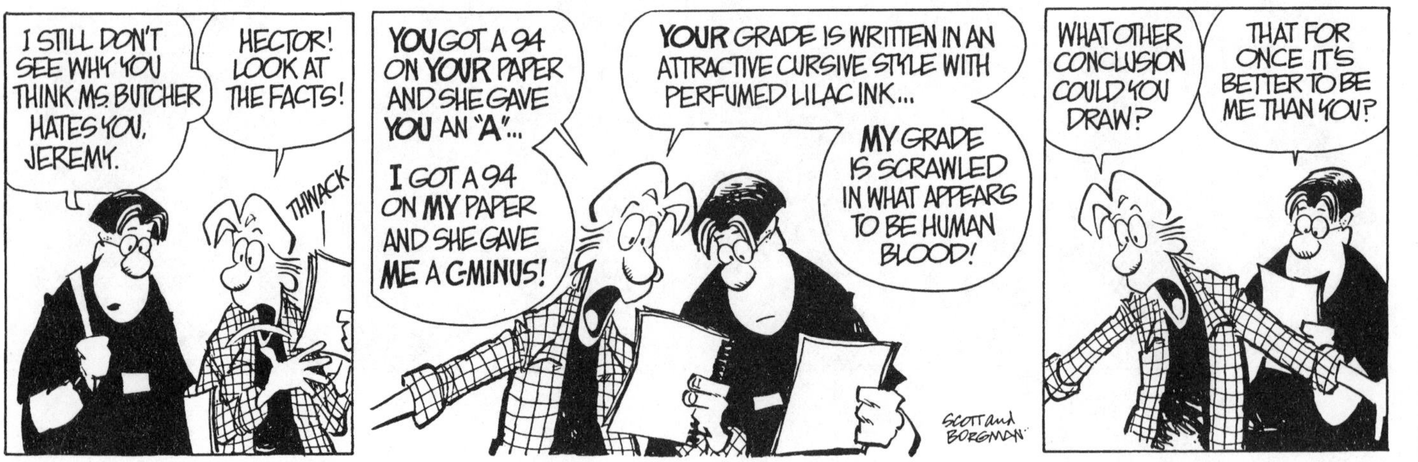
I STILL DON'T SEE WHY YOU THINK MS. BUTCHER HATES YOU, JEREMY.
HECTOR! LOOK AT THE FACTS!
THWACK
YOU GOT A 94 ON YOUR PAPER AND SHE GAVE YOU AN "A"...
I GOT A 94 ON MY PAPER AND SHE GAVE ME A C-MINUS!
YOUR GRADE IS WRITTEN IN AN ATTRACTIVE CURSIVE STYLE WITH PERFUMED LILAC INK...
MY GRADE IS SCRAWLED IN WHAT APPEARS TO BE HUMAN BLOOD!
SCOTT and BORGMAN
WHAT OTHER CONCLUSION COULD YOU DRAW?
THAT FOR ONCE IT'S BETTER TO BE ME THAN YOU?

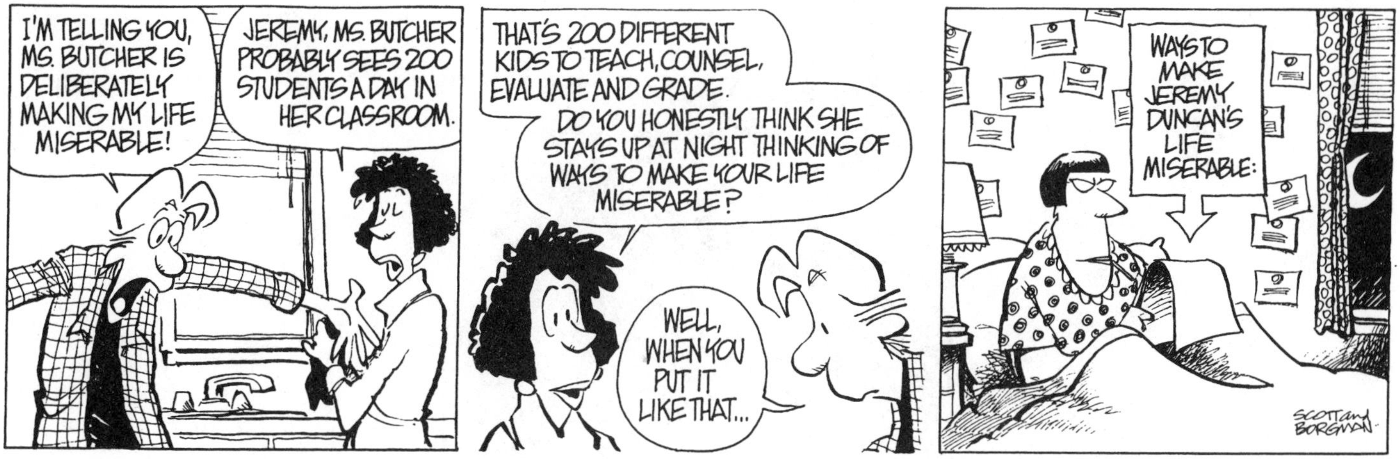
I'M TELLING YOU, MS. BUTCHER IS DELIBERATELY MAKING MY LIFE MISERABLE!
JEREMY, MS. BUTCHER PROBABLY SEES 200 STUDENTS A DAY IN HER CLASSROOM.
THAT'S 200 DIFFERENT KIDS TO TEACH, COUNSEL, EVALUATE AND GRADE.
DO YOU HONESTLY THINK SHE STAYS UP AT NIGHT THINKING OF WAYS TO MAKE YOUR LIFE MISERABLE?
WELL, WHEN YOU PUT IT LIKE THAT...
WAYS TO MAKE JEREMY DUNCAN'S LIFE MISERABLE:
SCOTT and BORGMAN

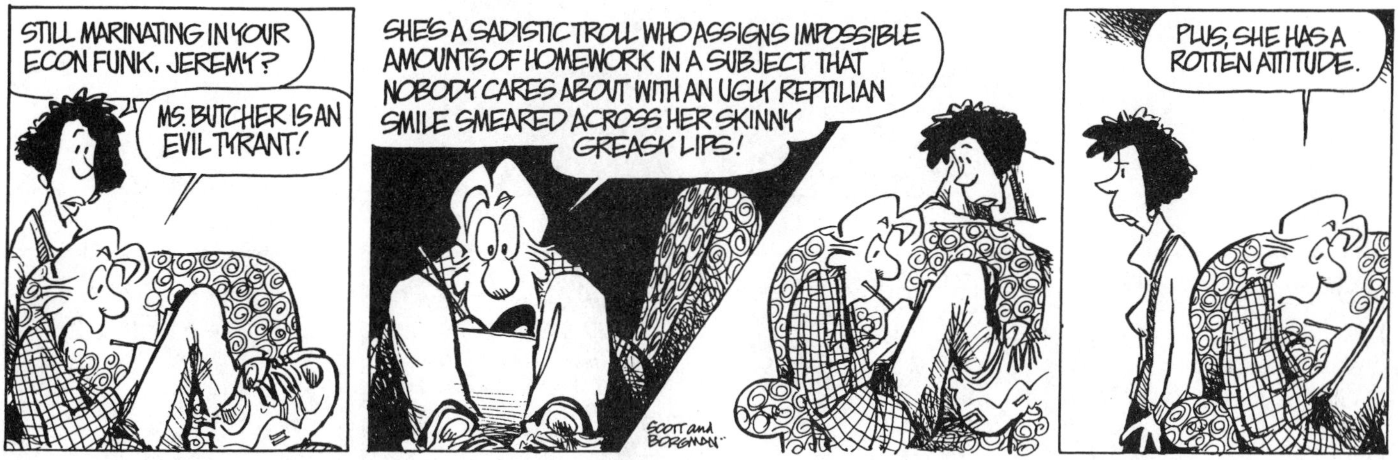
STILL MARINATING IN YOUR ECON FUNK, JEREMY?
MS. BUTCHER IS AN EVIL TYRANT!
SHE'S A SADISTIC TROLL WHO ASSIGNS IMPOSSIBLE AMOUNTS OF HOMEWORK IN A SUBJECT THAT NOBODY CARES ABOUT WITH AN UGLY REPTILIAN SMILE SMEARED ACROSS HER SKINNY GREASY LIPS!
SCOTT and BORGMAN
PLUS, SHE HAS A ROTTEN ATTITUDE.

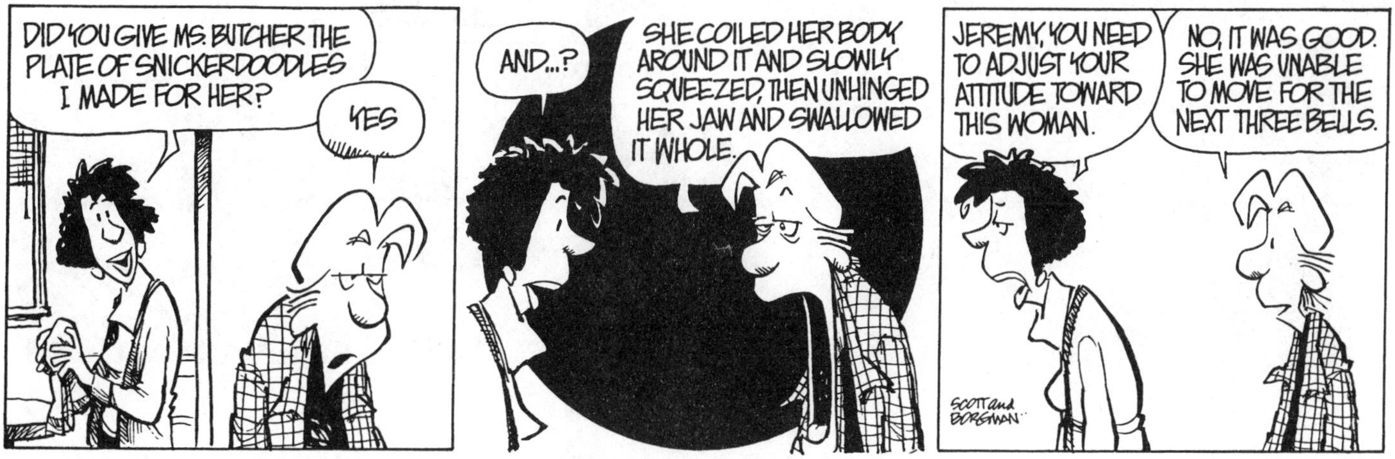
DID YOU GIVE MS. BUTCHER THE PLATE OF SNICKERDOODLES I MADE FOR HER?
YES
AND...?
SHE COILED HER BODY AROUND IT AND SLOWLY SQUEEZED, THEN UNHINGED HER JAW AND SWALLOWED IT WHOLE.
JEREMY, YOU NEED TO ADJUST YOUR ATTITUDE TOWARD THIS WOMAN.
NO, IT WAS GOOD. SHE WAS UNABLE TO MOVE FOR THE NEXT THREE BELLS.
SCOTT and BORGMAN

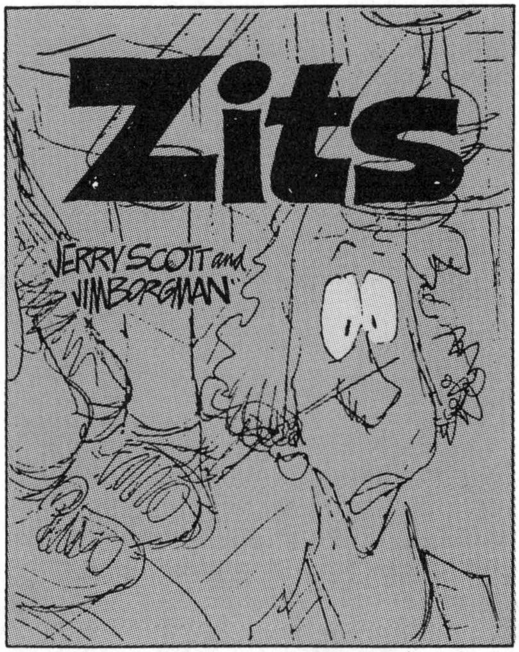
Zits
JERRY SCOTT and JIM BORGMAN

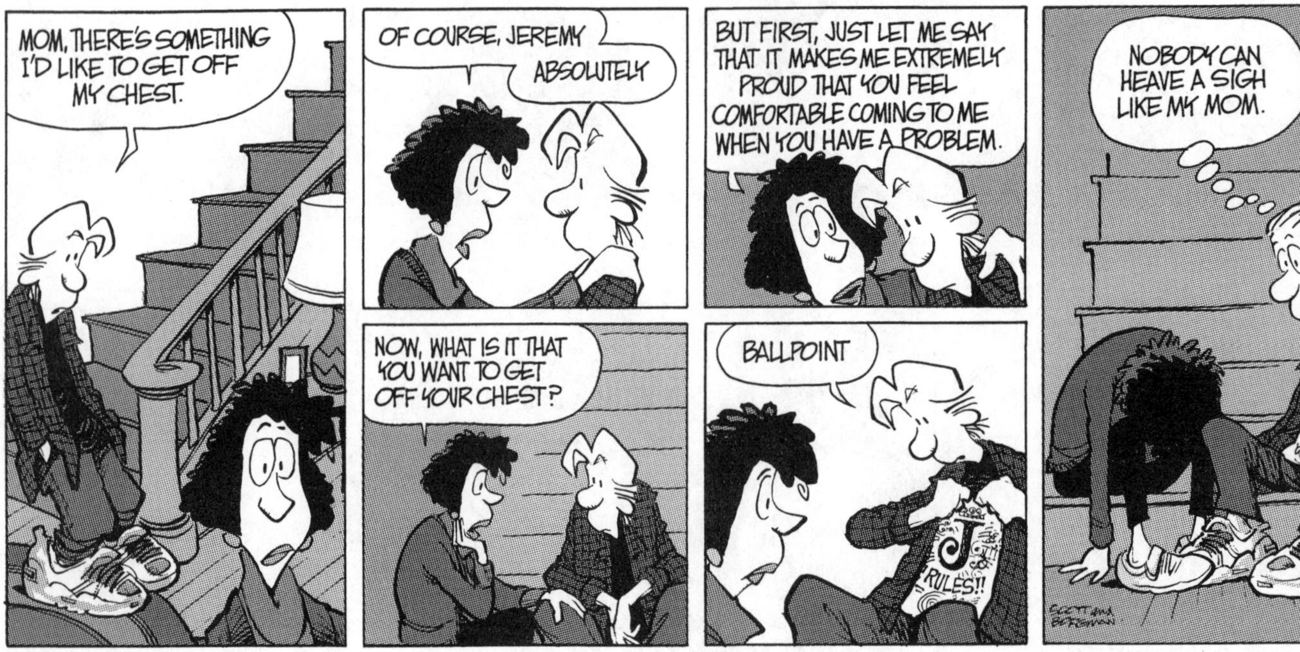
MOM, THERE'S SOMETHING I'D LIKE TO GET OFF MY CHEST.
OF COURSE, JEREMY
ABSOLUTELY
BUT FIRST, JUST LET ME SAY THAT IT MAKES ME EXTREMELY PROUD THAT YOU FEEL COMFORTABLE COMING TO ME WHEN YOU HAVE A PROBLEM.
NOW, WHAT IS IT THAT YOU WANT TO GET OFF YOUR CHEST?
BALLPOINT
J RULES!!
NOBODY CAN HEAVE A SIGH LIKE MY MOM.
SCOTT and BORGMAN

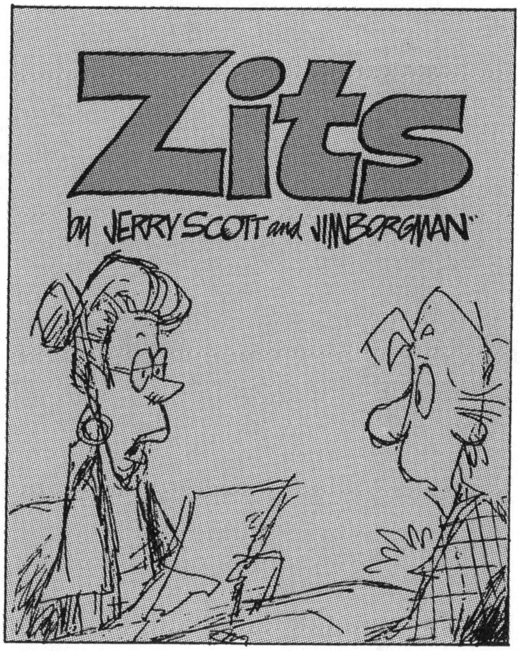
Zits
by JERRY SCOTT and JIM BORGMAN

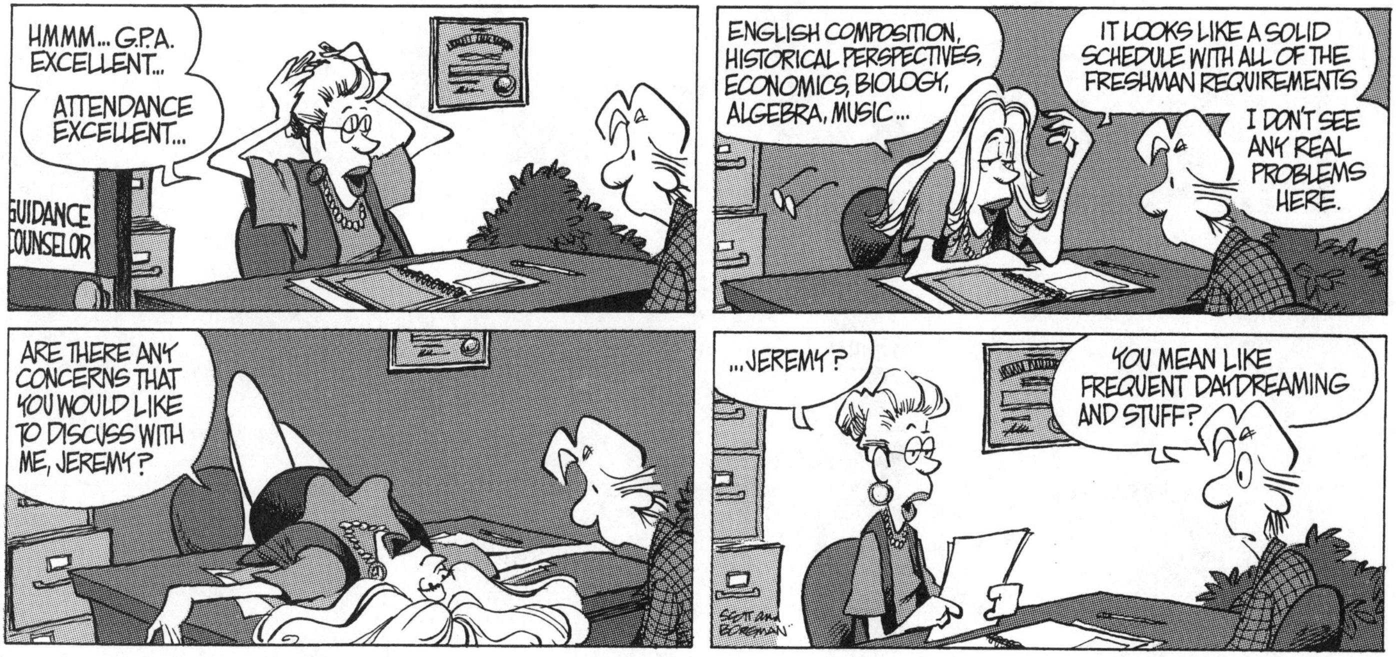
HMMM... G.P.A. EXCELLENT...
ATTENDANCE EXCELLENT...
GUIDANCE COUNSELOR
ENGLISH COMPOSITION, HISTORICAL PERSPECTIVES, ECONOMICS, BIOLOGY, ALGEBRA, MUSIC...
IT LOOKS LIKE A SOLID SCHEDULE WITH ALL OF THE FRESHMAN REQUIREMENTS
I DON'T SEE ANY REAL PROBLEMS HERE.
ARE THERE ANY CONCERNS THAT YOU WOULD LIKE TO DISCUSS WITH ME, JEREMY?
...JEREMY?
YOU MEAN LIKE FREQUENT DAYDREAMING AND STUFF?
SCOTT and BORGMAN

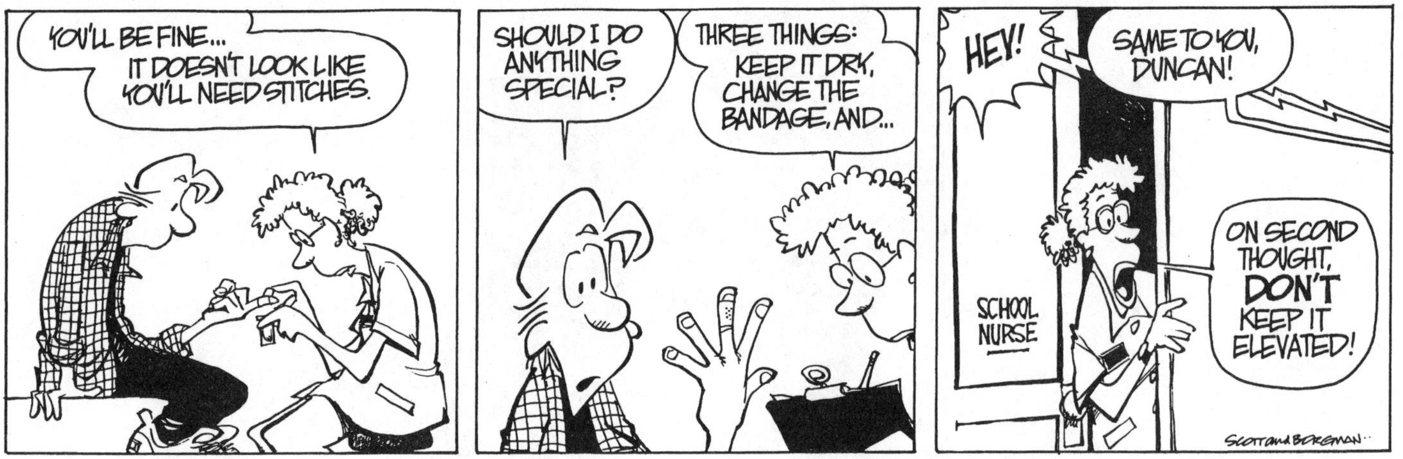
YOU'LL BE FINE... IT DOESN'T LOOK LIKE YOU'LL NEED STITCHES.
SHOULD I DO ANYTHING SPECIAL?
THREE THINGS: KEEP IT DRY, CHANGE THE BANDAGE, AND...
HEY!
SAME TO YOU, DUNCAN!
SCHOOL NURSE
ON SECOND THOUGHT, DON'T KEEP IT ELEVATED!
SCOTT and BORGMAN

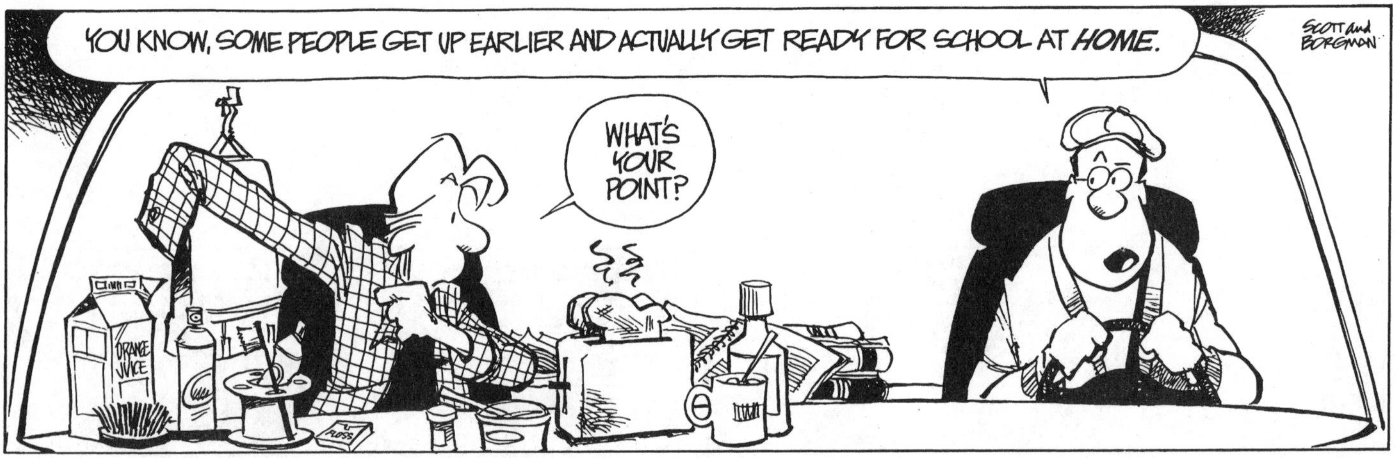
YOU KNOW, SOME PEOPLE GET UP EARLIER AND ACTUALLY GET READY FOR SCHOOL AT HOME.
WHAT'S YOUR POINT?
ORANGE JUICE
FLOSS
SCOTT and BORGMAN

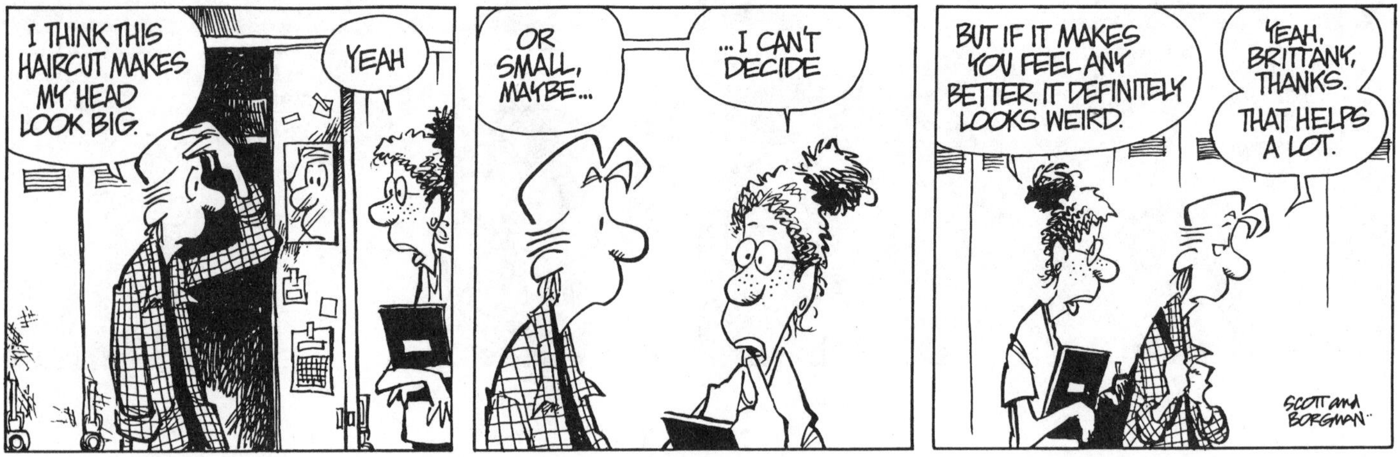
I THINK THIS HAIRCUT MAKES MY HEAD LOOK BIG.
YEAH
OR SMALL, MAYBE...
...I CAN'T DECIDE
BUT IF IT MAKES YOU FEEL ANY BETTER, IT DEFINITELY LOOKS WEIRD.
YEAH, BRITTANY, THANKS. THAT HELPS A LOT.
SCOTT and BORGMAN

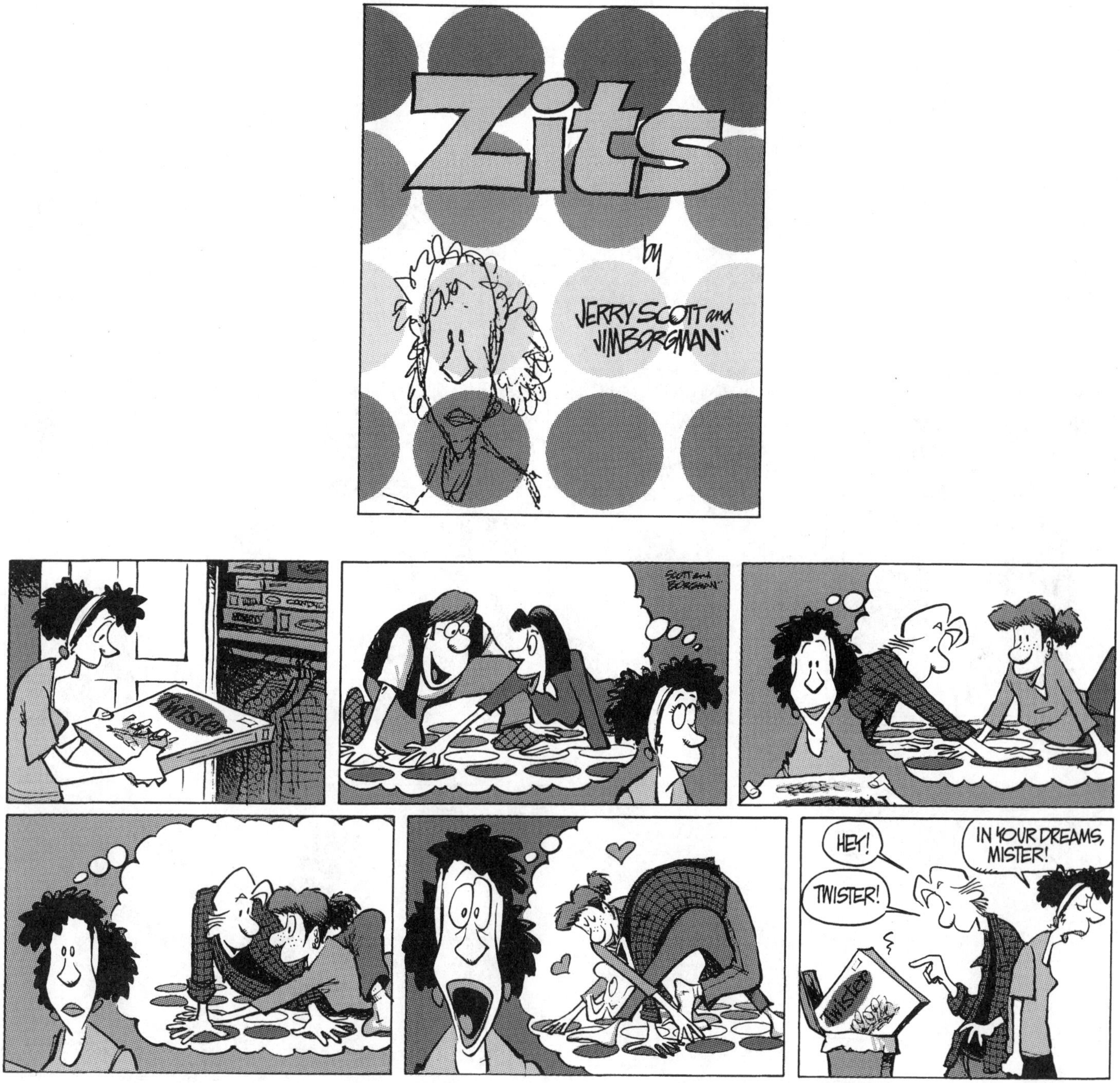
Zits
by
JERRY SCOTT and
JIM BORGMAN
HEY!
TWISTER!
IN YOUR DREAMS, MISTER!

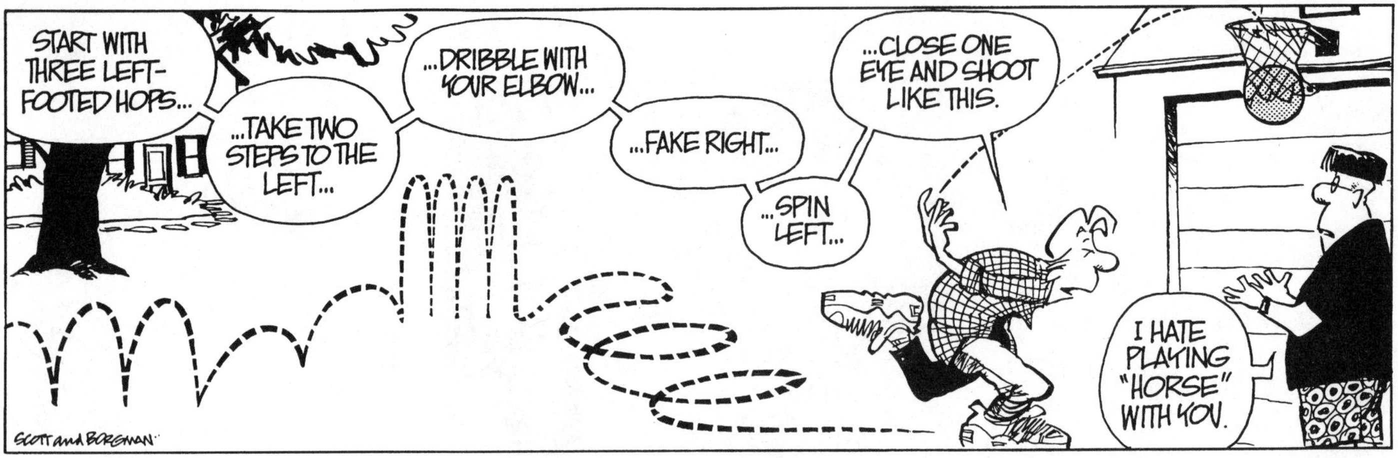
START WITH THREE LEFT-FOOTED HOPS...
...TAKE TWO STEPS TO THE LEFT...
...DRIBBLE WITH YOUR ELBOW...
...FAKE RIGHT...
...SPIN LEFT...
...CLOSE ONE EYE AND SHOOT LIKE THIS.
I HATE PLAYING "HORSE" WITH YOU.
SCOTT and BORGMAN

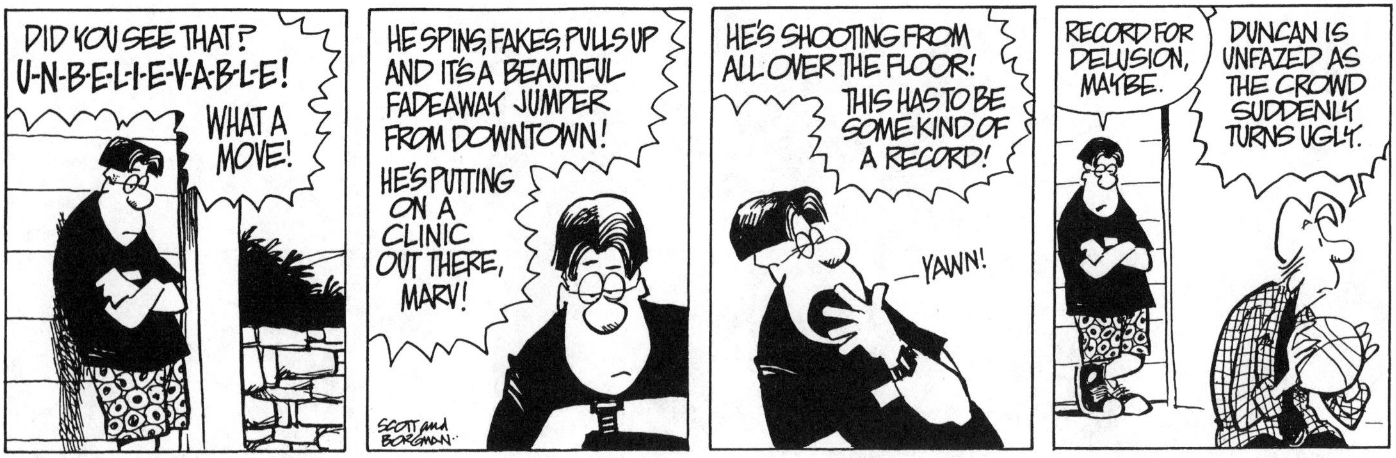
DID YOU SEE THAT? U-N-B-E-L-I-E-V-A-B-L-E!
WHAT A MOVE!
HE SPINS, FAKES, PULLS UP AND IT'S A BEAUTIFUL FADEAWAY JUMPER FROM DOWNTOWN!
HE'S PUTTING ON A CLINIC OUT THERE, MARV!
SCOTT and BORGMAN
HE'S SHOOTING FROM ALL OVER THE FLOOR!
THIS HAS TO BE SOME KIND OF A RECORD!
YAWN!
RECORD FOR DELUSION, MAYBE.
DUNCAN IS UNFAZED AS THE CROWD SUDDENLY TURNS UGLY.

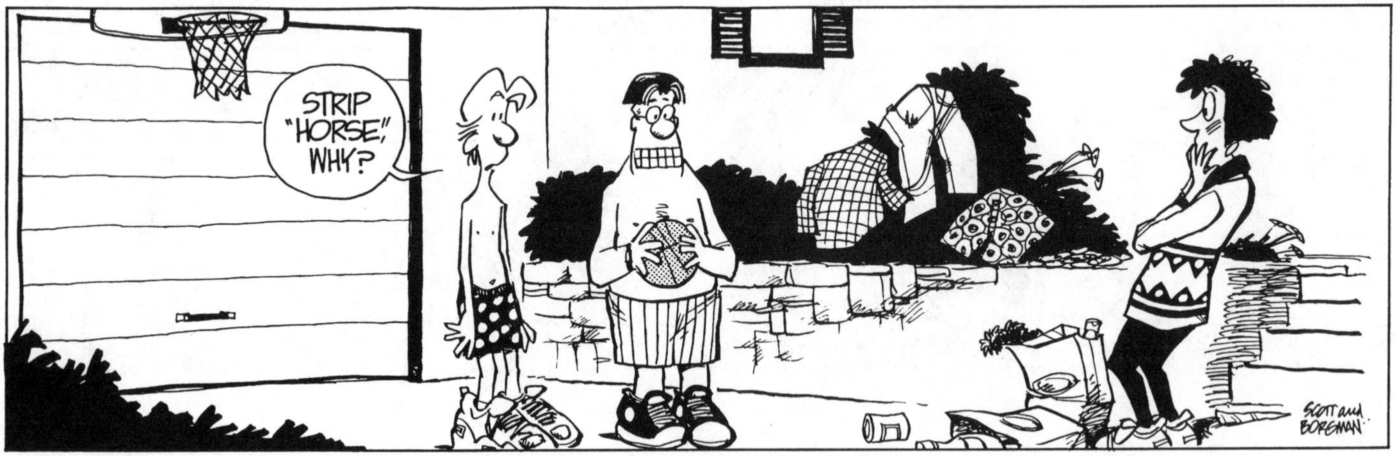
STRIP "HORSE," WHY?
SCOTT and BORGMAN

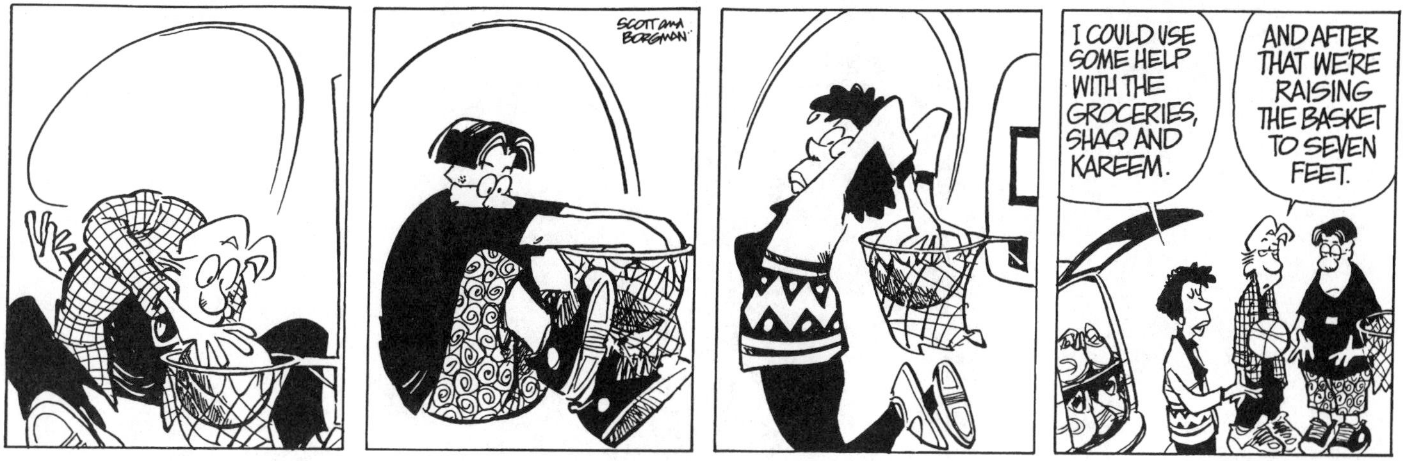
SCOTT and BORGMAN
I COULD USE SOME HELP WITH THE GROCERIES, SHAQ AND KAREEM.
AND AFTER THAT WE'RE RAISING THE BASKET TO SEVEN FEET.

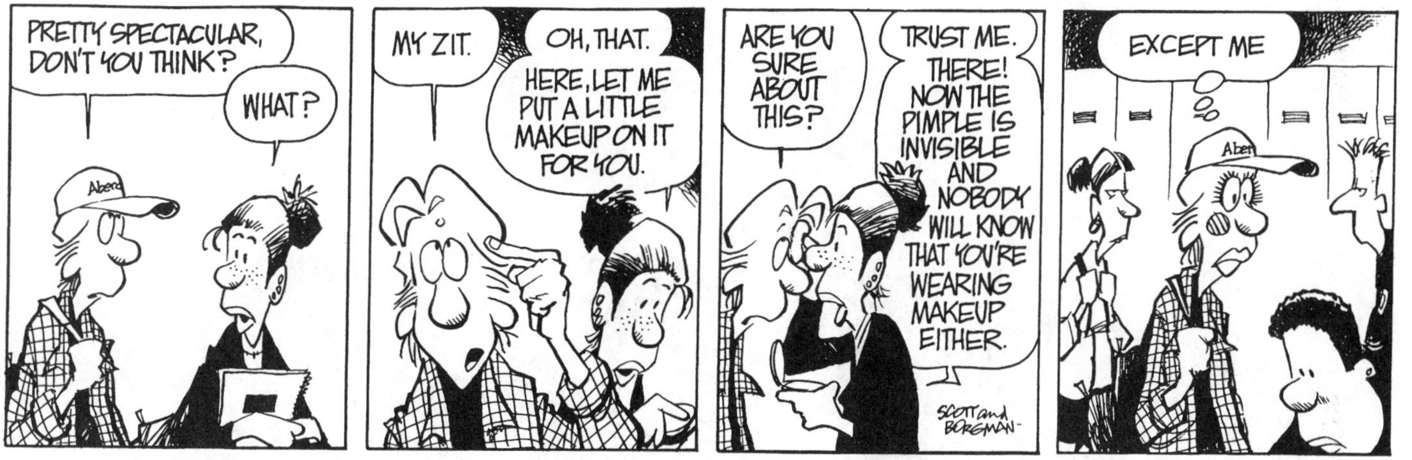
PRETTY SPECTACULAR, DON'T YOU THINK?
WHAT?
Aberd
MY ZIT.
OH, THAT.
HERE, LET ME PUT A LITTLE MAKEUP ON IT FOR YOU.
ARE YOU SURE ABOUT THIS?
TRUST ME.
THERE! NOW THE PIMPLE IS INVISIBLE AND NOBODY WILL KNOW THAT YOU'RE WEARING MAKEUP EITHER.
SCOTT and BORGMAN
EXCEPT ME

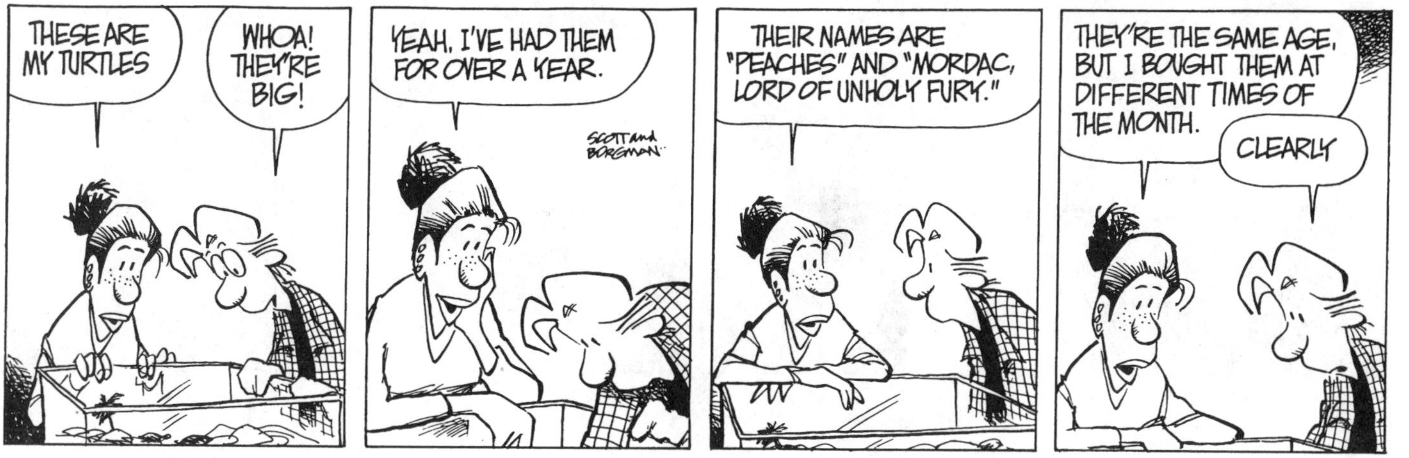
THESE ARE MY TURTLES
WHOA! THEY'RE BIG!
YEAH, I'VE HAD THEM FOR OVER A YEAR.
SCOTT and BORGMAN
THEIR NAMES ARE "PEACHES" AND "MORDAC, LORD OF UNHOLY FURY."
THEY'RE THE SAME AGE, BUT I BOUGHT THEM AT DIFFERENT TIMES OF THE MONTH.
CLEARLY

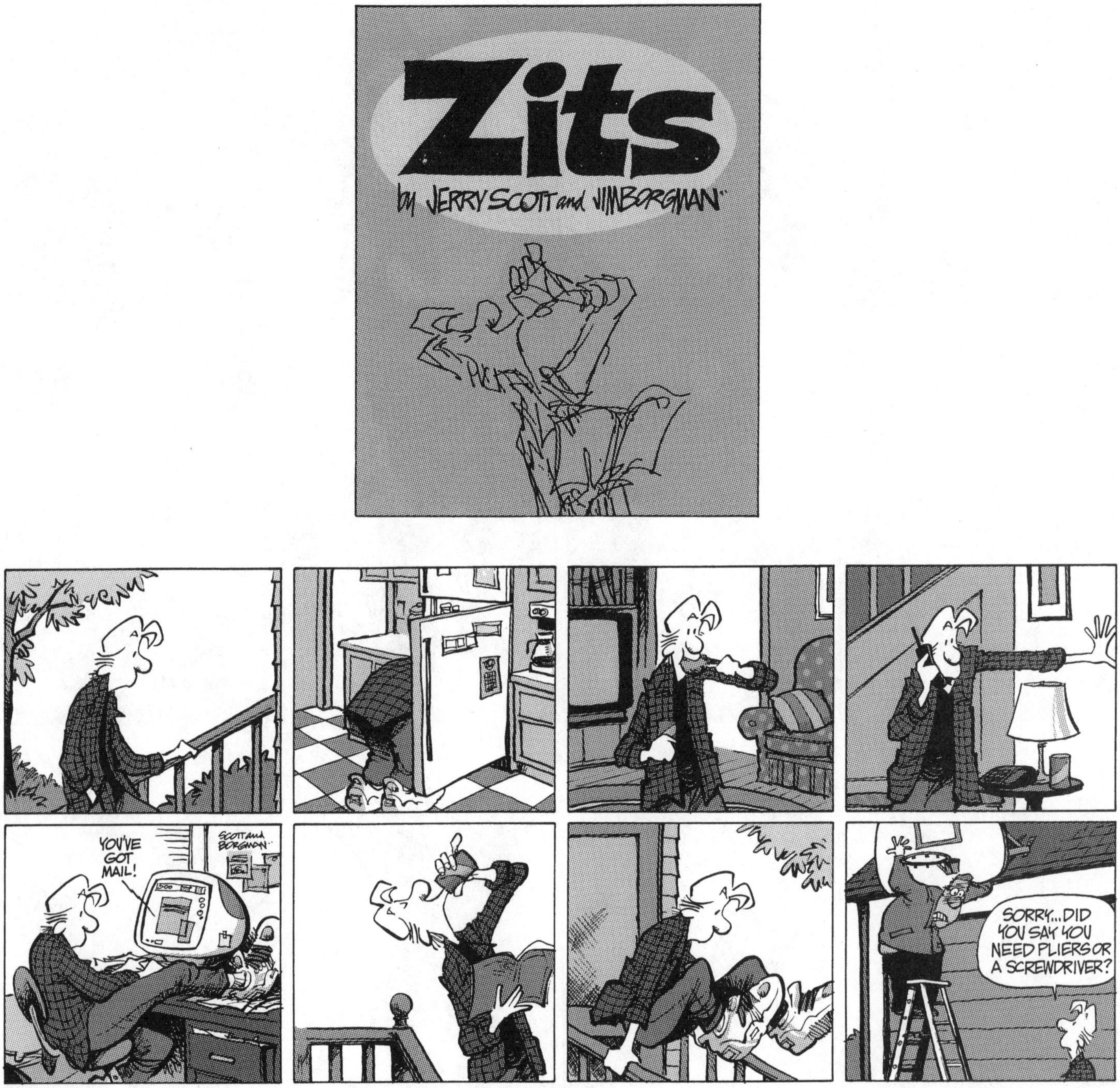
Zits
by JERRY SCOTT and JIM BORGMAN
YOU'VE GOT MAIL!
SCOTT and BORGMAN
SORRY... DID YOU SAY YOU NEED PLIERS OR A SCREWDRIVER?

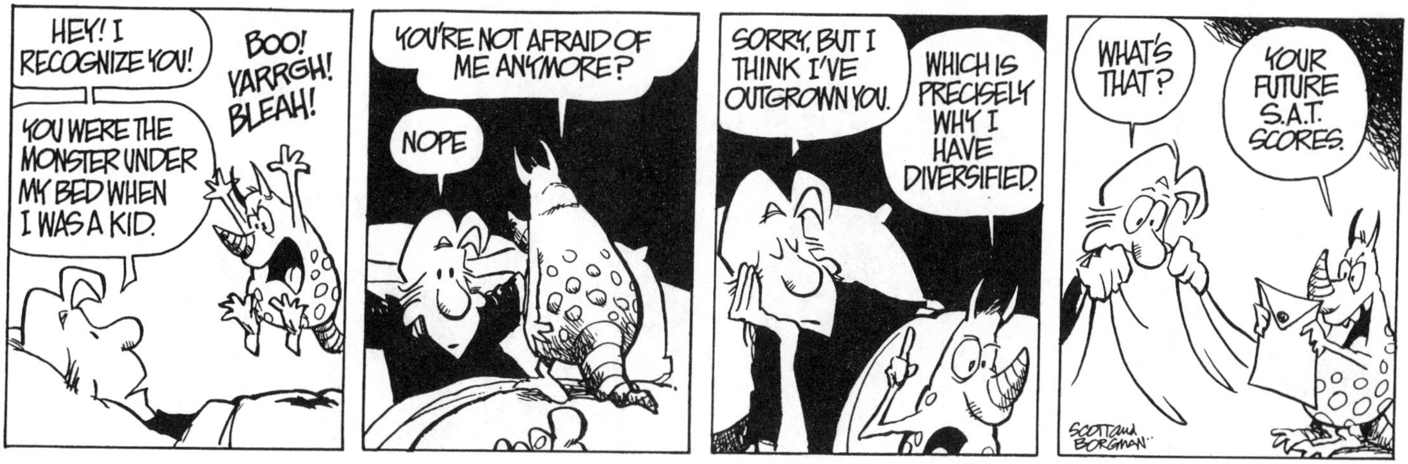
HEY! I RECOGNIZE YOU!
YOU WERE THE MONSTER UNDER MY BED WHEN I WAS A KID.
BOO! YARRGH! BLEAH!
YOU'RE NOT AFRAID OF ME ANYMORE?
NOPE
SORRY, BUT I THINK I'VE OUTGROWN YOU.
WHICH IS PRECISELY WHY I HAVE DIVERSIFIED.
WHAT'S THAT?
YOUR FUTURE S.A.T. SCORES.

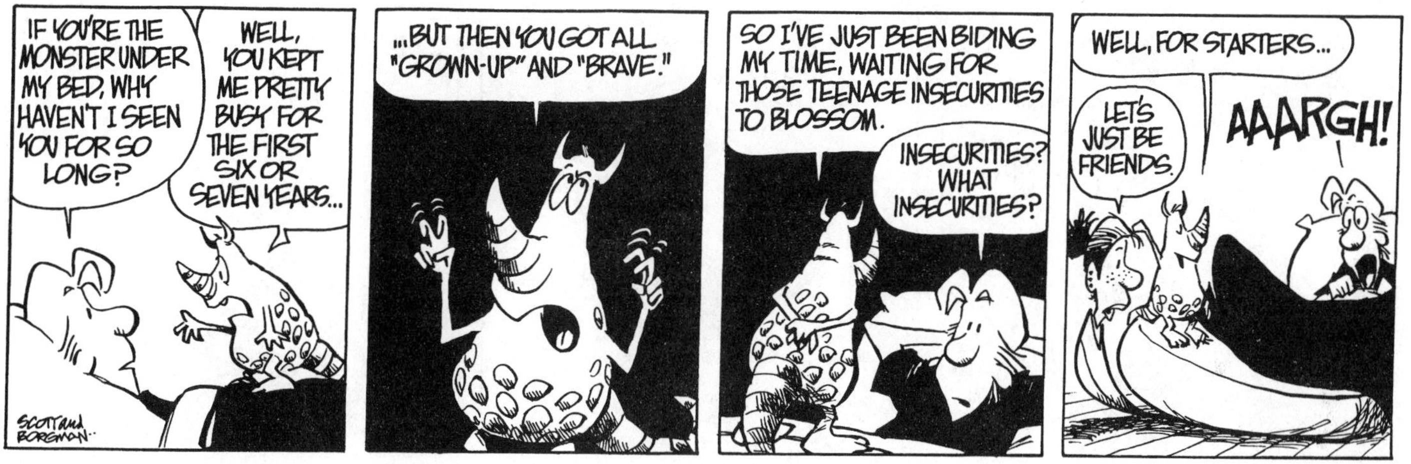
IF YOU'RE THE MONSTER UNDER MY BED, WHY HAVEN'T I SEEN YOU FOR SO LONG?
WELL, YOU KEPT ME PRETTY BUSY FOR THE FIRST SIX OR SEVEN YEARS...
...BUT THEN YOU GOT ALL "GROWN-UP" AND "BRAVE."
SO I'VE JUST BEEN BIDING MY TIME, WAITING FOR THOSE TEENAGE INSECURITIES TO BLOSSOM.
INSECURITIES? WHAT INSECURITIES?
WELL, FOR STARTERS...
LET'S JUST BE FRIENDS.
AAARGH!

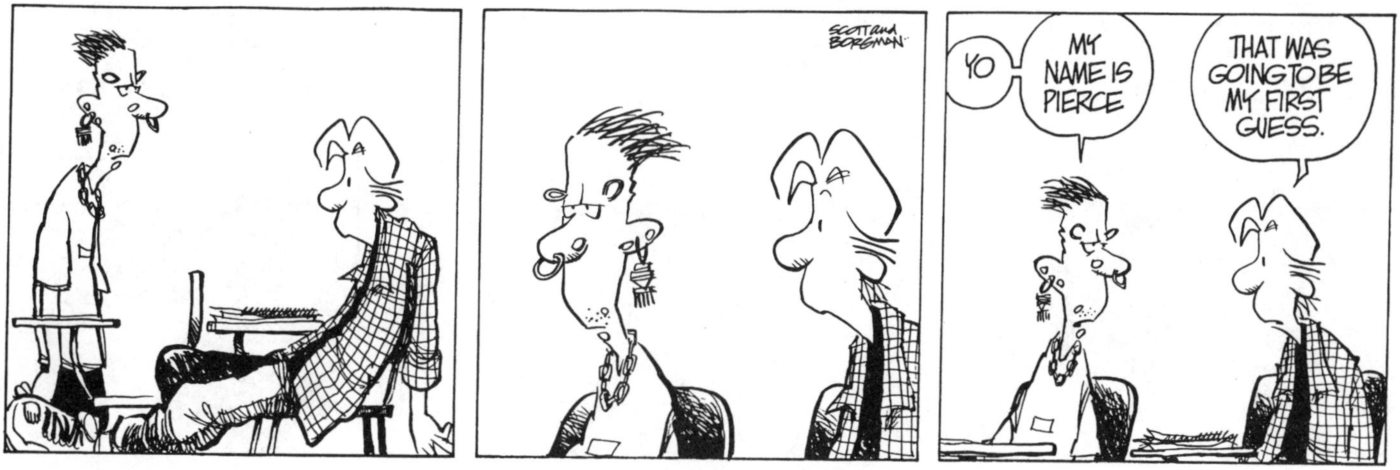
YO
MY NAME IS PIERCE
THAT WAS GOING TO BE MY FIRST GUESS.

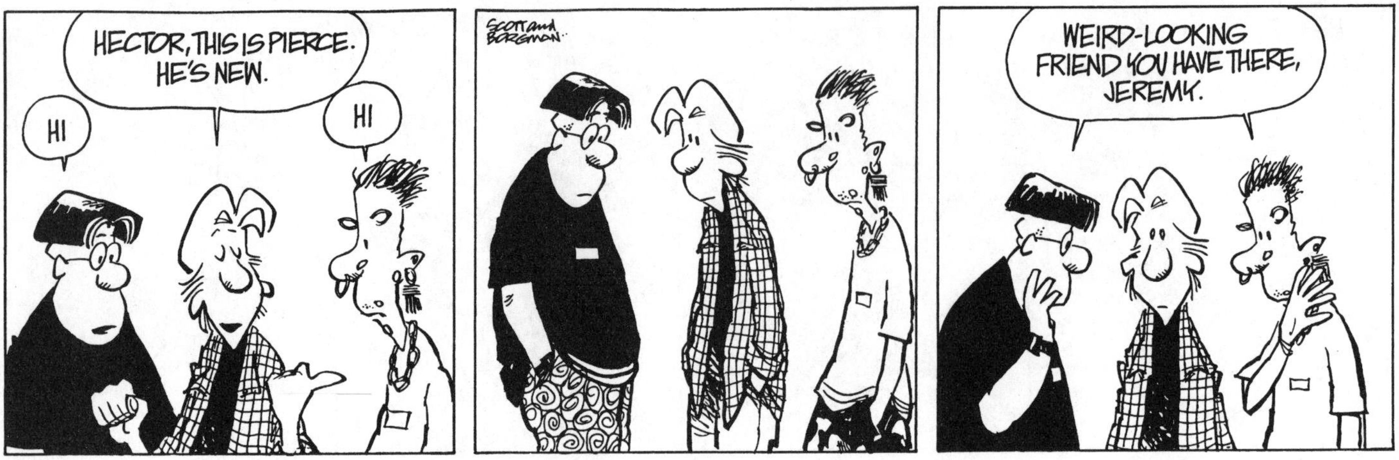
HECTOR, THIS IS PIERCE. HE'S NEW.
HI
HI
SCOTT and BORGMAN
WEIRD-LOOKING FRIEND YOU HAVE THERE, JEREMY.

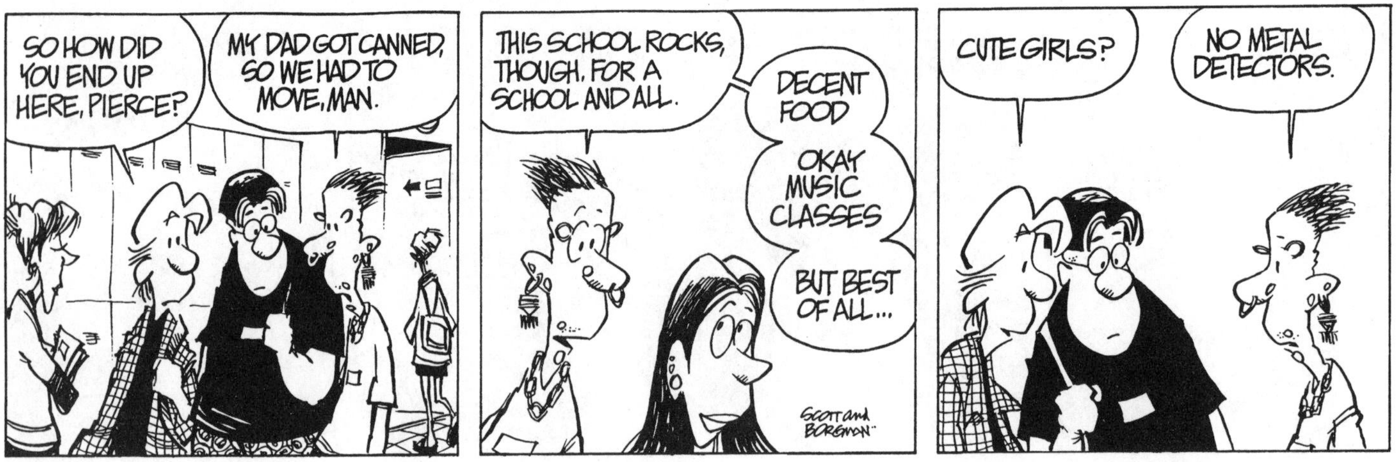
SO HOW DID YOU END UP HERE, PIERCE?
MY DAD GOT CANNED, SO WE HAD TO MOVE, MAN.
THIS SCHOOL ROCKS, THOUGH. FOR A SCHOOL AND ALL.
DECENT FOOD
OKAY MUSIC CLASSES
BUT BEST OF ALL...
SCOTT and BORGMAN
CUTE GIRLS?
NO METAL DETECTORS.

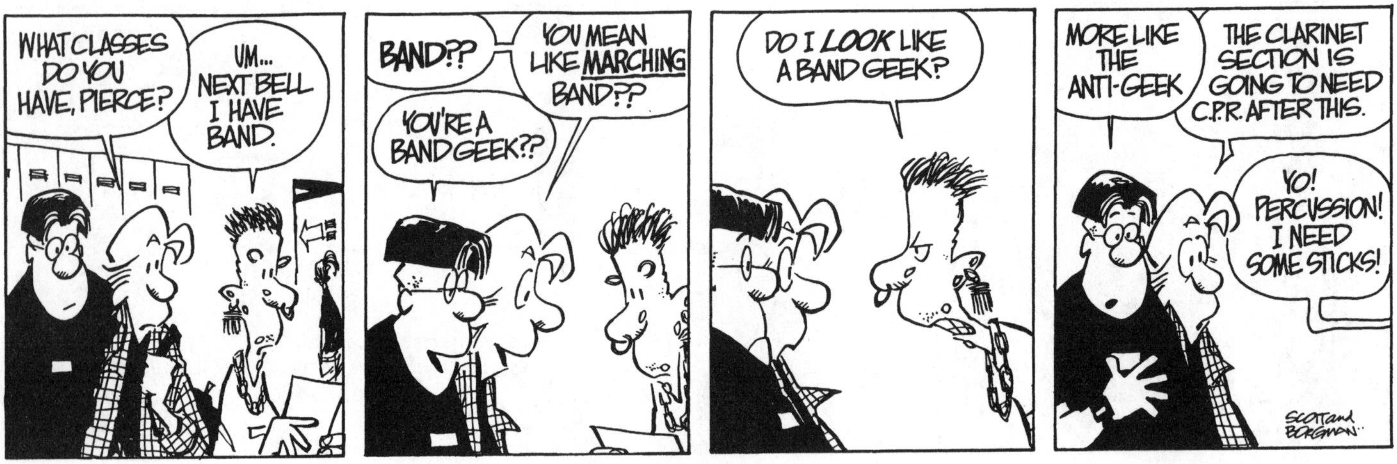
WHAT CLASSES DO YOU HAVE, PIERCE?
UM... NEXT BELL I HAVE BAND.
BAND??
YOU MEAN LIKE MARCHING BAND??
YOU'RE A BAND GEEK??
DO I LOOK LIKE A BAND GEEK?
MORE LIKE THE ANTI-GEEK
THE CLARINET SECTION IS GOING TO NEED C.P.R. AFTER THIS.
YO! PERCUSSION! I NEED SOME STICKS!
SCOTT and BORGMAN

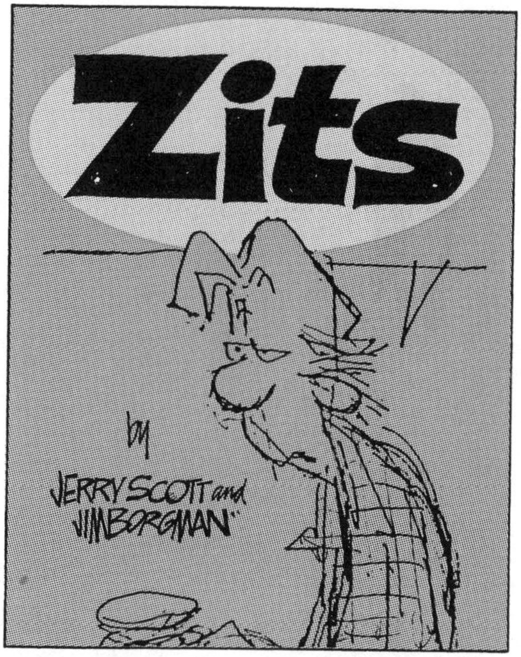
Zits
by
JERRY SCOTT and
JIM BORGMAN

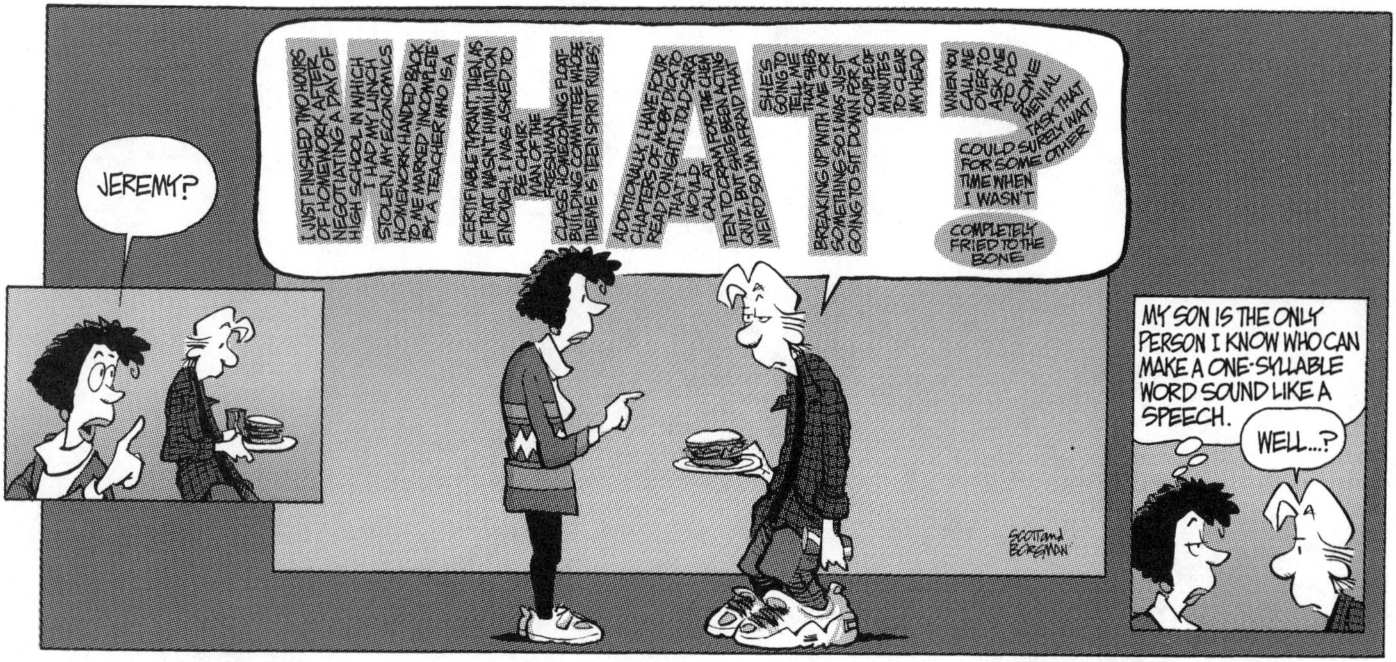
JEREMY?
WHAT?
I JUST FINISHED TWO HOURS OF HOMEWORK AFTER NEGOTIATING A DAY OF HIGH SCHOOL IN WHICH I HAD MY LUNCH STOLEN, MY ECONOMICS HOMEWORK HANDED BACK TO ME MARKED 'INCOMPLETE' BY A TEACHER WHO IS A
CERTIFIABLE TYRANT. THEN, AS IF THAT WASN'T HUMILIATION ENOUGH, I WAS ASKED TO BE CHAIRMAN OF THE FRESHMAN CLASS HOMECOMING FLOAT BUILDING COMMITTEE WHOSE THEME IS 'TEEN SPIRIT RULES!'
ADDITIONALLY, I HAVE FOUR CHAPTERS OF MOBY DICK TO READ TONIGHT. I TOLD SARA THAT I WOULD CALL AT TEN TO CRAM FOR THE CHEM QUIZ, BUT SHE'S BEEN ACTING WEIRD SO I'M AFRAID THAT
SHE'S GOING TO TELL ME THAT SHE'S BREAKING UP WITH ME OR SOMETHING SO I WAS JUST GOING TO SIT DOWN FOR A COUPLE OF MINUTES TO CLEAR MY HEAD
WHEN YOU CALL ME OVER TO ASK ME TO DO SOME MENIAL TASK THAT COULD SURELY WAIT FOR SOME OTHER TIME WHEN I WASN'T
COMPLETELY FRIED TO THE BONE
SCOTT and BORGMAN
MY SON IS THE ONLY PERSON I KNOW WHO CAN MAKE A ONE-SYLLABLE WORD SOUND LIKE A SPEECH.
WELL...?

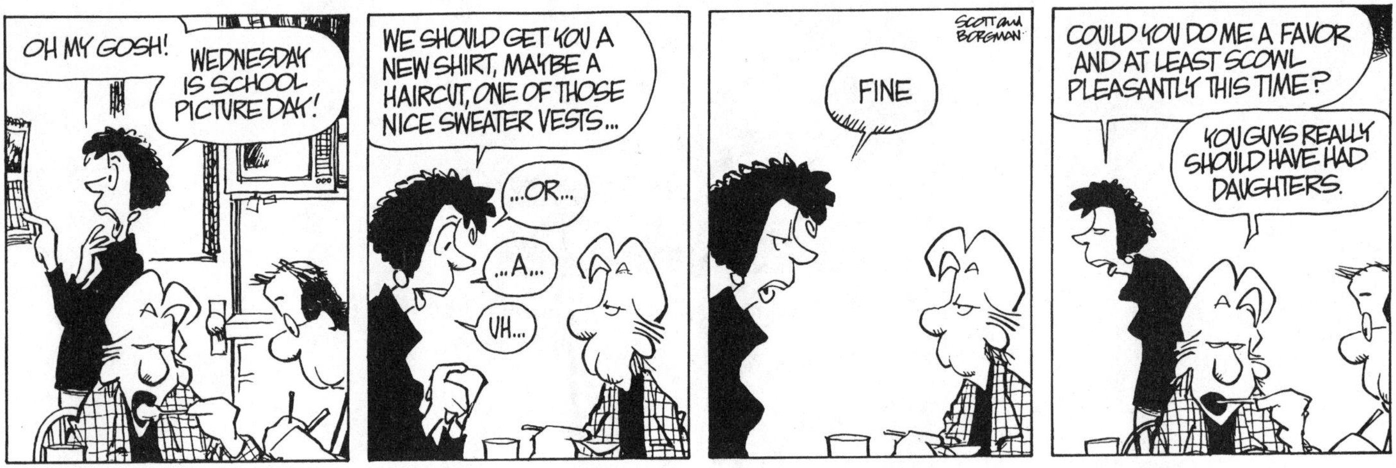
OH MY GOSH!
WEDNESDAY IS SCHOOL PICTURE DAY!
WE SHOULD GET YOU A NEW SHIRT, MAYBE A HAIRCUT, ONE OF THOSE NICE SWEATER VESTS...
...OR...
...A...
UH...
SCOTT AND BORGMAN
FINE
COULD YOU DO ME A FAVOR AND AT LEAST SCOWL PLEASANTLY THIS TIME?
YOU GUYS REALLY SHOULD HAVE HAD DAUGHTERS.

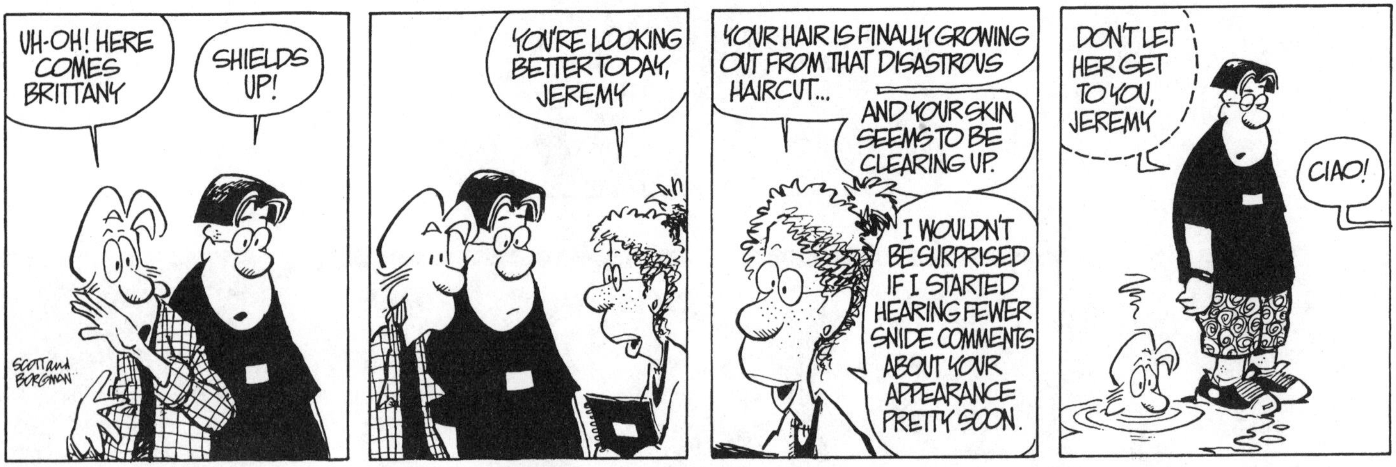
UH-OH! HERE COMES BRITTANY
SHIELDS UP!
SCOTT AND BORGMAN
YOU'RE LOOKING BETTER TODAY, JEREMY
YOUR HAIR IS FINALLY GROWING OUT FROM THAT DISASTROUS HAIRCUT...
AND YOUR SKIN SEEMS TO BE CLEARING UP.
I WOULDN'T BE SURPRISED IF I STARTED HEARING FEWER SNIDE COMMENTS ABOUT YOUR APPEARANCE PRETTY SOON.
DON'T LET HER GET TO YOU, JEREMY
CIAO!

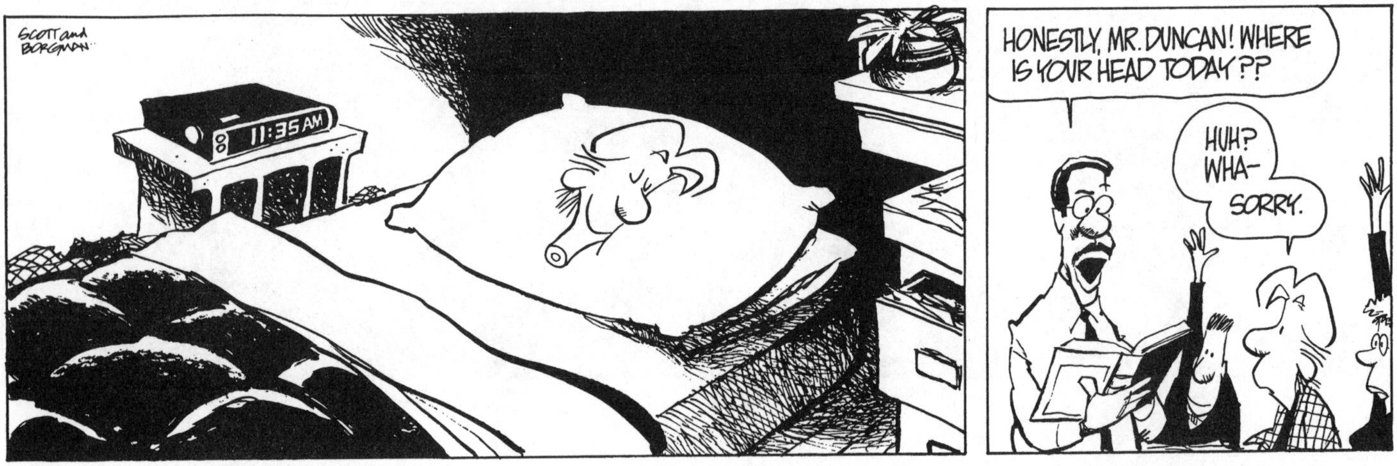
SCOTT AND BORGMAN
11:35 AM
HONESTLY, MR. DUNCAN! WHERE IS YOUR HEAD TODAY??
HUH? WHA- SORRY.

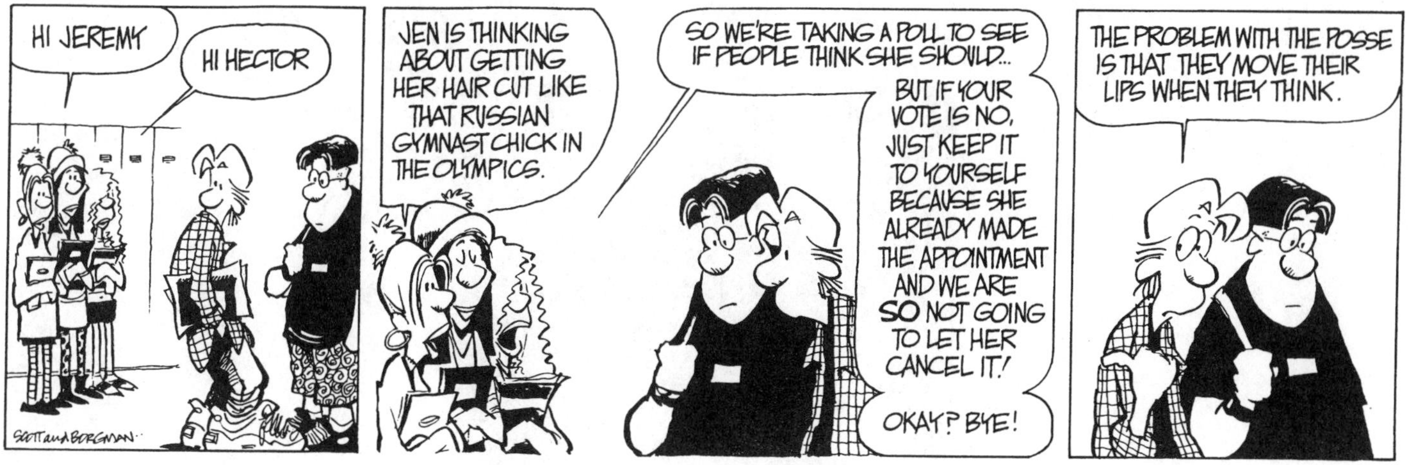
HI JEREMY
HI HECTOR
SCOTT and BORGMAN
JEN IS THINKING ABOUT GETTING HER HAIR CUT LIKE THAT RUSSIAN GYMNAST CHICK IN THE OLYMPICS.
SO WE'RE TAKING A POLL TO SEE IF PEOPLE THINK SHE SHOULD...
BUT IF YOUR VOTE IS NO, JUST KEEP IT TO YOURSELF BECAUSE SHE ALREADY MADE THE APPOINTMENT AND WE ARE SO NOT GOING TO LET HER CANCEL IT!
OKAY? BYE!
THE PROBLEM WITH THE POSSE IS THAT THEY MOVE THEIR LIPS WHEN THEY THINK.

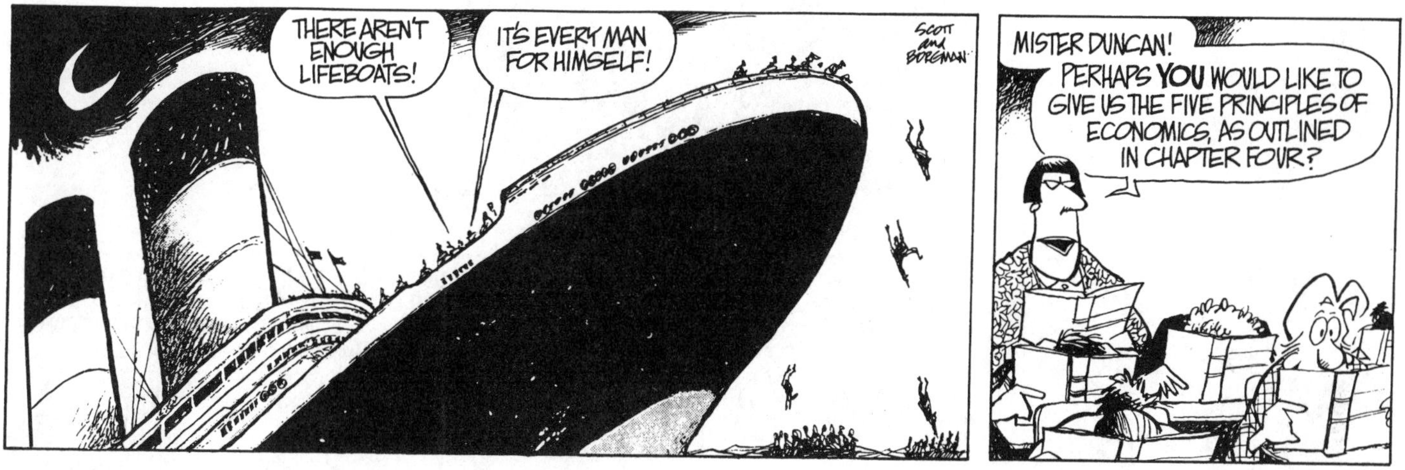
THERE AREN'T ENOUGH LIFEBOATS!
IT'S EVERY MAN FOR HIMSELF!
SCOTT and BORGMAN
MISTER DUNCAN!
PERHAPS YOU WOULD LIKE TO GIVE US THE FIVE PRINCIPLES OF ECONOMICS, AS OUTLINED IN CHAPTER FOUR?

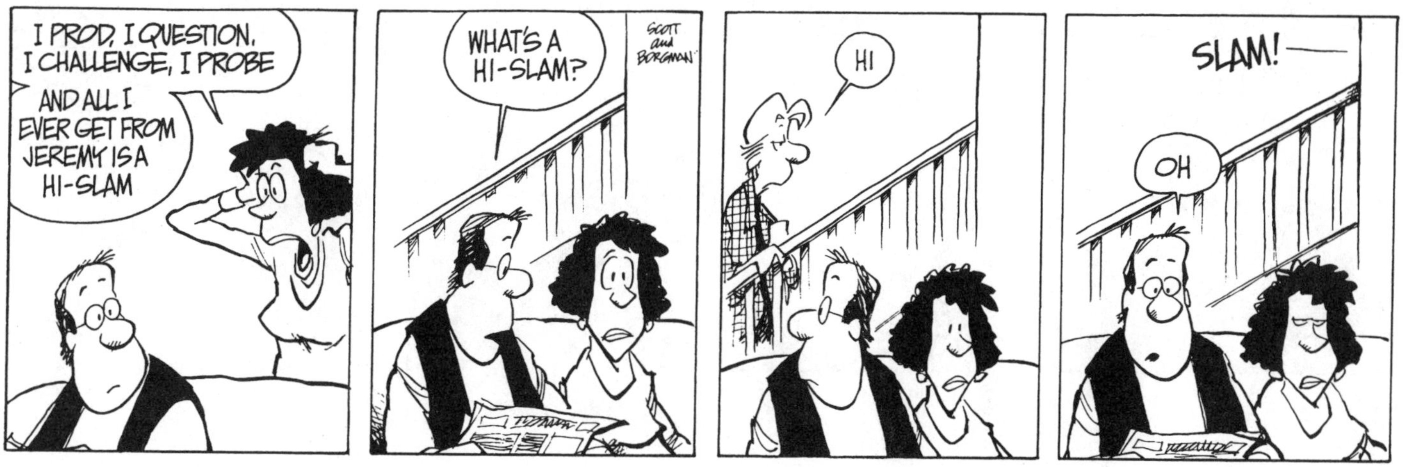
I PROD, I QUESTION, I CHALLENGE, I PROBE
AND ALL I EVER GET FROM JEREMY IS A HI-SLAM
WHAT'S A HI-SLAM?
SCOTT and BORGMAN
HI
SLAM!
OH

Zits
by JERRY SCOTT and JIM BORGMAN

THIS HAS BEEN THE FIFTH-BEST DAY OF MY LIFE!
REALLY? FIFTH?
WORLD HISTORY
A+
WELL, THE FIRST WOULD BE THE DAY I WAS BORN, OF COURSE.
OF COURSE
SECOND WAS THE DAY OF THE 'N SYNC CONCERT WHEN JUSTIN— I SWEAR—LOOKED STRAIGHT AT ME!
OKAY
THIRD WOULD BE THE DAY WE GOT PIZZA FOR MARGO'S BIRTHDAY IN THIRD GRADE AND WE GOT TO DANCE IN OUR BARE FEET IN THE GYM.
UM-HMM
AND THE FOURTH WAS THE TIME MY DAD AND I SPENT THE WHOLE DAY AT THE MALL AND NEITHER OF US MENTIONED THE DIVORCE ONCE.
WHAT WAS THE SIXTH?
THE SIXTH BEST DAY OF MY LIFE WAS THE DAY WE MET.
REALLY?
REALLY.
BECAUSE THAT WAS THE DAY THEY CAME OUT WITH PEANUT BUTTER COOKIE DOUGH ICE CREAM AT GRAETER'S, WHICH I CAN TOTALLY NOT LIVE WITHOUT UNDER ANY CIRCUMSTANCES BECAUSE THE STUFF IS WAY BEYOND GOOD. IT'S LIKE A RELIGIOUS EXPERIENCE! AND WHENEVER
sigh

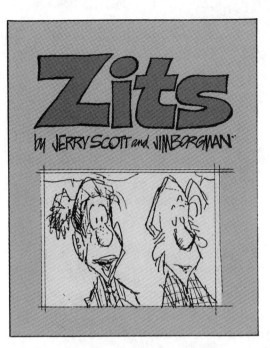

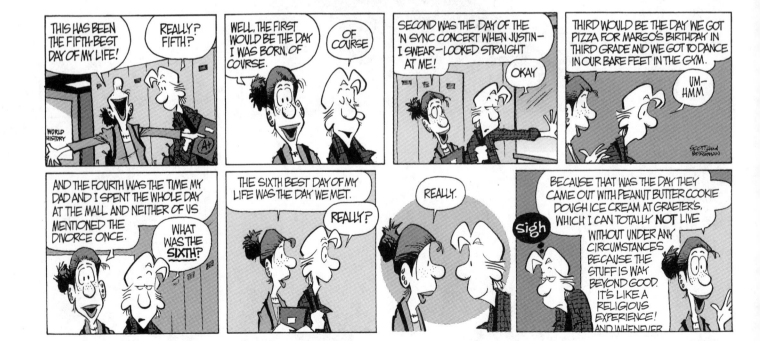

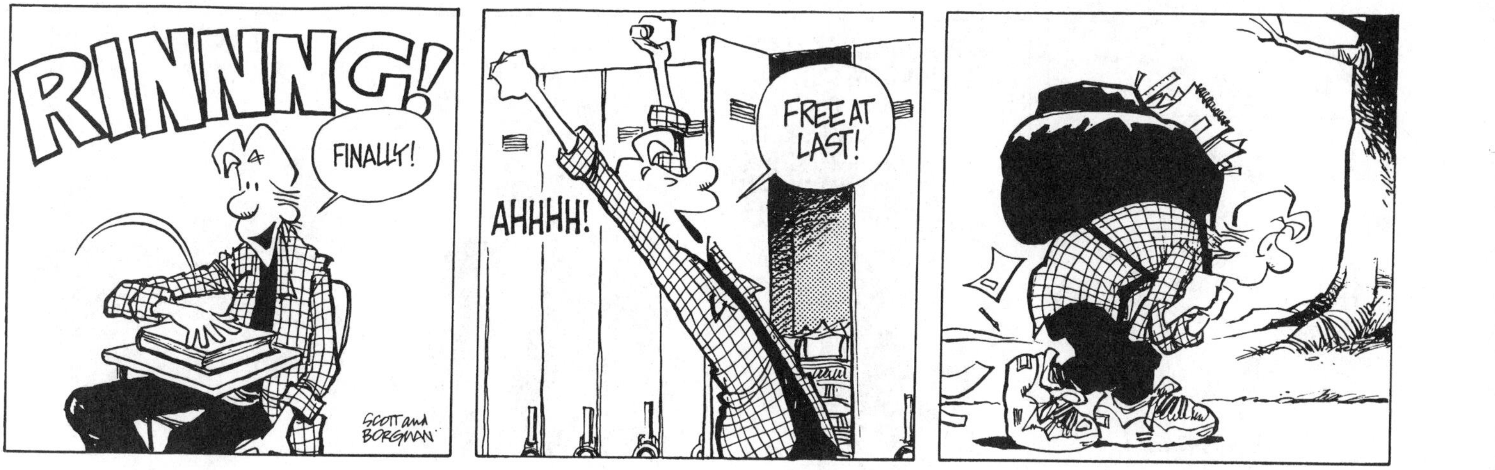
RINNNG!
FINALLY!
SCOTT and BORGMAN
AHHHH!
FREE AT LAST!

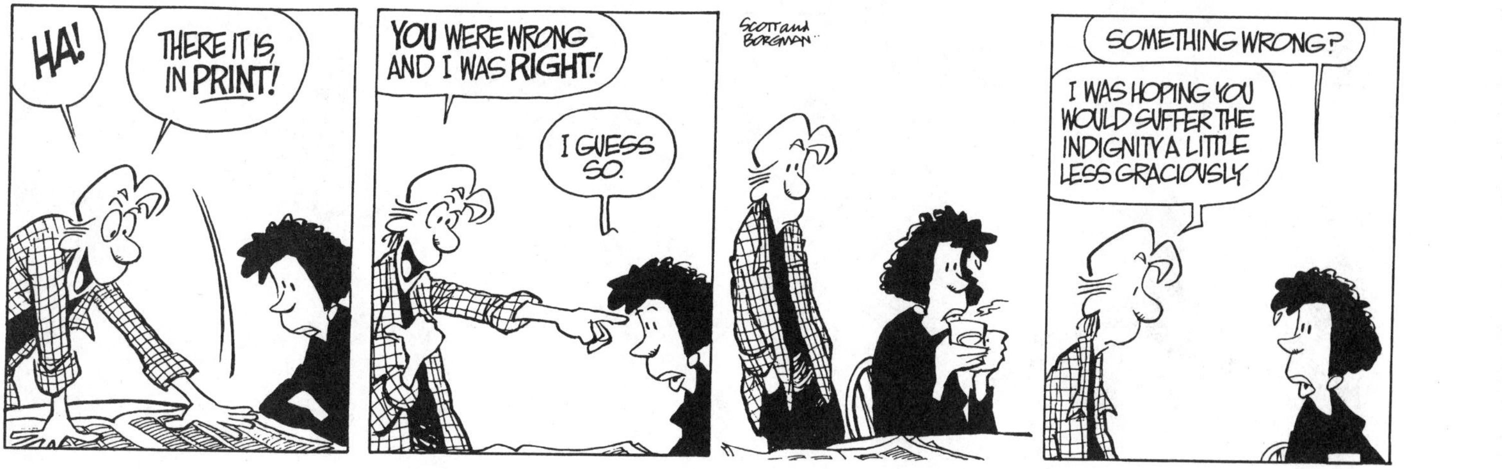
HA!
THERE IT IS, IN PRINT!
YOU WERE WRONG AND I WAS RIGHT!
I GUESS SO.
SCOTT and BORGMAN
SOMETHING WRONG?
I WAS HOPING YOU WOULD SUFFER THE INDIGNITY A LITTLE LESS GRACIOUSLY

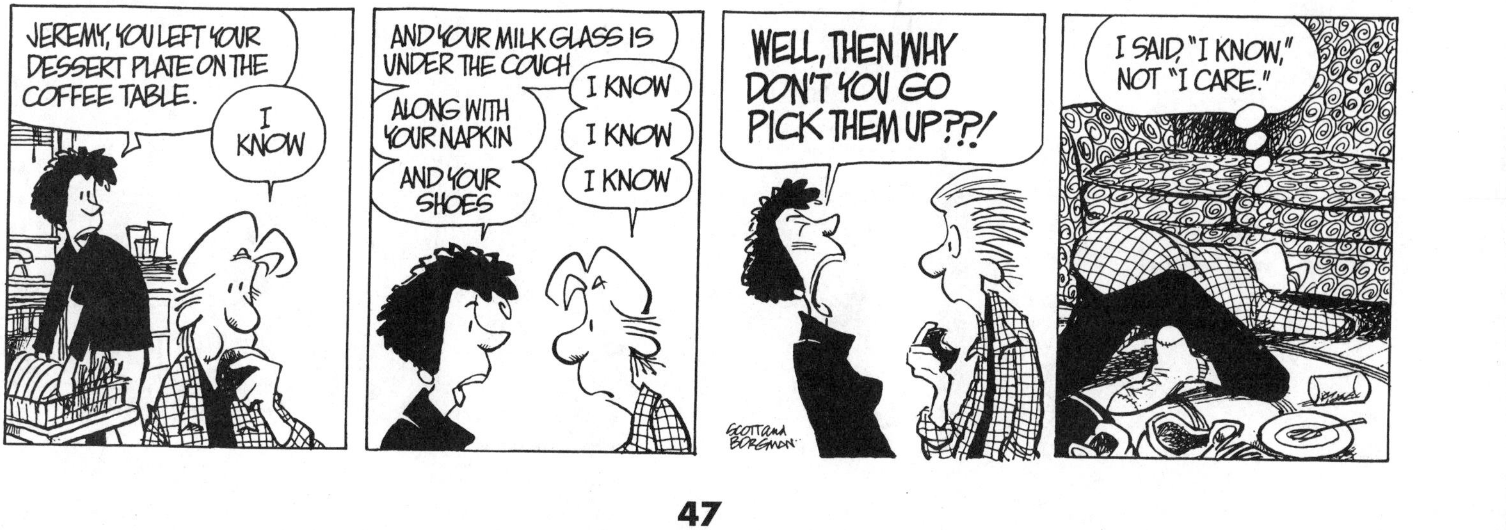
JEREMY, YOU LEFT YOUR DESSERT PLATE ON THE COFFEE TABLE.
I KNOW
AND YOUR MILK GLASS IS UNDER THE COUCH
I KNOW
ALONG WITH YOUR NAPKIN
I KNOW
AND YOUR SHOES
I KNOW
WELL, THEN WHY DON'T YOU GO PICK THEM UP??!
SCOTT and BORGMAN
I SAID, "I KNOW," NOT "I CARE."

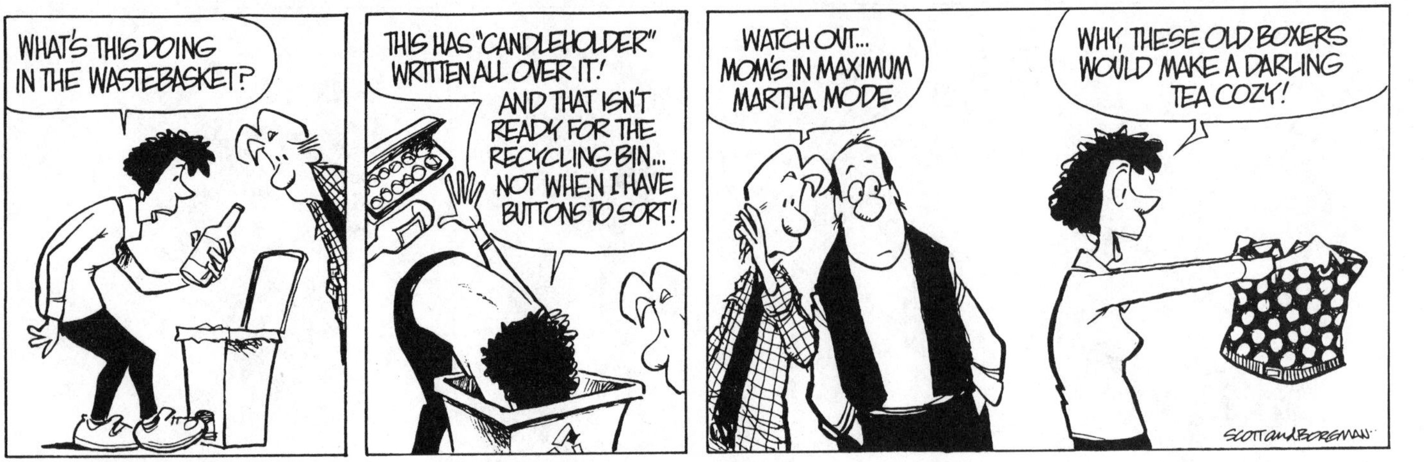
WHAT'S THIS DOING IN THE WASTEBASKET?
THIS HAS "CANDLEHOLDER" WRITTEN ALL OVER IT!
AND THAT ISN'T READY FOR THE RECYCLING BIN... NOT WHEN I HAVE BUTTONS TO SORT!
WATCH OUT... MOM'S IN MAXIMUM MARTHA MODE
WHY, THESE OLD BOXERS WOULD MAKE A DARLING TEA COZY!
SCOTT and BORGMAN

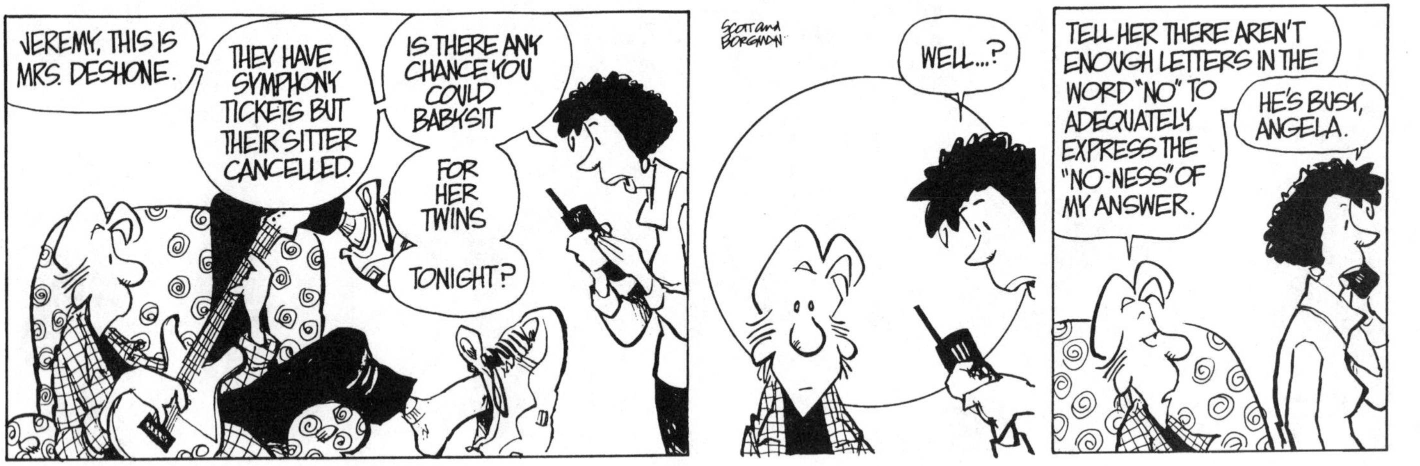
JEREMY, THIS IS MRS. DESHONE.
THEY HAVE SYMPHONY TICKETS BUT THEIR SITTER CANCELLED.
IS THERE ANY CHANCE YOU COULD BABYSIT
FOR HER TWINS
TONIGHT?
SCOTT and BORGMAN
WELL...?
TELL HER THERE AREN'T ENOUGH LETTERS IN THE WORD "NO" TO ADEQUATELY EXPRESS THE "NO-NESS" OF MY ANSWER.
HE'S BUSY, ANGELA.

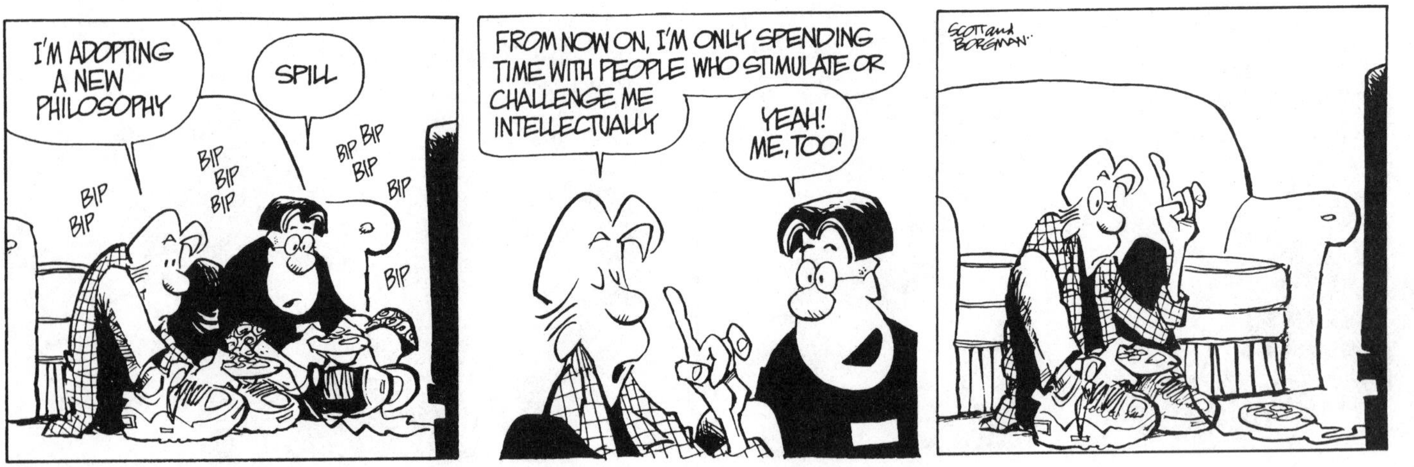
I'M ADOPTING A NEW PHILOSOPHY
SPILL
BIP BIP
BIP BIP BIP
BIP BIP BIP
BIP
BIP
FROM NOW ON, I'M ONLY SPENDING TIME WITH PEOPLE WHO STIMULATE OR CHALLENGE ME INTELLECTUALLY
YEAH! ME, TOO!
SCOTT and BORGMAN

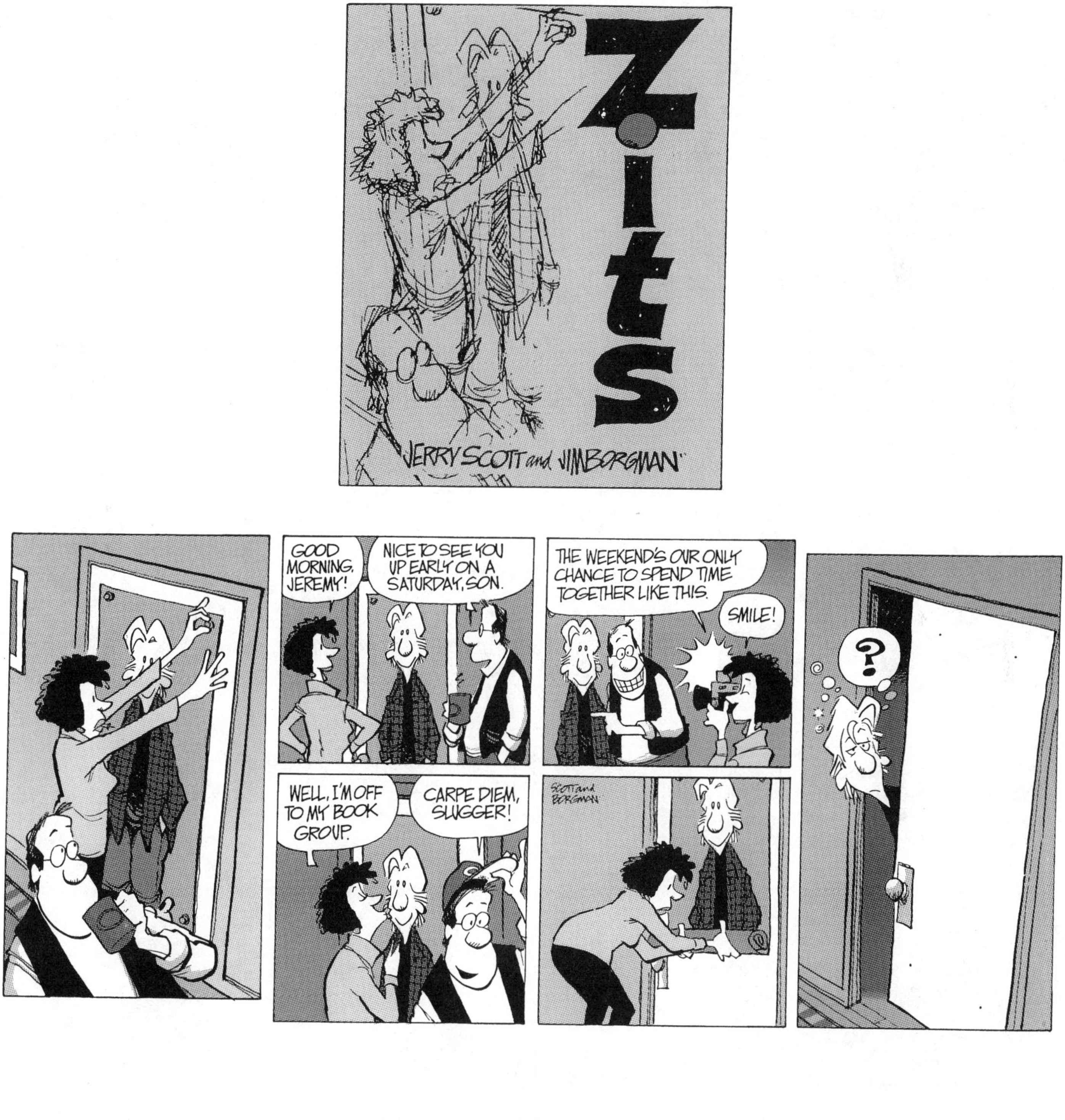
Zits
JERRY SCOTT and JIM BORGMAN
GOOD MORNING, JEREMY!
NICE TO SEE YOU UP EARLY ON A SATURDAY, SON.
THE WEEKEND'S OUR ONLY CHANCE TO SPEND TIME TOGETHER LIKE THIS.
SMILE!
WELL, I'M OFF TO MY BOOK GROUP.
CARPE DIEM, SLUGGER!
SCOTT and BORGMAN
?

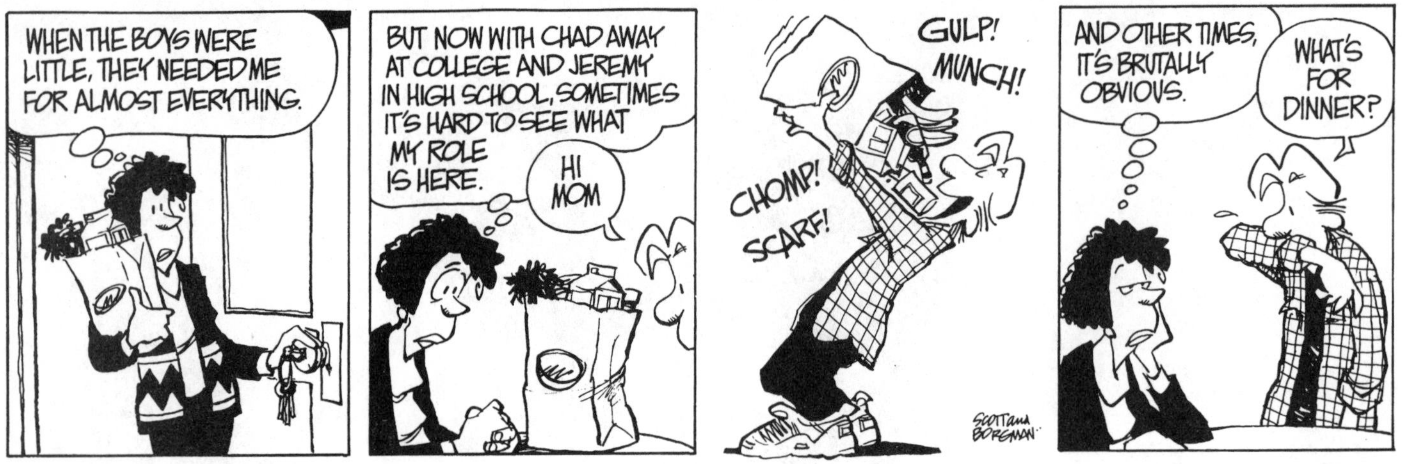
WHEN THE BOYS WERE LITTLE, THEY NEEDED ME FOR ALMOST EVERYTHING.
BUT NOW WITH CHAD AWAY AT COLLEGE AND JEREMY IN HIGH SCHOOL, SOMETIMES IT'S HARD TO SEE WHAT MY ROLE IS HERE.
HI MOM
GULP!
MUNCH!
CHOMP!
SCARF!
SCOTT and BORGMAN
AND OTHER TIMES, IT'S BRUTALLY OBVIOUS.
WHAT'S FOR DINNER?

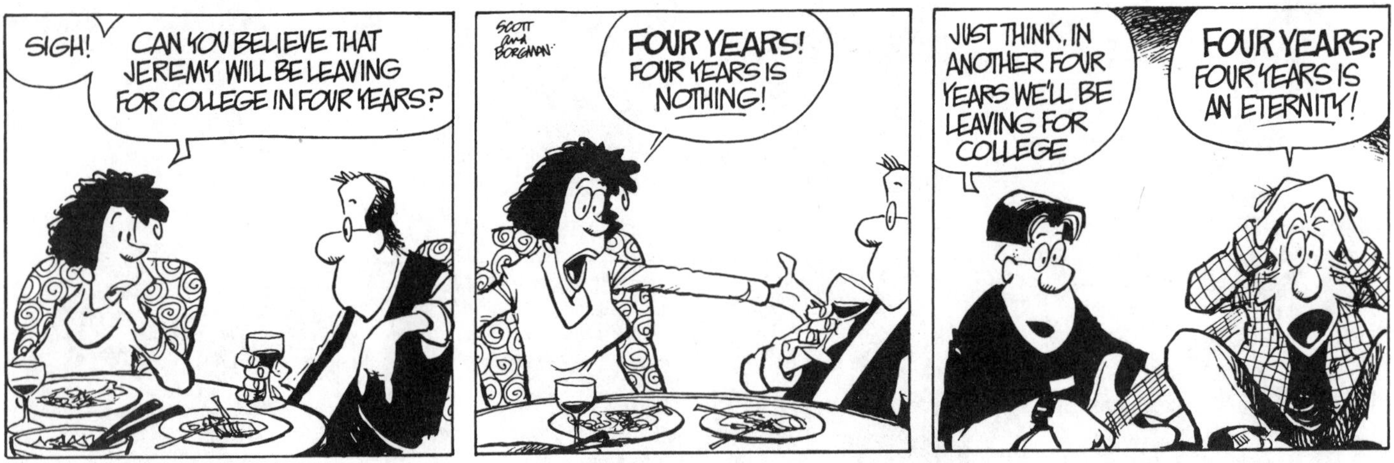
SIGH!
CAN YOU BELIEVE THAT JEREMY WILL BE LEAVING FOR COLLEGE IN FOUR YEARS?
SCOTT and BORGMAN
FOUR YEARS! FOUR YEARS IS NOTHING!
JUST THINK, IN ANOTHER FOUR YEARS WE'LL BE LEAVING FOR COLLEGE
FOUR YEARS? FOUR YEARS IS AN ETERNITY!

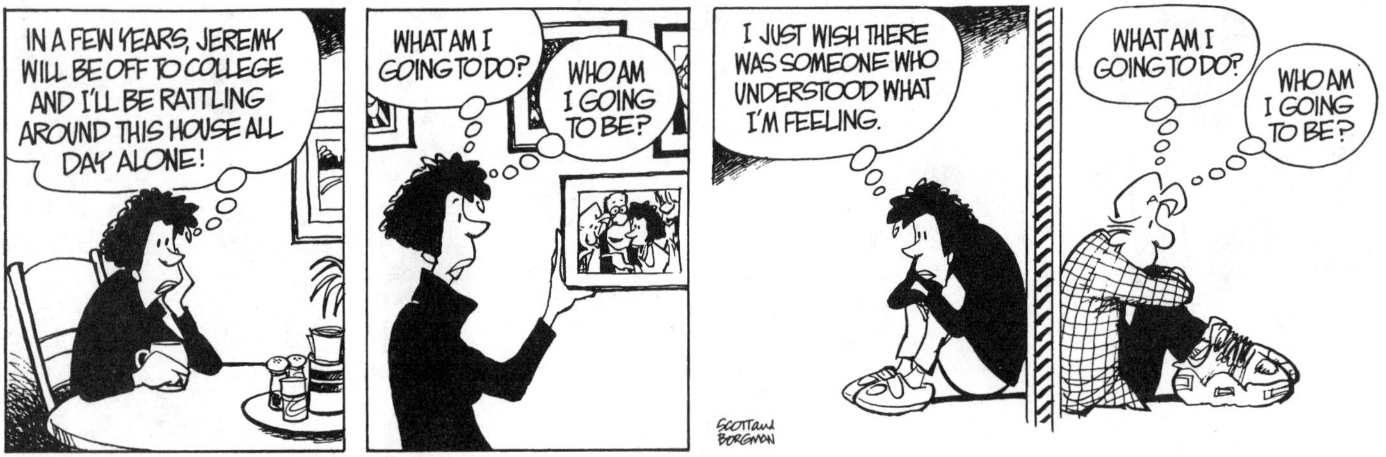
IN A FEW YEARS, JEREMY WILL BE OFF TO COLLEGE AND I'LL BE RATTLING AROUND THIS HOUSE ALL DAY ALONE!
WHAT AM I GOING TO DO?
WHO AM I GOING TO BE?
I JUST WISH THERE WAS SOMEONE WHO UNDERSTOOD WHAT I'M FEELING.
WHAT AM I GOING TO DO?
WHO AM I GOING TO BE?
SCOTT and BORGMAN

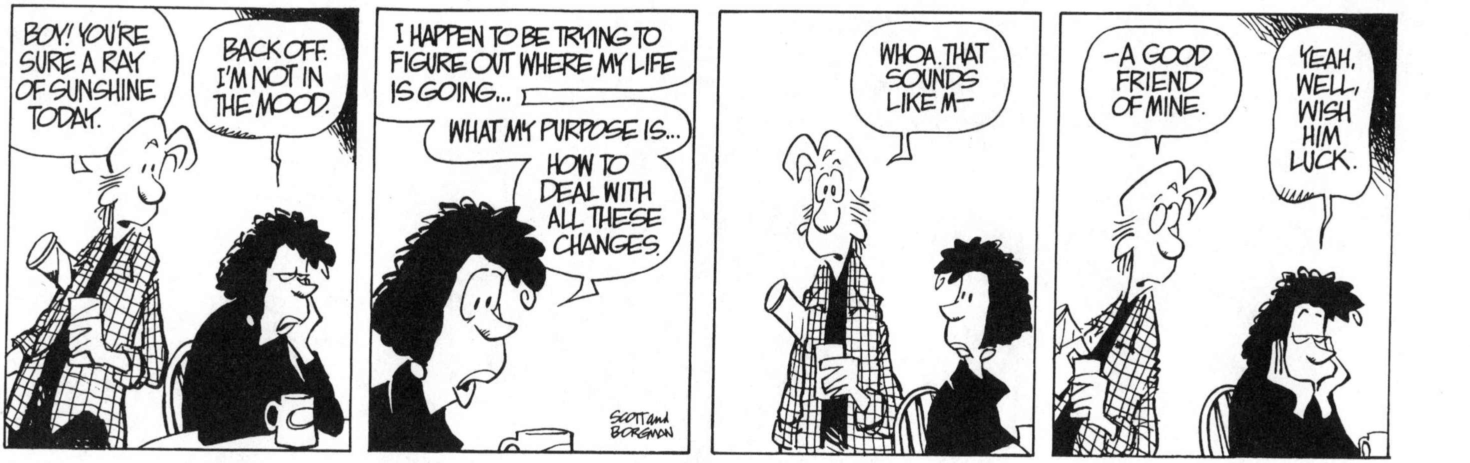
BOY! YOU'RE SURE A RAY OF SUNSHINE TODAY.
BACK OFF. I'M NOT IN THE MOOD.
I HAPPEN TO BE TRYING TO FIGURE OUT WHERE MY LIFE IS GOING...
WHAT MY PURPOSE IS...
HOW TO DEAL WITH ALL THESE CHANGES.
SCOTT and BORGMAN
WHOA. THAT SOUNDS LIKE M—
—A GOOD FRIEND OF MINE.
YEAH, WELL, WISH HIM LUCK.

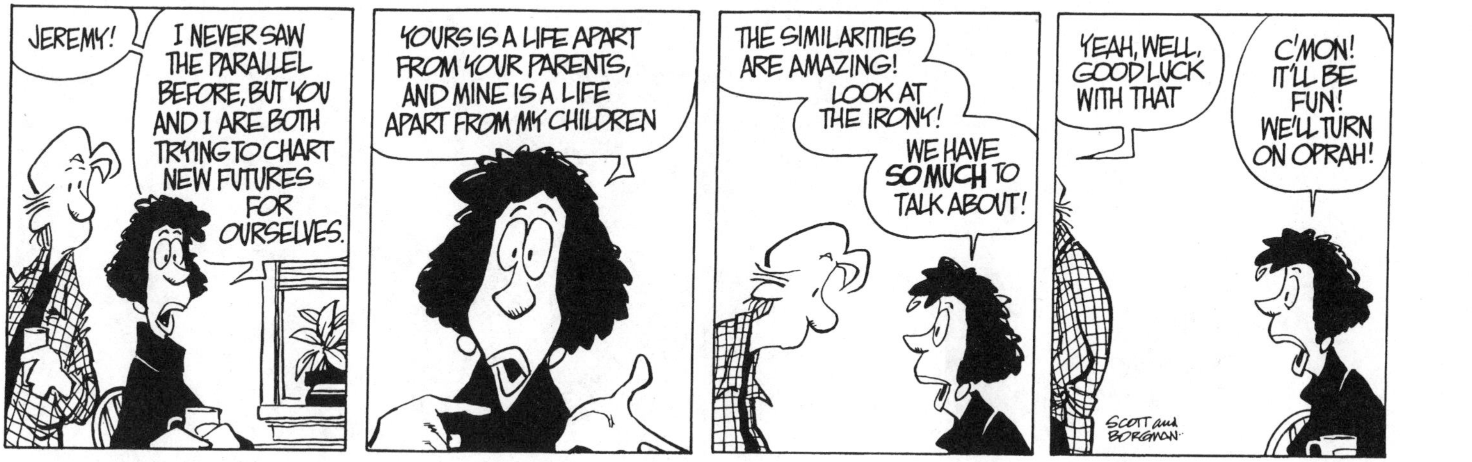
JEREMY!
I NEVER SAW THE PARALLEL BEFORE, BUT YOU AND I ARE BOTH TRYING TO CHART NEW FUTURES FOR OURSELVES.
YOURS IS A LIFE APART FROM YOUR PARENTS, AND MINE IS A LIFE APART FROM MY CHILDREN
THE SIMILARITIES ARE AMAZING!
LOOK AT THE IRONY!
WE HAVE **SO MUCH** TO TALK ABOUT!
YEAH, WELL, GOOD LUCK WITH THAT
C'MON! IT'LL BE FUN! WE'LL TURN ON OPRAH!
SCOTT and BORGMAN

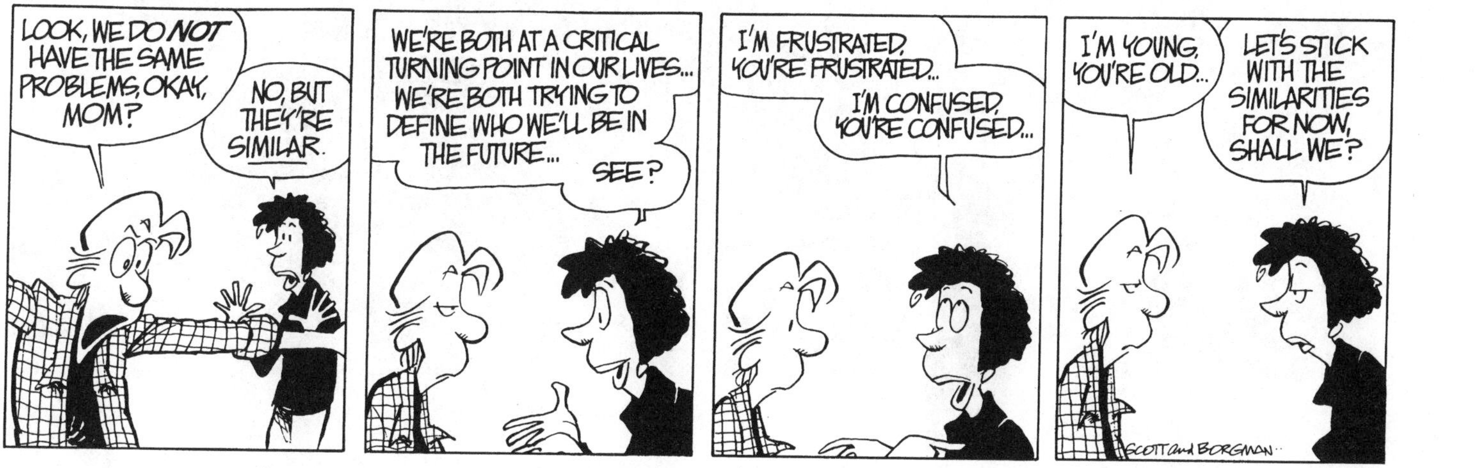
LOOK, WE DO ***NOT*** HAVE THE SAME PROBLEMS, OKAY, MOM?
NO, BUT THEY'RE SIMILAR.
WE'RE BOTH AT A CRITICAL TURNING POINT IN OUR LIVES... WE'RE BOTH TRYING TO DEFINE WHO WE'LL BE IN THE FUTURE...
SEE?
I'M FRUSTRATED, YOU'RE FRUSTRATED...
I'M CONFUSED, YOU'RE CONFUSED...
I'M YOUNG, YOU'RE OLD...
LET'S STICK WITH THE SIMILARITIES FOR NOW, SHALL WE?
SCOTT and BORGMAN

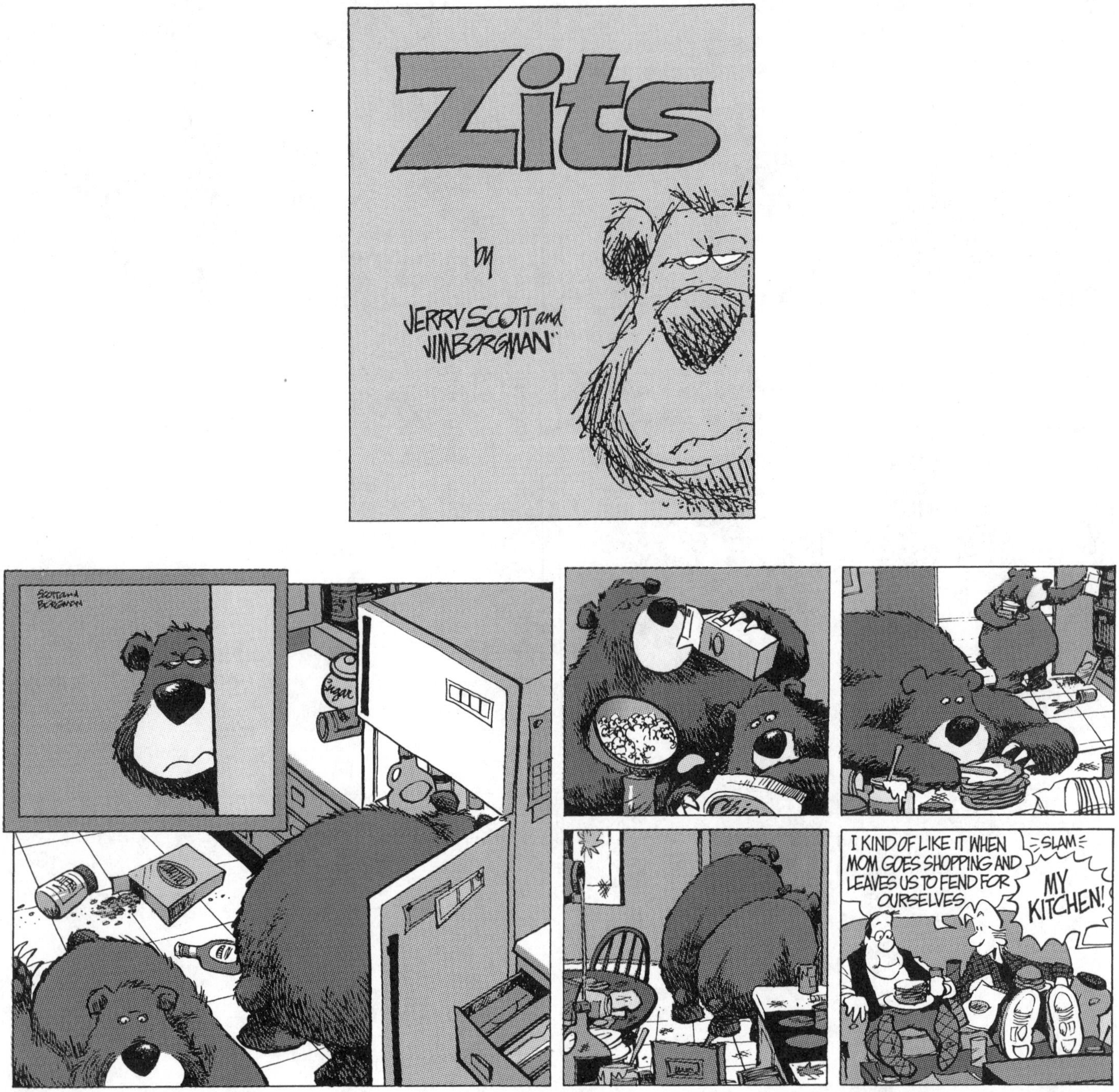
Zits
by
JERRY SCOTT and
JIM BORGMAN
I KIND OF LIKE IT WHEN MOM GOES SHOPPING AND LEAVES US TO FEND FOR OURSELVES.
SLAM
MY KITCHEN!

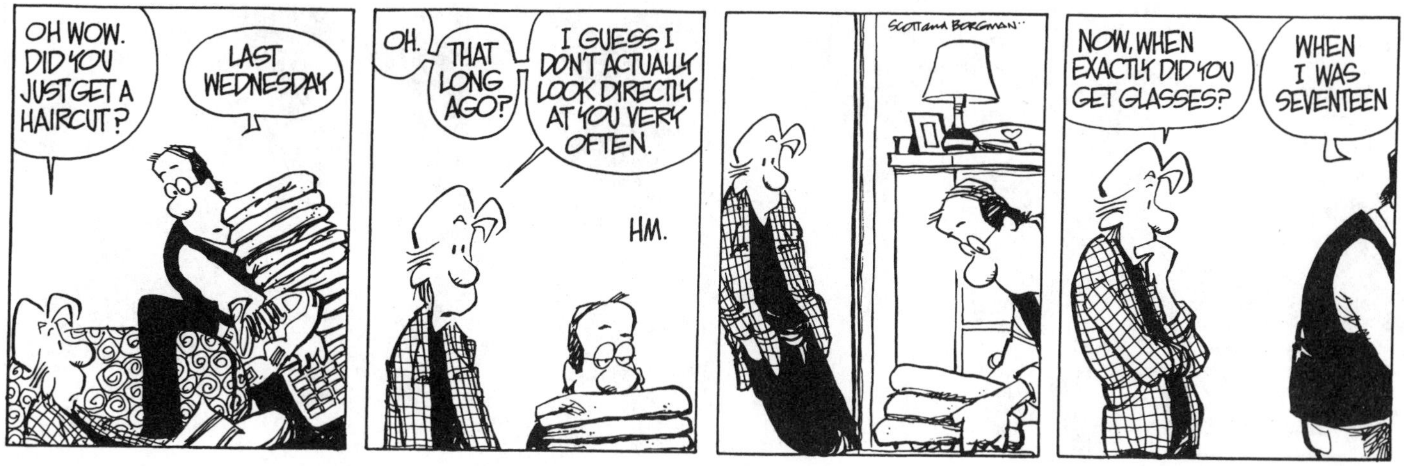
OH WOW. DID YOU JUST GET A HAIRCUT?
LAST WEDNESDAY
OH.
THAT LONG AGO?
I GUESS I DON'T ACTUALLY LOOK DIRECTLY AT YOU VERY OFTEN.
HM.
SCOTT and BORGMAN
NOW, WHEN EXACTLY DID YOU GET GLASSES?
WHEN I WAS SEVENTEEN

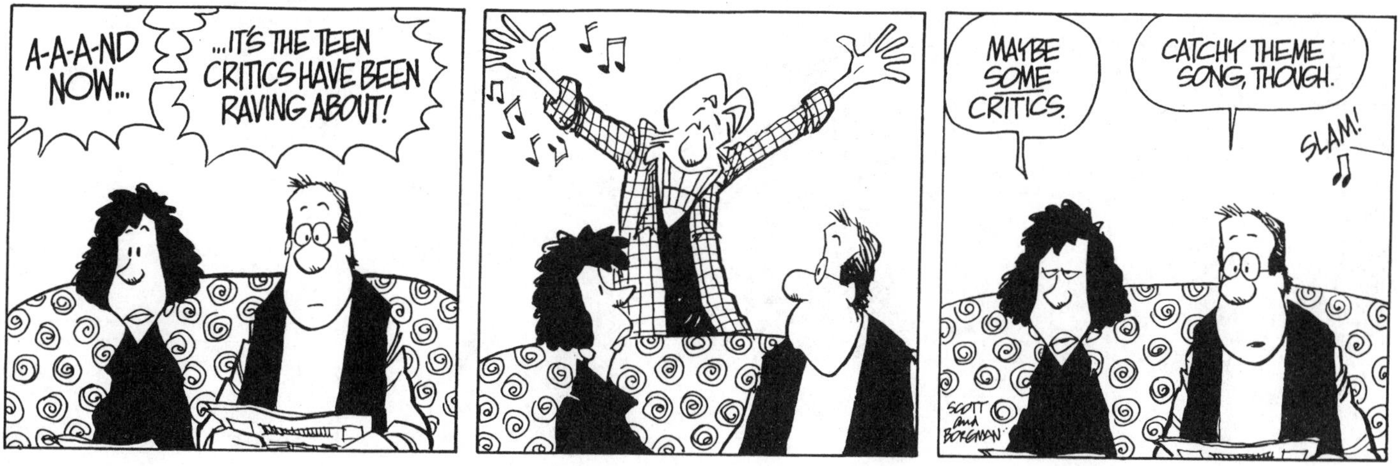
A-A-A-ND NOW...
...IT'S THE TEEN CRITICS HAVE BEEN RAVING ABOUT!
MAYBE SOME CRITICS.
CATCHY THEME SONG, THOUGH.
SLAM!
SCOTT and BORGMAN

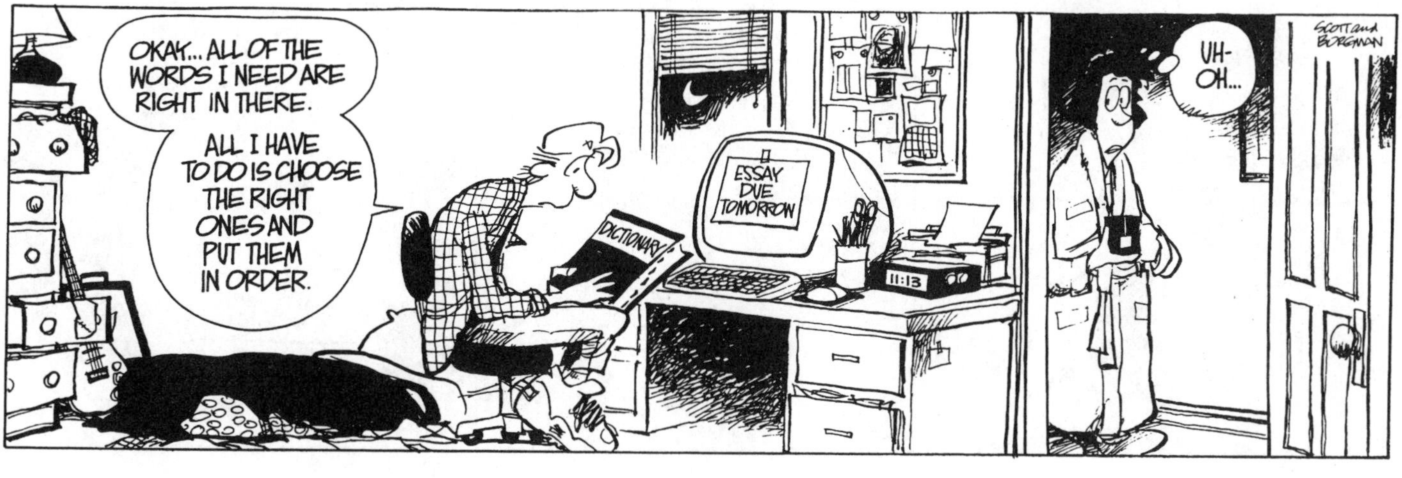
OKAY... ALL OF THE WORDS I NEED ARE RIGHT IN THERE.
ALL I HAVE TO DO IS CHOOSE THE RIGHT ONES AND PUT THEM IN ORDER.
ESSAY DUE TOMORROW
DICTIONARY
11:13
UH-OH...
SCOTT and BORGMAN

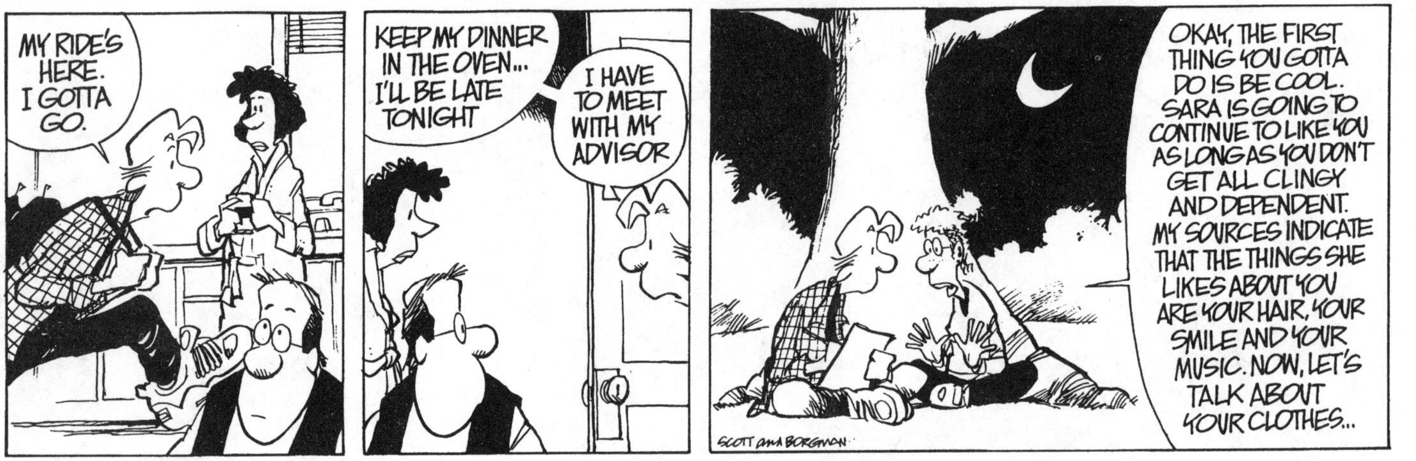
MY RIDE'S HERE. I GOTTA GO.
KEEP MY DINNER IN THE OVEN... I'LL BE LATE TONIGHT
I HAVE TO MEET WITH MY ADVISOR
OKAY, THE FIRST THING YOU GOTTA DO IS BE COOL. SARA IS GOING TO CONTINUE TO LIKE YOU AS LONG AS YOU DON'T GET ALL CLINGY AND DEPENDENT. MY SOURCES INDICATE THAT THE THINGS SHE LIKES ABOUT YOU ARE YOUR HAIR, YOUR SMILE AND YOUR MUSIC. NOW, LET'S TALK ABOUT YOUR CLOTHES...
SCOTT and BORGMAN

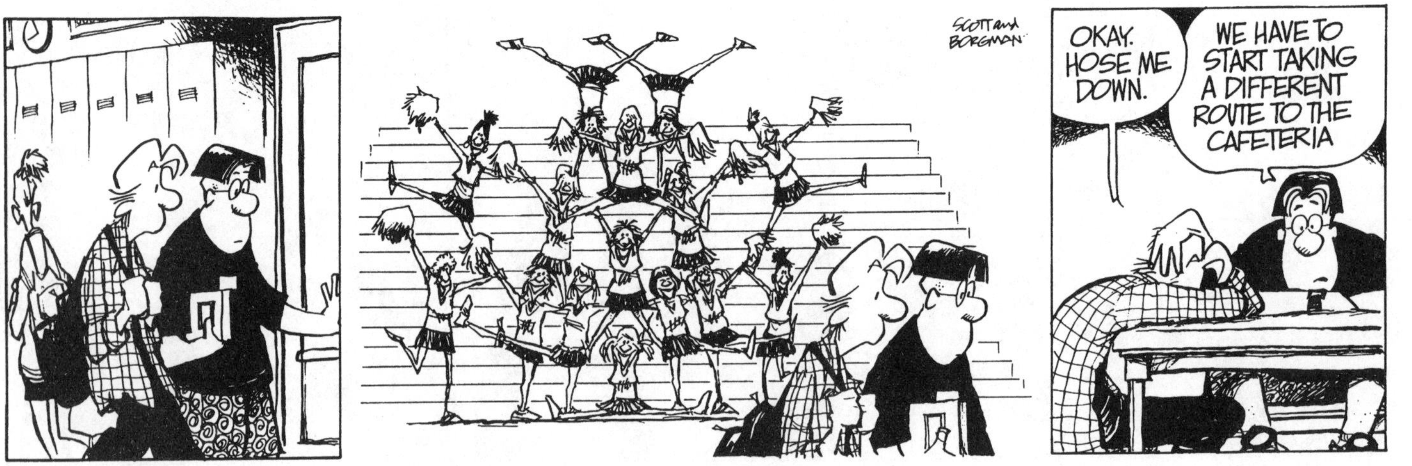
SCOTT and BORGMAN
OKAY. HOSE ME DOWN.
WE HAVE TO START TAKING A DIFFERENT ROUTE TO THE CAFETERIA

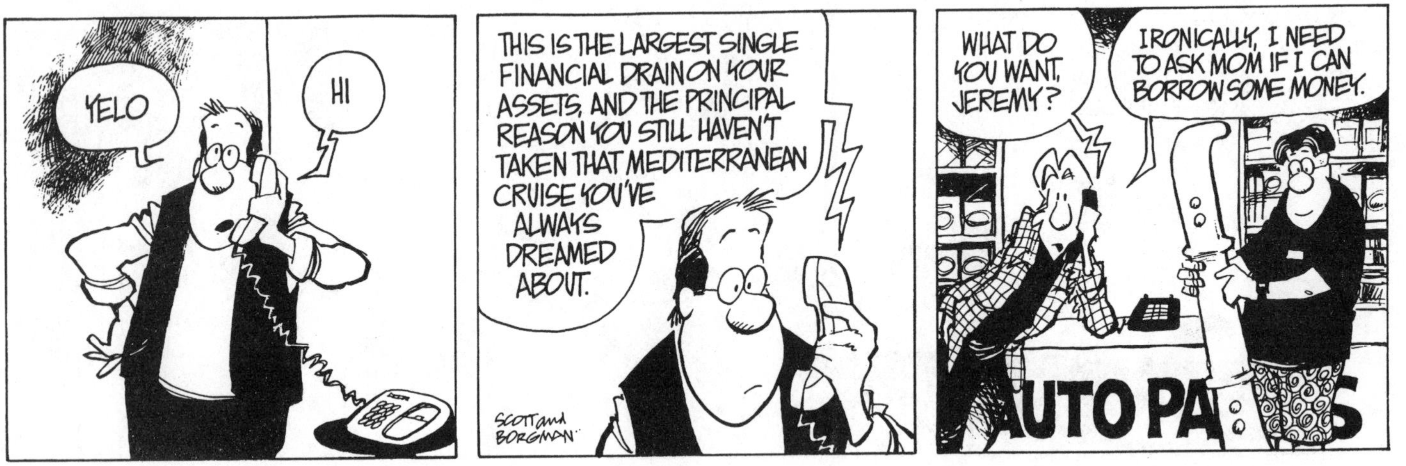
YELO
HI
THIS IS THE LARGEST SINGLE FINANCIAL DRAIN ON YOUR ASSETS, AND THE PRINCIPAL REASON YOU STILL HAVEN'T TAKEN THAT MEDITERRANEAN CRUISE YOU'VE ALWAYS DREAMED ABOUT.
SCOTT and BORGMAN
WHAT DO YOU WANT, JEREMY?
IRONICALLY, I NEED TO ASK MOM IF I CAN BORROW SOME MONEY.
AUTO PA S

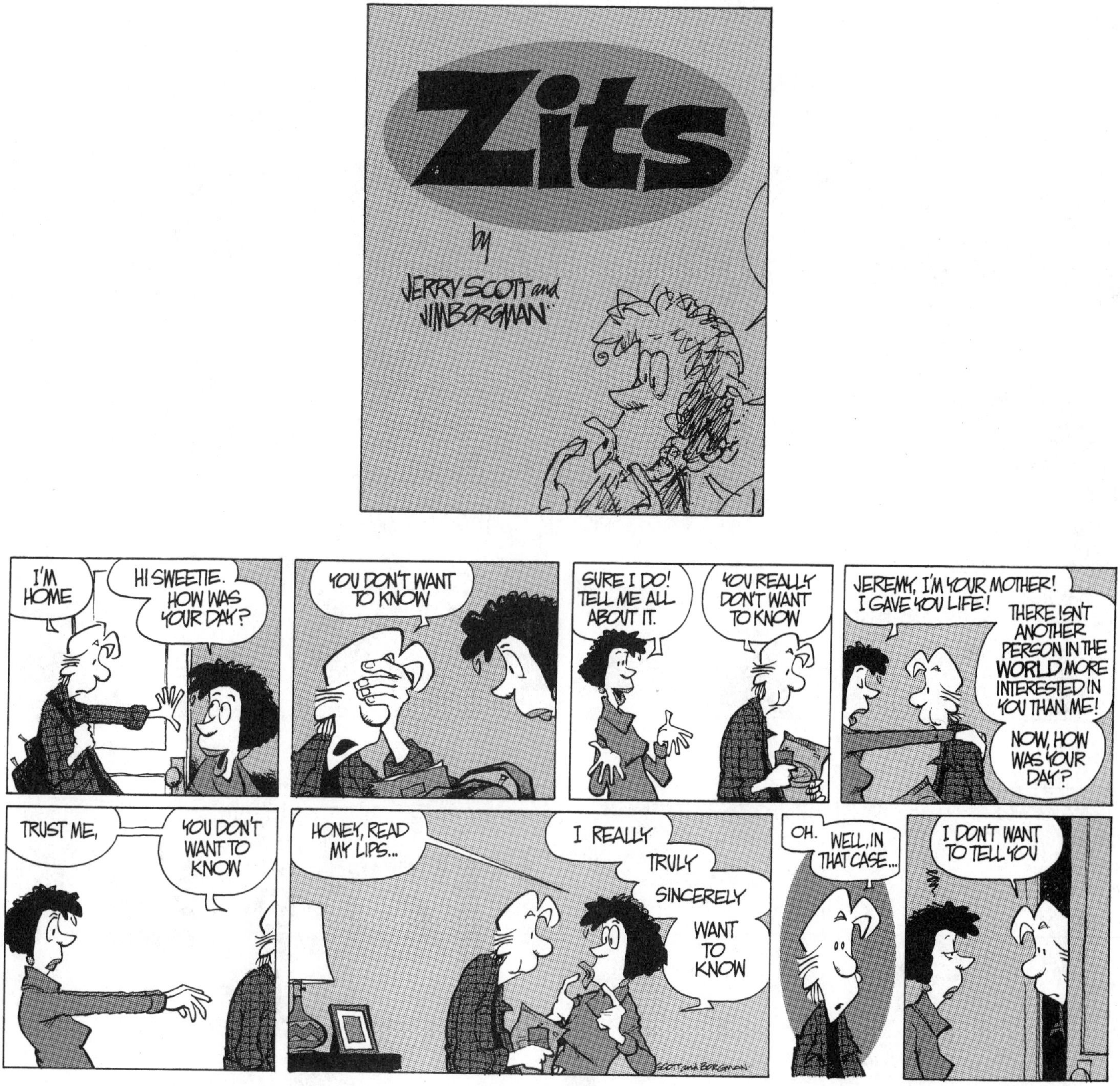
Zits
by
JERRY SCOTT and JIM BORGMAN
I'M HOME
HI SWEETIE. HOW WAS YOUR DAY?
YOU DON'T WANT TO KNOW
SURE I DO! TELL ME ALL ABOUT IT.
YOU REALLY DON'T WANT TO KNOW
JEREMY, I'M YOUR MOTHER! I GAVE YOU LIFE!
THERE ISN'T ANOTHER PERSON IN THE WORLD MORE INTERESTED IN YOU THAN ME!
NOW, HOW WAS YOUR DAY?
TRUST ME,
YOU DON'T WANT TO KNOW
HONEY, READ MY LIPS...
I REALLY
TRULY
SINCERELY
WANT TO KNOW
OH.
WELL, IN THAT CASE...
I DON'T WANT TO TELL YOU

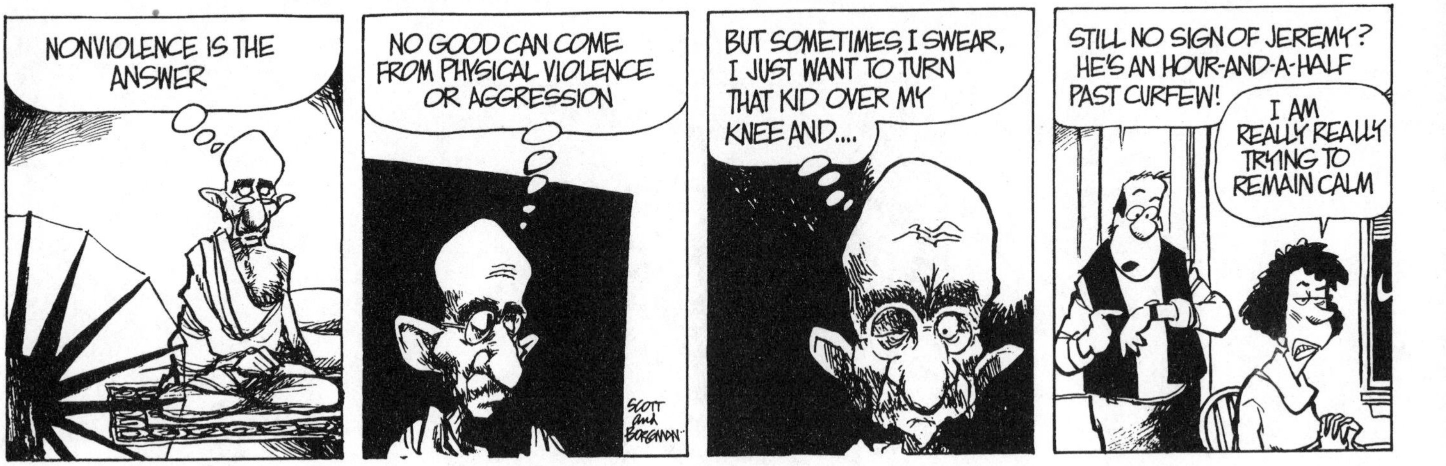
NONVIOLENCE IS THE ANSWER
NO GOOD CAN COME FROM PHYSICAL VIOLENCE OR AGGRESSION
BUT SOMETIMES, I SWEAR, I JUST WANT TO TURN THAT KID OVER MY KNEE AND....
STILL NO SIGN OF JEREMY? HE'S AN HOUR-AND-A-HALF PAST CURFEW!
I AM REALLY REALLY TRYING TO REMAIN CALM

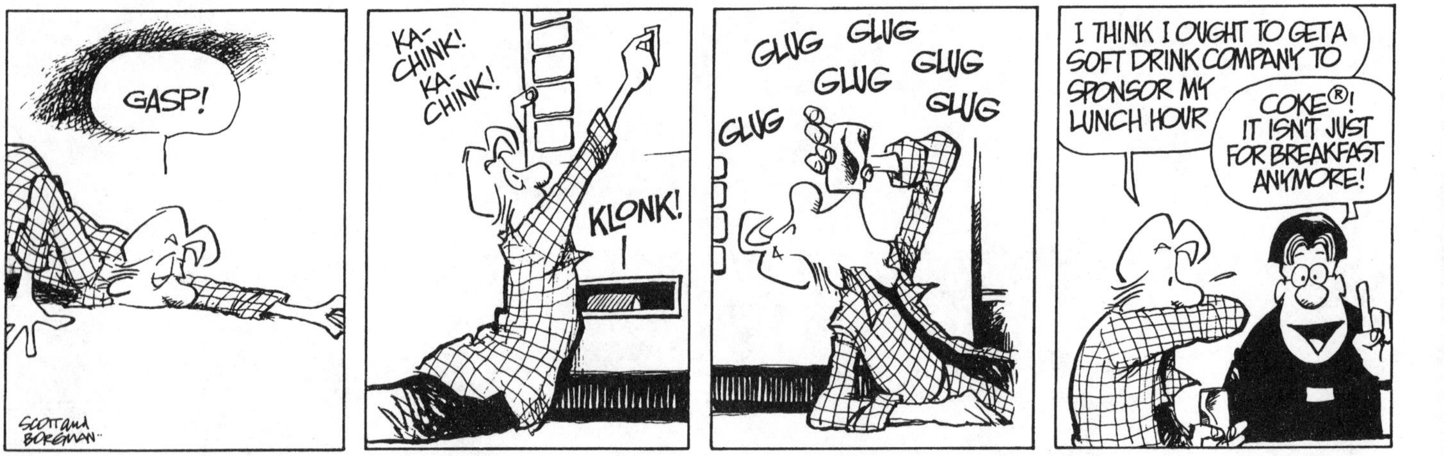
GASP!
KA-CHINK! KA-CHINK!
KLONK!
GLUG GLUG GLUG GLUG GLUG GLUG
I THINK I OUGHT TO GET A SOFT DRINK COMPANY TO SPONSOR MY LUNCH HOUR
COKE®! IT ISN'T JUST FOR BREAKFAST ANYMORE!

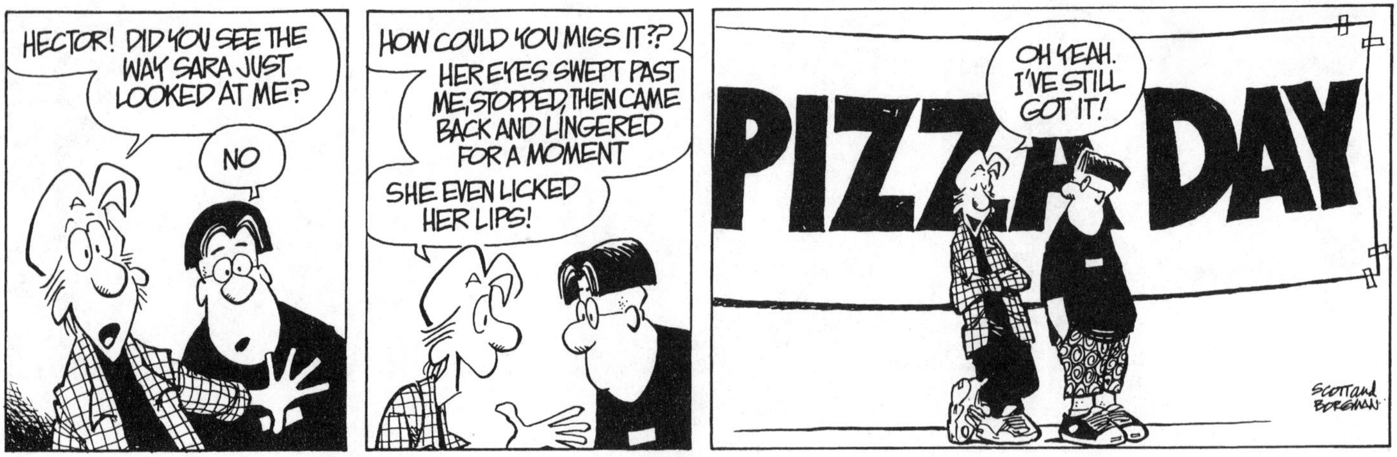
HECTOR! DID YOU SEE THE WAY SARA JUST LOOKED AT ME?
NO
HOW COULD YOU MISS IT??
HER EYES SWEPT PAST ME, STOPPED, THEN CAME BACK AND LINGERED FOR A MOMENT
SHE EVEN LICKED HER LIPS!
PIZZA DAY
OH YEAH. I'VE STILL GOT IT!

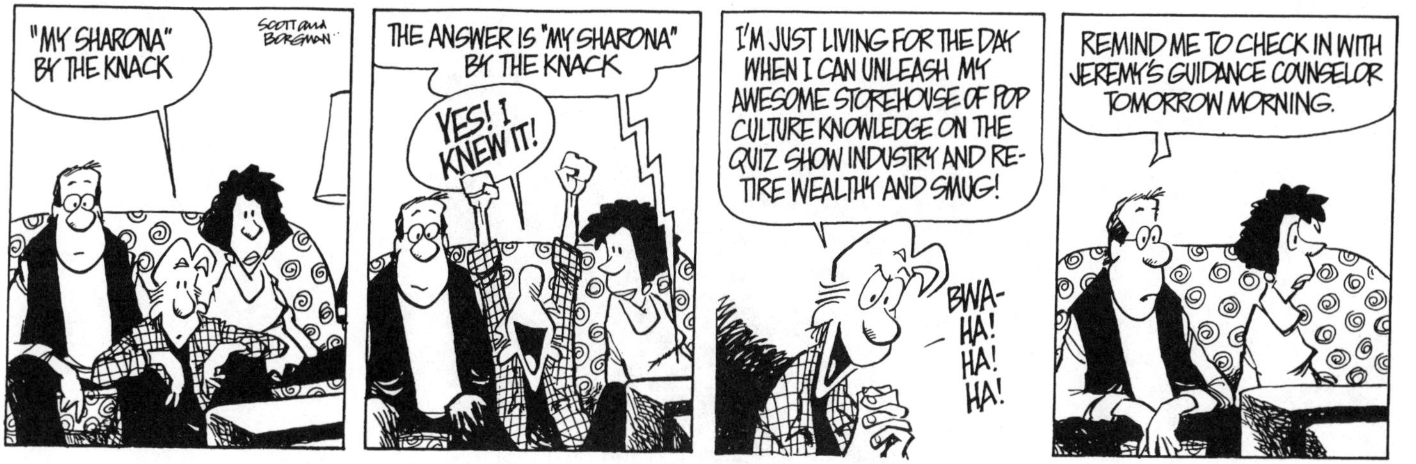
"MY SHARONA" BY THE KNACK
SCOTT and BORGMAN
THE ANSWER IS "MY SHARONA" BY THE KNACK
YES! I KNEW IT!
I'M JUST LIVING FOR THE DAY WHEN I CAN UNLEASH MY AWESOME STOREHOUSE OF POP CULTURE KNOWLEDGE ON THE QUIZ SHOW INDUSTRY AND RETIRE WEALTHY AND SMUG!
BWA-HA! HA! HA!
REMIND ME TO CHECK IN WITH JEREMY'S GUIDANCE COUNSELOR TOMORROW MORNING.

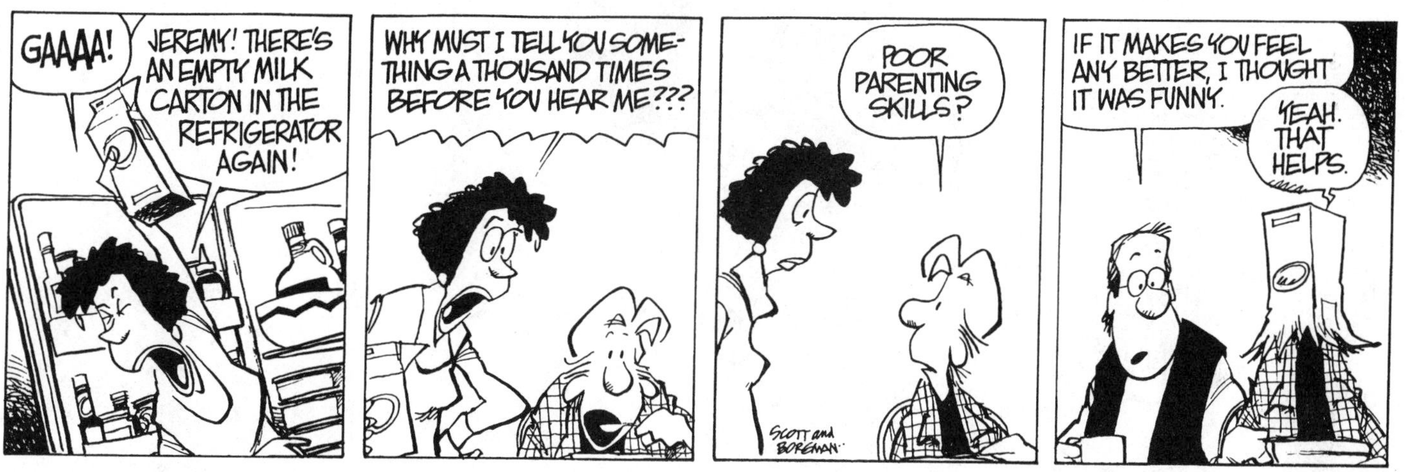
GAAAA!
JEREMY! THERE'S AN EMPTY MILK CARTON IN THE REFRIGERATOR AGAIN!
WHY MUST I TELL YOU SOMETHING A THOUSAND TIMES BEFORE YOU HEAR ME???
POOR PARENTING SKILLS?
SCOTT and BORGMAN
IF IT MAKES YOU FEEL ANY BETTER, I THOUGHT IT WAS FUNNY.
YEAH. THAT HELPS.

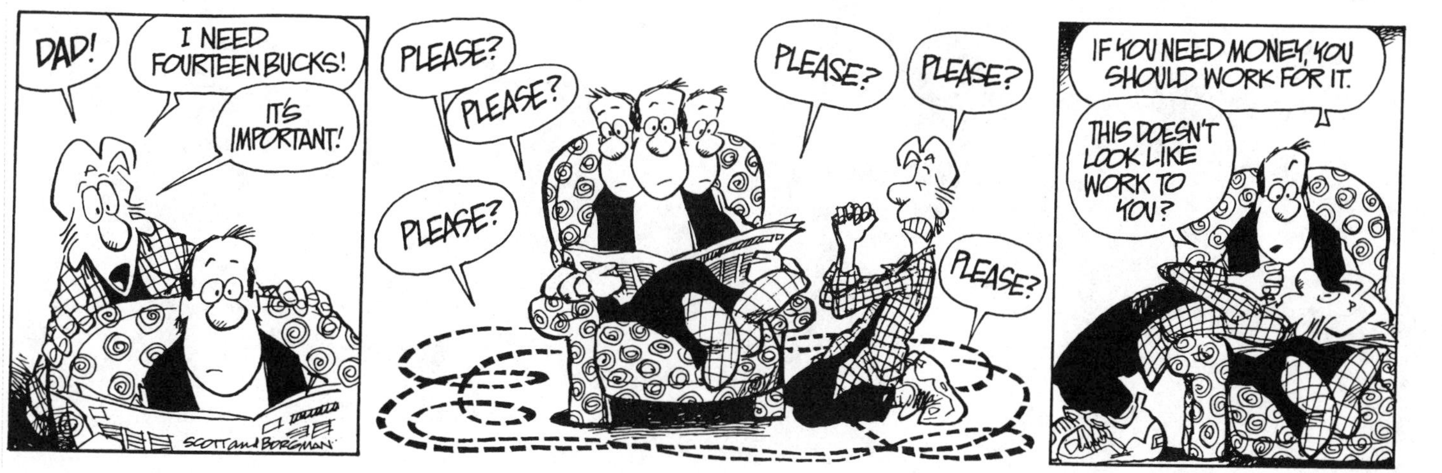
DAD!
I NEED FOURTEEN BUCKS!
IT'S IMPORTANT!
SCOTT and BORGMAN
PLEASE?
PLEASE?
PLEASE?
PLEASE?
PLEASE?
PLEASE?
IF YOU NEED MONEY, YOU SHOULD WORK FOR IT.
THIS DOESN'T LOOK LIKE WORK TO YOU?

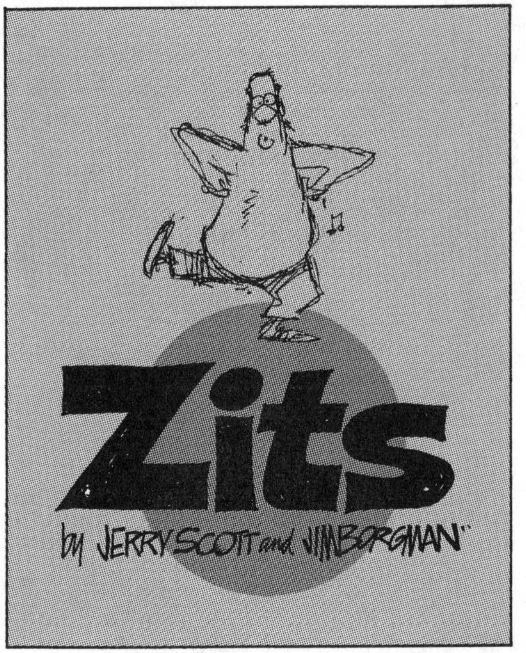
Zits
by JERRY SCOTT and JIM BORGMAN

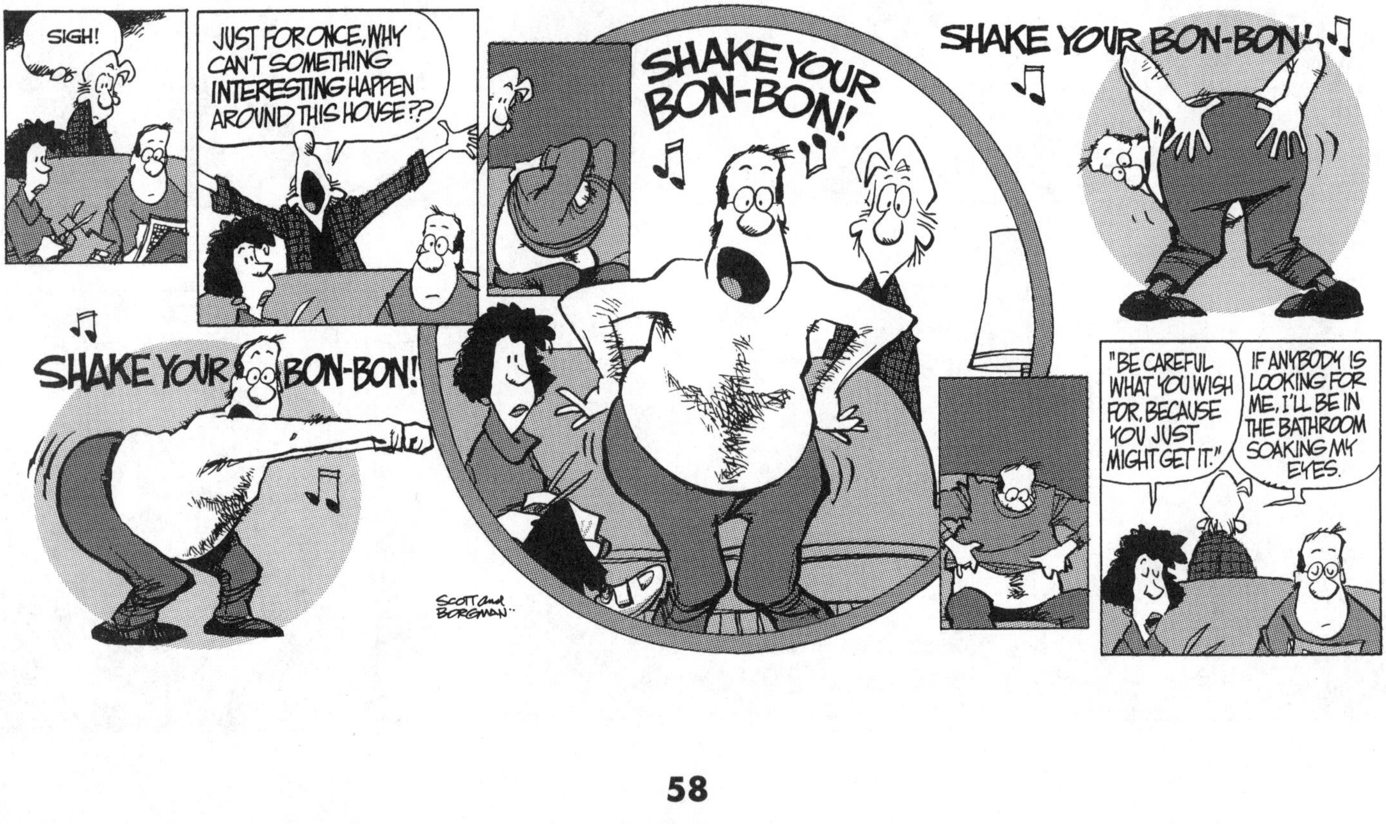
SIGH!
JUST FOR ONCE, WHY CAN'T SOMETHING INTERESTING HAPPEN AROUND THIS HOUSE??
SHAKE YOUR BON-BON!
SHAKE YOUR BON-BON!
SHAKE YOUR BON-BON!
"BE CAREFUL WHAT YOU WISH FOR, BECAUSE YOU JUST MIGHT GET IT."
IF ANYBODY IS LOOKING FOR ME, I'LL BE IN THE BATHROOM SOAKING MY EYES.
SCOTT and BORGMAN

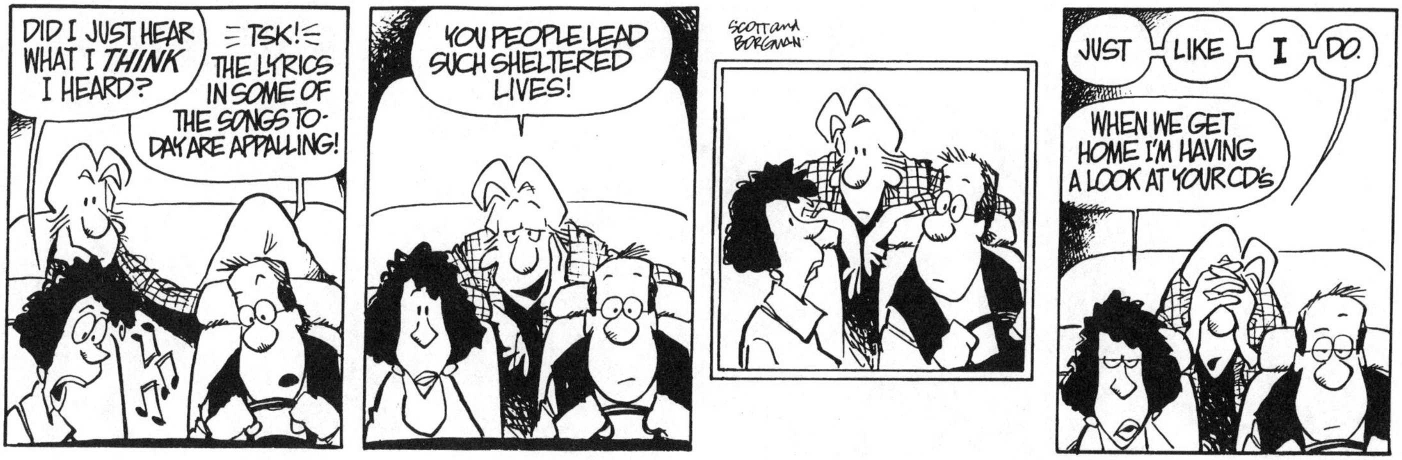
DID I JUST HEAR WHAT I THINK I HEARD?
≡TSK!≡ THE LYRICS IN SOME OF THE SONGS TO-DAY ARE APPALLING!
YOU PEOPLE LEAD SUCH SHELTERED LIVES!
SCOTT AND BORGMAN
JUST LIKE I DO.
WHEN WE GET HOME I'M HAVING A LOOK AT YOUR CD's

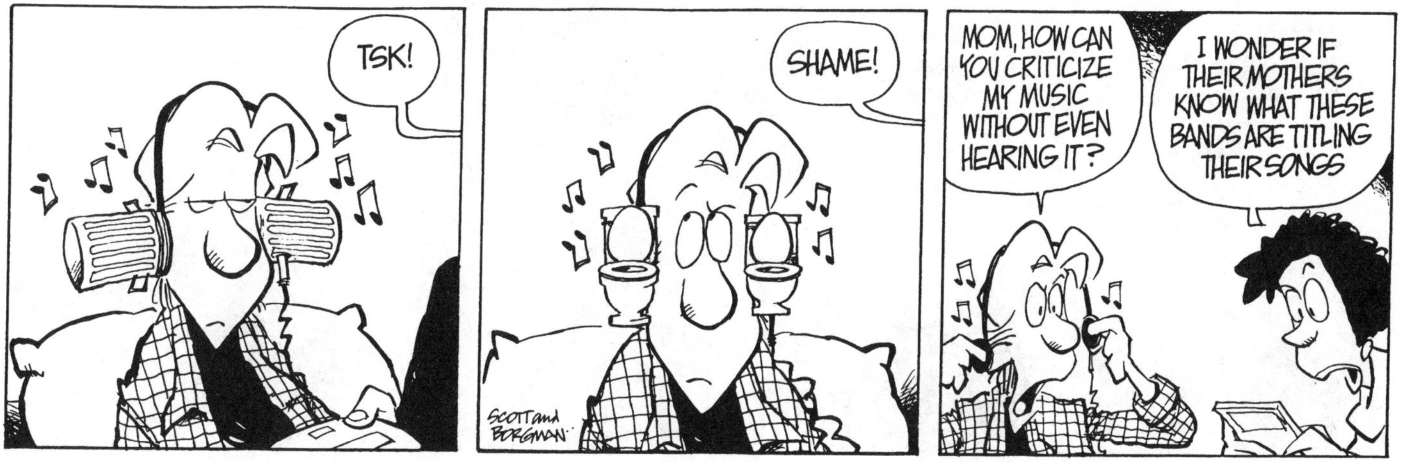
TSK!
SHAME!
SCOTT AND BORGMAN
MOM, HOW CAN YOU CRITICIZE MY MUSIC WITHOUT EVEN HEARING IT?
I WONDER IF THEIR MOTHERS KNOW WHAT THESE BANDS ARE TITLING THEIR SONGS

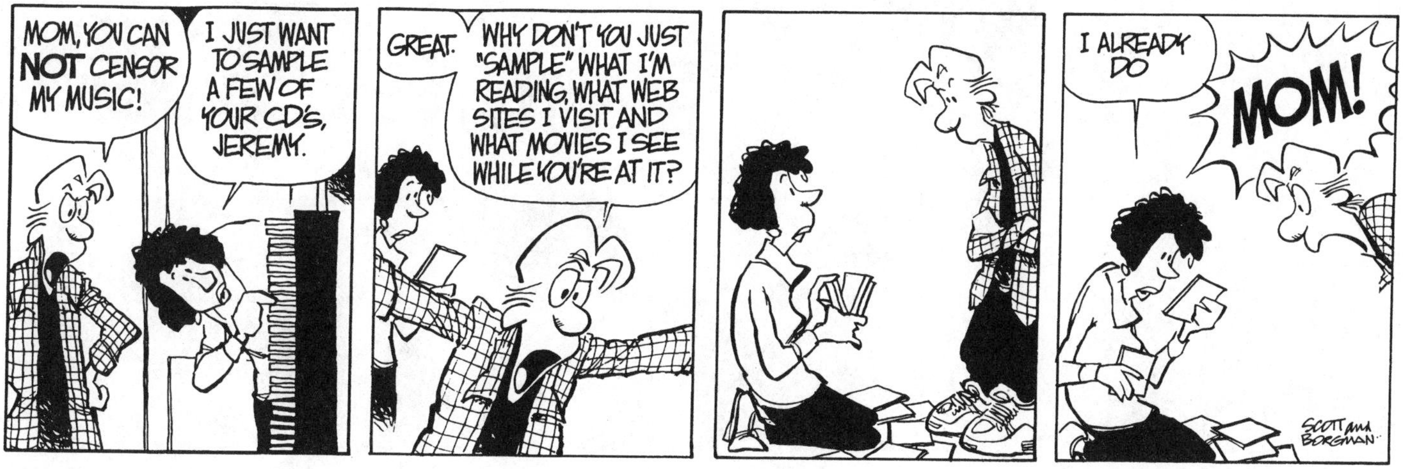
MOM, YOU CAN NOT CENSOR MY MUSIC!
I JUST WANT TO SAMPLE A FEW OF YOUR CD's, JEREMY.
GREAT.
WHY DON'T YOU JUST "SAMPLE" WHAT I'M READING, WHAT WEB SITES I VISIT AND WHAT MOVIES I SEE WHILE YOU'RE AT IT?
I ALREADY DO
MOM!
SCOTT AND BORGMAN

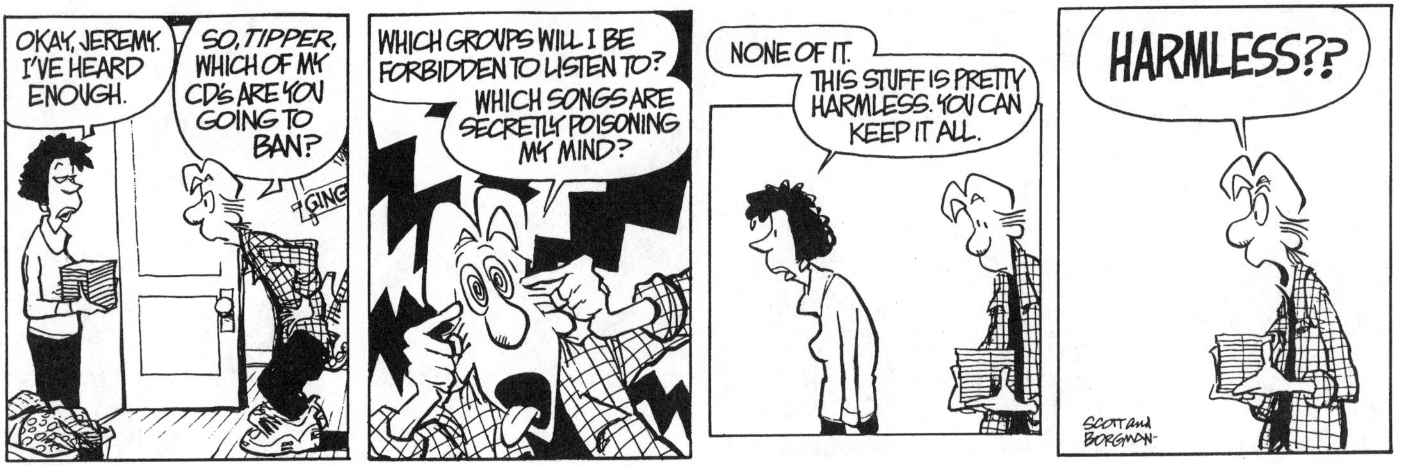
OKAY, JEREMY. I'VE HEARD ENOUGH.
SO, TIPPER, WHICH OF MY CD'S ARE YOU GOING TO BAN?
WHICH GROUPS WILL I BE FORBIDDEN TO LISTEN TO?
WHICH SONGS ARE SECRETLY POISONING MY MIND?
NONE OF IT.
THIS STUFF IS PRETTY HARMLESS. YOU CAN KEEP IT ALL.
HARMLESS??
SCOTT and BORGMAN

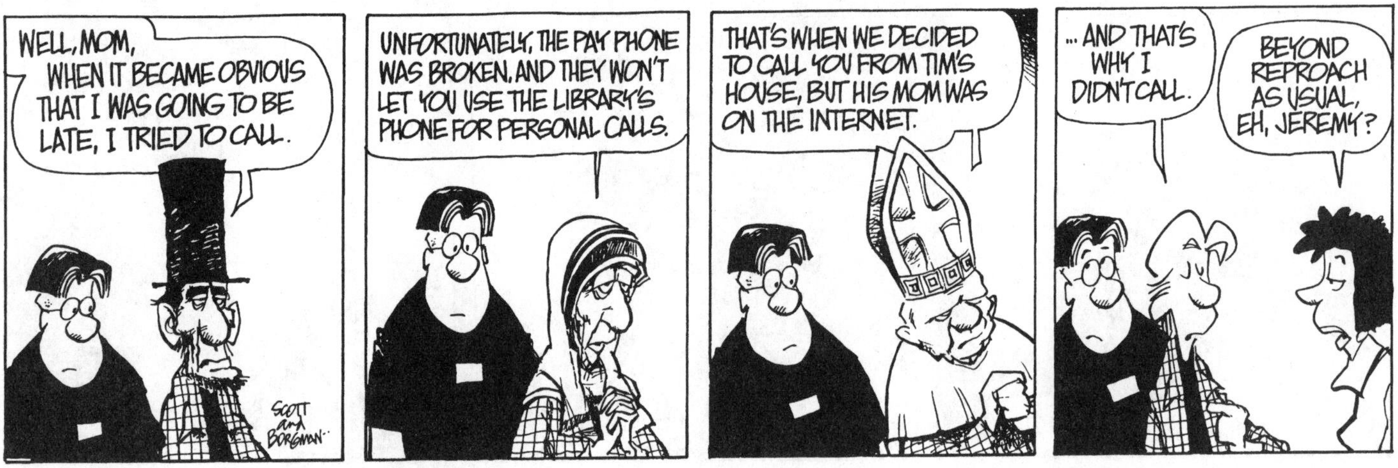
WELL, MOM,
WHEN IT BECAME OBVIOUS THAT I WAS GOING TO BE LATE, I TRIED TO CALL.
SCOTT and BORGMAN
UNFORTUNATELY, THE PAY PHONE WAS BROKEN, AND THEY WON'T LET YOU USE THE LIBRARY'S PHONE FOR PERSONAL CALLS.
THAT'S WHEN WE DECIDED TO CALL YOU FROM TIM'S HOUSE, BUT HIS MOM WAS ON THE INTERNET.
... AND THAT'S WHY I DIDN'T CALL.
BEYOND REPROACH AS USUAL, EH, JEREMY?

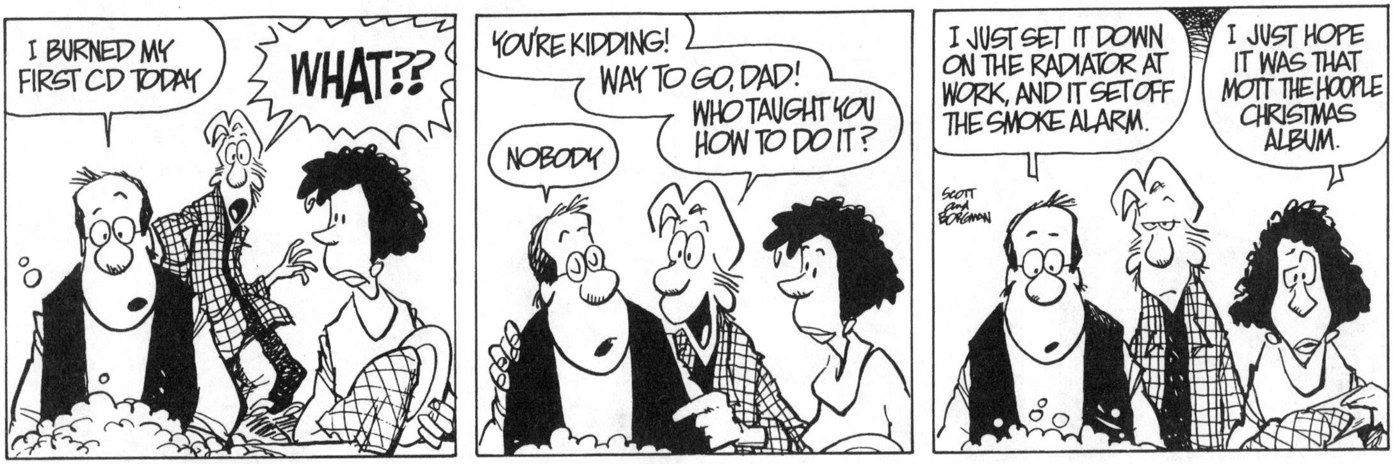
I BURNED MY FIRST CD TODAY
WHAT??
YOU'RE KIDDING!
WAY TO GO, DAD!
WHO TAUGHT YOU HOW TO DO IT?
NOBODY
I JUST SET IT DOWN ON THE RADIATOR AT WORK, AND IT SET OFF THE SMOKE ALARM.
I JUST HOPE IT WAS THAT MOTT THE HOOPLE CHRISTMAS ALBUM.
SCOTT and BORGMAN

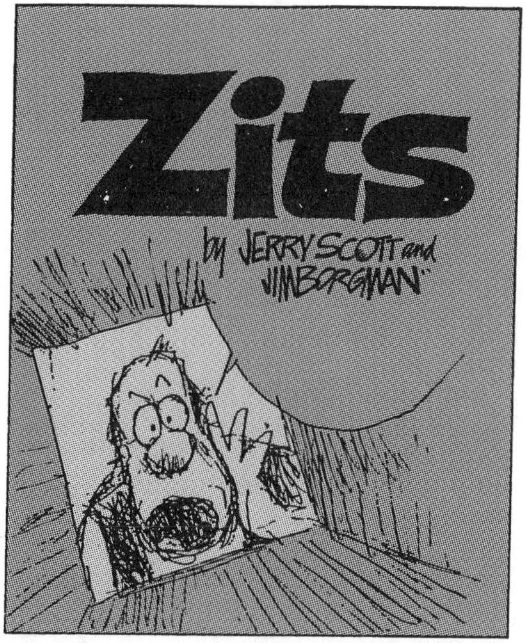
Zits
by JERRY SCOTT and JIM BORGMAN

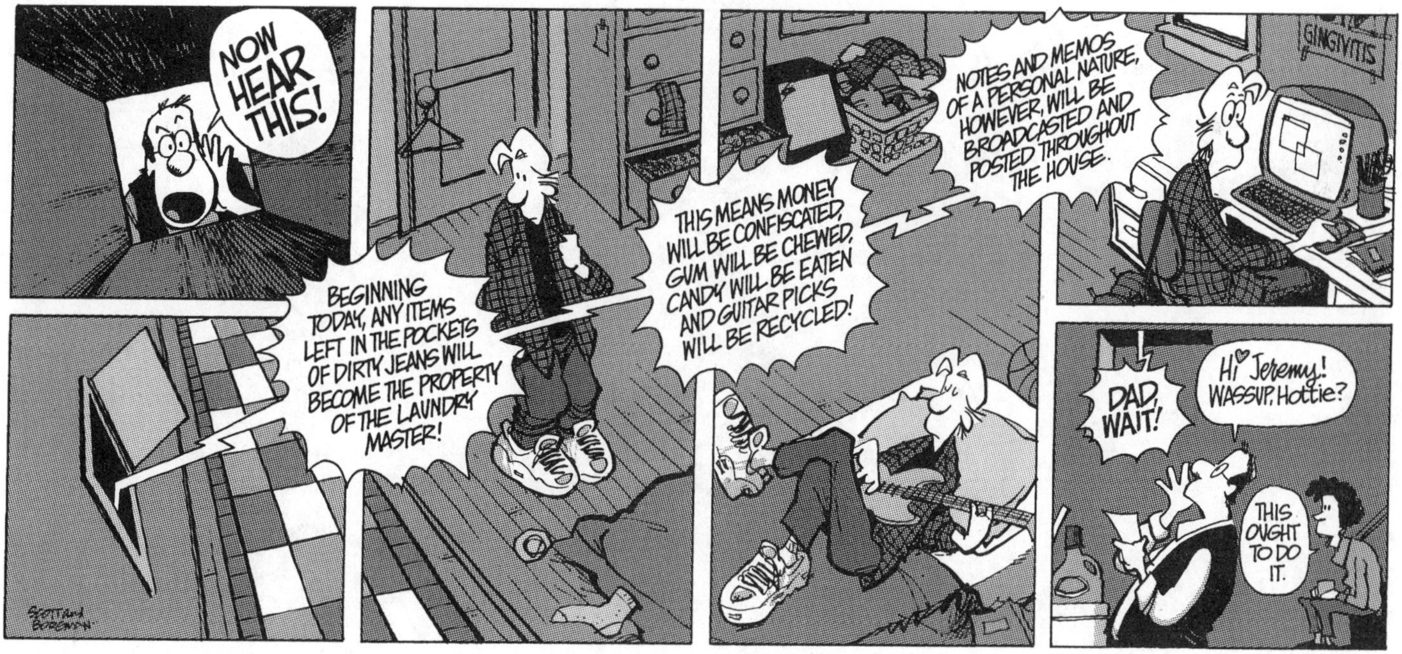
NOW HEAR THIS!
BEGINNING TODAY, ANY ITEMS LEFT IN THE POCKETS OF DIRTY JEANS WILL BECOME THE PROPERTY OF THE LAUNDRY MASTER!
THIS MEANS MONEY WILL BE CONFISCATED, GUM WILL BE CHEWED, CANDY WILL BE EATEN AND GUITAR PICKS WILL BE RECYCLED!
NOTES AND MEMOS OF A PERSONAL NATURE, HOWEVER, WILL BE BROADCASTED AND POSTED THROUGHOUT THE HOUSE.
GINGIVITIS
DAD, WAIT!
Hi Jeremy! WASSUP, Hottie?
THIS OUGHT TO DO IT.

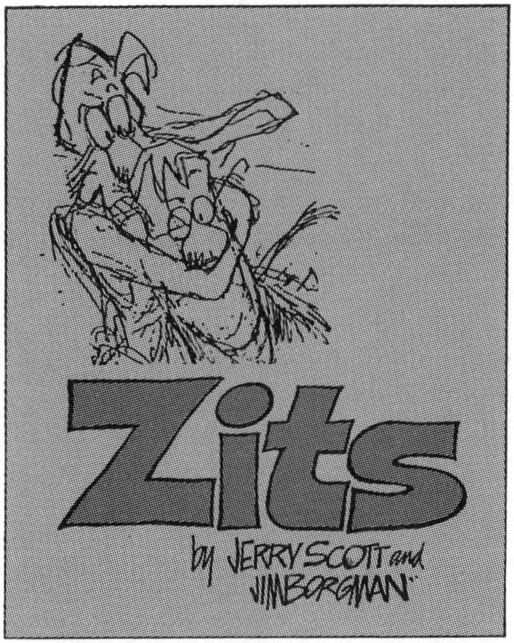
Zits
by JERRY SCOTT and JIM BORGMAN

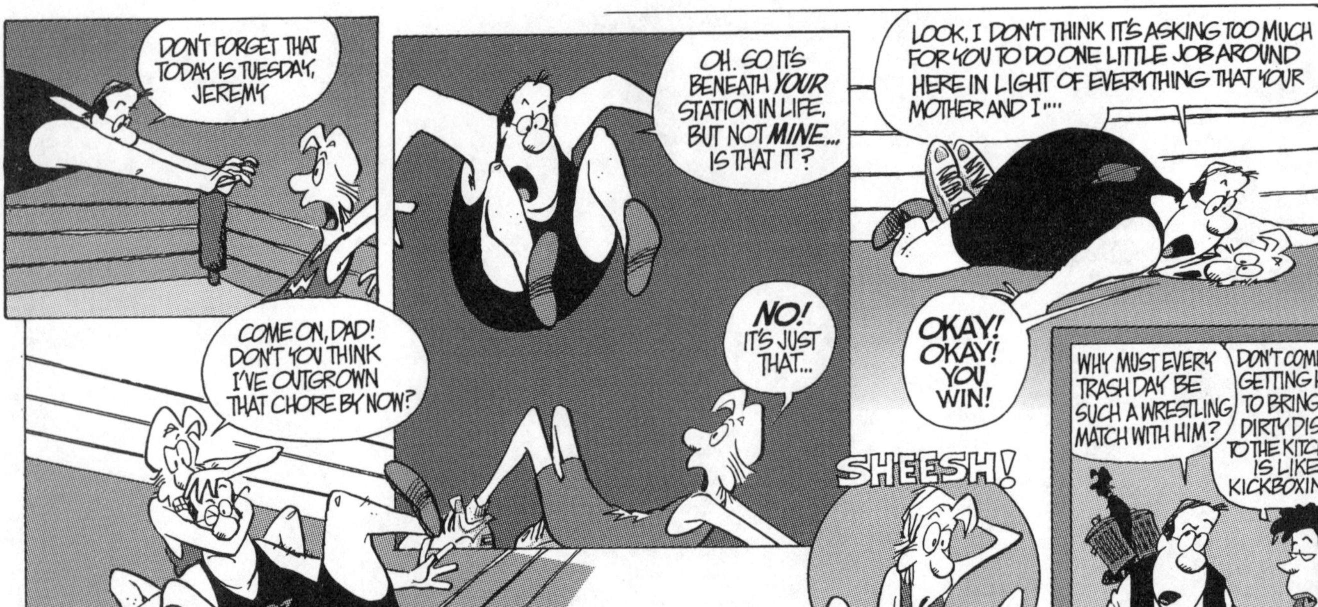
DON'T FORGET THAT TODAY IS TUESDAY, JEREMY
COME ON, DAD! DON'T YOU THINK I'VE OUTGROWN THAT CHORE BY NOW?
OH. SO IT'S BENEATH YOUR STATION IN LIFE, BUT NOT MINE... IS THAT IT?
NO! IT'S JUST THAT...
LOOK, I DON'T THINK IT'S ASKING TOO MUCH FOR YOU TO DO ONE LITTLE JOB AROUND HERE IN LIGHT OF EVERYTHING THAT YOUR MOTHER AND I....
OKAY! OKAY! YOU WIN!
SHEESH!
WHY MUST EVERY TRASH DAY BE SUCH A WRESTLING MATCH WITH HIM?
DON'T COMPLAIN. GETTING HIM TO BRING HIS DIRTY DISHES TO THE KITCHEN IS LIKE KICKBOXING.

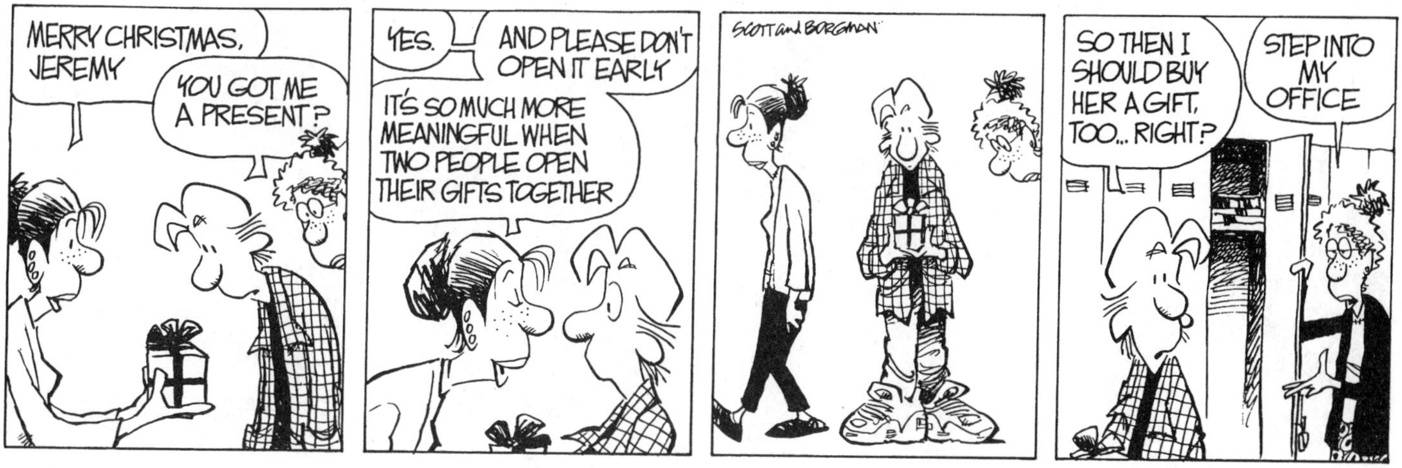
MERRY CHRISTMAS, JEREMY
YOU GOT ME A PRESENT?
YES.
AND PLEASE DON'T OPEN IT EARLY
IT'S SO MUCH MORE MEANINGFUL WHEN TWO PEOPLE OPEN THEIR GIFTS TOGETHER
SCOTT and BORGMAN
SO THEN I SHOULD BUY HER A GIFT, TOO... RIGHT?
STEP INTO MY OFFICE

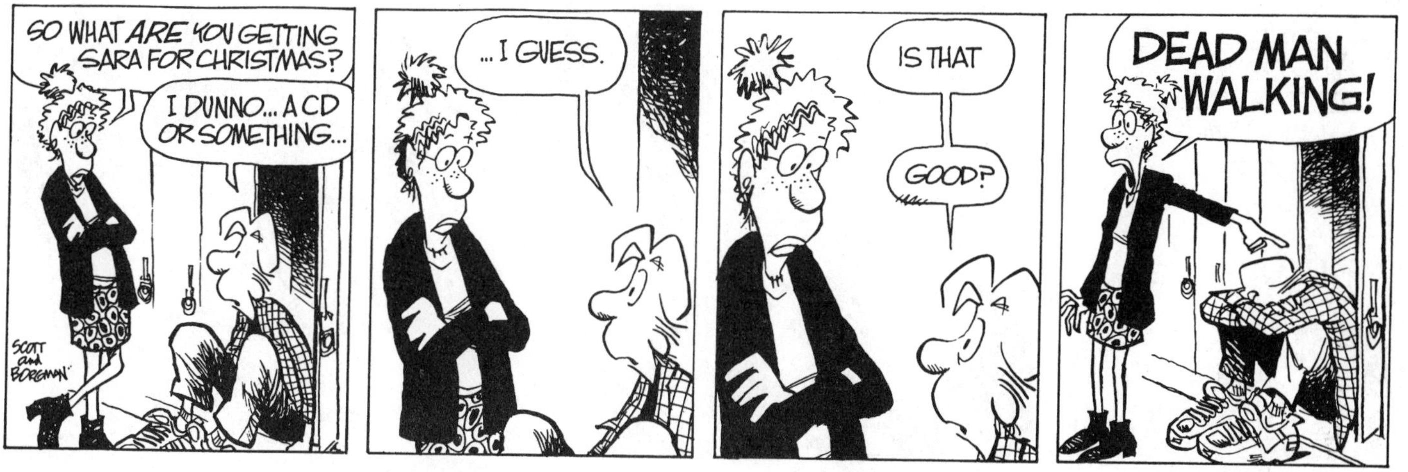
SO WHAT *ARE* YOU GETTING SARA FOR CHRISTMAS?
I DUNNO... A CD OR SOMETHING...
SCOTT and BORGMAN
... I GUESS.
IS THAT
GOOD?
DEAD MAN WALKING!

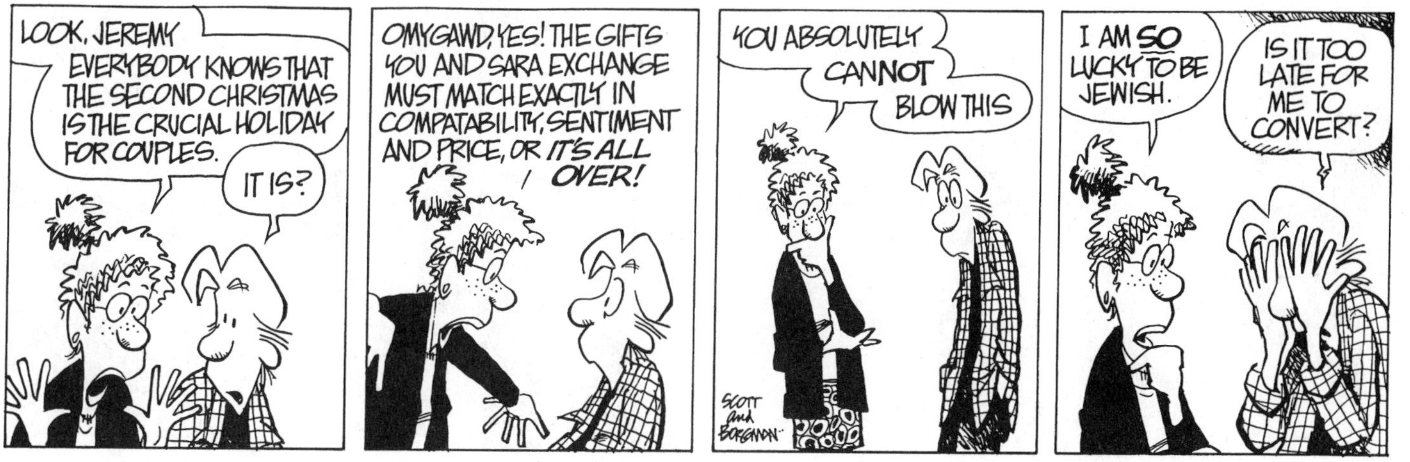
LOOK, JEREMY
EVERYBODY KNOWS THAT THE SECOND CHRISTMAS IS THE CRUCIAL HOLIDAY FOR COUPLES.
IT IS?
OMYGAWD, YES! THE GIFTS YOU AND SARA EXCHANGE MUST MATCH EXACTLY IN COMPATABILITY, SENTIMENT AND PRICE, OR *IT'S ALL OVER!*
YOU ABSOLUTELY
CAN**NOT**
BLOW THIS
SCOTT and BORGMAN
I AM **SO** LUCKY TO BE JEWISH.
IS IT TOO LATE FOR ME TO CONVERT?

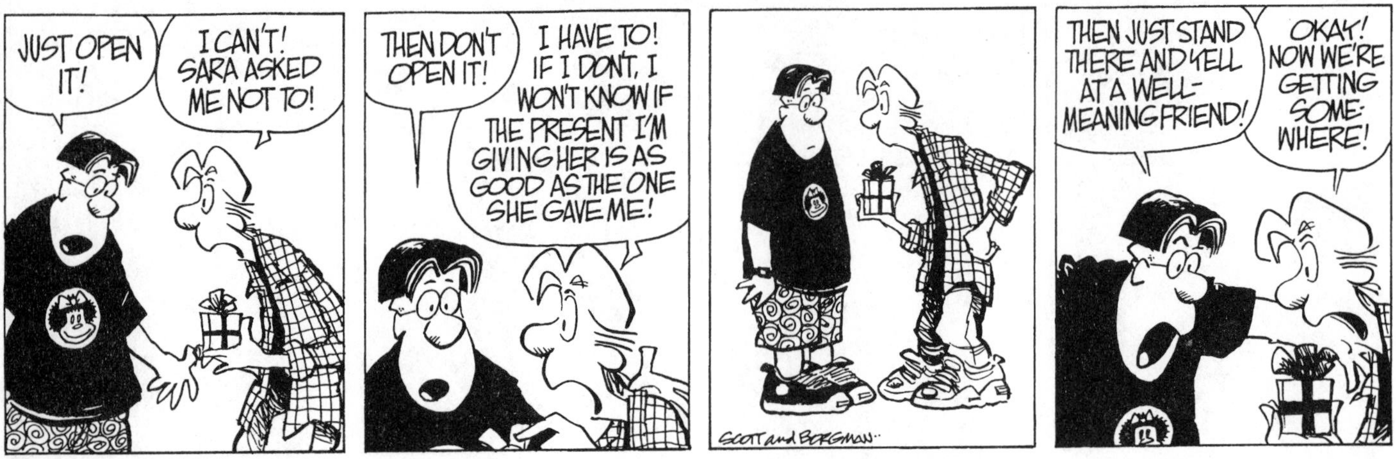
JUST OPEN IT!
I CAN'T! SARA ASKED ME NOT TO!
THEN DON'T OPEN IT!
I HAVE TO! IF I DON'T, I WON'T KNOW IF THE PRESENT I'M GIVING HER IS AS GOOD AS THE ONE SHE GAVE ME!
SCOTT and BORGMAN
THEN JUST STAND THERE AND YELL AT A WELL-MEANING FRIEND!
OKAY! NOW WE'RE GETTING SOME-WHERE!

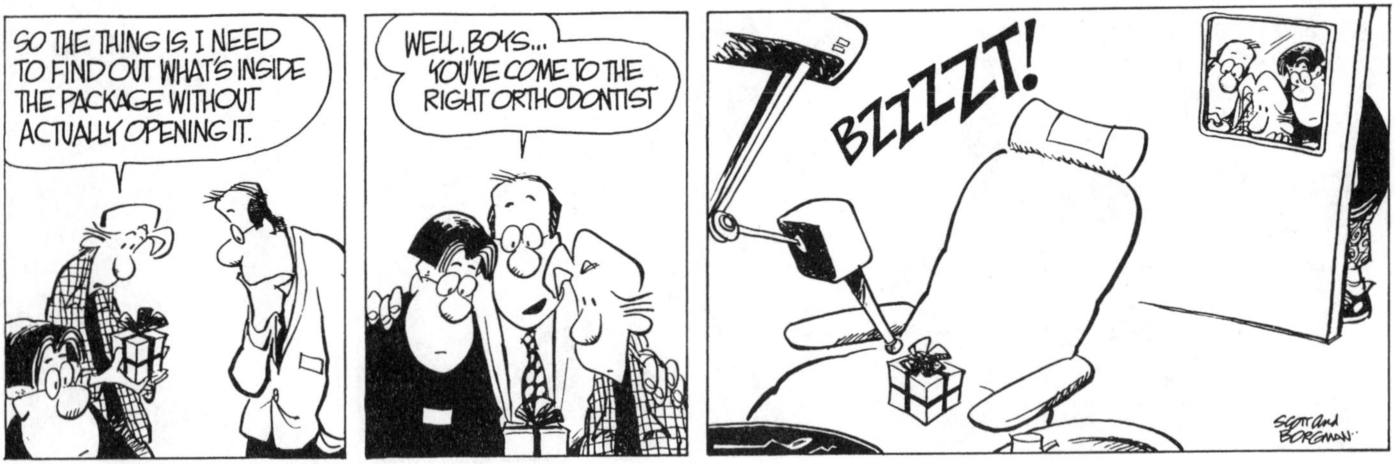
SO THE THING IS, I NEED TO FIND OUT WHAT'S INSIDE THE PACKAGE WITHOUT ACTUALLY OPENING IT.
WELL, BOYS... YOU'VE COME TO THE RIGHT ORTHODONTIST
BZZZZT!
SCOTT and BORGMAN

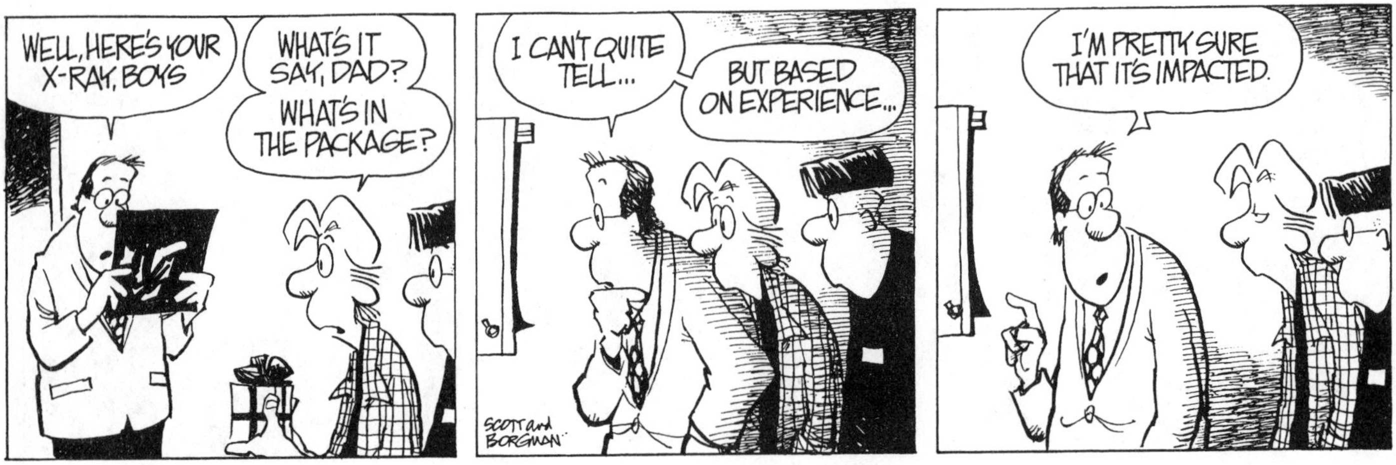
WELL, HERE'S YOUR X-RAY, BOYS
WHAT'S IT SAY, DAD? WHAT'S IN THE PACKAGE?
I CAN'T QUITE TELL...
BUT BASED ON EXPERIENCE...
SCOTT and BORGMAN
I'M PRETTY SURE THAT IT'S IMPACTED.

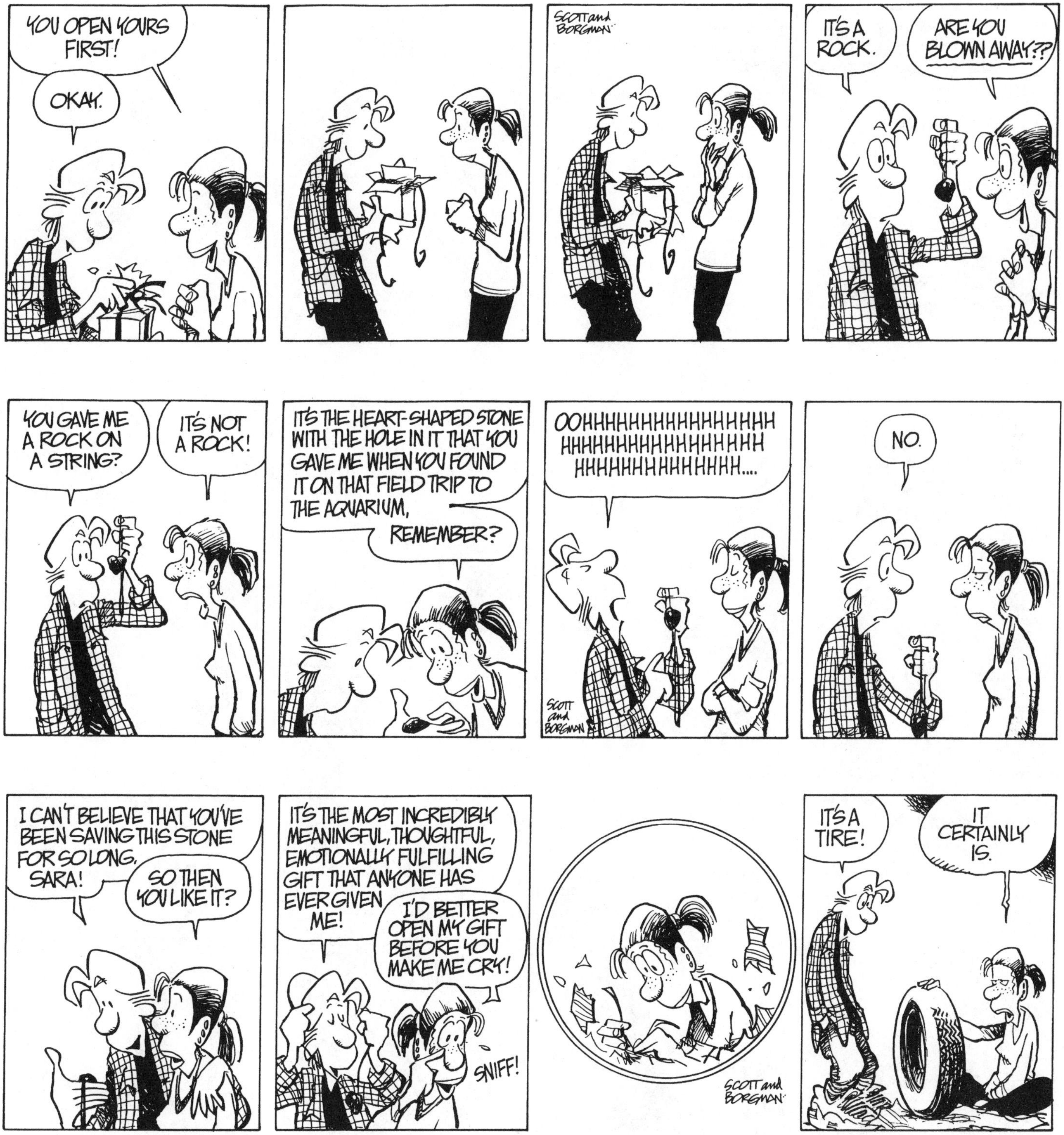
YOU OPEN YOURS FIRST!
OKAY.
SCOTT and BORGMAN
IT'S A ROCK.
ARE YOU BLOWN AWAY??
YOU GAVE ME A ROCK ON A STRING?
IT'S NOT A ROCK!
IT'S THE HEART-SHAPED STONE WITH THE HOLE IN IT THAT YOU GAVE ME WHEN YOU FOUND IT ON THAT FIELD TRIP TO THE AQUARIUM,
REMEMBER?
OOHHHHHHHHHHHHHHHH HHHHHHHHHHHHHHHH HHHHHHHHHHHHHH....
SCOTT and BORGMAN
NO.
I CAN'T BELIEVE THAT YOU'VE BEEN SAVING THIS STONE FOR SO LONG, SARA!
SO THEN YOU LIKE IT?
IT'S THE MOST INCREDIBLY MEANINGFUL, THOUGHTFUL, EMOTIONALLY FULFILLING GIFT THAT ANYONE HAS EVER GIVEN ME!
I'D BETTER OPEN MY GIFT BEFORE YOU MAKE ME CRY!
SNIFF!
SCOTT and BORGMAN
IT'S A TIRE!
IT CERTAINLY IS.

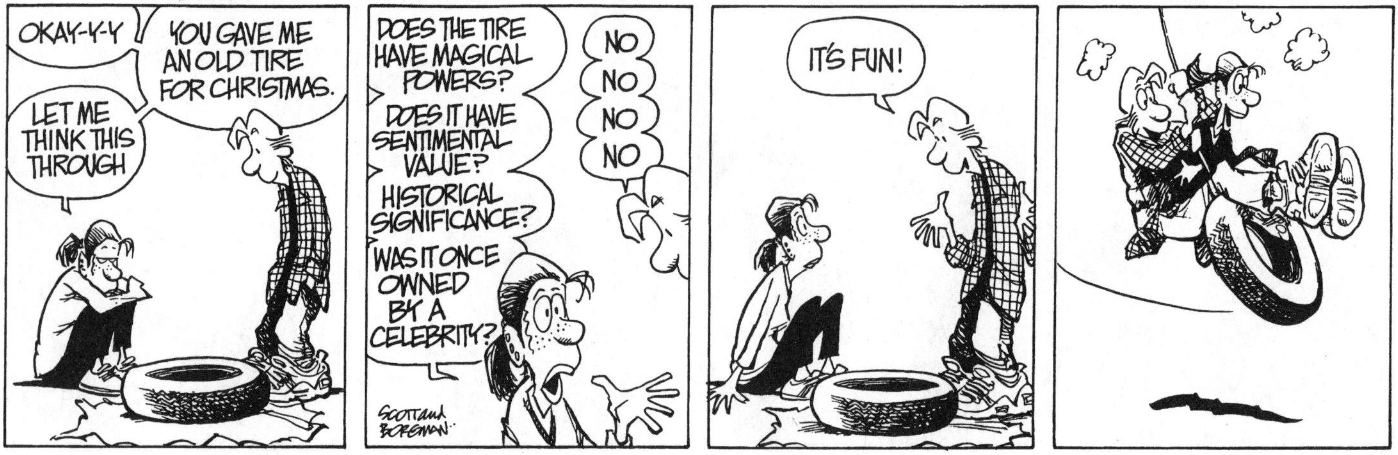
OKAY-Y-Y
LET ME THINK THIS THROUGH
YOU GAVE ME AN OLD TIRE FOR CHRISTMAS.
DOES THE TIRE HAVE MAGICAL POWERS?
NO
DOES IT HAVE SENTIMENTAL VALUE?
NO
HISTORICAL SIGNIFICANCE?
NO
WAS IT ONCE OWNED BY A CELEBRITY?
NO
SCOTT AND BORGMAN
IT'S FUN!

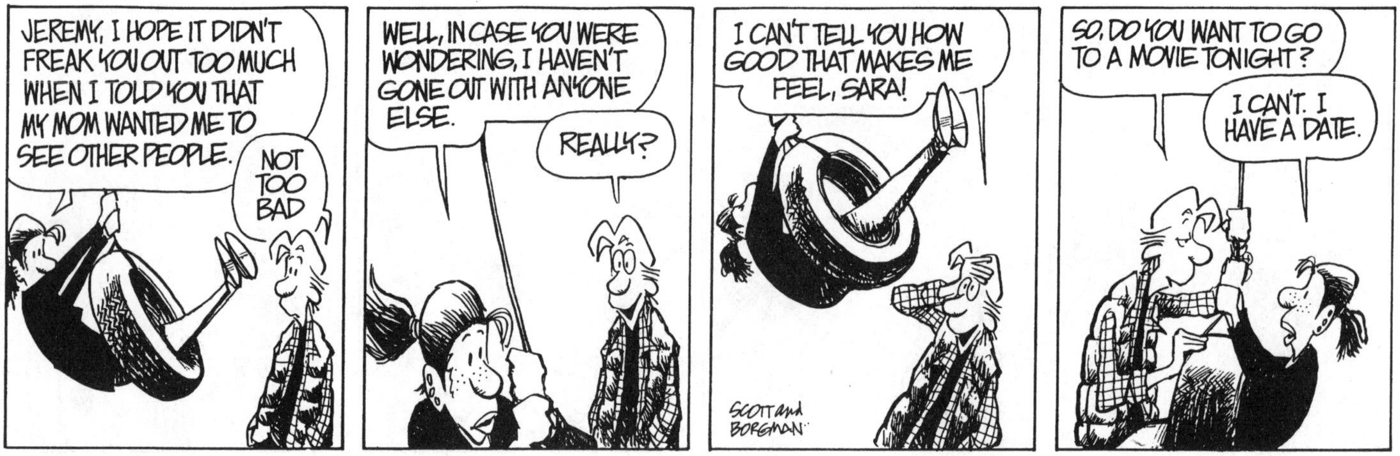
JEREMY, I HOPE IT DIDN'T FREAK YOU OUT TOO MUCH WHEN I TOLD YOU THAT MY MOM WANTED ME TO SEE OTHER PEOPLE.
NOT TOO BAD
WELL, IN CASE YOU WERE WONDERING, I HAVEN'T GONE OUT WITH ANYONE ELSE.
REALLY?
I CAN'T TELL YOU HOW GOOD THAT MAKES ME FEEL, SARA!
SCOTT AND BORGMAN
SO, DO YOU WANT TO GO TO A MOVIE TONIGHT?
I CAN'T. I HAVE A DATE.

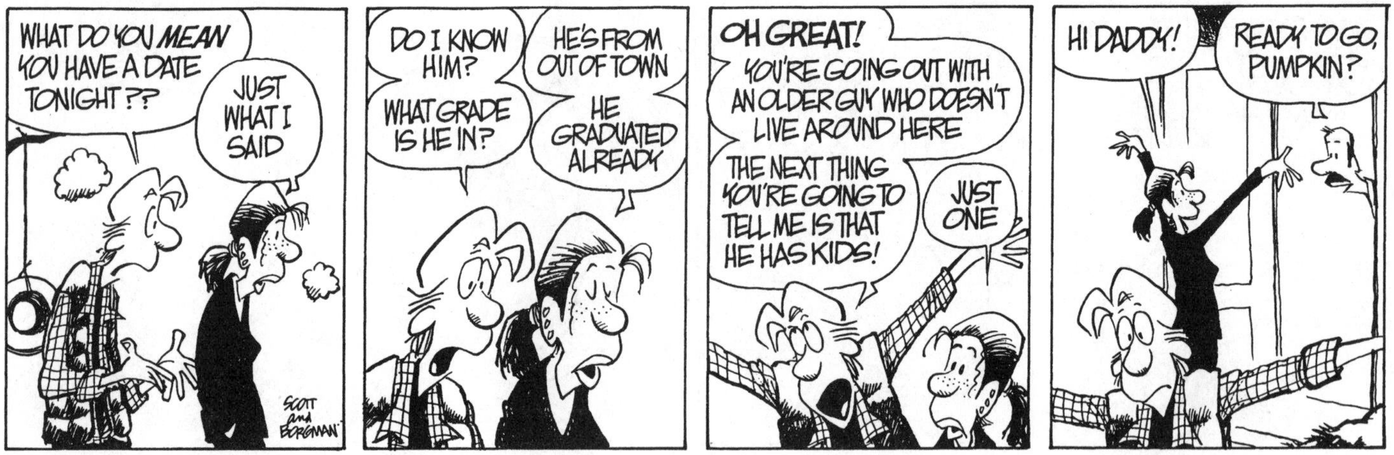
WHAT DO YOU *MEAN* YOU HAVE A DATE TONIGHT??
JUST WHAT I SAID
SCOTT AND BORGMAN
DO I KNOW HIM?
HE'S FROM OUT OF TOWN
WHAT GRADE IS HE IN?
HE GRADUATED ALREADY
OH GREAT!
YOU'RE GOING OUT WITH AN OLDER GUY WHO DOESN'T LIVE AROUND HERE
THE NEXT THING YOU'RE GOING TO TELL ME IS THAT HE HAS KIDS!
JUST ONE
HI DADDY!
READY TO GO, PUMPKIN?

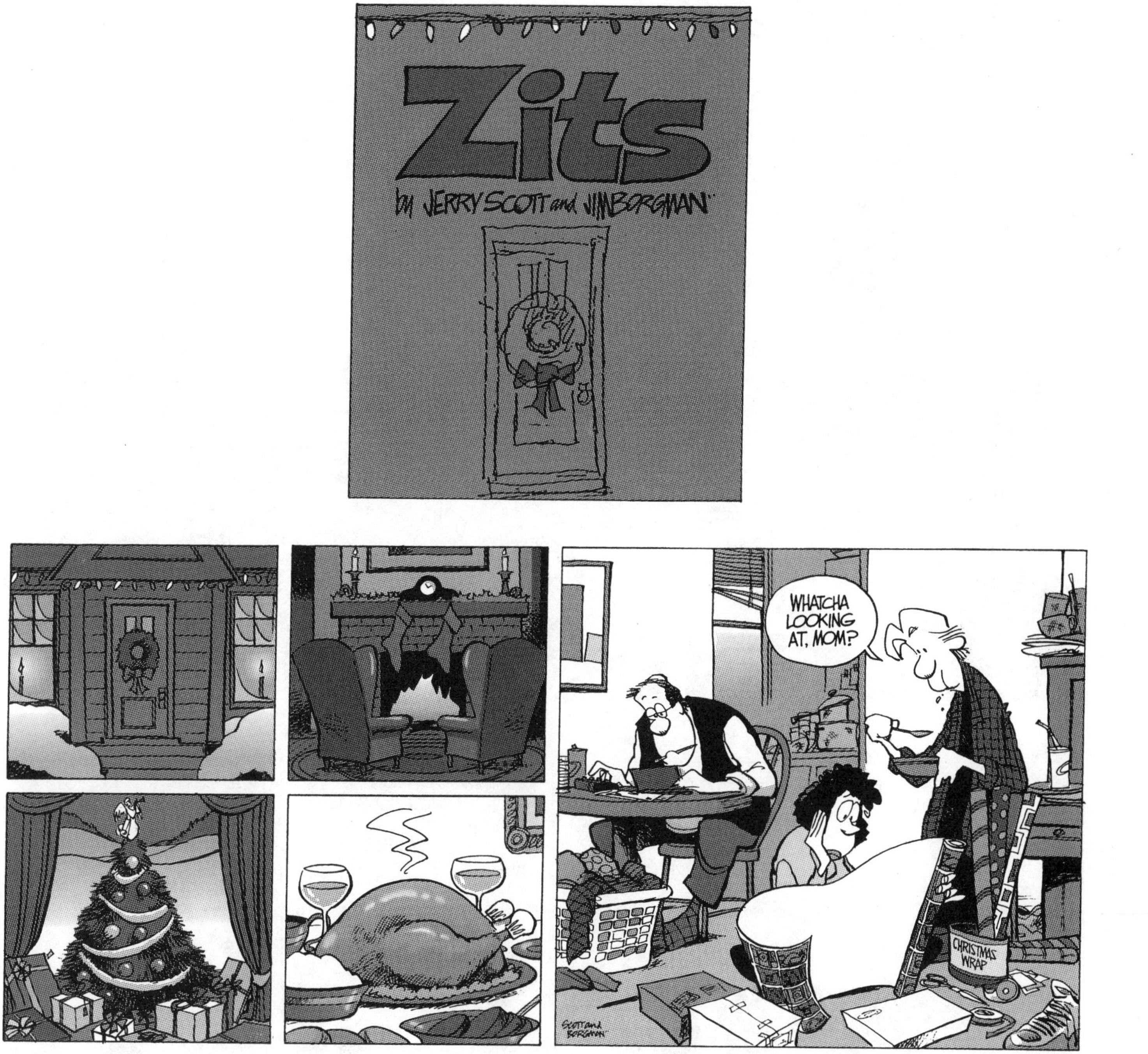
Zits
by JERRY SCOTT and JIM BORGMAN
WHATCHA LOOKING AT, MOM?
CHRISTMAS WRAP
SCOTT and BORGMAN

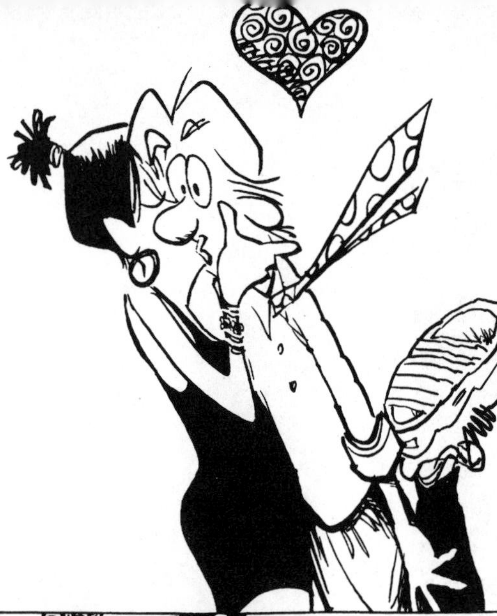

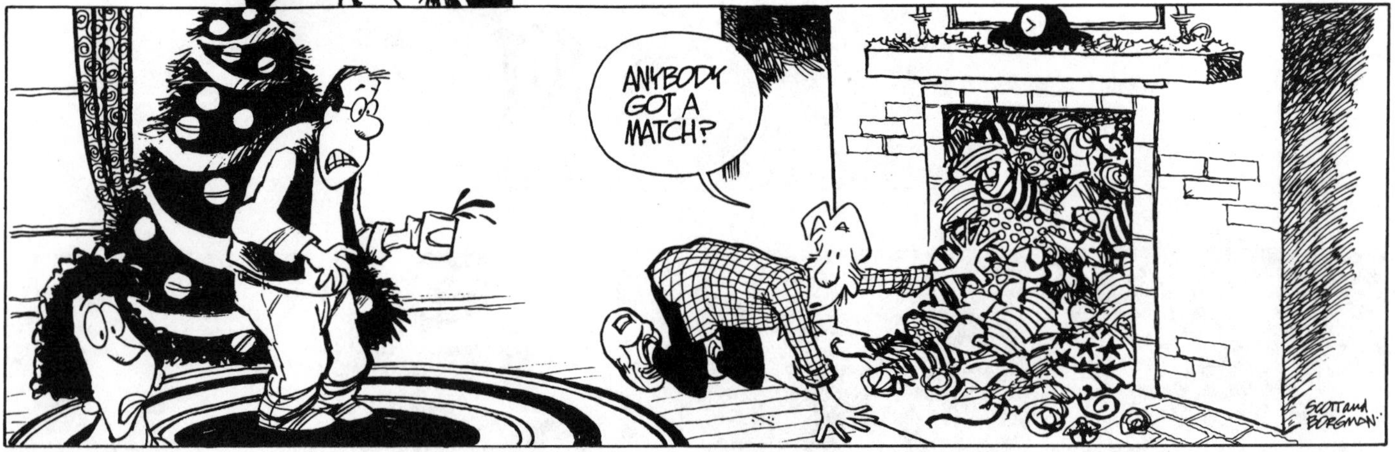
ANYBODY GOT A MATCH?

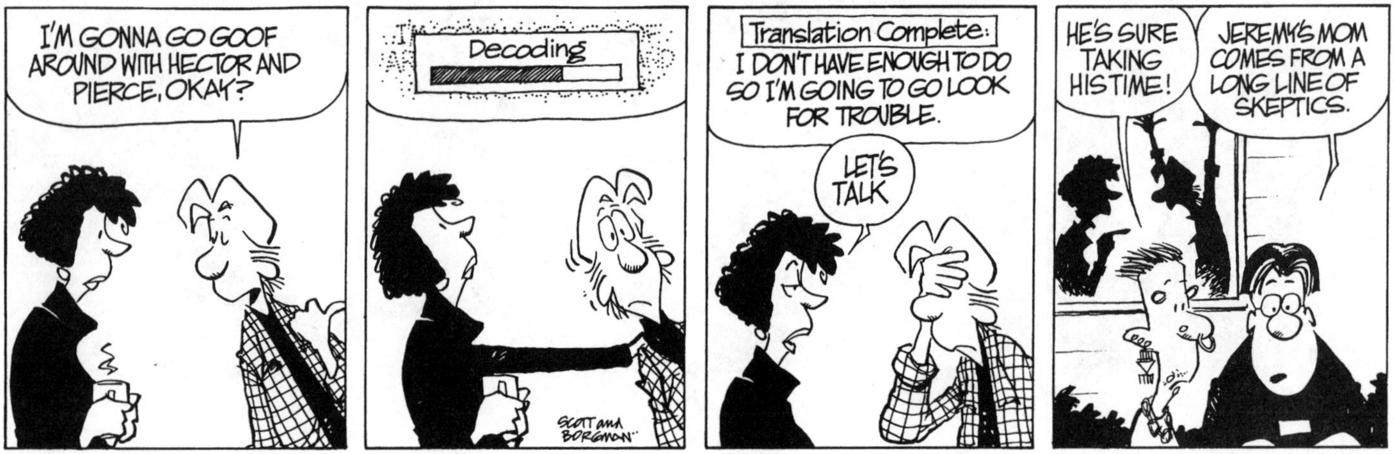
I'M GONNA GO GOOF AROUND WITH HECTOR AND PIERCE, OKAY?
Decoding
Translation Complete:
I DON'T HAVE ENOUGH TO DO SO I'M GOING TO GO LOOK FOR TROUBLE.
LET'S TALK
HE'S SURE TAKING HIS TIME!
JEREMY'S MOM COMES FROM A LONG LINE OF SKEPTICS.

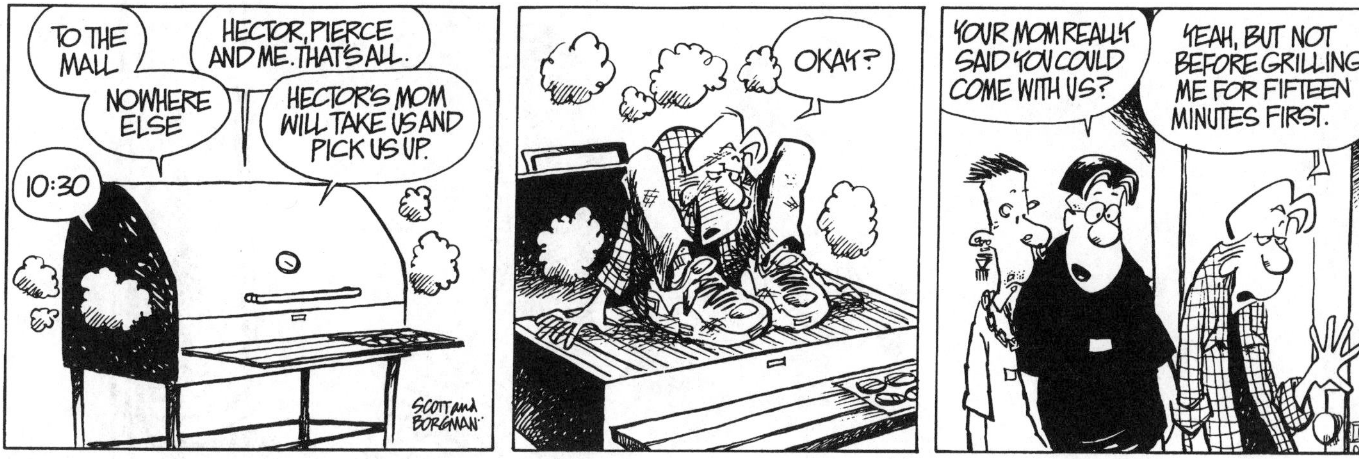
TO THE MALL
NOWHERE ELSE
HECTOR, PIERCE AND ME. THAT'S ALL.
HECTOR'S MOM WILL TAKE US AND PICK US UP.
10:30
SCOTT and BORGMAN
OKAY?
YOUR MOM REALLY SAID YOU COULD COME WITH US?
YEAH, BUT NOT BEFORE GRILLING ME FOR FIFTEEN MINUTES FIRST.

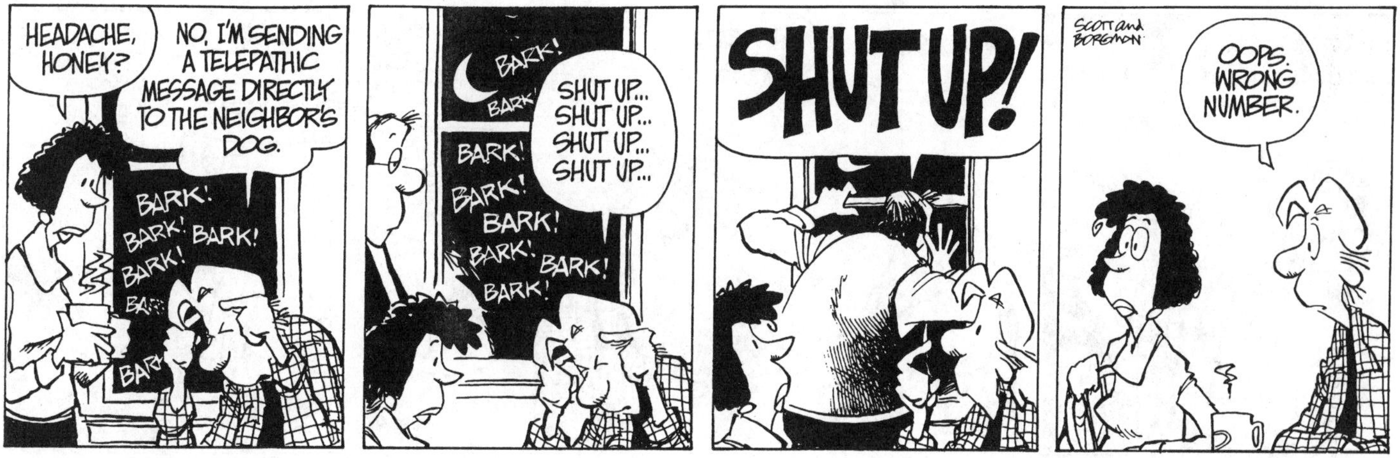
HEADACHE, HONEY?
NO, I'M SENDING A TELEPATHIC MESSAGE DIRECTLY TO THE NEIGHBOR'S DOG.
BARK! BARK! BARK! BARK!
BARK! BARK!
BARK! BARK! BARK! BARK! BARK! BARK!
SHUT UP... SHUT UP... SHUT UP... SHUT UP...
SHUT UP!
SCOTT and BORGMAN
OOPS. WRONG NUMBER.

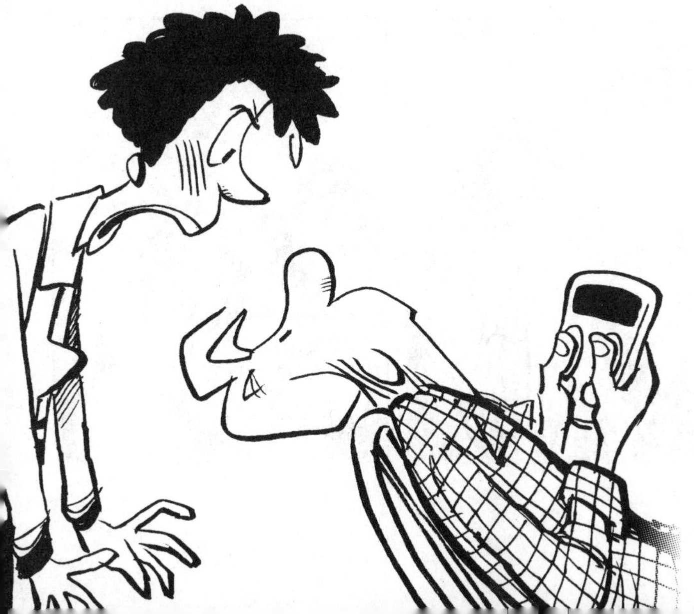

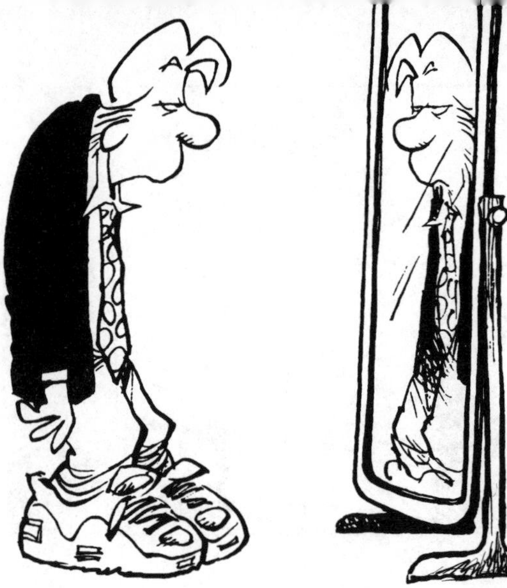

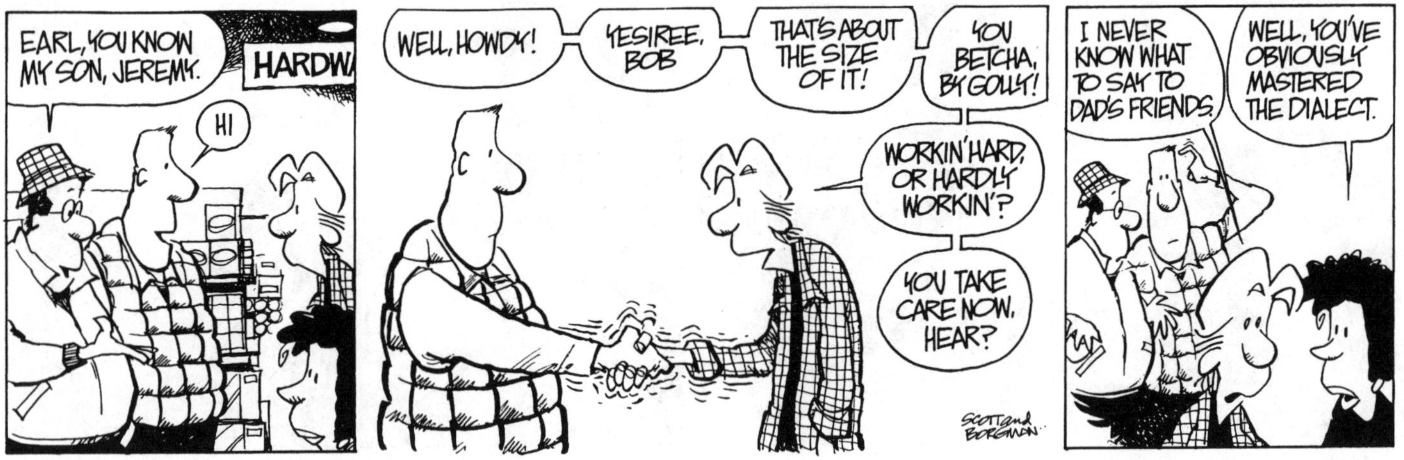
EARL, YOU KNOW MY SON, JEREMY.
HI
WELL, HOWDY!
YESIREE, BOB
THAT'S ABOUT THE SIZE OF IT!
YOU BETCHA, BY GOLLY!
WORKIN' HARD, OR HARDLY WORKIN'?
YOU TAKE CARE NOW, HEAR?
I NEVER KNOW WHAT TO SAY TO DAD'S FRIENDS.
WELL, YOU'VE OBVIOUSLY MASTERED THE DIALECT.

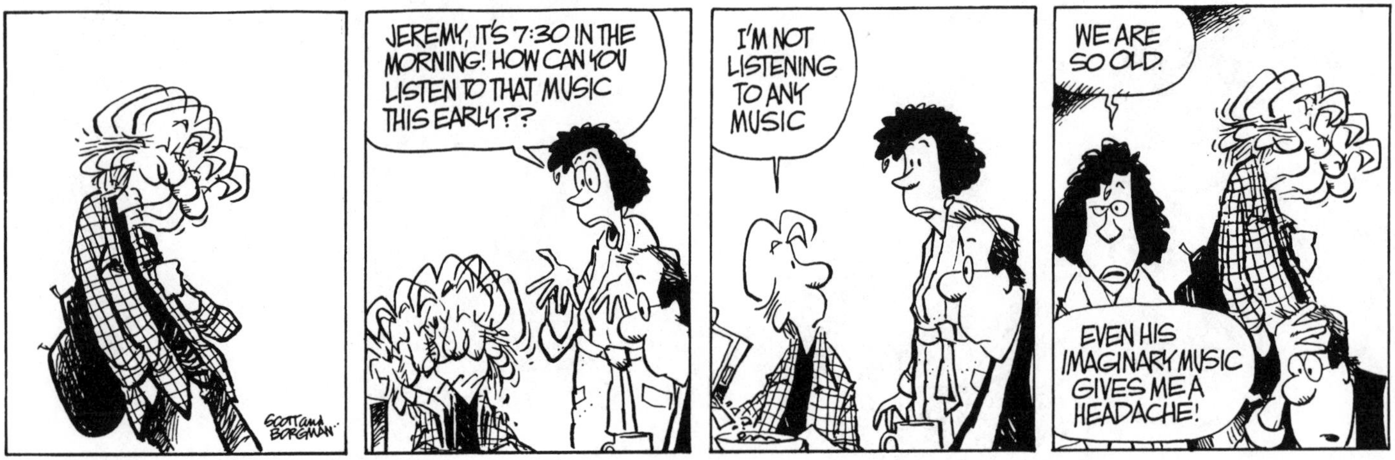
JEREMY, IT'S 7:30 IN THE MORNING! HOW CAN YOU LISTEN TO THAT MUSIC THIS EARLY??
I'M NOT LISTENING TO ANY MUSIC
WE ARE SO OLD.
EVEN HIS IMAGINARY MUSIC GIVES ME A HEADACHE!

Zits
by JERRY SCOTT and JIM BORGMAN

DO YOU HAVE ANY PLANS FOR TONIGHT, JEREMY?
ARE YOU KIDDING? IT'S NEW YEAR'S EVE!
FIRST, I'M GOING TO DRESS UP IN A TOP HAT AND TAILS LIKE THE LITTLE GUY ON THE MONOPOLY BOX.
THEN I'LL GO TO A PARTY WHERE THEY'LL SERVE CHAMPAGNE IN PLASTIC GLASSES AND COCKTAIL WEENIES ON MYLAR PLATTERS.
AND AT MIDNIGHT WE'LL ALL TOOT NOISEMAKERS LIKE IDIOTS, EXCHANGE BIG, SLOPPY, MEANINGLESS KISSES AND SING AULD LANG SYNE UNTIL WE PUKE!
THAT'S MY IDEA OF FUN!
IT SOUNDS LIKE SOMEBODY HAS BEEN DOING SOME RESEARCH.
I THOUGHT WE HID THOSE OLD PHOTO ALBUMS!
LIGHTS
DOCUMENTS

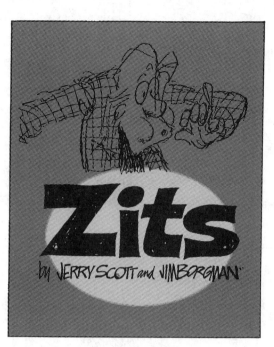

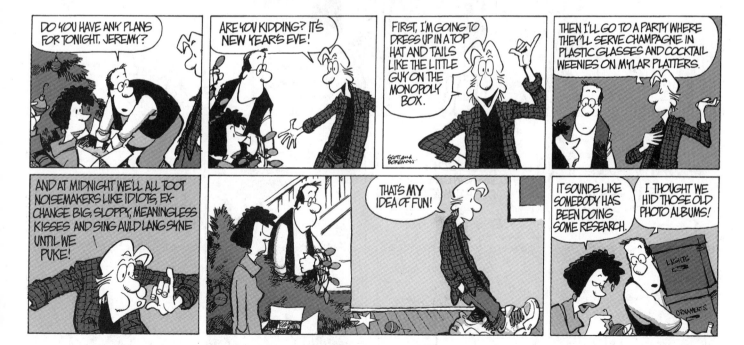

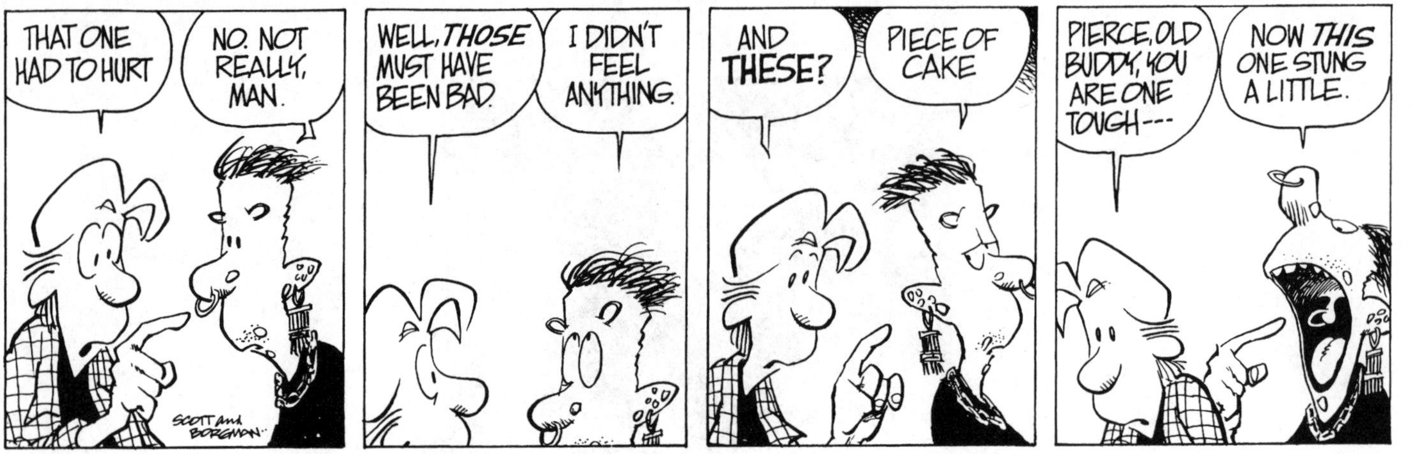
THAT ONE HAD TO HURT
NO. NOT REALLY, MAN.
SCOTT AND BORGMAN
WELL, *THOSE* MUST HAVE BEEN BAD.
I DIDN'T FEEL ANYTHING.
AND **THESE**?
PIECE OF CAKE
PIERCE, OLD BUDDY, YOU ARE ONE TOUGH---
NOW *THIS* ONE STUNG A LITTLE.

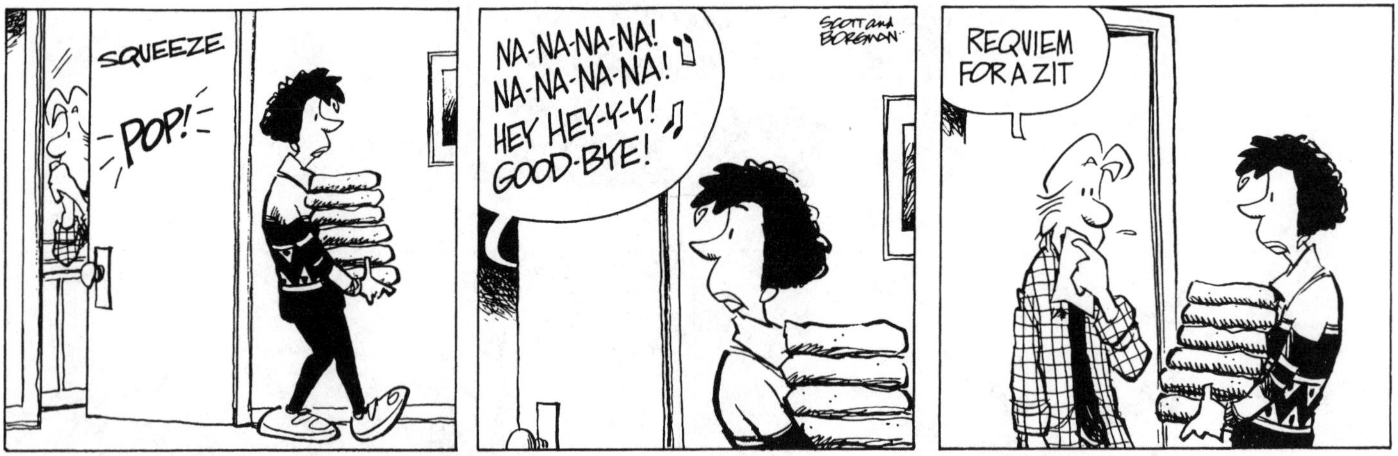
SQUEEZE
POP!
SCOTT AND BORGMAN
NA-NA-NA-NA! NA-NA-NA-NA! HEY HEY-Y-Y! GOOD-BYE!
REQUIEM FOR A ZIT

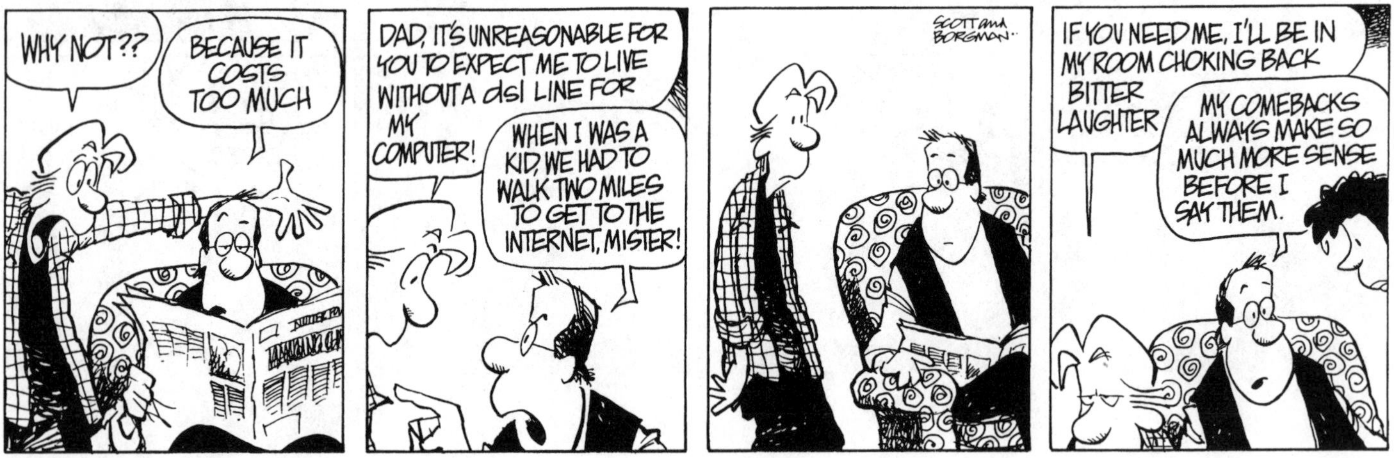
WHY NOT??
BECAUSE IT COSTS TOO MUCH
DAD, IT'S UNREASONABLE FOR YOU TO EXPECT ME TO LIVE WITHOUT A dsl LINE FOR MY COMPUTER!
WHEN I WAS A KID, WE HAD TO WALK TWO MILES TO GET TO THE INTERNET, MISTER!
SCOTT AND BORGMAN
IF YOU NEED ME, I'LL BE IN MY ROOM CHOKING BACK BITTER LAUGHTER
MY COMEBACKS ALWAYS MAKE SO MUCH MORE SENSE BEFORE I SAY THEM.

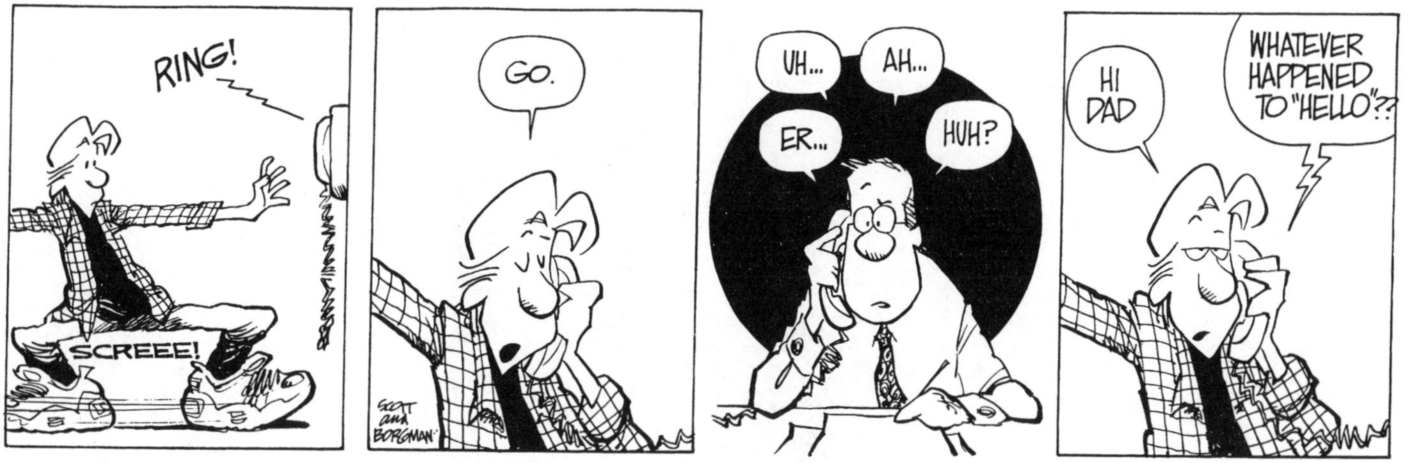
RING!
SCREEEE!
GO.
SCOTT and BORGMAN
UH...
AH...
ER...
HUH?
HI DAD
WHATEVER HAPPENED TO "HELLO"??

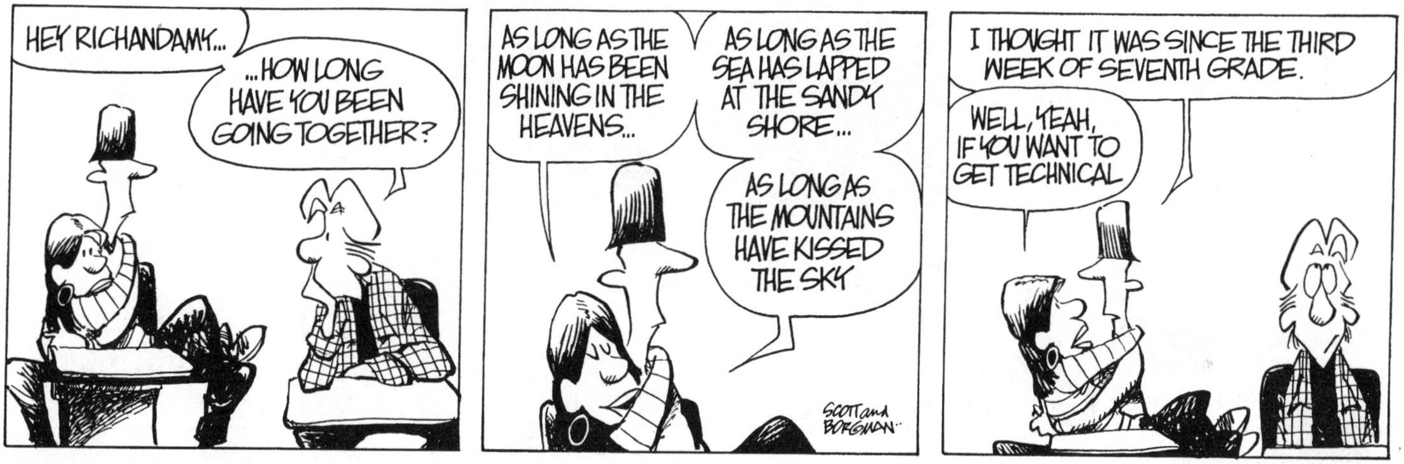
HEY RICHANDAMY...
...HOW LONG HAVE YOU BEEN GOING TOGETHER?
AS LONG AS THE MOON HAS BEEN SHINING IN THE HEAVENS...
AS LONG AS THE SEA HAS LAPPED AT THE SANDY SHORE...
AS LONG AS THE MOUNTAINS HAVE KISSED THE SKY
SCOTT and BORGMAN
I THOUGHT IT WAS SINCE THE THIRD WEEK OF SEVENTH GRADE.
WELL, YEAH, IF YOU WANT TO GET TECHNICAL

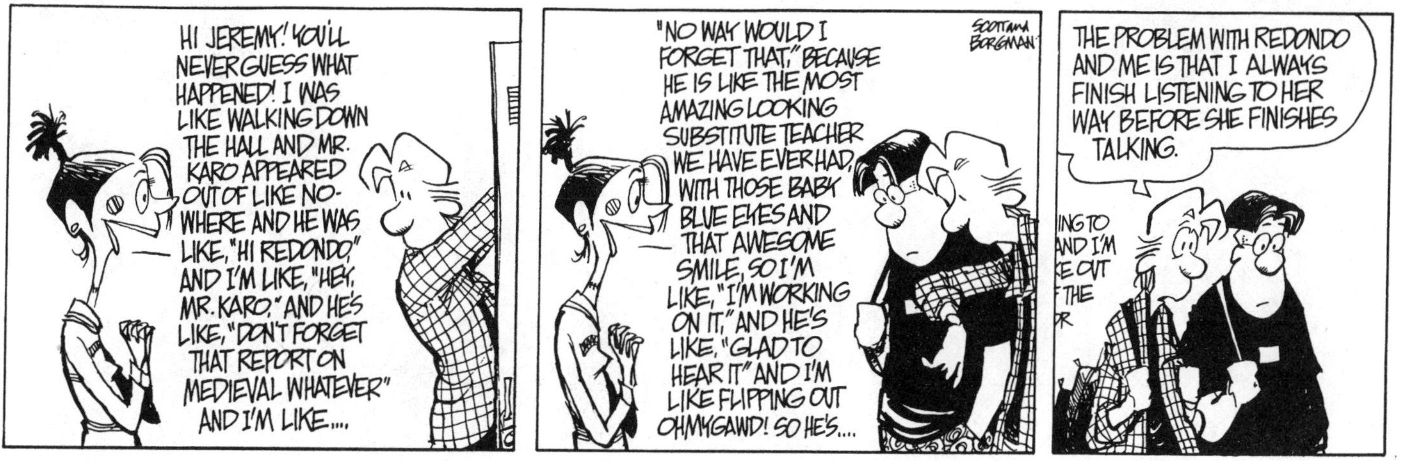
HI JEREMY! YOU'LL NEVER GUESS WHAT HAPPENED! I WAS LIKE WALKING DOWN THE HALL AND MR. KARO APPEARED OUT OF LIKE NO-WHERE AND HE WAS LIKE, "HI REDONDO," AND I'M LIKE, "HEY, MR. KARO." AND HE'S LIKE, "DON'T FORGET THAT REPORT ON MEDIEVAL WHATEVER" AND I'M LIKE....
"NO WAY WOULD I FORGET THAT," BECAUSE HE IS LIKE THE MOST AMAZING LOOKING SUBSTITUTE TEACHER WE HAVE EVER HAD, WITH THOSE BABY BLUE EYES AND THAT AWESOME SMILE, SO I'M LIKE, "I'M WORKING ON IT," AND HE'S LIKE, "GLAD TO HEAR IT" AND I'M LIKE FLIPPING OUT OHMYGAWD! SO HE'S....
SCOTT and BORGMAN
THE PROBLEM WITH REDONDO AND ME IS THAT I ALWAYS FINISH LISTENING TO HER WAY BEFORE SHE FINISHES TALKING.

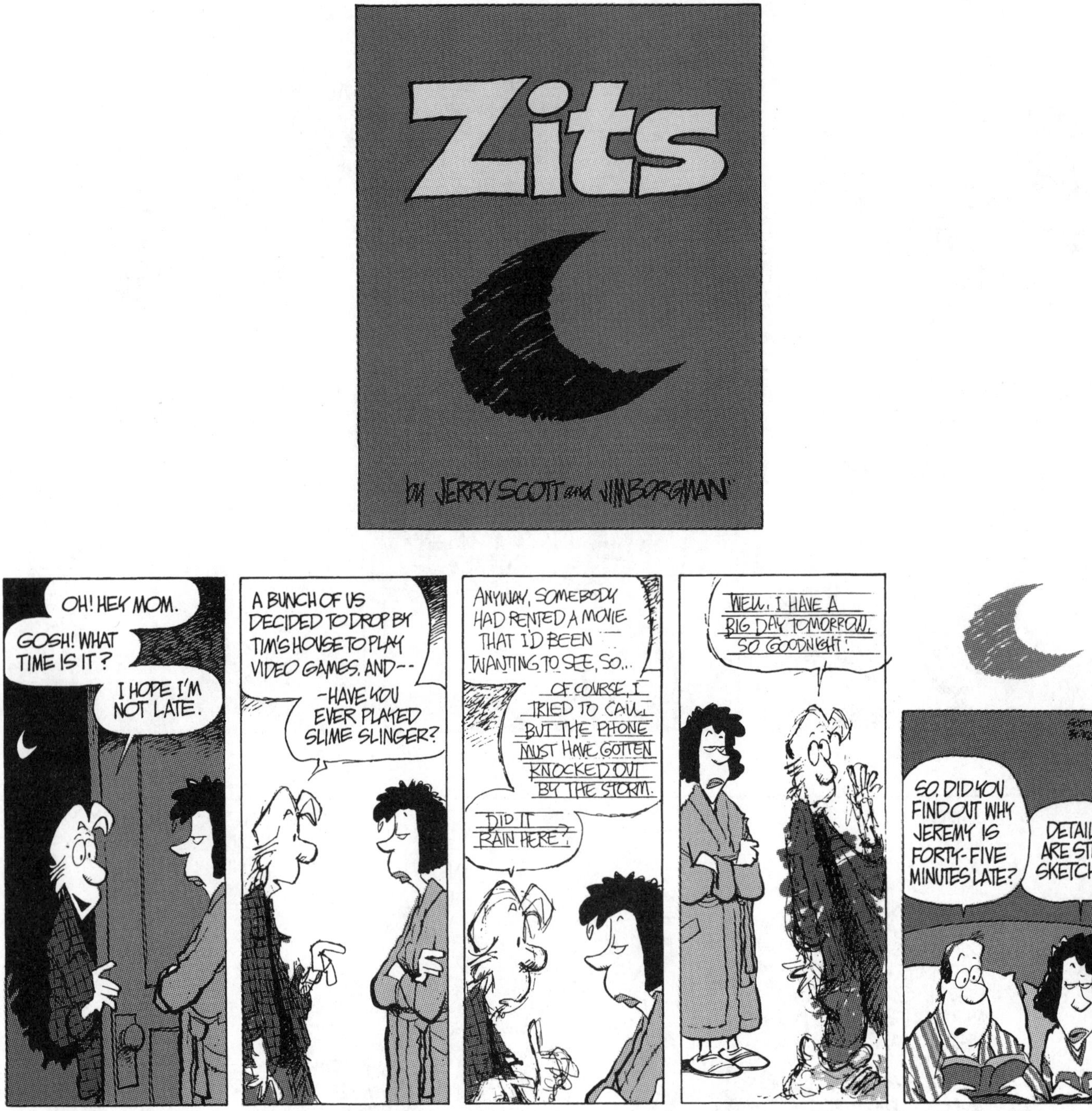
Zits
by JERRY SCOTT and JIM BORGMAN
OH! HEY MOM.
GOSH! WHAT TIME IS IT?
I HOPE I'M NOT LATE.
A BUNCH OF US DECIDED TO DROP BY TIM'S HOUSE TO PLAY VIDEO GAMES, AND--
-HAVE YOU EVER PLAYED SLIME SLINGER?
ANYWAY, SOMEBODY HAD RENTED A MOVIE THAT I'D BEEN WANTING TO SEE, SO...
OF COURSE, I TRIED TO CALL BUT THE PHONE MUST HAVE GOTTEN KNOCKED OUT BY THE STORM.
DID IT RAIN HERE?
WELL, I HAVE A BIG DAY TOMORROW, SO GOODNIGHT!
SO, DID YOU FIND OUT WHY JEREMY IS FORTY-FIVE MINUTES LATE?
DETAILS ARE STILL SKETCHY.

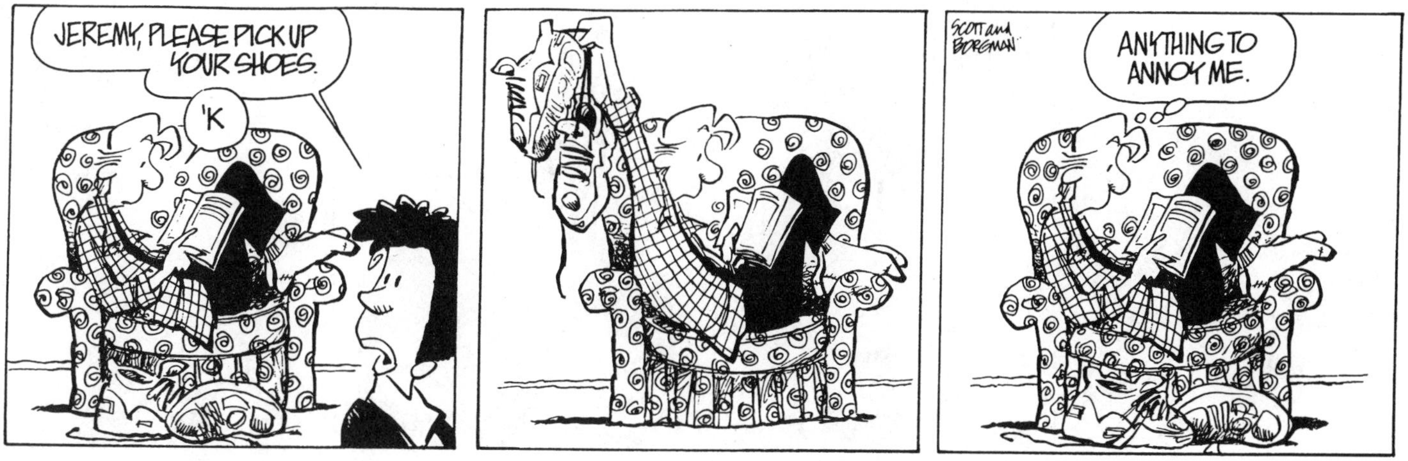
JEREMY, PLEASE PICK UP YOUR SHOES.
'K
SCOTT and BORGMAN
ANYTHING TO ANNOY ME.

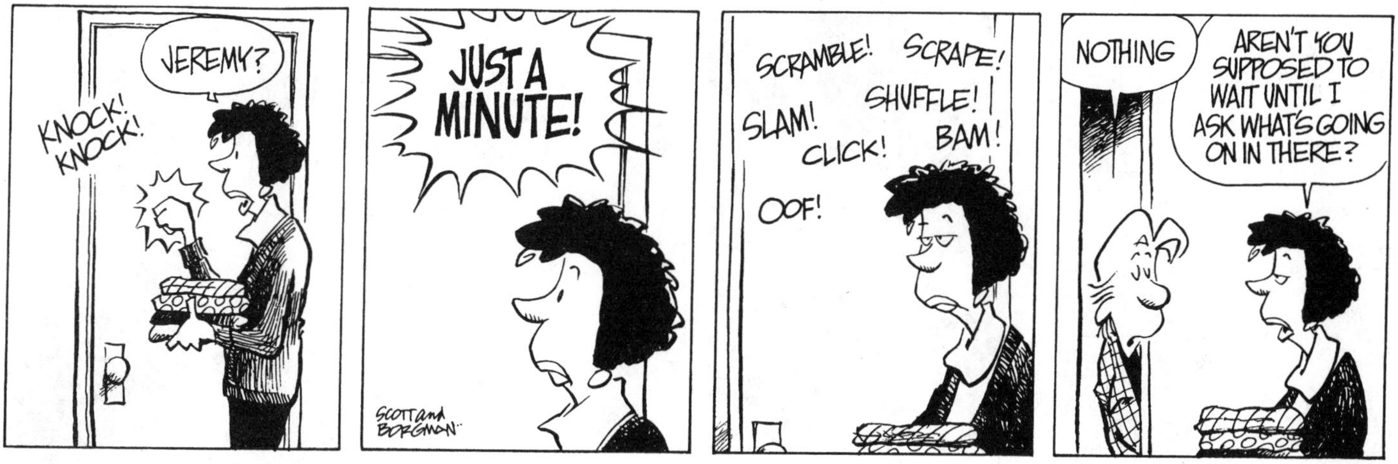
KNOCK! KNOCK!
JEREMY?
JUST A MINUTE!
SCOTT and BORGMAN
SCRAMBLE! SCRAPE!
SLAM! SHUFFLE!
CLICK! BAM!
OOF!
NOTHING
AREN'T YOU SUPPOSED TO WAIT UNTIL I ASK WHAT'S GOING ON IN THERE?

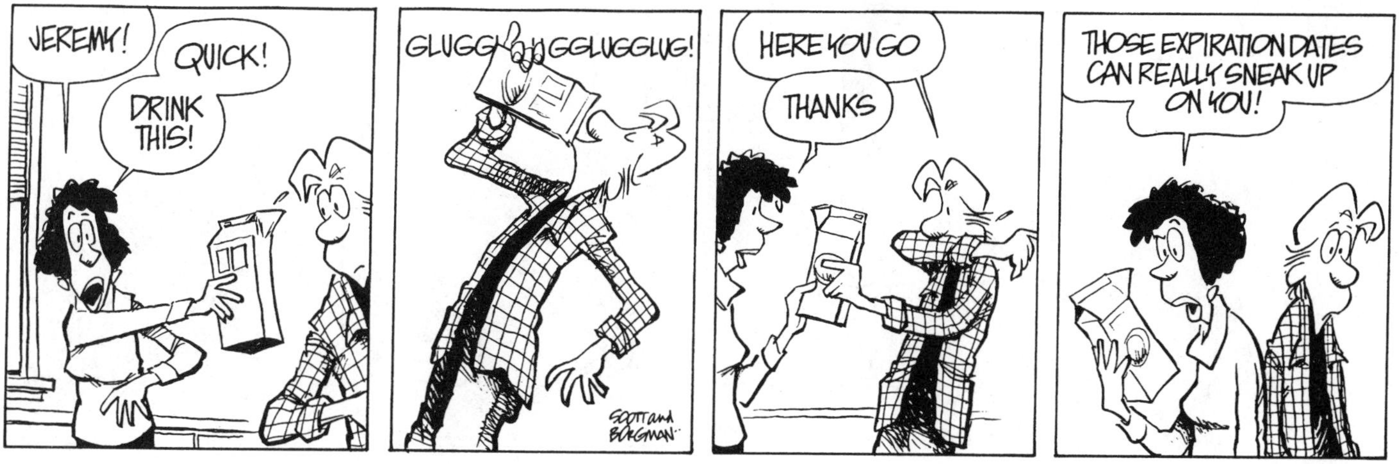
JEREMY!
QUICK!
DRINK THIS!
GLUGG
GGLUGGLUG!
SCOTT and BORGMAN
HERE YOU GO
THANKS
THOSE EXPIRATION DATES CAN REALLY SNEAK UP ON YOU!

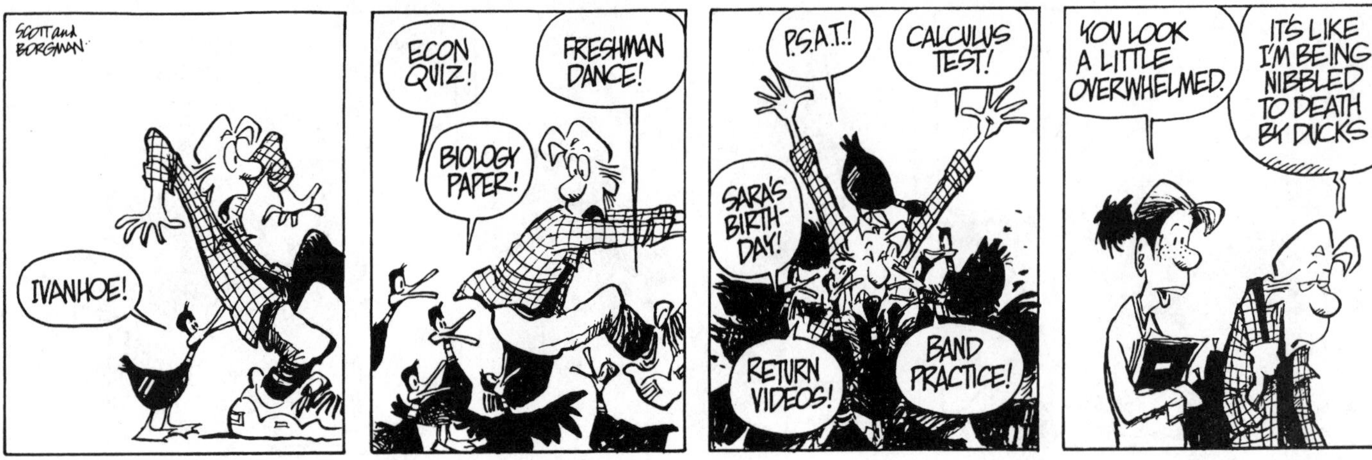
SCOTT and BORGMAN
IVANHOE!
ECON QUIZ!
FRESHMAN DANCE!
BIOLOGY PAPER!
P.S.A.T.!
CALCULUS TEST!
SARA'S BIRTH-DAY!
RETURN VIDEOS!
BAND PRACTICE!
YOU LOOK A LITTLE OVERWHELMED.
IT'S LIKE I'M BEING NIBBLED TO DEATH BY DUCKS

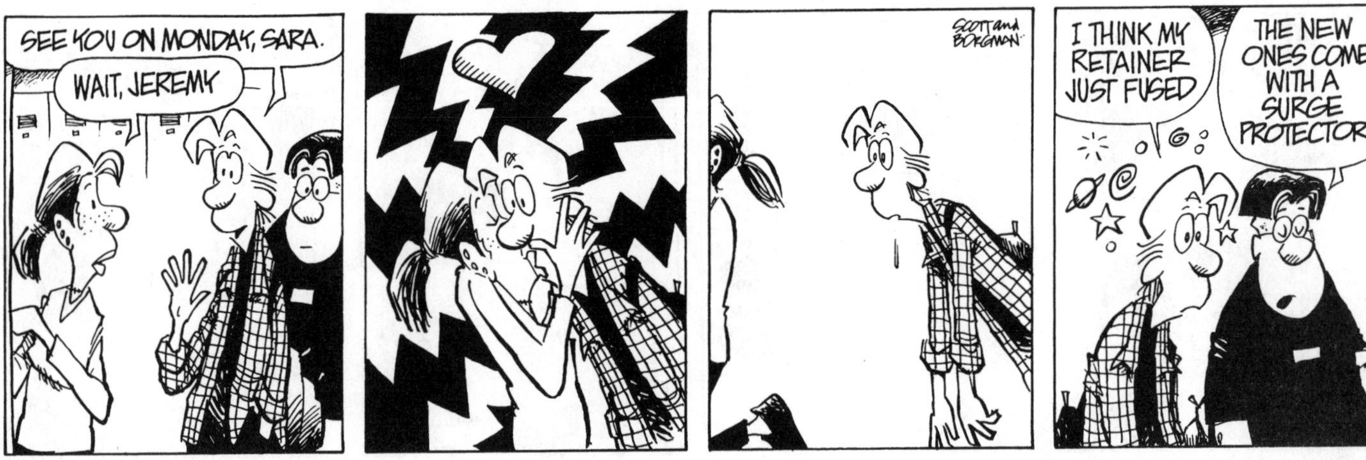
SEE YOU ON MONDAY, SARA.
WAIT, JEREMY
SCOTT and BORGMAN
I THINK MY RETAINER JUST FUSED
THE NEW ONES COME WITH A SURGE PROTECTOR

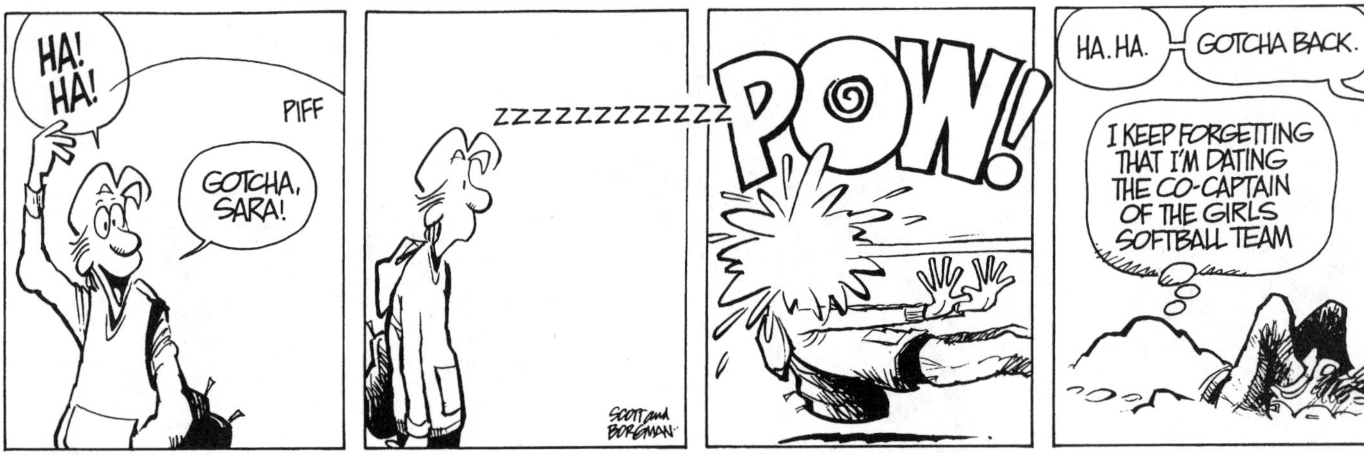
HA! HA!
PIFF
GOTCHA, SARA!
ZZZZZZZZZZZZ
SCOTT and BORGMAN
POW!
HA. HA.
GOTCHA BACK.
I KEEP FORGETTING THAT I'M DATING THE CO-CAPTAIN OF THE GIRLS SOFTBALL TEAM

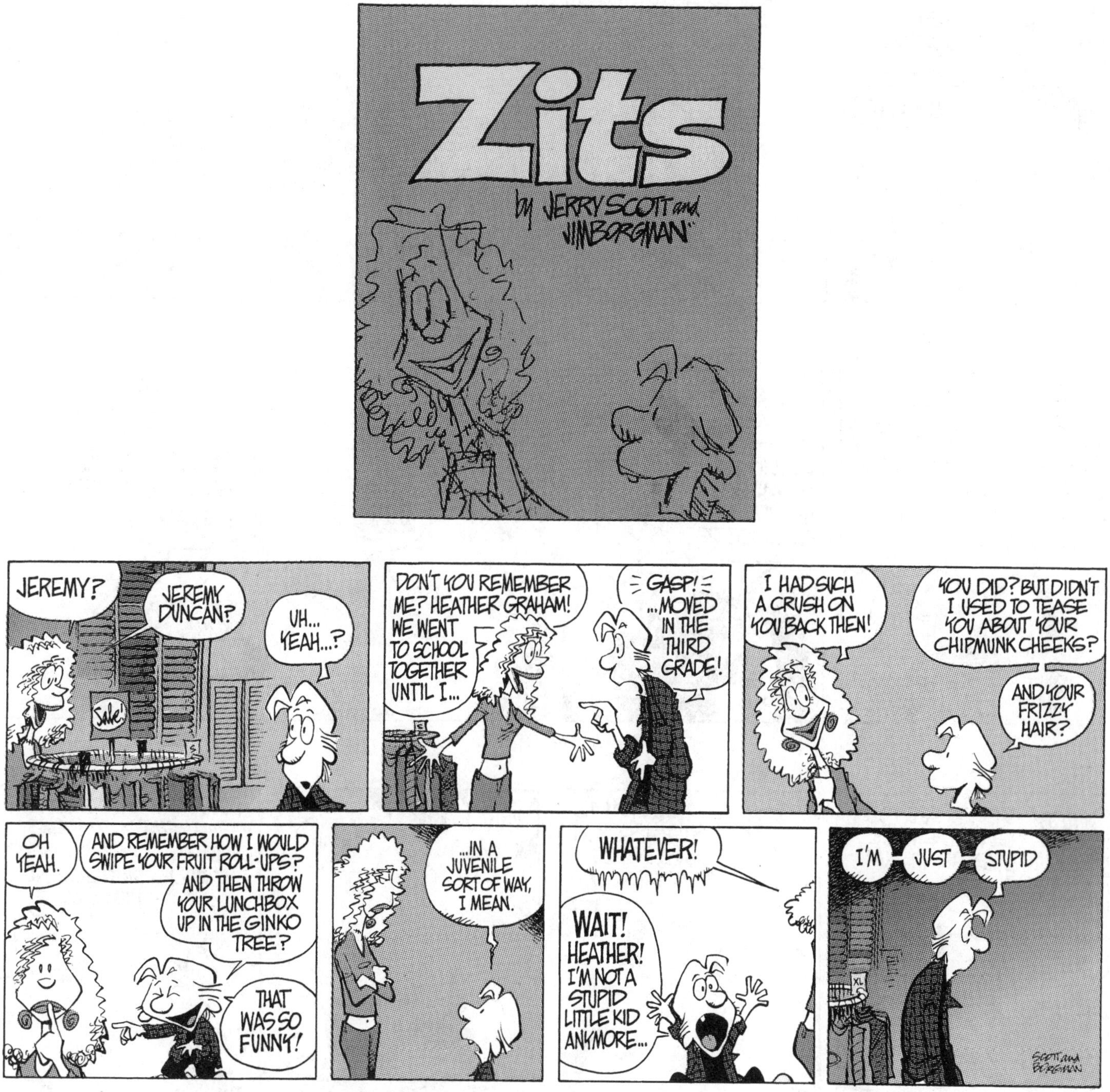
Zits
by JERRY SCOTT and JIM BORGMAN
JEREMY?
JEREMY DUNCAN?
UH... YEAH...?
Sale!
DON'T YOU REMEMBER ME? HEATHER GRAHAM! WE WENT TO SCHOOL TOGETHER UNTIL I...
GASP!
...MOVED IN THE THIRD GRADE!
I HAD SUCH A CRUSH ON YOU BACK THEN!
YOU DID? BUT DIDN'T I USED TO TEASE YOU ABOUT YOUR CHIPMUNK CHEEKS?
AND YOUR FRIZZY HAIR?
OH YEAH.
AND REMEMBER HOW I WOULD SWIPE YOUR FRUIT ROLL-UPS?
AND THEN THROW YOUR LUNCHBOX UP IN THE GINKO TREE?
THAT WAS SO FUNNY!
...IN A JUVENILE SORT OF WAY, I MEAN.
WHATEVER!
WAIT! HEATHER! I'M NOT A STUPID LITTLE KID ANYMORE...
XL
I'M
JUST
STUPID
SCOTT and BORGMAN

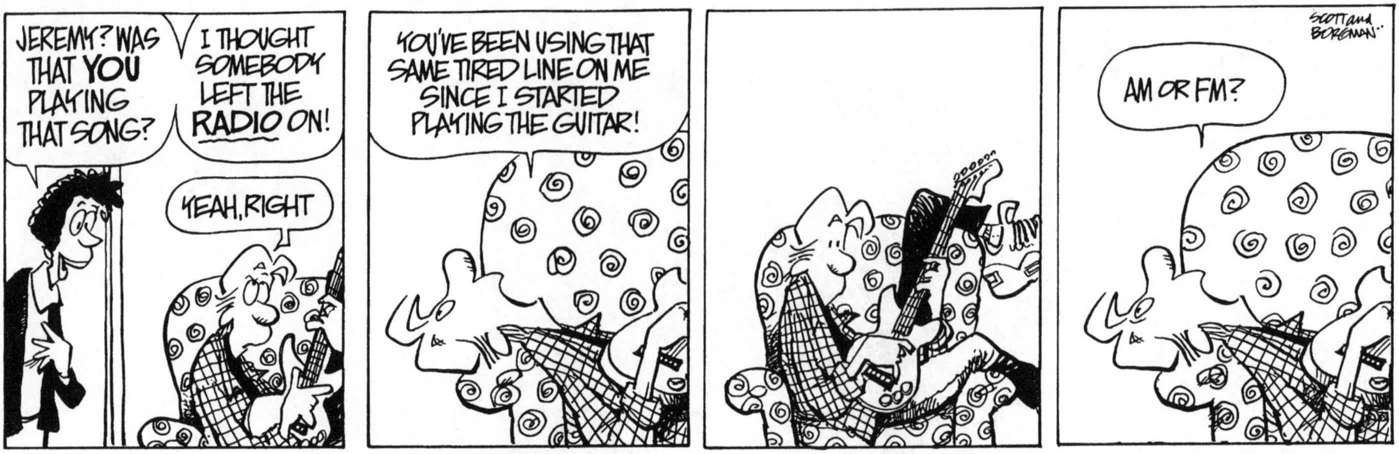
JEREMY? WAS THAT YOU PLAYING THAT SONG?
I THOUGHT SOMEBODY LEFT THE RADIO ON!
YEAH, RIGHT
YOU'VE BEEN USING THAT SAME TIRED LINE ON ME SINCE I STARTED PLAYING THE GUITAR!
SCOTT and BORGMAN
AM OR FM?

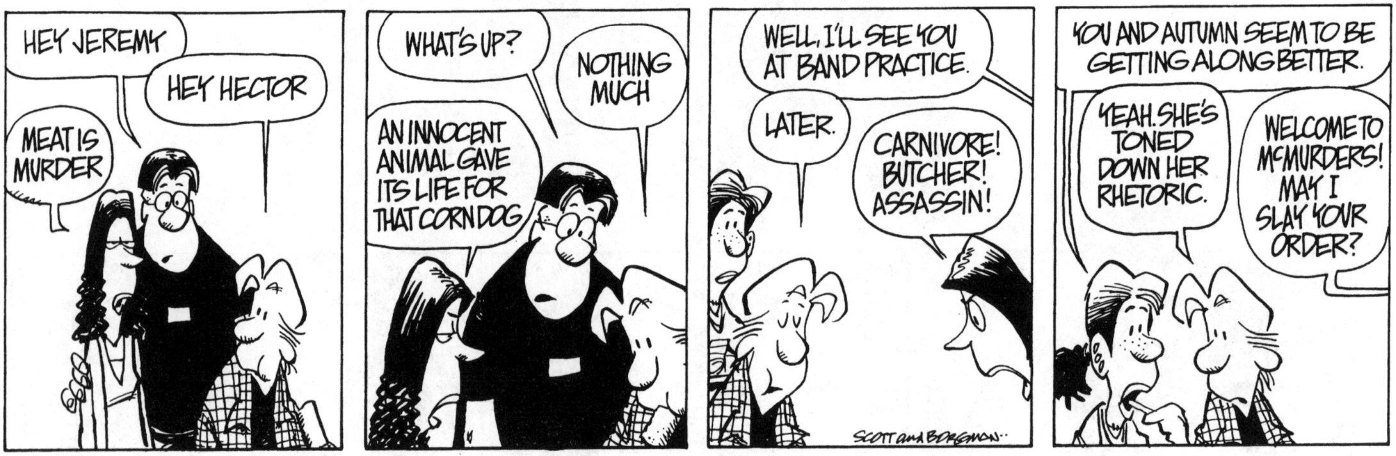
HEY JEREMY
HEY HECTOR
MEAT IS MURDER
WHAT'S UP?
NOTHING MUCH
AN INNOCENT ANIMAL GAVE ITS LIFE FOR THAT CORN DOG
WELL, I'LL SEE YOU AT BAND PRACTICE.
LATER.
CARNIVORE! BUTCHER! ASSASSIN!
SCOTT and BORGMAN
YOU AND AUTUMN SEEM TO BE GETTING ALONG BETTER.
YEAH. SHE'S TONED DOWN HER RHETORIC.
WELCOME TO McMURDERS! MAY I SLAY YOUR ORDER?

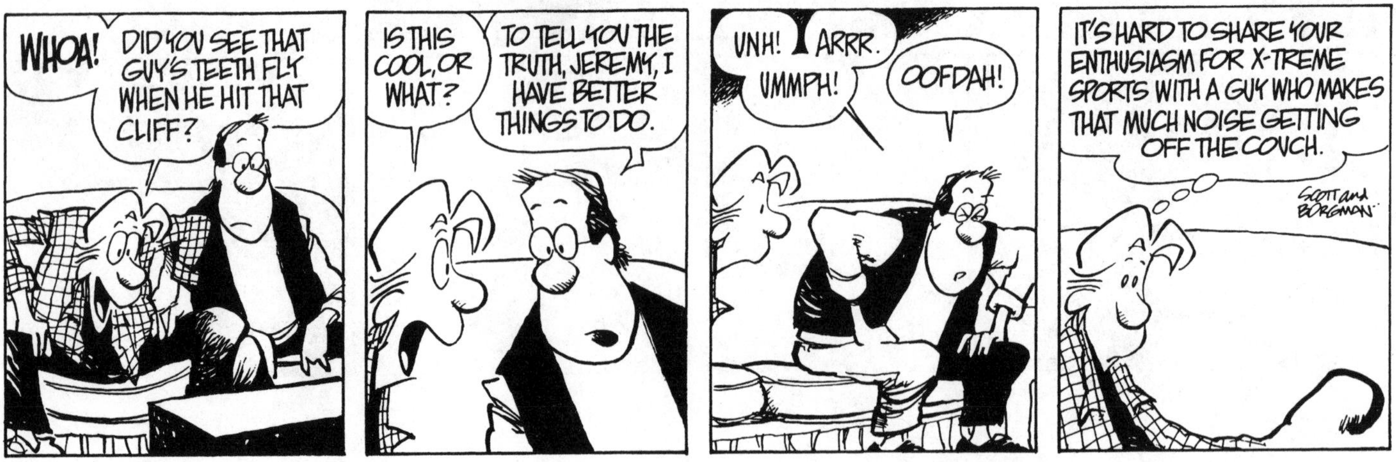
WHOA!
DID YOU SEE THAT GUY'S TEETH FLY WHEN HE HIT THAT CLIFF?
IS THIS COOL, OR WHAT?
TO TELL YOU THE TRUTH, JEREMY, I HAVE BETTER THINGS TO DO.
UNH!
ARRR.
UMMPH!
OOFDAH!
IT'S HARD TO SHARE YOUR ENTHUSIASM FOR X-TREME SPORTS WITH A GUY WHO MAKES THAT MUCH NOISE GETTING OFF THE COUCH.
SCOTT and BORGMAN

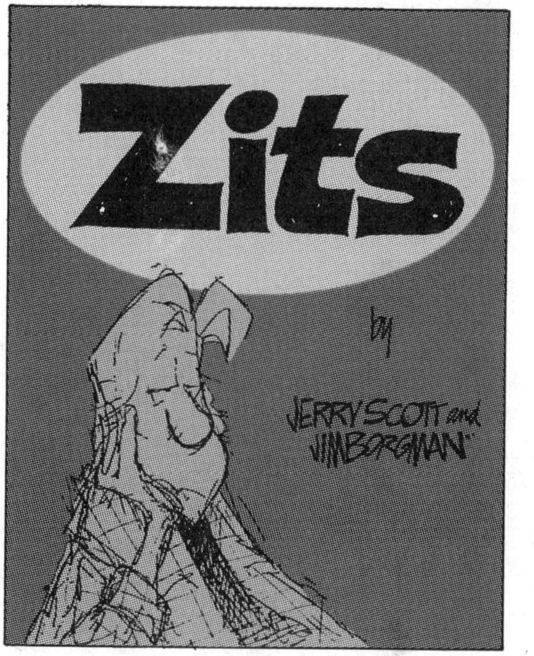
Zits
by
JERRY SCOTT and JIM BORGMAN

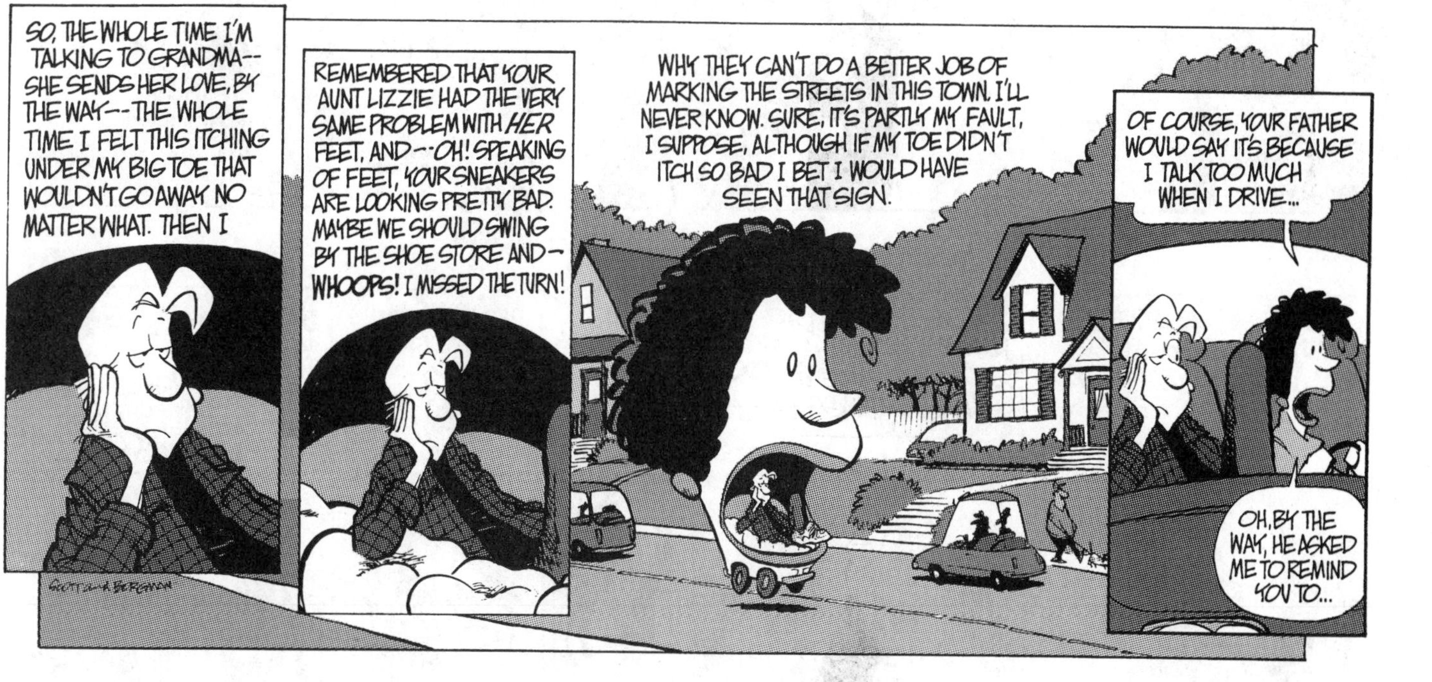
SO, THE WHOLE TIME I'M TALKING TO GRANDMA-- SHE SENDS HER LOVE, BY THE WAY-- THE WHOLE TIME I FELT THIS ITCHING UNDER MY BIG TOE THAT WOULDN'T GO AWAY NO MATTER WHAT. THEN I
REMEMBERED THAT YOUR AUNT LIZZIE HAD THE VERY SAME PROBLEM WITH HER FEET, AND--OH! SPEAKING OF FEET, YOUR SNEAKERS ARE LOOKING PRETTY BAD. MAYBE WE SHOULD SWING BY THE SHOE STORE AND-- WHOOPS! I MISSED THE TURN!
WHY THEY CAN'T DO A BETTER JOB OF MARKING THE STREETS IN THIS TOWN, I'LL NEVER KNOW. SURE, IT'S PARTLY MY FAULT, I SUPPOSE, ALTHOUGH IF MY TOE DIDN'T ITCH SO BAD I BET I WOULD HAVE SEEN THAT SIGN.
OF COURSE, YOUR FATHER WOULD SAY IT'S BECAUSE I TALK TOO MUCH WHEN I DRIVE...
OH, BY THE WAY, HE ASKED ME TO REMIND YOU TO...

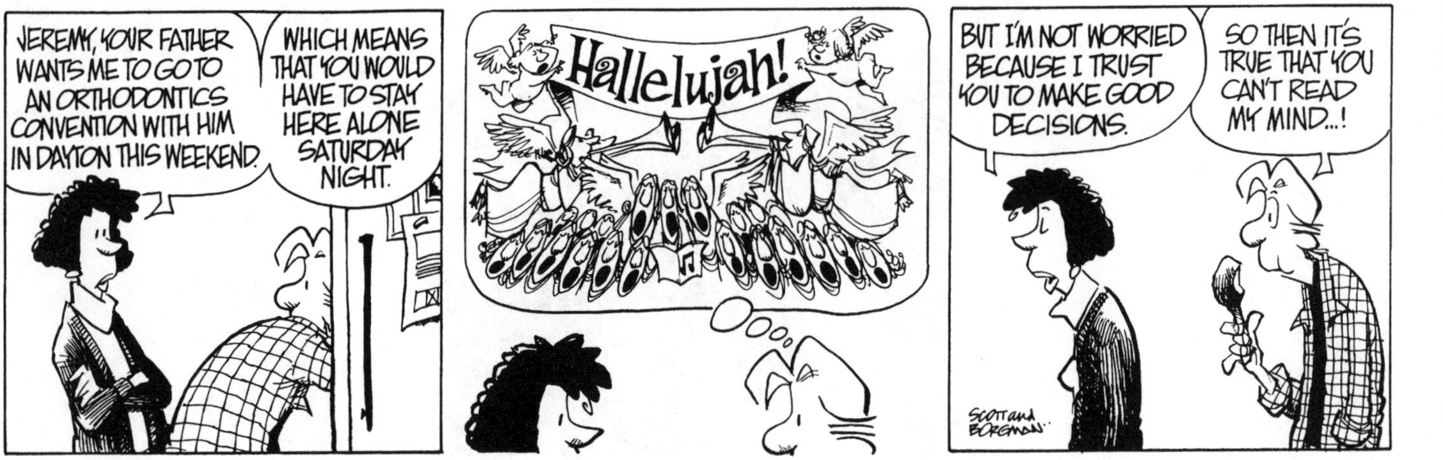
JEREMY, YOUR FATHER WANTS ME TO GO TO AN ORTHODONTICS CONVENTION WITH HIM IN DAYTON THIS WEEKEND.
WHICH MEANS THAT YOU WOULD HAVE TO STAY HERE ALONE SATURDAY NIGHT.
Hallelujah!
BUT I'M NOT WORRIED BECAUSE I TRUST YOU TO MAKE GOOD DECISIONS.
SO THEN IT'S TRUE THAT YOU CAN'T READ MY MIND...!
SCOTT and BORGMAN

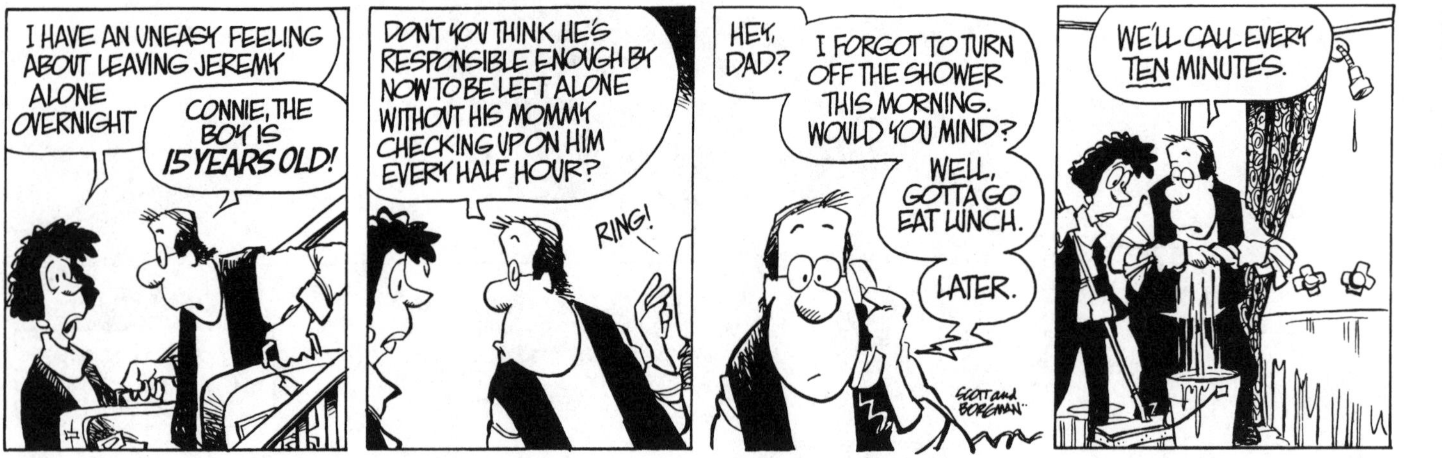
I HAVE AN UNEASY FEELING ABOUT LEAVING JEREMY ALONE OVERNIGHT
CONNIE, THE BOY IS **15 YEARS OLD!**
DON'T YOU THINK HE'S RESPONSIBLE ENOUGH BY NOW TO BE LEFT ALONE WITHOUT HIS MOMMY CHECKING UP ON HIM EVERY HALF HOUR?
RING!
HEY, DAD?
I FORGOT TO TURN OFF THE SHOWER THIS MORNING. WOULD YOU MIND?
WELL, GOTTA GO EAT LUNCH.
LATER.
SCOTT and BORGMAN
WE'LL CALL EVERY TEN MINUTES.

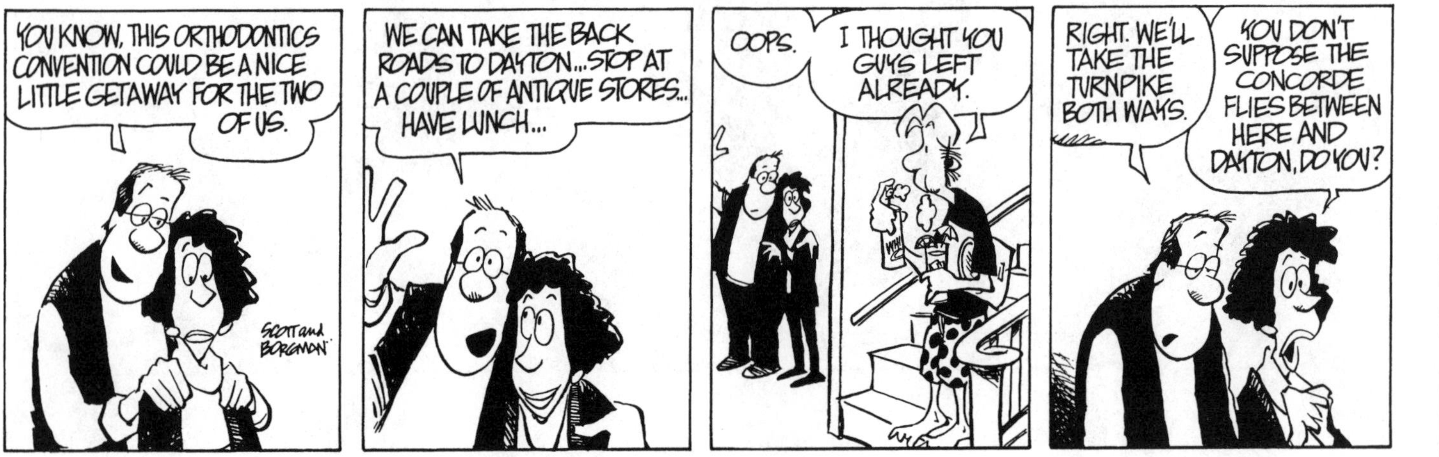
YOU KNOW, THIS ORTHODONTICS CONVENTION COULD BE A NICE LITTLE GETAWAY FOR THE TWO OF US.
SCOTT and BORGMAN
WE CAN TAKE THE BACK ROADS TO DAYTON... STOP AT A COUPLE OF ANTIQUE STORES... HAVE LUNCH...
OOPS.
I THOUGHT YOU GUYS LEFT ALREADY.
RIGHT. WE'LL TAKE THE TURNPIKE BOTH WAYS.
YOU DON'T SUPPOSE THE CONCORDE FLIES BETWEEN HERE AND DAYTON, DO YOU?

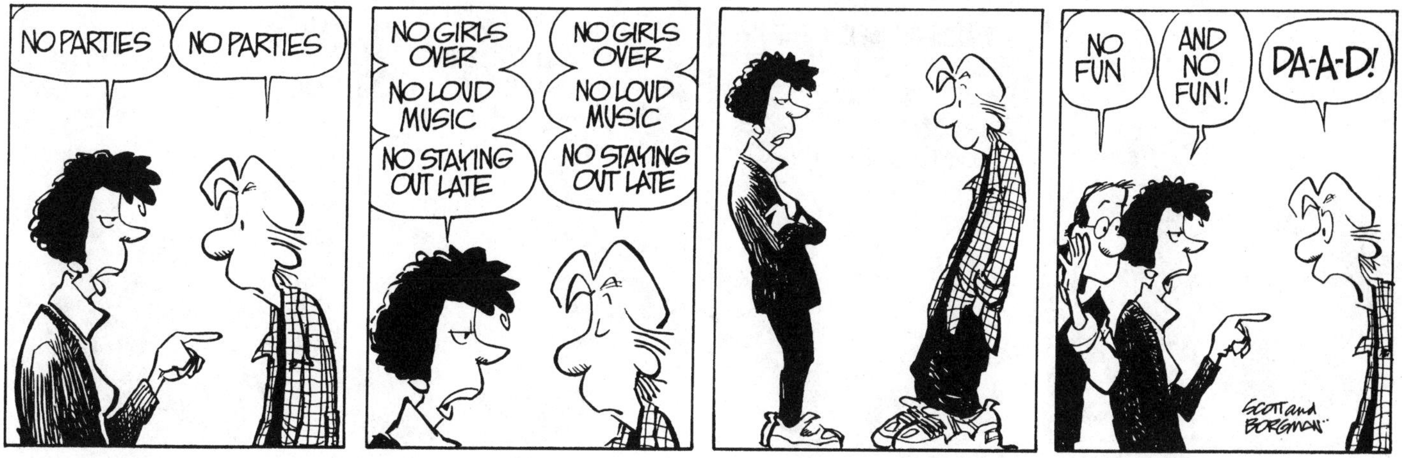
NO PARTIES
NO PARTIES
NO GIRLS OVER
NO LOUD MUSIC
NO STAYING OUT LATE
NO GIRLS OVER
NO LOUD MUSIC
NO STAYING OUT LATE
NO FUN
AND NO FUN!
DA-A-D!
SCOTT and BORGMAN

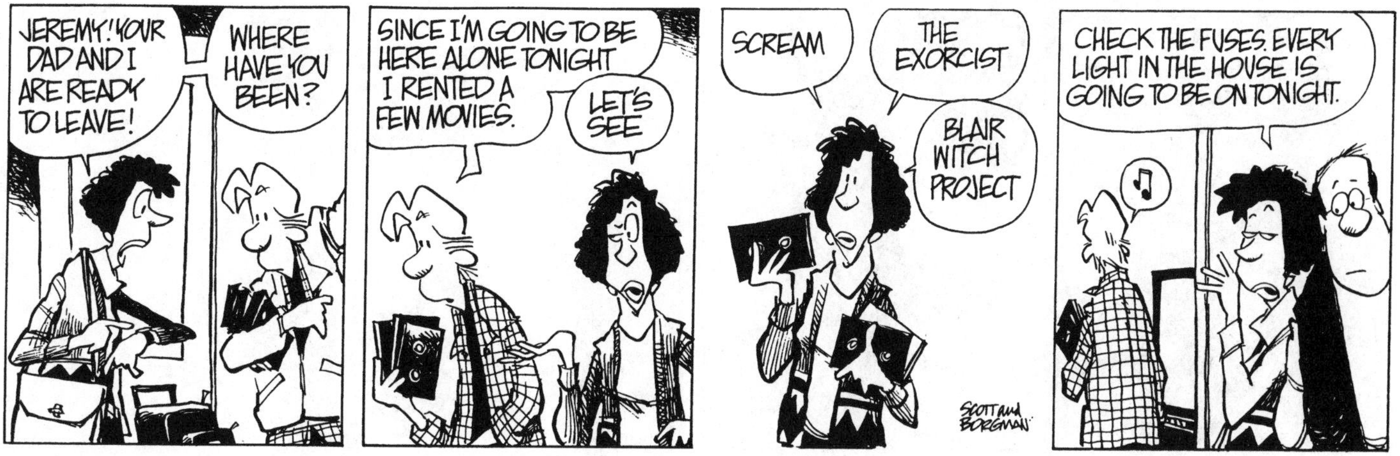
JEREMY! YOUR DAD AND I ARE READY TO LEAVE!
WHERE HAVE YOU BEEN?
SINCE I'M GOING TO BE HERE ALONE TONIGHT I RENTED A FEW MOVIES.
LET'S SEE
SCREAM
THE EXORCIST
BLAIR WITCH PROJECT
SCOTT and BORGMAN
CHECK THE FUSES. EVERY LIGHT IN THE HOUSE IS GOING TO BE ON TONIGHT.

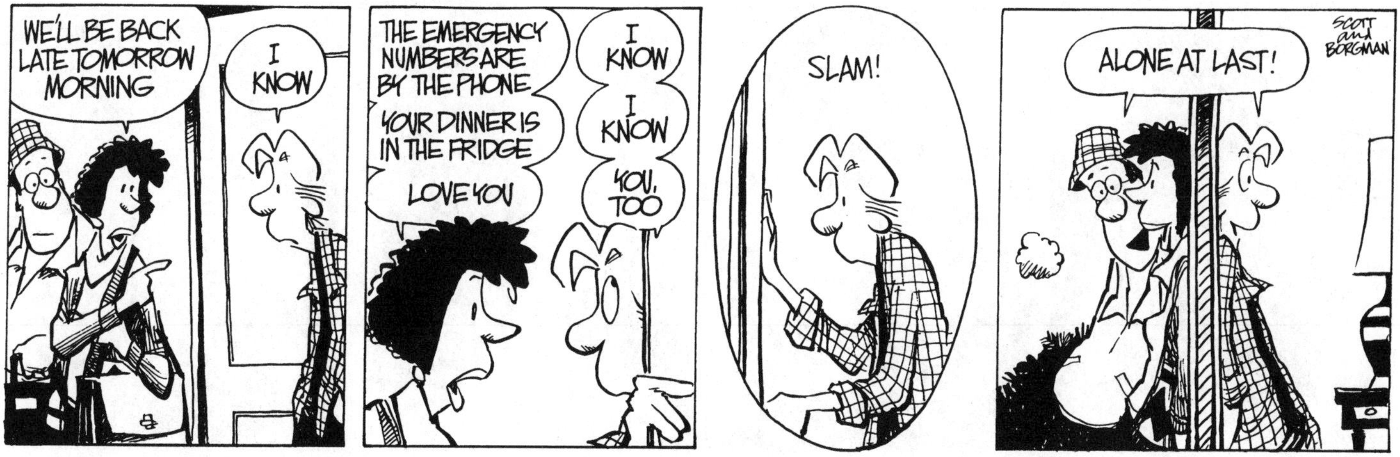
WE'LL BE BACK LATE TOMORROW MORNING
I KNOW
THE EMERGENCY NUMBERS ARE BY THE PHONE
YOUR DINNER IS IN THE FRIDGE
LOVE YOU
I KNOW
I KNOW
YOU, TOO
SLAM!
SCOTT and BORGMAN
ALONE AT LAST!

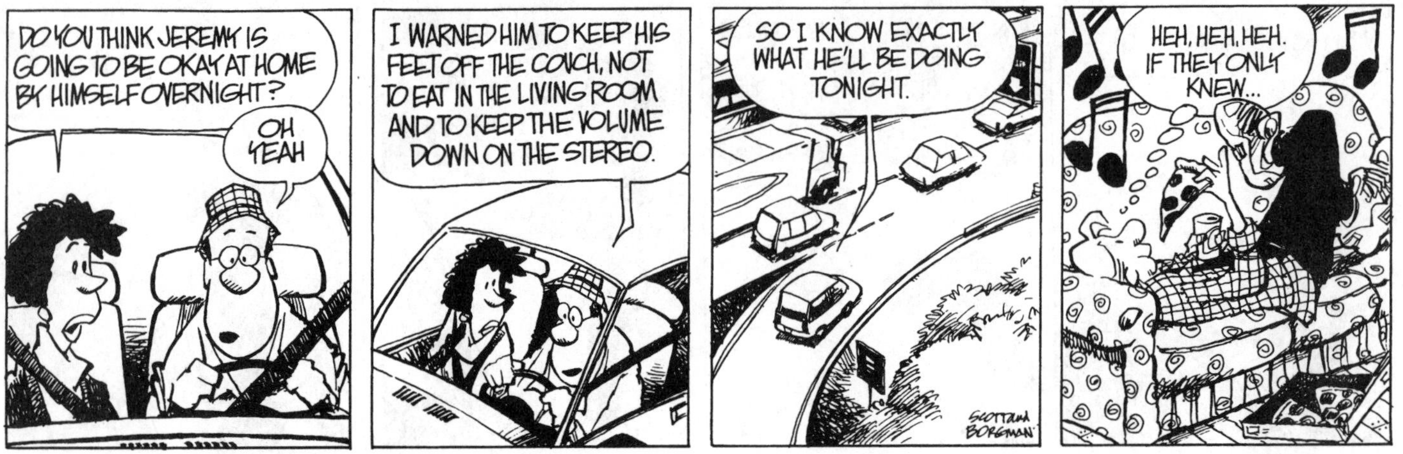
DO YOU THINK JEREMY IS GOING TO BE OKAY AT HOME BY HIMSELF OVERNIGHT?
OH YEAH
I WARNED HIM TO KEEP HIS FEET OFF THE COUCH, NOT TO EAT IN THE LIVING ROOM AND TO KEEP THE VOLUME DOWN ON THE STEREO.
SO I KNOW EXACTLY WHAT HE'LL BE DOING TONIGHT.
SCOTT AND BORGMAN
HEH, HEH, HEH. IF THEY ONLY KNEW...

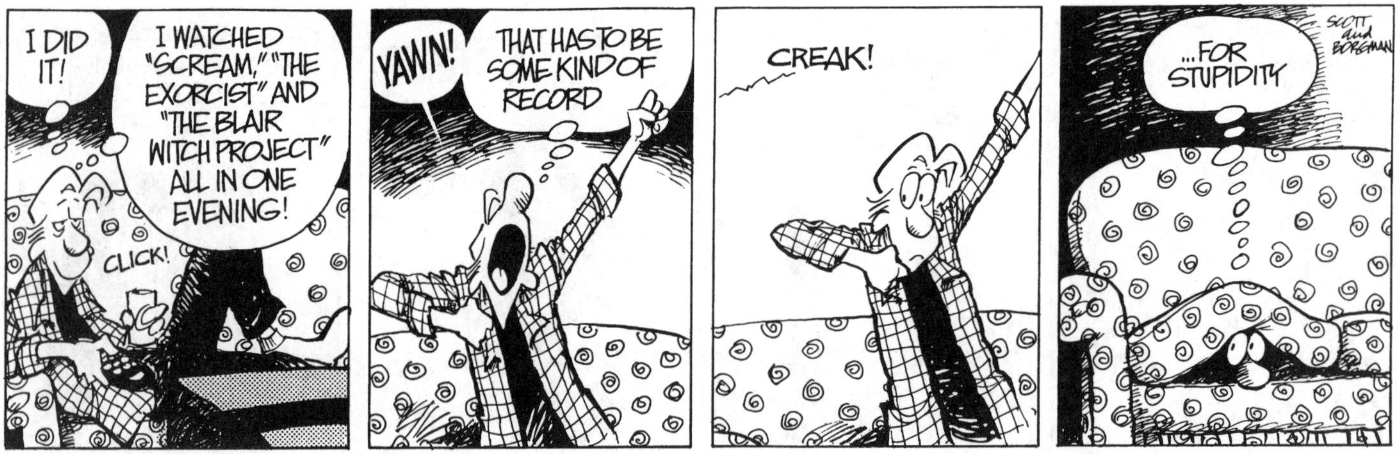
I DID IT!
I WATCHED "SCREAM," "THE EXORCIST" AND "THE BLAIR WITCH PROJECT" ALL IN ONE EVENING!
CLICK!
YAWN!
THAT HAS TO BE SOME KIND OF RECORD
CREAK!
SCOTT and BORGMAN
...FOR STUPIDITY

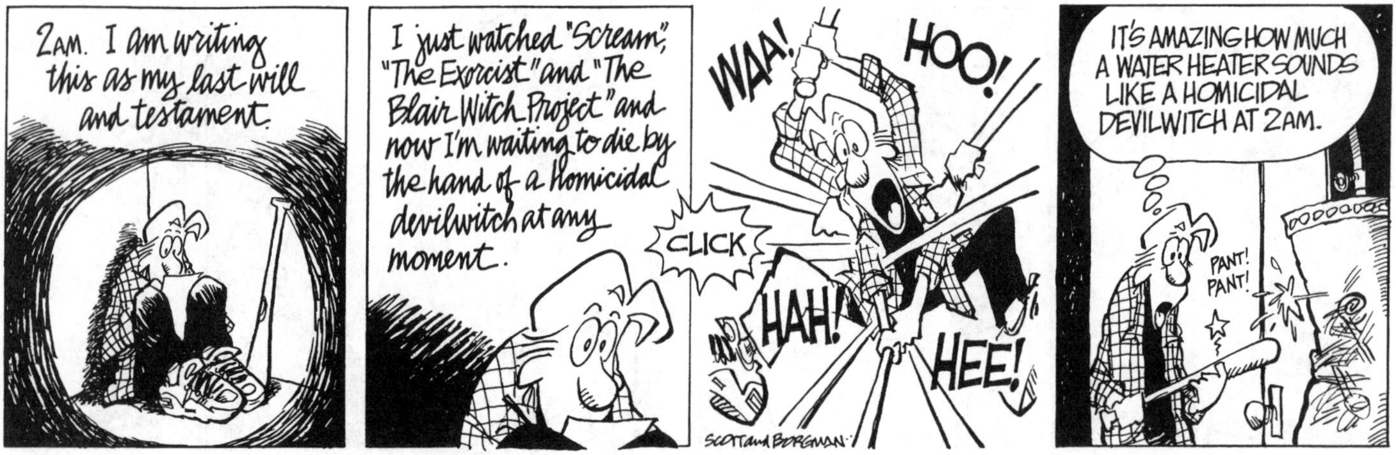
2AM. I am writing this as my last will and testament.
I just watched "Scream", "The Exorcist" and "The Blair Witch Project" and now I'm waiting to die by the hand of a Homicidal devilwitch at any moment.
CLICK
WAA! HOO!
HAH! HEE!
SCOTT AND BORGMAN
IT'S AMAZING HOW MUCH A WATER HEATER SOUNDS LIKE A HOMICIDAL DEVILWITCH AT 2AM.
PANT! PANT!

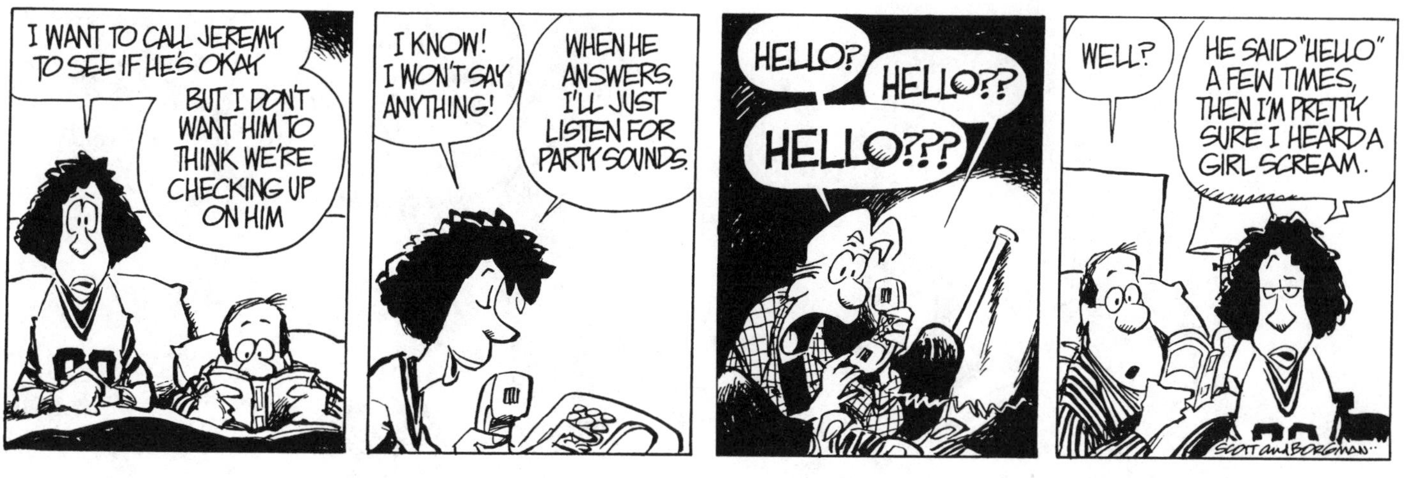
I WANT TO CALL JEREMY TO SEE IF HE'S OKAY
BUT I DON'T WANT HIM TO THINK WE'RE CHECKING UP ON HIM
I KNOW! I WON'T SAY ANYTHING!
WHEN HE ANSWERS, I'LL JUST LISTEN FOR PARTY SOUNDS.
HELLO?
HELLO??
HELLO???
WELL?
HE SAID "HELLO" A FEW TIMES, THEN I'M PRETTY SURE I HEARD A GIRL SCREAM.
SCOTT and BORGMAN

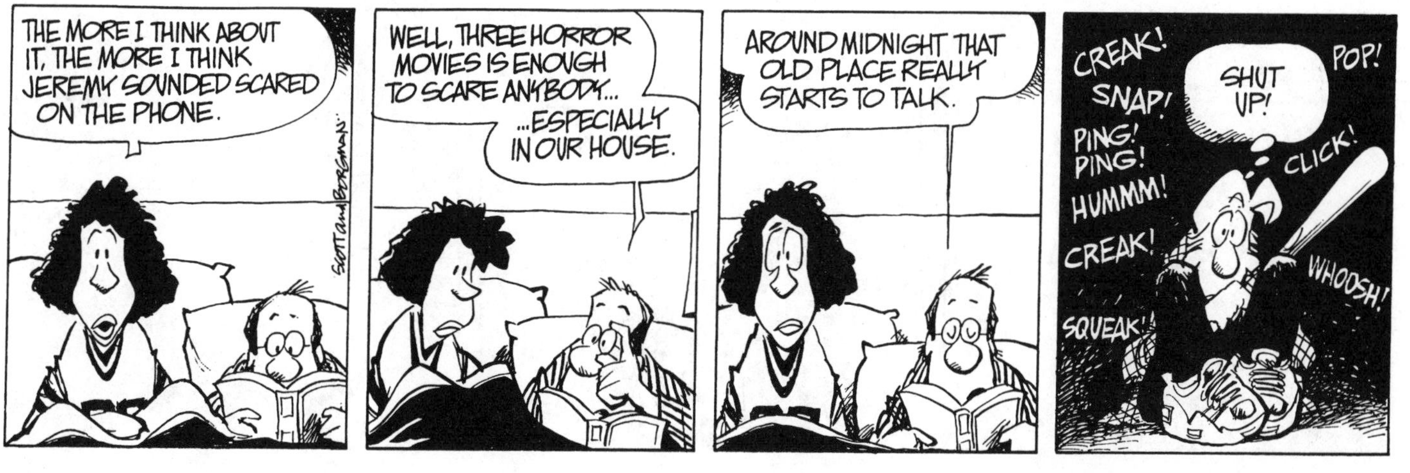
THE MORE I THINK ABOUT IT, THE MORE I THINK JEREMY SOUNDED SCARED ON THE PHONE.
SCOTT and BORGMAN
WELL, THREE HORROR MOVIES IS ENOUGH TO SCARE ANYBODY...
...ESPECIALLY IN OUR HOUSE.
AROUND MIDNIGHT THAT OLD PLACE REALLY STARTS TO TALK.
CREAK!
SNAP!
SHUT UP!
POP!
PING! PING!
CLICK!
HUMMM!
CREAK!
WHOOSH!
SQUEAK!

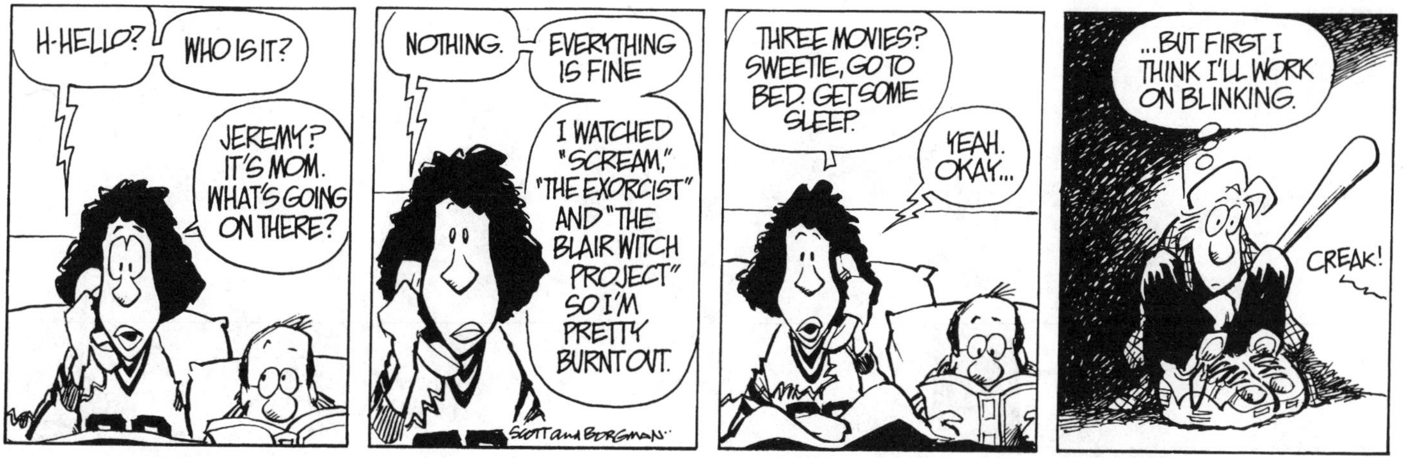
H-HELLO?
WHO IS IT?
JEREMY? IT'S MOM. WHAT'S GOING ON THERE?
NOTHING.
EVERYTHING IS FINE
I WATCHED "SCREAM," "THE EXORCIST" AND "THE BLAIR WITCH PROJECT" SO I'M PRETTY BURNT OUT.
SCOTT and BORGMAN
THREE MOVIES? SWEETIE, GO TO BED. GET SOME SLEEP.
YEAH. OKAY...
...BUT FIRST I THINK I'LL WORK ON BLINKING.
CREAK!

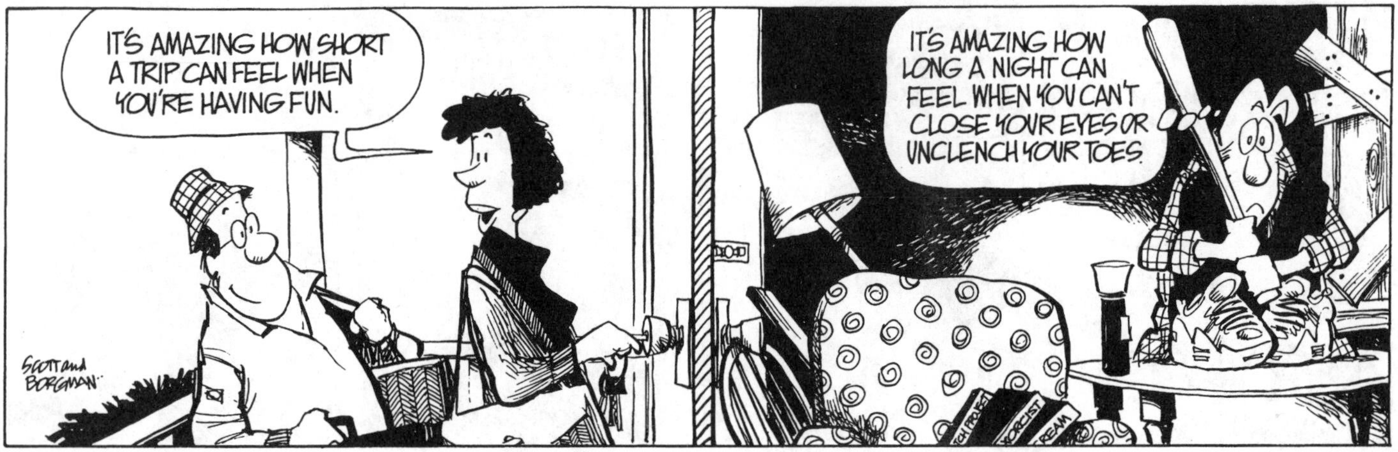
SCOTT and BORGMAN
IT'S AMAZING HOW SHORT A TRIP CAN FEEL WHEN YOU'RE HAVING FUN.
IT'S AMAZING HOW LONG A NIGHT CAN FEEL WHEN YOU CAN'T CLOSE YOUR EYES OR UNCLENCH YOUR TOES.

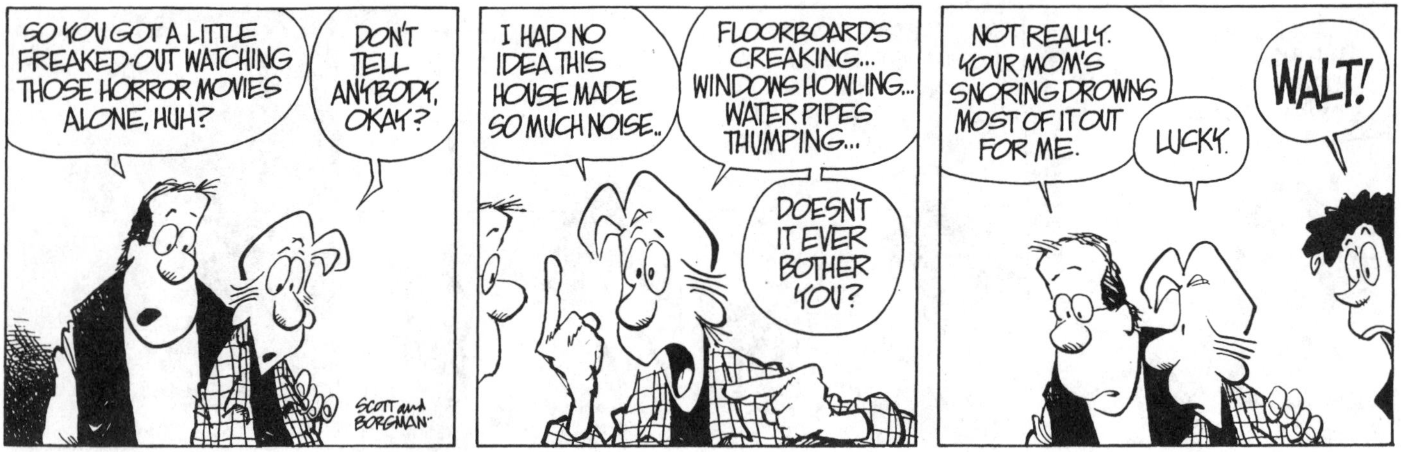
SO YOU GOT A LITTLE FREAKED-OUT WATCHING THOSE HORROR MOVIES ALONE, HUH?
DON'T TELL ANYBODY, OKAY?
SCOTT and BORGMAN
I HAD NO IDEA THIS HOUSE MADE SO MUCH NOISE..
FLOORBOARDS CREAKING... WINDOWS HOWLING... WATER PIPES THUMPING...
DOESN'T IT EVER BOTHER YOU?
NOT REALLY. YOUR MOM'S SNORING DROWNS MOST OF IT OUT FOR ME.
LUCKY.
WALT!

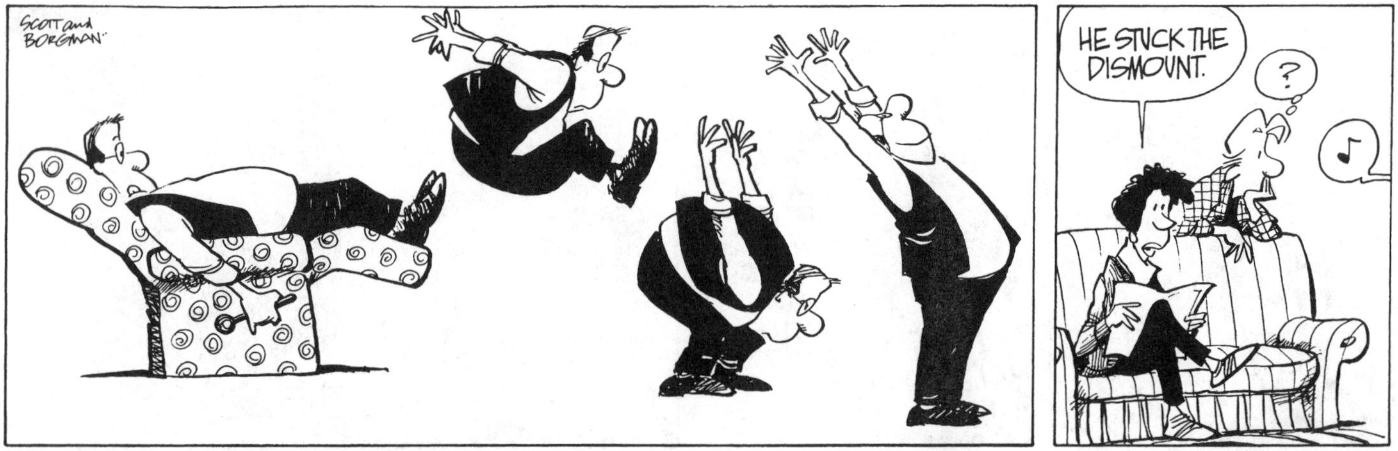
SCOTT and BORGMAN
HE STUCK THE DISMOUNT.
?

Zits
by JERRY SCOTT and JIM BORGMAN

SCOTT and BORGMAN
HI SWEETIE! HOW WAS YOUR DAY?
OK
WOULD IT KILL HIM TO SMILE?
ONLY IF WE SAW HIM

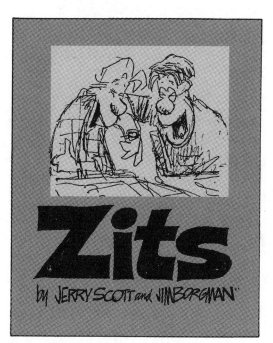

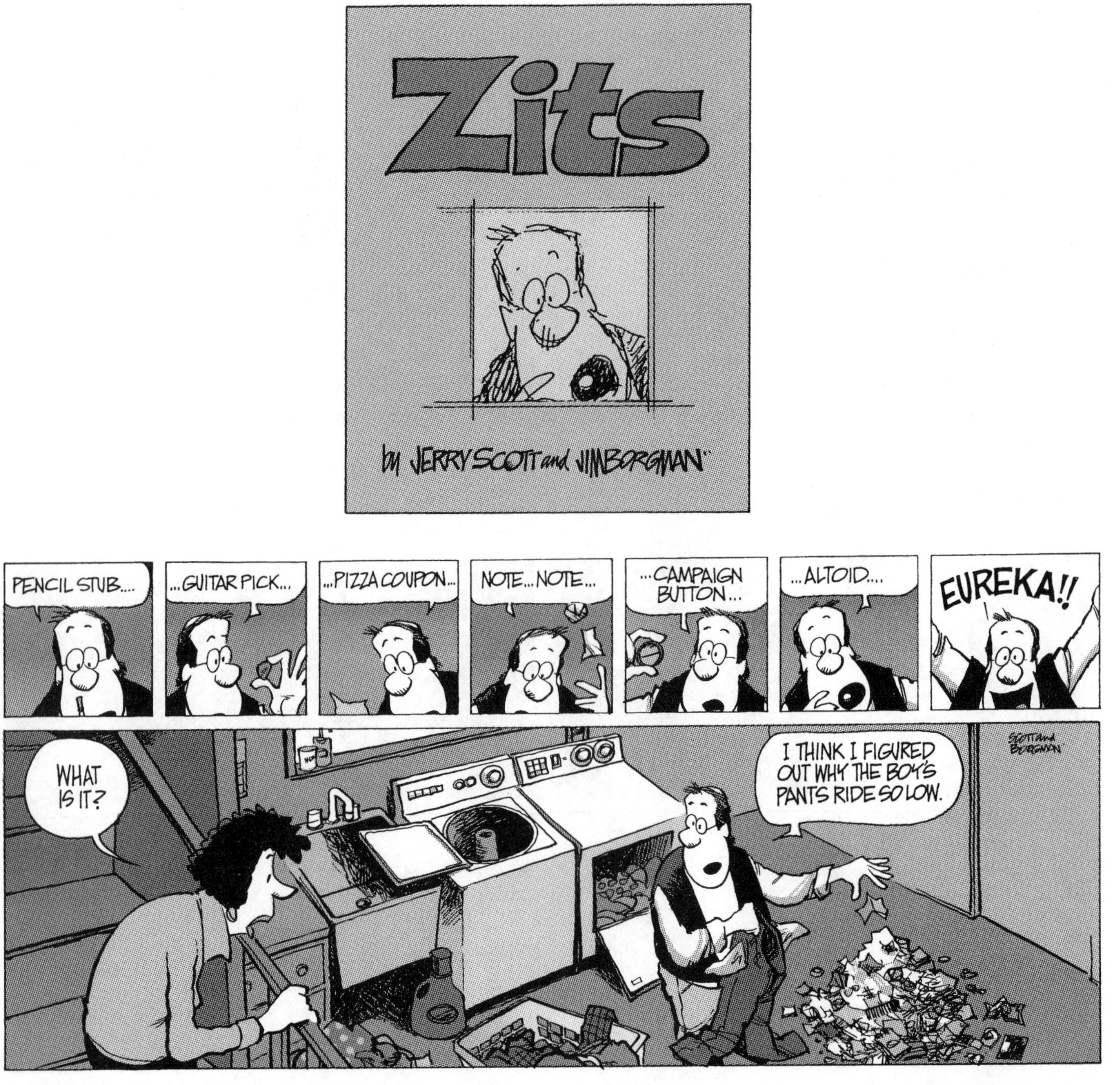
Zits
by JERRY SCOTT and JIM BORGMAN
PENCIL STUB....
...GUITAR PICK...
...PIZZA COUPON...
NOTE...NOTE...
...CAMPAIGN BUTTON...
...ALTOID....
EUREKA!!
WHAT IS IT?
I THINK I FIGURED OUT WHY THE BOY'S PANTS RIDE SO LOW.
SCOTT and BORGMAN

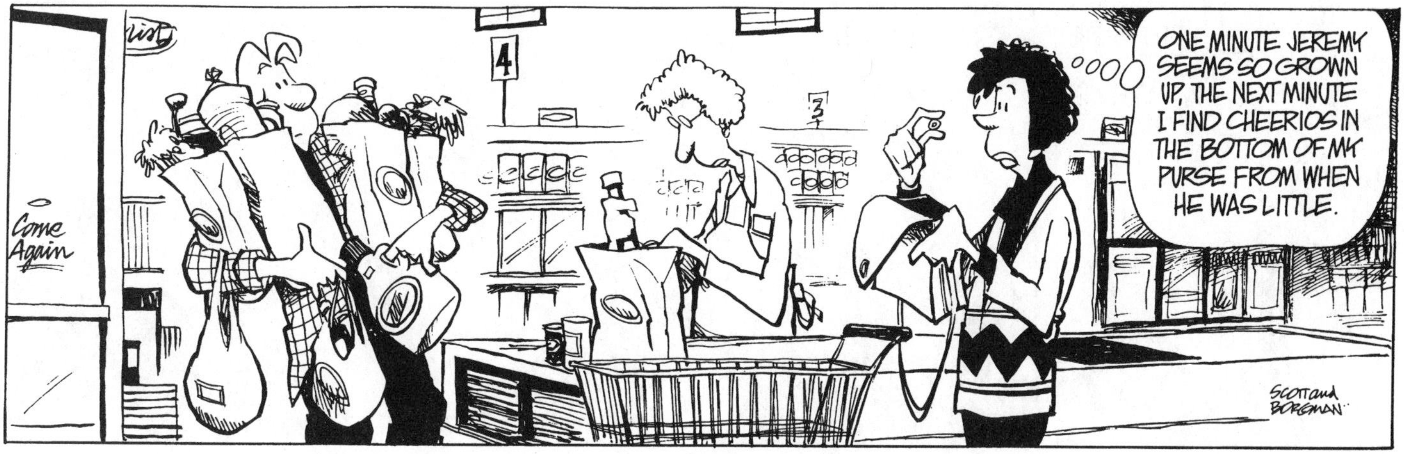
Come Again
4
ONE MINUTE JEREMY SEEMS SO GROWN UP, THE NEXT MINUTE I FIND CHEERIOS IN THE BOTTOM OF MY PURSE FROM WHEN HE WAS LITTLE.
SCOTT and BORGMAN

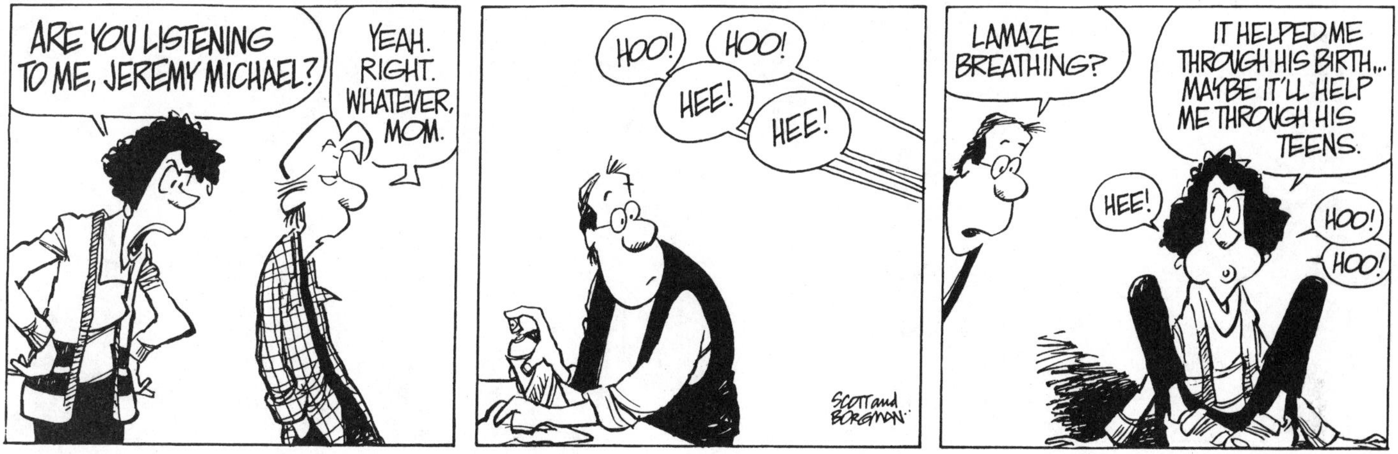
ARE YOU LISTENING TO ME, JEREMY MICHAEL?
YEAH. RIGHT. WHATEVER, MOM.
HOO!
HOO!
HEE!
HEE!
SCOTT and BORGMAN
LAMAZE BREATHING?
IT HELPED ME THROUGH HIS BIRTH... MAYBE IT'LL HELP ME THROUGH HIS TEENS.
HEE!
HOO!
HOO!

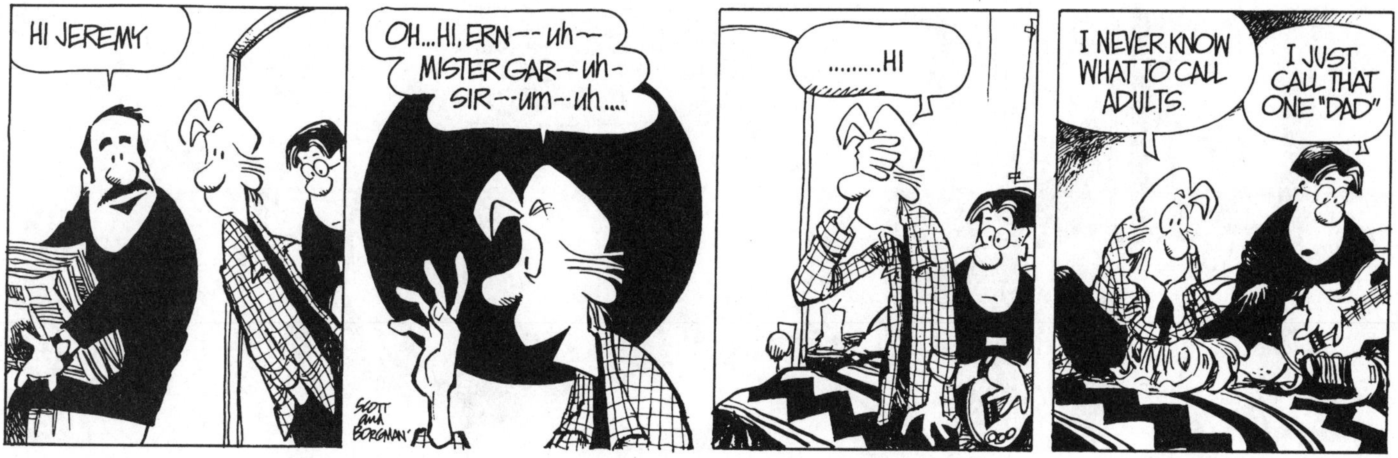
HI JEREMY
OH...HI, ERN-- uh-- MISTER GAR-- uh- SIR--um--uh....
SCOTT and BORGMAN
.........HI
I NEVER KNOW WHAT TO CALL ADULTS.
I JUST CALL THAT ONE "DAD"

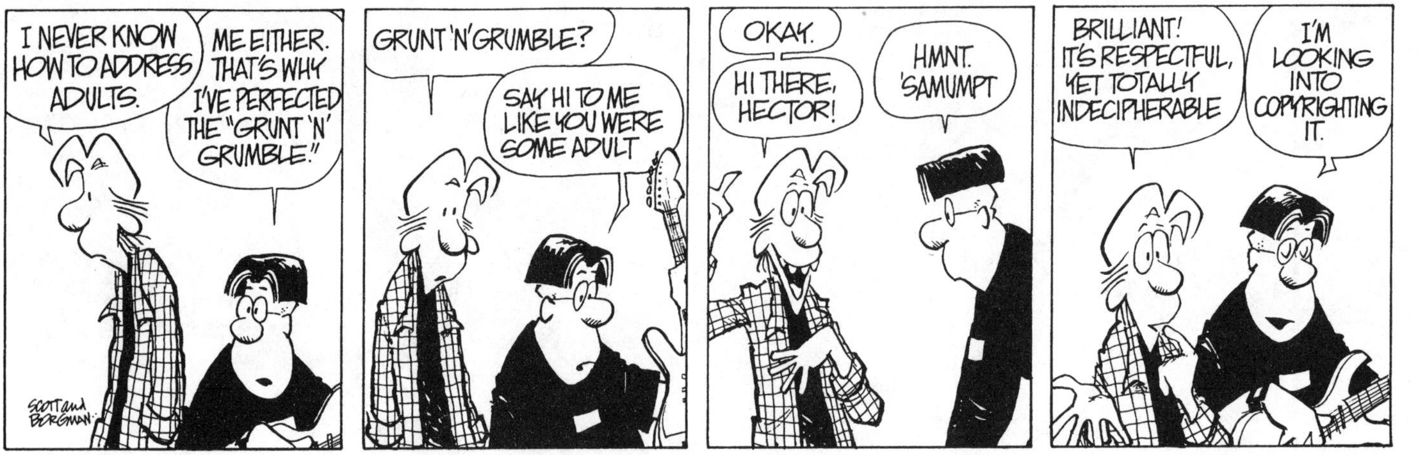
I NEVER KNOW HOW TO ADDRESS ADULTS.
ME EITHER. THAT'S WHY I'VE PERFECTED THE "GRUNT 'N' GRUMBLE."
SCOTT and BORGMAN
GRUNT 'N' GRUMBLE?
SAY HI TO ME LIKE YOU WERE SOME ADULT
OKAY.
HI THERE, HECTOR!
HMNT. 'SAMUMPT
BRILLIANT! IT'S RESPECTFUL, YET TOTALLY INDECIPHERABLE
I'M LOOKING INTO COPYRIGHTING IT.

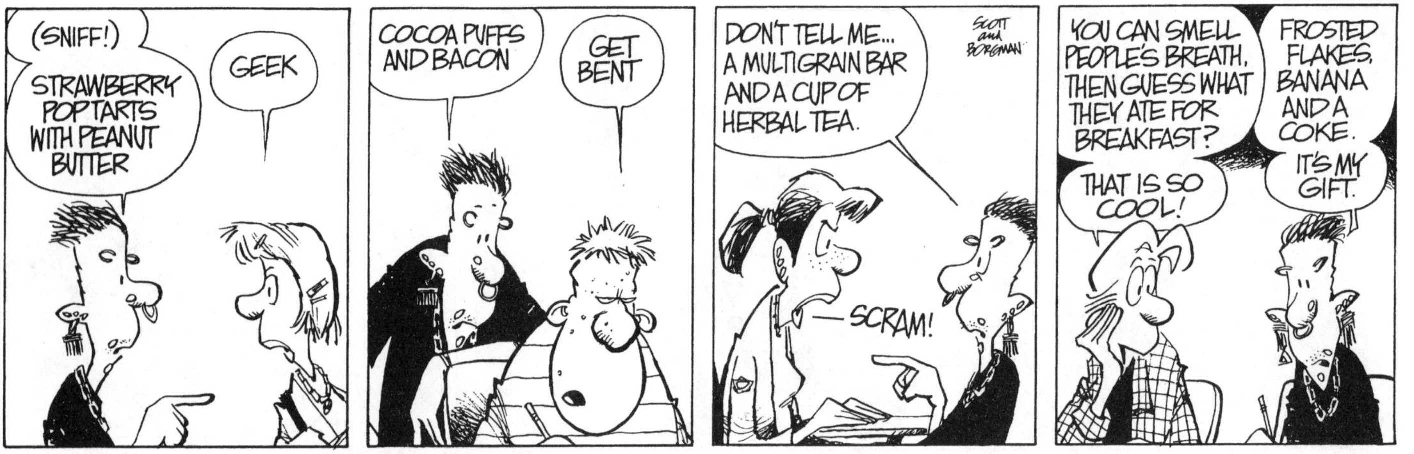
(SNIFF!)
STRAWBERRY POP TARTS WITH PEANUT BUTTER
GEEK
COCOA PUFFS AND BACON
GET BENT
DON'T TELL ME... A MULTIGRAIN BAR AND A CUP OF HERBAL TEA.
SCOTT and BORGMAN
SCRAM!
YOU CAN SMELL PEOPLE'S BREATH, THEN GUESS WHAT THEY ATE FOR BREAKFAST?
FROSTED FLAKES, BANANA AND A COKE.
THAT IS SO COOL!
IT'S MY GIFT.

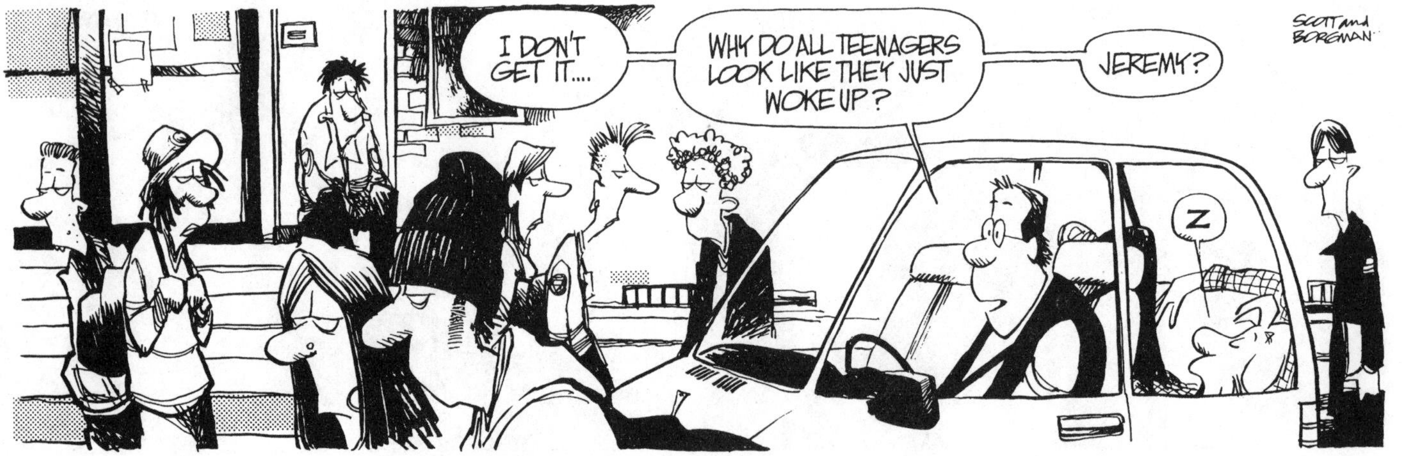
I DON'T GET IT....
WHY DO ALL TEENAGERS LOOK LIKE THEY JUST WOKE UP?
JEREMY?
Z
SCOTT and BORGMAN

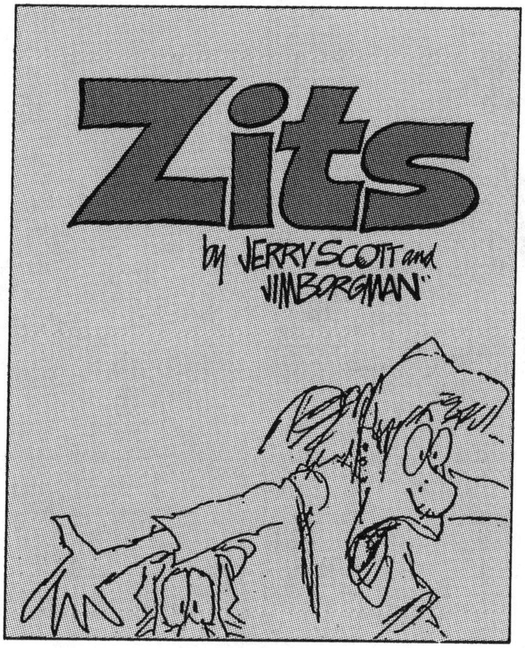
Zits
by JERRY SCOTT and JIM BORGMAN

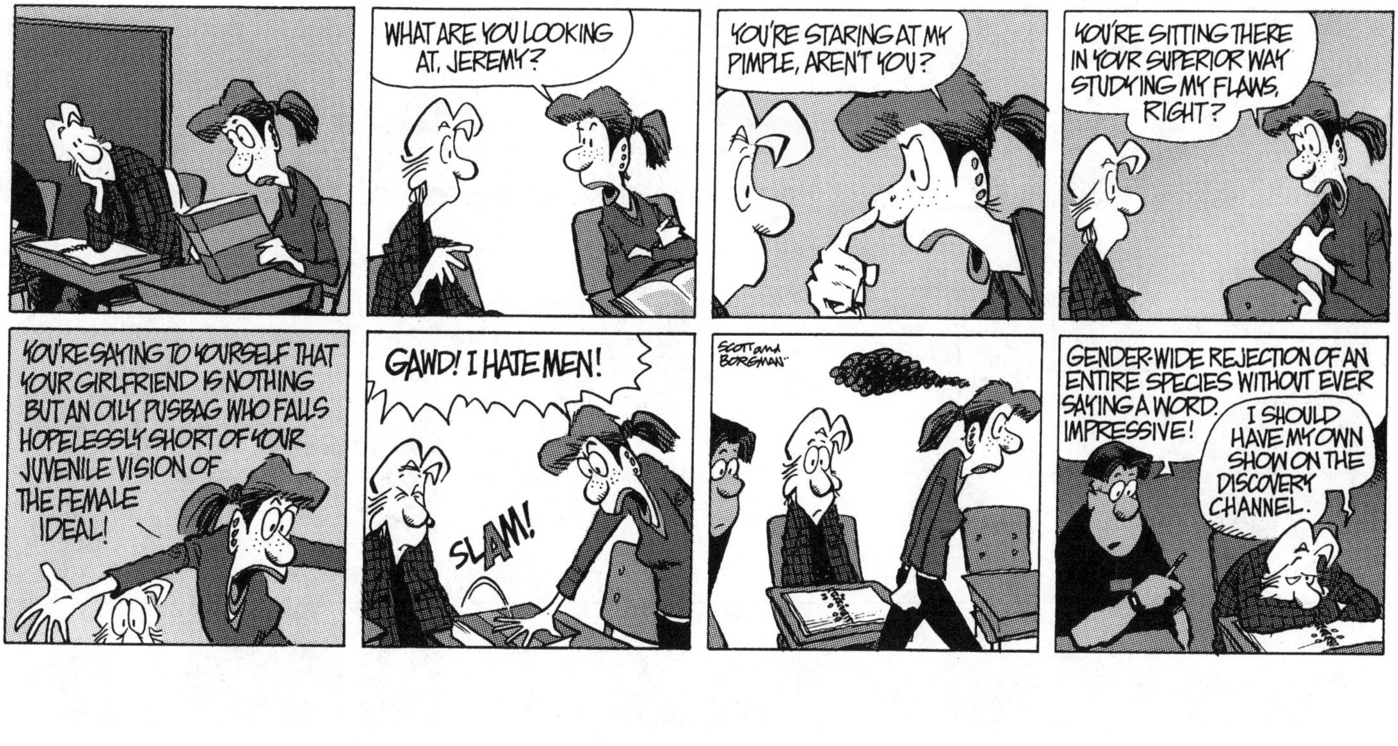
WHAT ARE YOU LOOKING AT, JEREMY?
YOU'RE STARING AT MY PIMPLE, AREN'T YOU?
YOU'RE SITTING THERE IN YOUR SUPERIOR WAY STUDYING MY FLAWS, RIGHT?
YOU'RE SAYING TO YOURSELF THAT YOUR GIRLFRIEND IS NOTHING BUT AN OILY PUSBAG WHO FALLS HOPELESSLY SHORT OF YOUR JUVENILE VISION OF THE FEMALE IDEAL!
GAWD! I HATE MEN!
SLAM!
SCOTT and BORGMAN
GENDER-WIDE REJECTION OF AN ENTIRE SPECIES WITHOUT EVER SAYING A WORD. IMPRESSIVE!
I SHOULD HAVE MY OWN SHOW ON THE DISCOVERY CHANNEL.

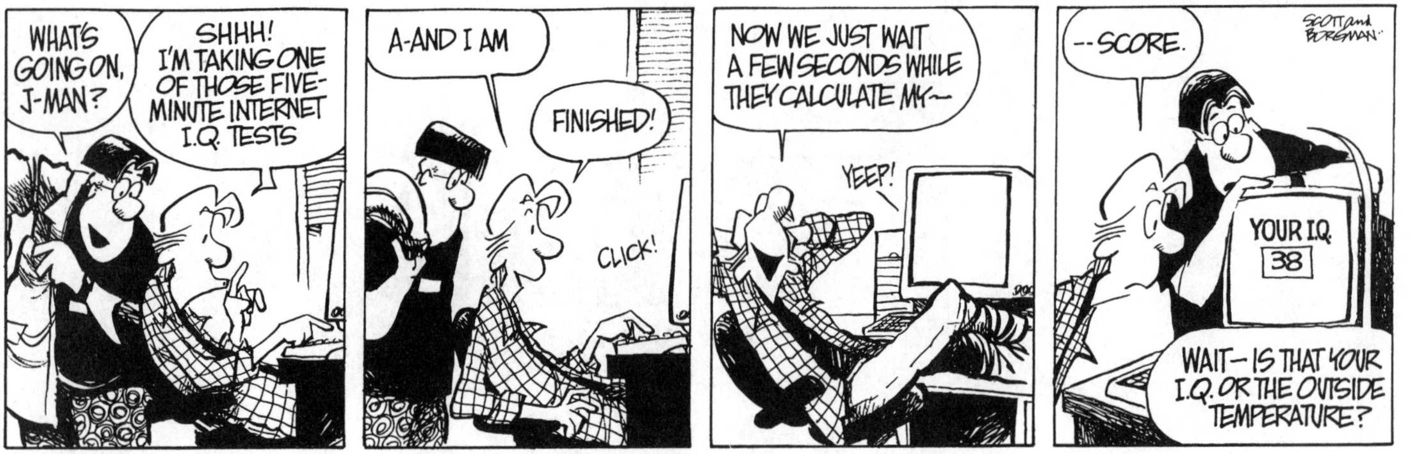
WHAT'S GOING ON, J-MAN?
SHHH! I'M TAKING ONE OF THOSE FIVE-MINUTE INTERNET I.Q. TESTS
A-AND I AM
FINISHED!
CLICK!
NOW WE JUST WAIT A FEW SECONDS WHILE THEY CALCULATE MY—
YEEP!
--SCORE.
YOUR I.Q.
38
WAIT— IS THAT YOUR I.Q. OR THE OUTSIDE TEMPERATURE?

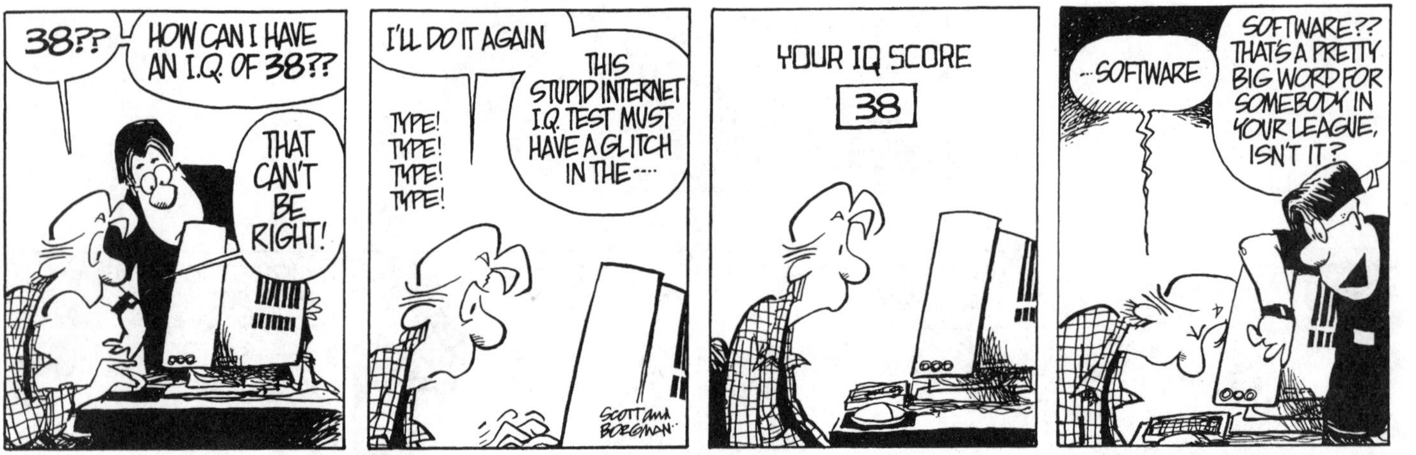
38??
HOW CAN I HAVE AN I.Q. OF 38??
THAT CAN'T BE RIGHT!
I'LL DO IT AGAIN
TYPE! TYPE! TYPE! TYPE!
THIS STUPID INTERNET I.Q. TEST MUST HAVE A GLITCH IN THE----
YOUR IQ SCORE
38
...SOFTWARE
SOFTWARE?? THAT'S A PRETTY BIG WORD FOR SOMEBODY IN YOUR LEAGUE, ISN'T IT?

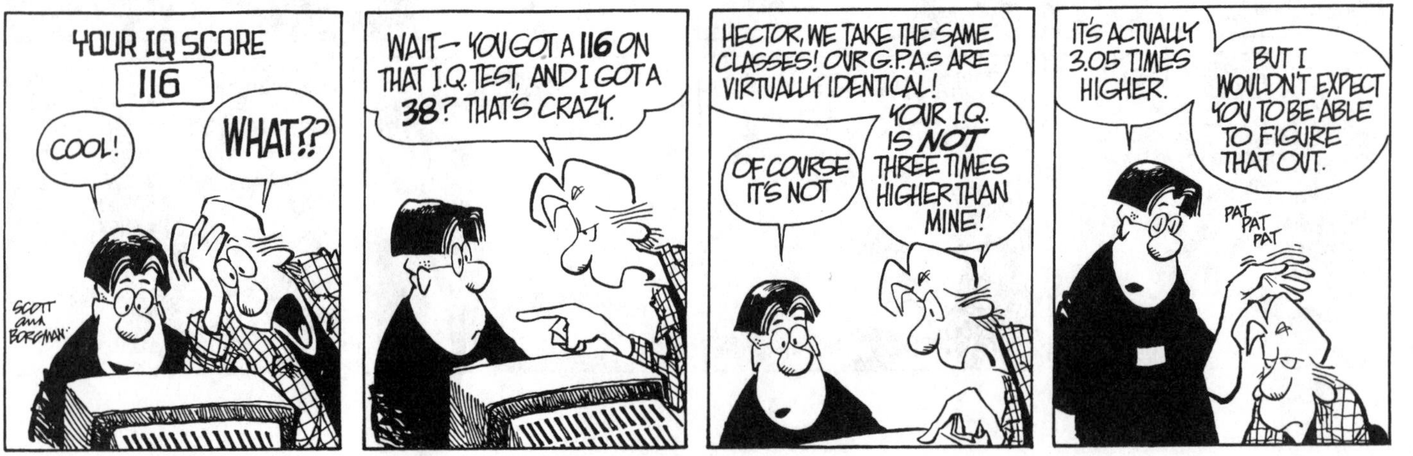
YOUR IQ SCORE
116
COOL!
WHAT??
WAIT— YOU GOT A 116 ON THAT I.Q. TEST, AND I GOT A 38? THAT'S CRAZY.
HECTOR, WE TAKE THE SAME CLASSES! OUR G.P.A.s ARE VIRTUALLY IDENTICAL!
YOUR I.Q. IS NOT THREE TIMES HIGHER THAN MINE!
OF COURSE IT'S NOT
IT'S ACTUALLY 3.05 TIMES HIGHER.
BUT I WOULDN'T EXPECT YOU TO BE ABLE TO FIGURE THAT OUT.
PAT PAT PAT

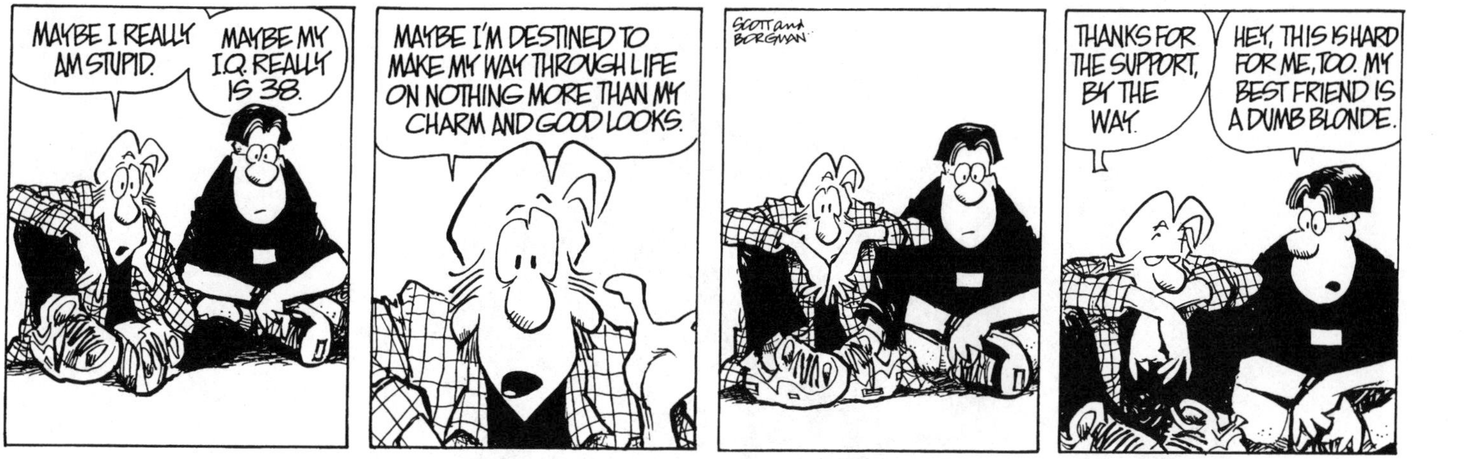
MAYBE I REALLY AM STUPID.
MAYBE MY I.Q. REALLY IS 38.
MAYBE I'M DESTINED TO MAKE MY WAY THROUGH LIFE ON NOTHING MORE THAN MY CHARM AND GOOD LOOKS.
SCOTT and BORGMAN
THANKS FOR THE SUPPORT, BY THE WAY.
HEY, THIS IS HARD FOR ME, TOO. MY BEST FRIEND IS A DUMB BLONDE.

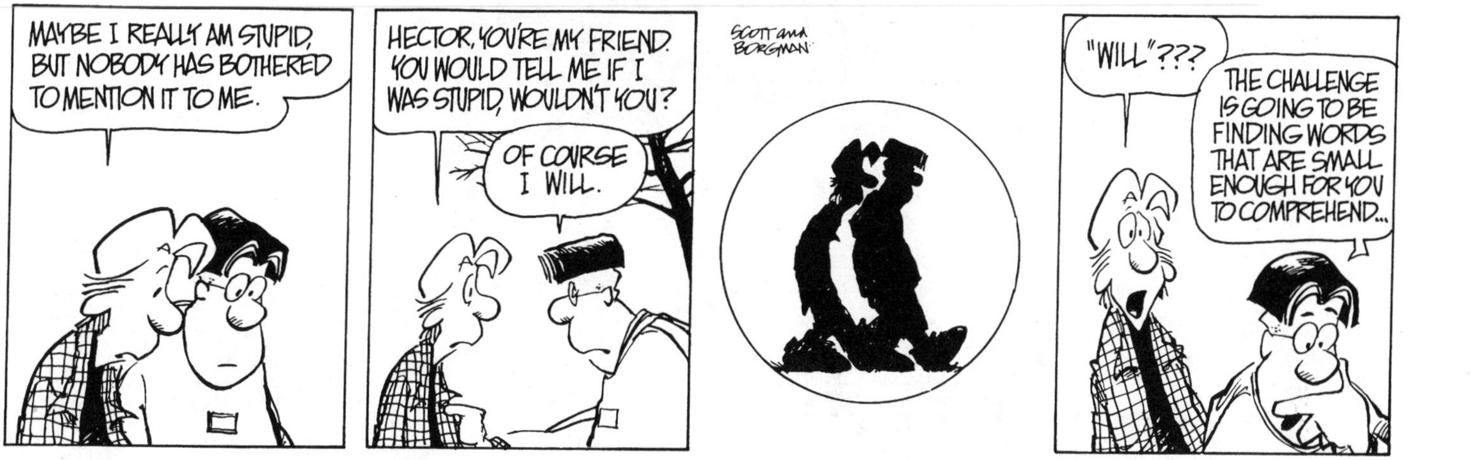
MAYBE I REALLY AM STUPID, BUT NOBODY HAS BOTHERED TO MENTION IT TO ME.
HECTOR, YOU'RE MY FRIEND. YOU WOULD TELL ME IF I WAS STUPID, WOULDN'T YOU?
OF COURSE I WILL.
SCOTT and BORGMAN
"WILL"???
THE CHALLENGE IS GOING TO BE FINDING WORDS THAT ARE SMALL ENOUGH FOR YOU TO COMPREHEND...

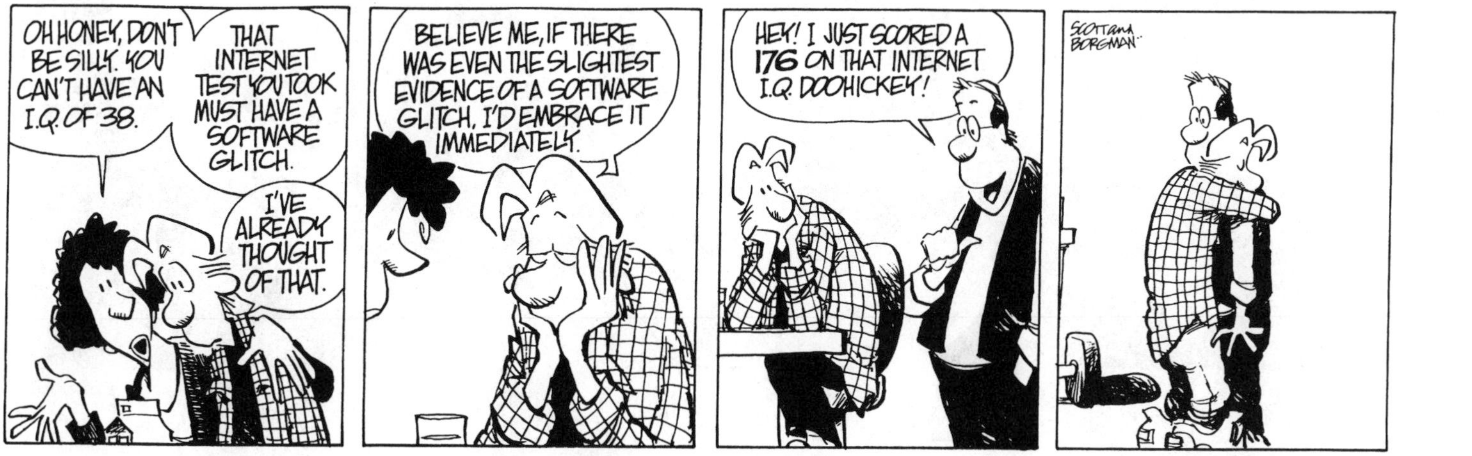
OH HONEY, DON'T BE SILLY. YOU CAN'T HAVE AN I.Q. OF 38.
THAT INTERNET TEST YOU TOOK MUST HAVE A SOFTWARE GLITCH.
I'VE ALREADY THOUGHT OF THAT.
BELIEVE ME, IF THERE WAS EVEN THE SLIGHTEST EVIDENCE OF A SOFTWARE GLITCH, I'D EMBRACE IT IMMEDIATELY.
HEY! I JUST SCORED A 176 ON THAT INTERNET I.Q. DOOHICKEY!
SCOTT and BORGMAN

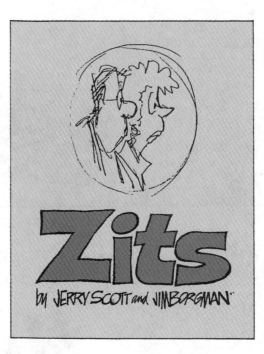

# Zits
## by Jerry Scott and Jim Borgman

YOU DIDN'T ASK ME HOW SCHOOL WAS TODAY.

OKA·A·AY... HOW WAS SCHOOL TODAY, JEREMY?

AMAZING.

I WAS REALLY WORRIED ABOUT HOW MY SEMESTER PROJECT IN BIOLOGY WAS GOING, BUT I LAID IT ALL OUT FOR MR. GONZALES, AND IT TURNS OUT THAT I'M RIGHT ON TRACK. HE EVEN SAID SOME OF MY IDEAS ARE EXCITING AND ORIGINAL!

I DON'T KNOW IF I MENTIONED IT, BUT SARA HAS BEEN ACTING A LITTLE DISTANT LATELY. BUT IT TURNS OUT THAT SHE'S JUST BEEN STRESSED ABOUT SCHOOL. SHE EVEN KISSED ME ON THE WAY TO OUR 4TH BELL CLASS, WHICH WAS REASSURING.

IT'S AMAZING HOW MUCH PRESSURE WE PUT ON OURSELVES WHEN WE ASSIGN THE SAME DEGREE OF IMPORTANCE TO EVERYTHING, Y'KNOW? WELL, I'D BETTER HIT THE BOOKS.

SEE YA.

I JUST HAD THE WEIRDEST DREAM

NO! NO! IT WAS REAL! I THINK HE ACTUALLY VOLUNTEERED INFORMATION!

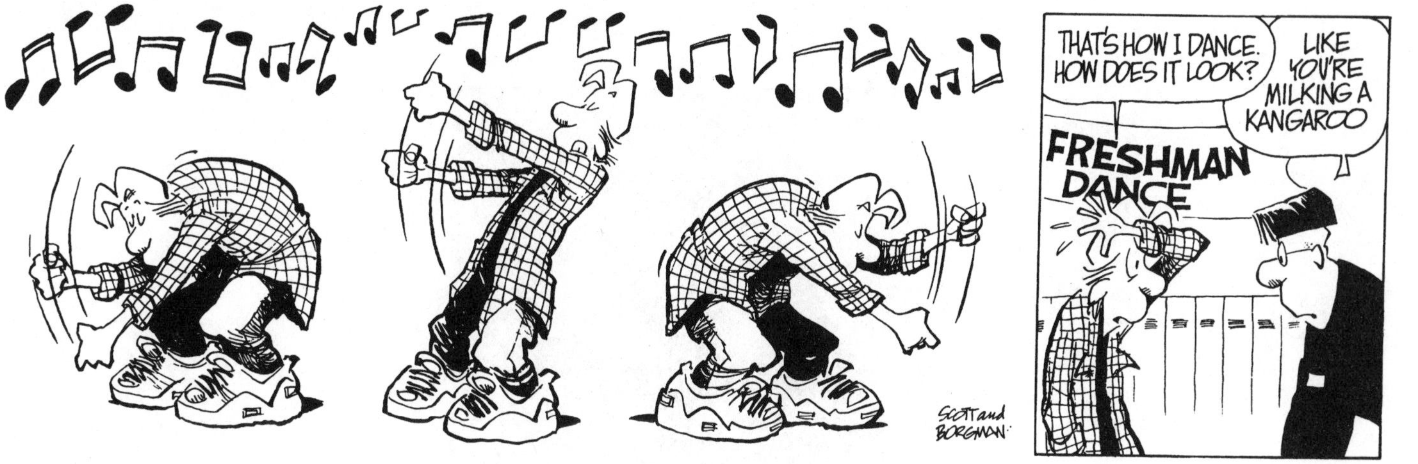
SCOTT and BORGMAN
THAT'S HOW I DANCE. HOW DOES IT LOOK?
LIKE YOU'RE MILKING A KANGAROO
FRESHMAN DANCE

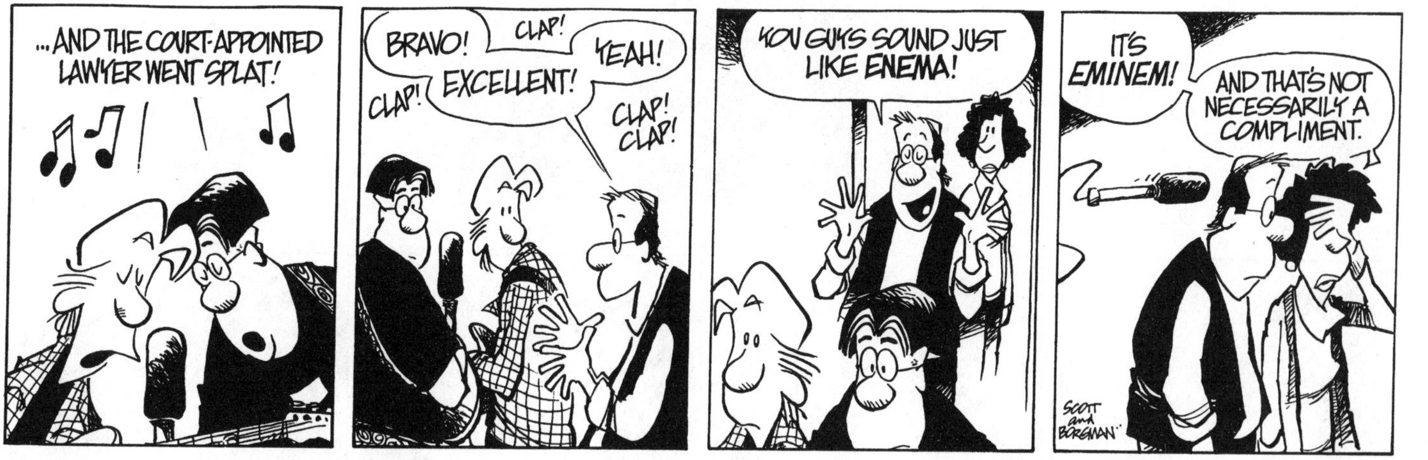
...AND THE COURT-APPOINTED LAWYER WENT SPLAT!
BRAVO!
CLAP!
YEAH!
CLAP!
EXCELLENT!
CLAP! CLAP!
YOU GUYS SOUND JUST LIKE ENEMA!
IT'S EMINEM!
AND THAT'S NOT NECESSARILY A COMPLIMENT.
SCOTT and BORGMAN

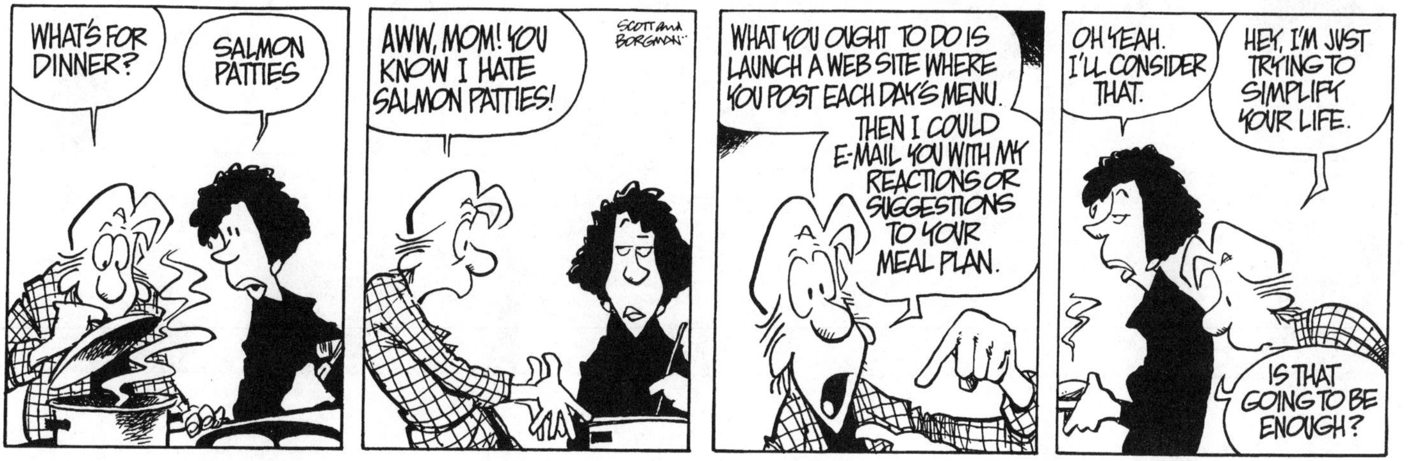
WHAT'S FOR DINNER?
SALMON PATTIES
AWW, MOM! YOU KNOW I HATE SALMON PATTIES!
SCOTT and BORGMAN
WHAT YOU OUGHT TO DO IS LAUNCH A WEB SITE WHERE YOU POST EACH DAY'S MENU.
THEN I COULD E-MAIL YOU WITH MY REACTIONS OR SUGGESTIONS TO YOUR MEAL PLAN.
OH YEAH. I'LL CONSIDER THAT.
HEY, I'M JUST TRYING TO SIMPLIFY YOUR LIFE.
IS THAT GOING TO BE ENOUGH?

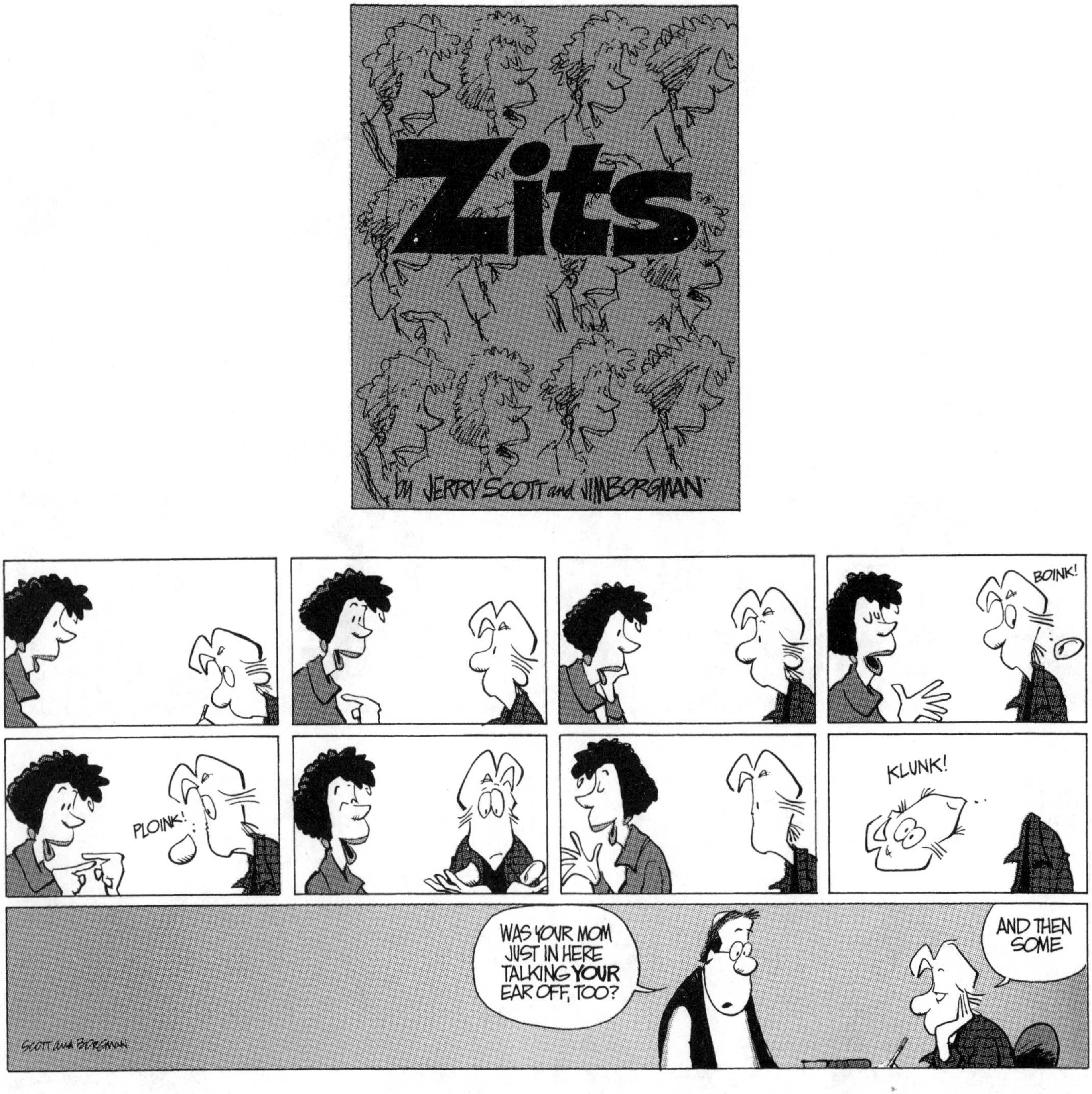
Zits
by JERRY SCOTT and JIM BORGMAN
BOINK!
PLOINK!
KLUNK!
WAS YOUR MOM JUST IN HERE TALKING **YOUR** EAR OFF, TOO?
AND THEN SOME
SCOTT AND BORGMAN

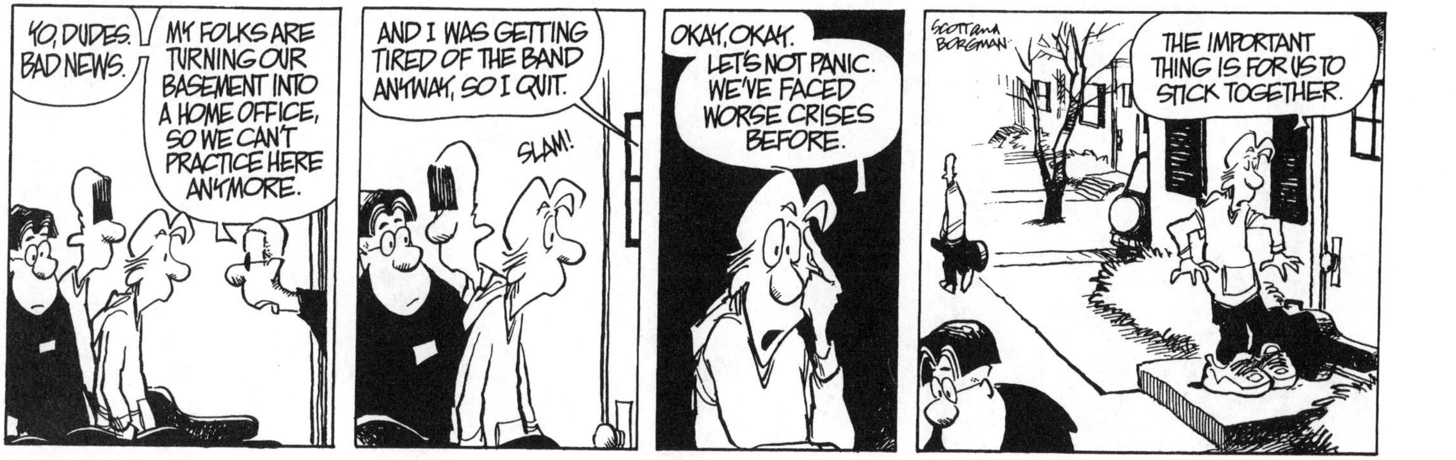
YO, DUDES. BAD NEWS.
MY FOLKS ARE TURNING OUR BASEMENT INTO A HOME OFFICE, SO WE CAN'T PRACTICE HERE ANYMORE.
AND I WAS GETTING TIRED OF THE BAND ANYWAY, SO I QUIT.
SLAM!
OKAY, OKAY.
LET'S NOT PANIC. WE'VE FACED WORSE CRISES BEFORE.
SCOTT AND BORGMAN
THE IMPORTANT THING IS FOR US TO STICK TOGETHER.

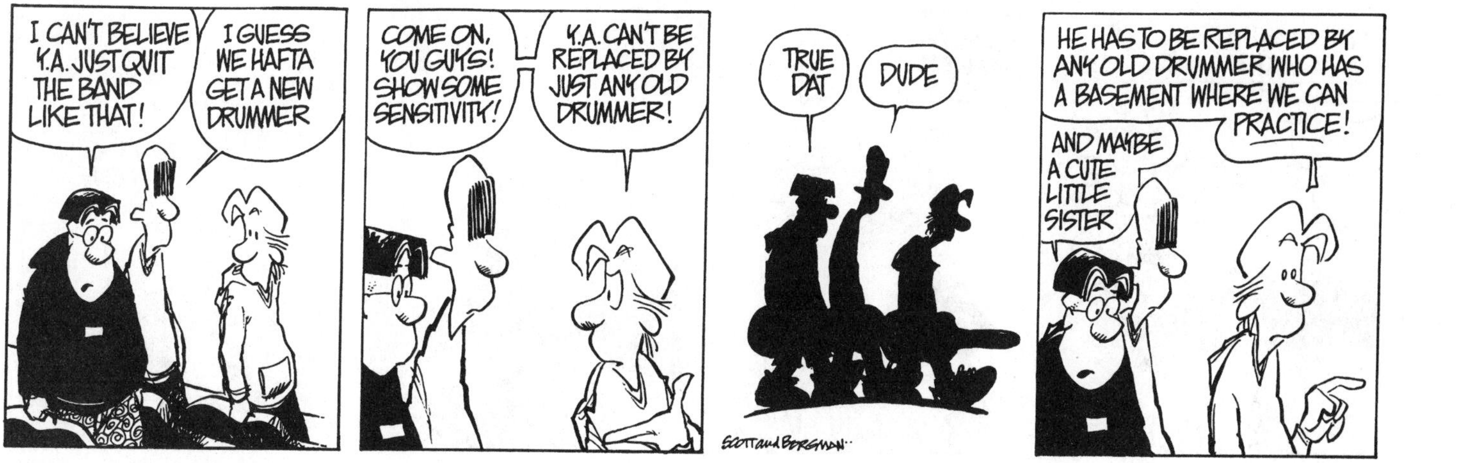
I CAN'T BELIEVE Y.A. JUST QUIT THE BAND LIKE THAT!
I GUESS WE HAFTA GET A NEW DRUMMER
COME ON, YOU GUYS! SHOW SOME SENSITIVITY!
Y.A. CAN'T BE REPLACED BY JUST ANY OLD DRUMMER!
TRUE DAT
DUDE
SCOTT AND BORGMAN
HE HAS TO BE REPLACED BY ANY OLD DRUMMER WHO HAS A BASEMENT WHERE WE CAN PRACTICE!
AND MAYBE A CUTE LITTLE SISTER

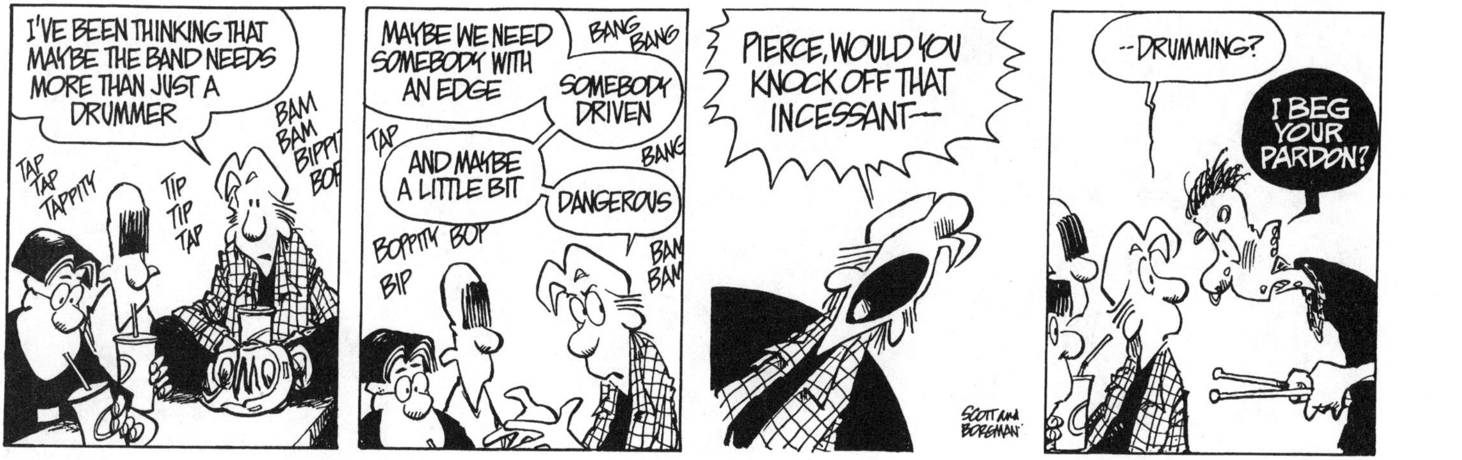
I'VE BEEN THINKING THAT MAYBE THE BAND NEEDS MORE THAN JUST A DRUMMER
TAP TAP TAPPITY
TIP TIP TAP
BAM BAM BIPPITY BOP
MAYBE WE NEED SOMEBODY WITH AN EDGE
BANG BANG
SOMEBODY DRIVEN
TAP
BANG
AND MAYBE A LITTLE BIT
DANGEROUS
BOPPITY BOP
BIP
BAM BAM
PIERCE, WOULD YOU KNOCK OFF THAT INCESSANT--
SCOTT AND BORGMAN
--DRUMMING?
I BEG YOUR PARDON?

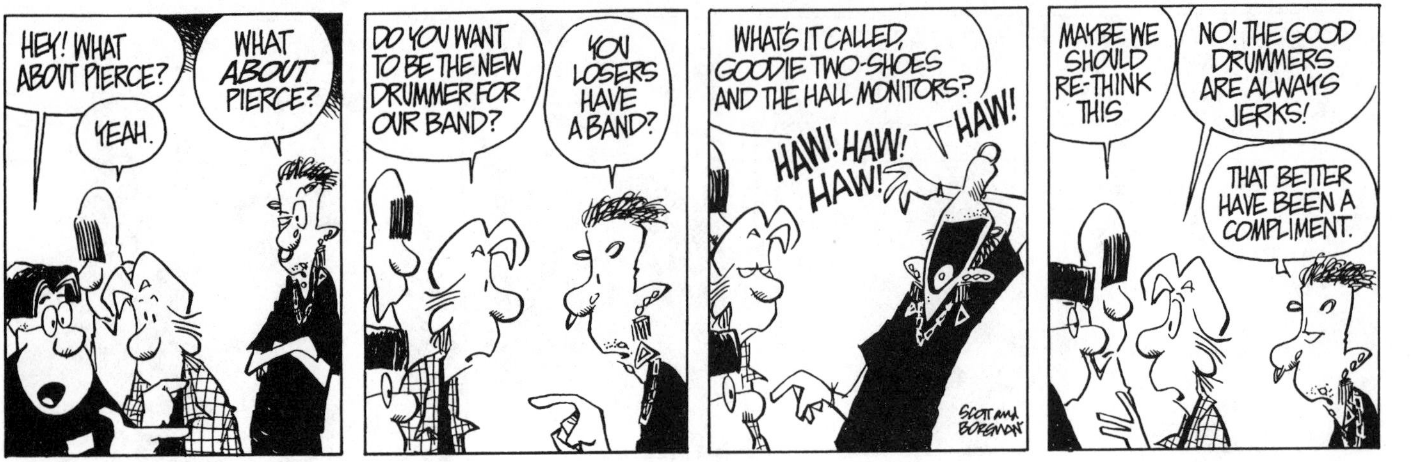
HEY! WHAT ABOUT PIERCE?
YEAH.
WHAT ABOUT PIERCE?
DO YOU WANT TO BE THE NEW DRUMMER FOR OUR BAND?
YOU LOSERS HAVE A BAND?
WHAT'S IT CALLED, GOODIE TWO-SHOES AND THE HALL MONITORS?
HAW! HAW! HAW! HAW! HAW!
SCOTT AND BORGMAN
MAYBE WE SHOULD RE-THINK THIS
NO! THE GOOD DRUMMERS ARE ALWAYS JERKS!
THAT BETTER HAVE BEEN A COMPLIMENT.

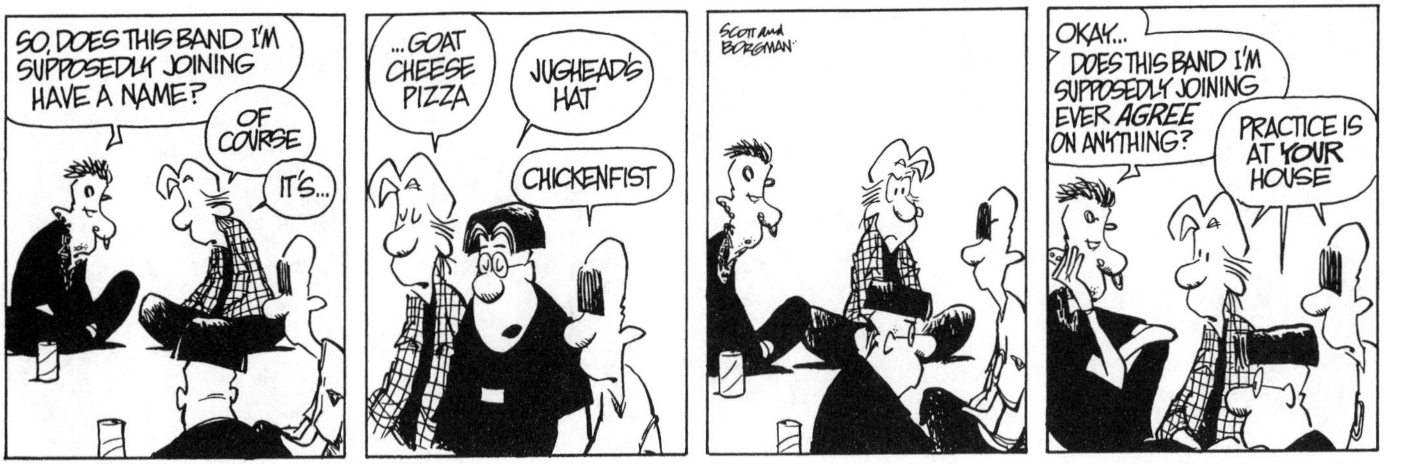
SO, DOES THIS BAND I'M SUPPOSEDLY JOINING HAVE A NAME?
OF COURSE
IT'S...
...GOAT CHEESE PIZZA
JUGHEAD'S HAT
CHICKENFIST
SCOTT AND BORGMAN
OKAY... DOES THIS BAND I'M SUPPOSEDLY JOINING EVER AGREE ON ANYTHING?
PRACTICE IS AT YOUR HOUSE

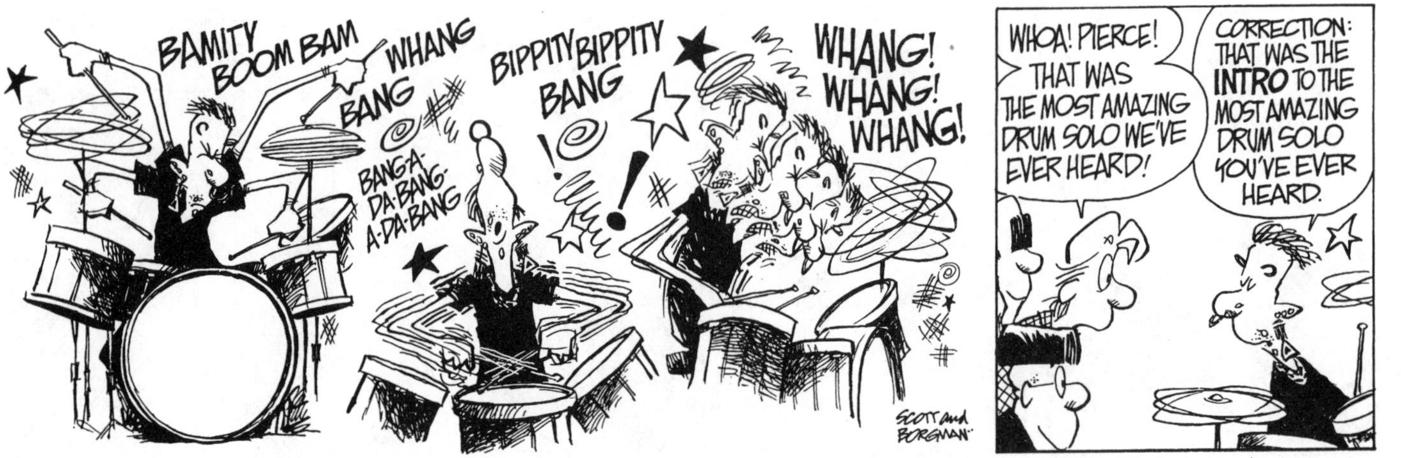
BAMITY BOOM BAM
WHANG BANG
BIPPITY BIPPITY BANG
WHANG! WHANG! WHANG!
BANG-A-DA-BANG-A-DA-BANG
SCOTT AND BORGMAN
WHOA! PIERCE! THAT WAS THE MOST AMAZING DRUM SOLO WE'VE EVER HEARD!
CORRECTION: THAT WAS THE INTRO TO THE MOST AMAZING DRUM SOLO YOU'VE EVER HEARD.

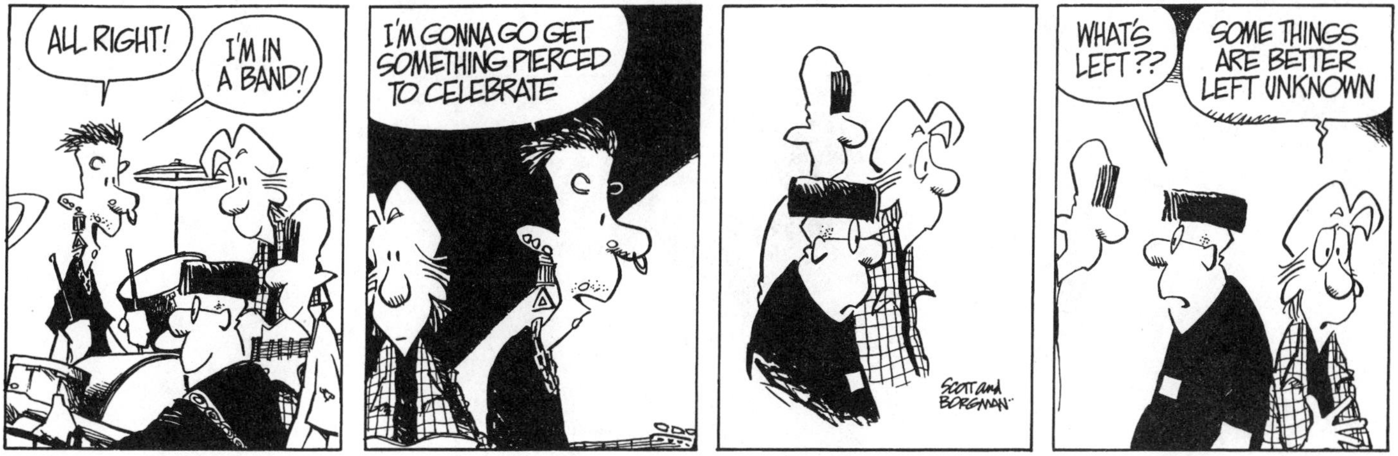
ALL RIGHT!
I'M IN A BAND!
I'M GONNA GO GET SOMETHING PIERCED TO CELEBRATE
WHAT'S LEFT??
SOME THINGS ARE BETTER LEFT UNKNOWN
SCOTT and BORGMAN

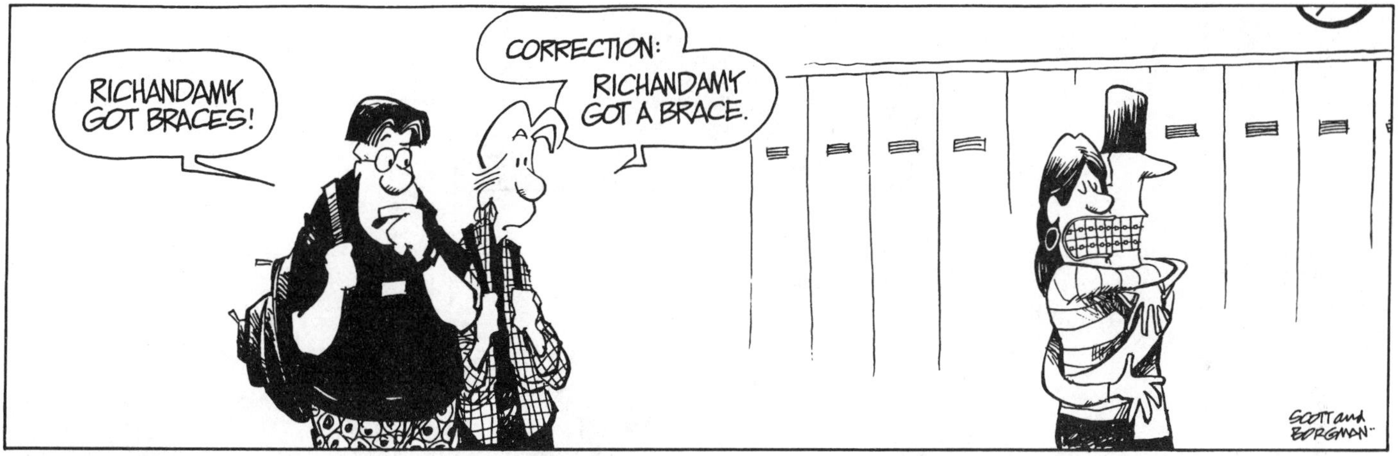
RICHANDAMY GOT BRACES!
CORRECTION:
RICHANDAMY GOT A BRACE.
SCOTT and BORGMAN

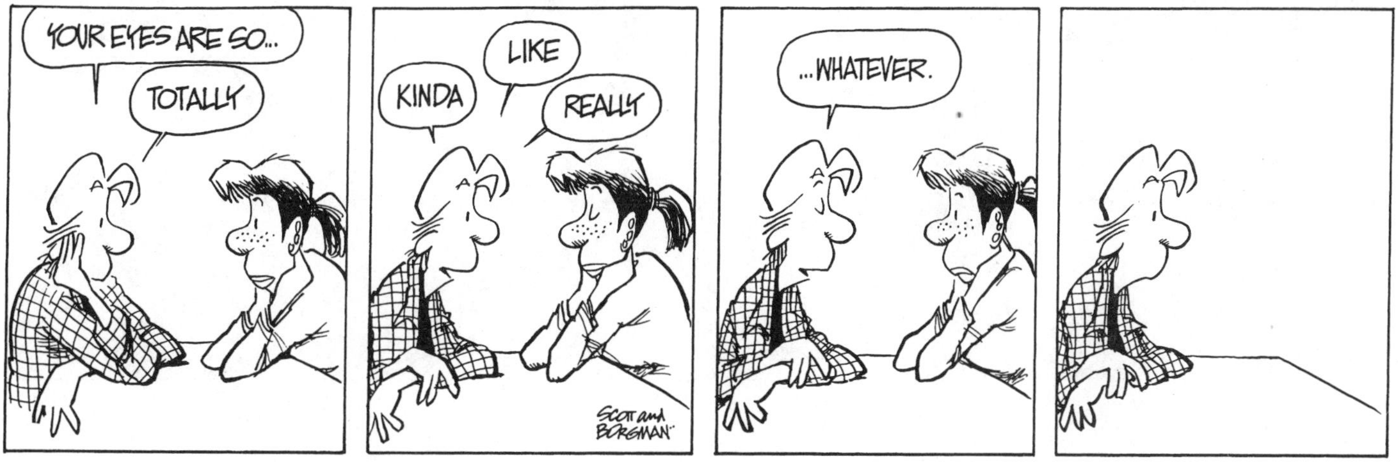
YOUR EYES ARE SO...
TOTALLY
KINDA
LIKE
REALLY
SCOTT and BORGMAN
...WHATEVER.

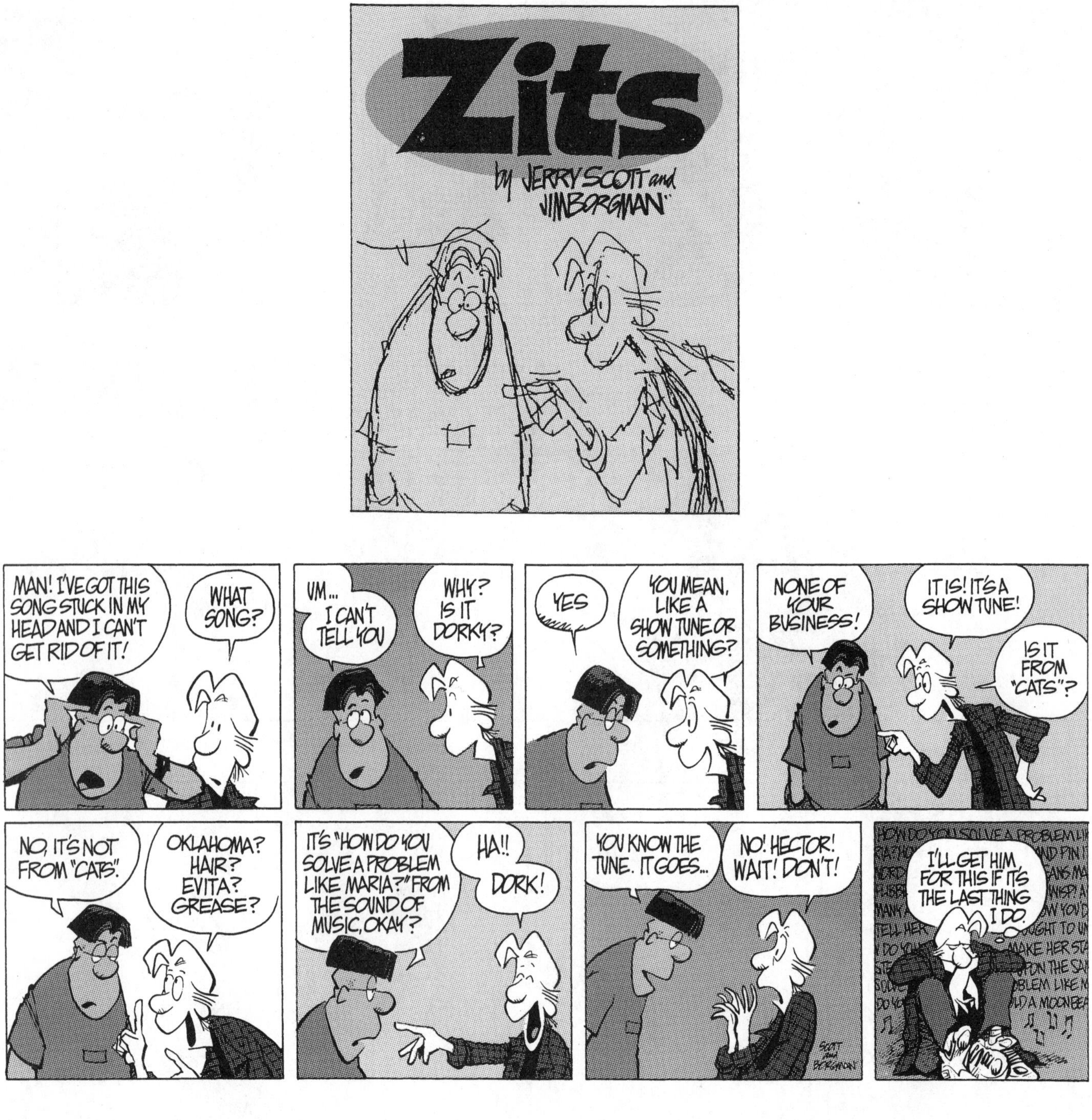

Zits
by JERRY SCOTT and JIM BORGMAN
MAN! I'VE GOT THIS SONG STUCK IN MY HEAD AND I CAN'T GET RID OF IT!
WHAT SONG?
UM... I CAN'T TELL YOU
WHY? IS IT DORKY?
YES
YOU MEAN, LIKE A SHOW TUNE OR SOMETHING?
NONE OF YOUR BUSINESS!
IT IS! IT'S A SHOW TUNE!
IS IT FROM "CATS"?
NO, IT'S NOT FROM "CATS".
OKLAHOMA? HAIR? EVITA? GREASE?
IT'S "HOW DO YOU SOLVE A PROBLEM LIKE MARIA?" FROM THE SOUND OF MUSIC, OKAY?
HA!!
DORK!
YOU KNOW THE TUNE. IT GOES...
NO! HECTOR! WAIT! DON'T!
I'LL GET HIM, FOR THIS IF IT'S THE LAST THING I DO.

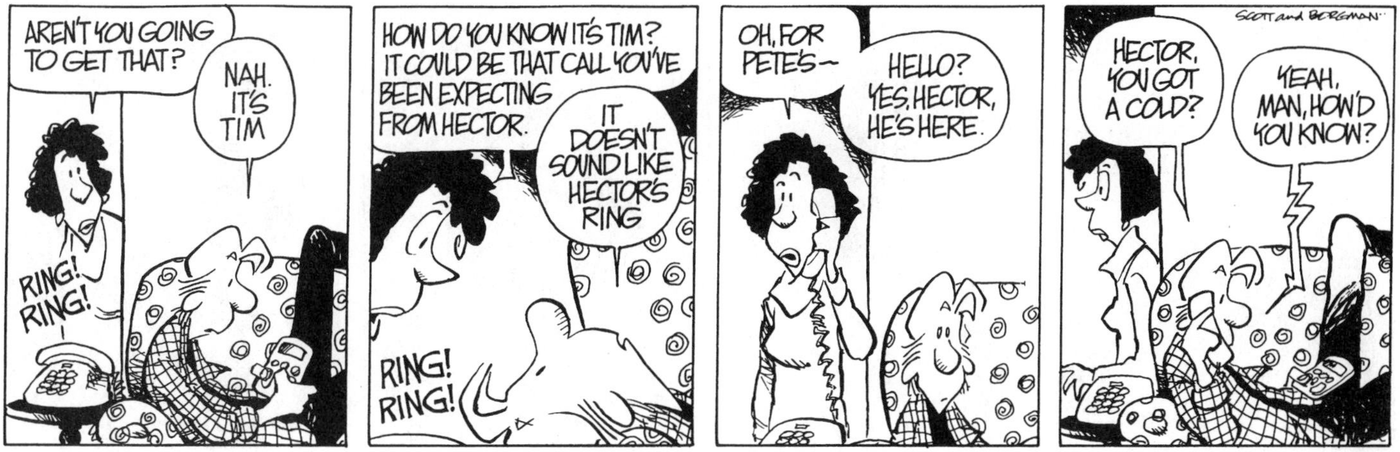
AREN'T YOU GOING TO GET THAT?
NAH. IT'S TIM
RING! RING!
HOW DO YOU KNOW IT'S TIM? IT COULD BE THAT CALL YOU'VE BEEN EXPECTING FROM HECTOR.
IT DOESN'T SOUND LIKE HECTOR'S RING
RING! RING!
OH, FOR PETE'S~
HELLO? YES, HECTOR, HE'S HERE.
SCOTT and BORGMAN
HECTOR, YOU GOT A COLD?
YEAH, MAN, HOW'D YOU KNOW?

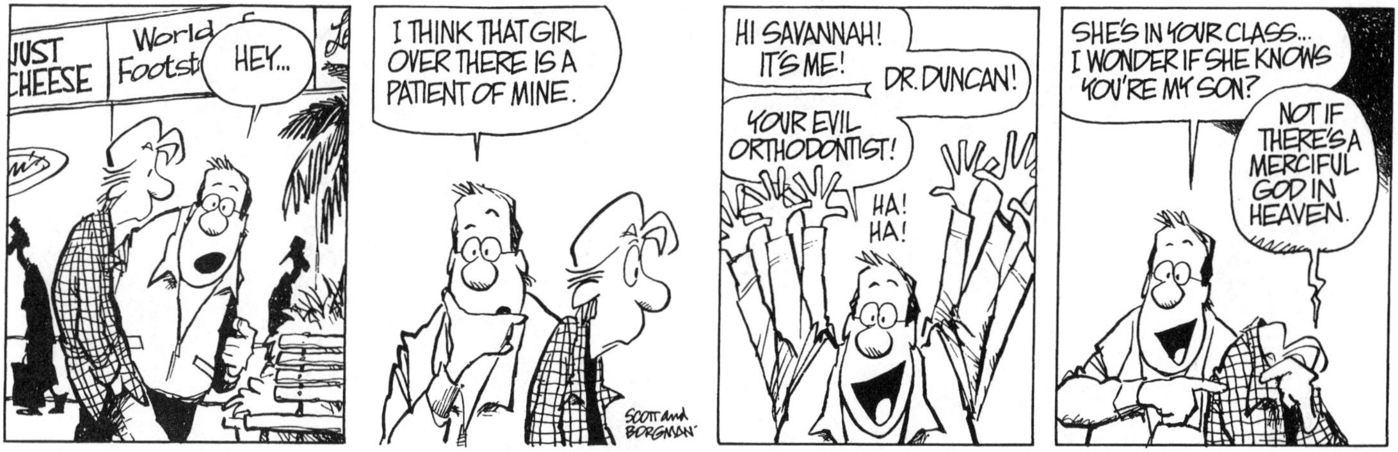
JUST CHEESE
World Footst
HEY...
I THINK THAT GIRL OVER THERE IS A PATIENT OF MINE.
SCOTT AND BORGMAN
HI SAVANNAH! IT'S ME!
DR. DUNCAN!
YOUR EVIL ORTHODONTIST!
HA! HA!
SHE'S IN YOUR CLASS... I WONDER IF SHE KNOWS YOU'RE MY SON?
NOT IF THERE'S A MERCIFUL GOD IN HEAVEN.

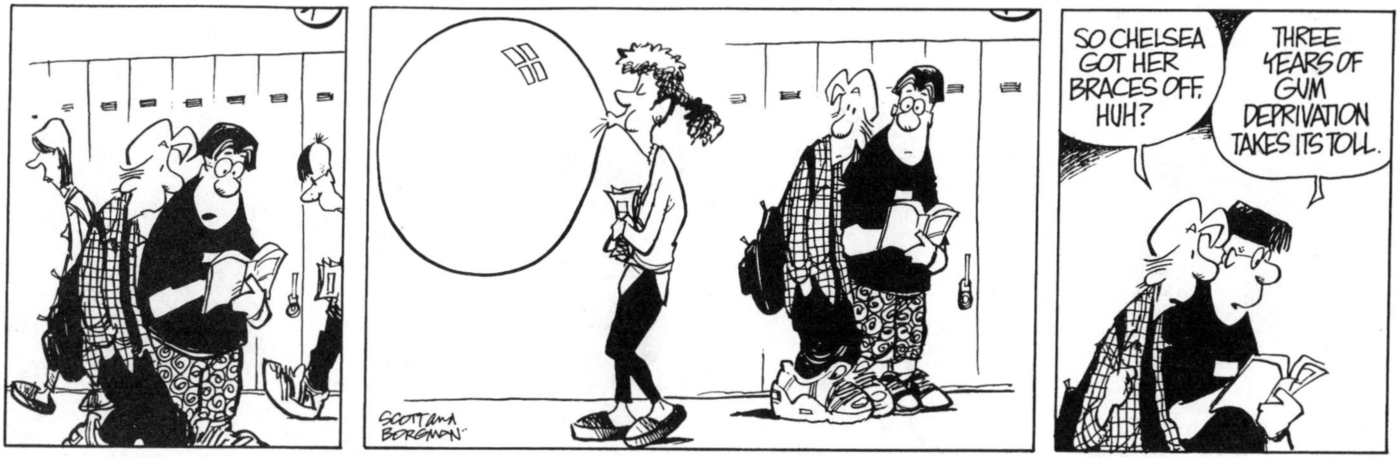
SCOTT AND BORGMAN
SO CHELSEA GOT HER BRACES OFF, HUH?
THREE YEARS OF GUM DEPRIVATION TAKES ITS TOLL.

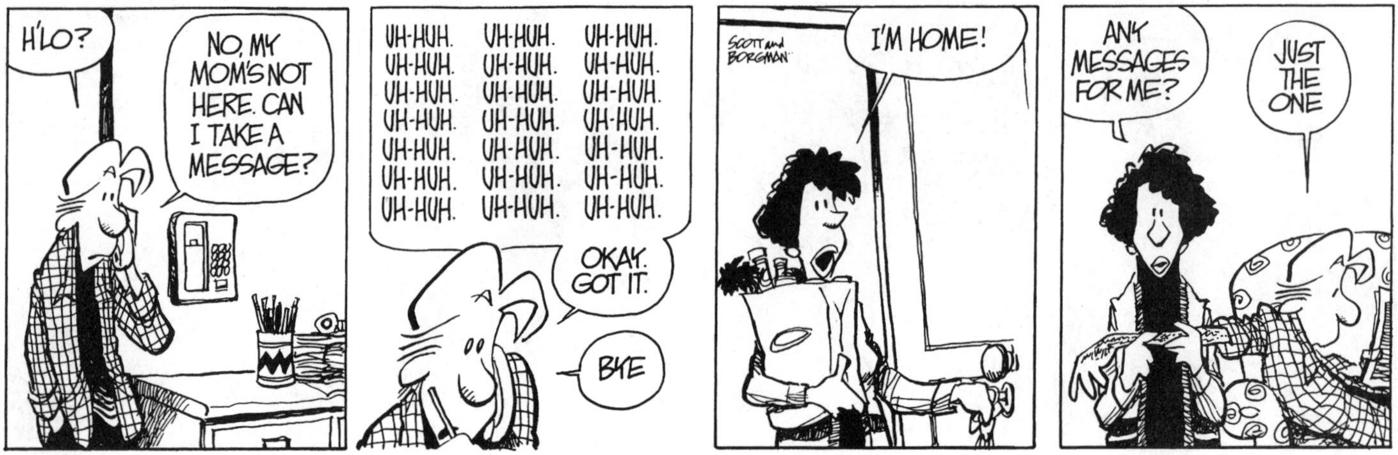
H'LO?
NO, MY MOM'S NOT HERE. CAN I TAKE A MESSAGE?
UH-HUH. UH-HUH. UH-HUH. UH-HUH. UH-HUH. UH-HUH. UH-HUH. UH-HUH. UH-HUH. UH-HUH. UH-HUH. UH-HUH. UH-HUH. UH-HUH. UH-HUH. UH-HUH. UH-HUH. UH-HUH. UH-HUH. UH-HUH. UH-HUH.
OKAY. GOT IT.
BYE
SCOTT and BORGMAN
I'M HOME!
ANY MESSAGES FOR ME?
JUST THE ONE

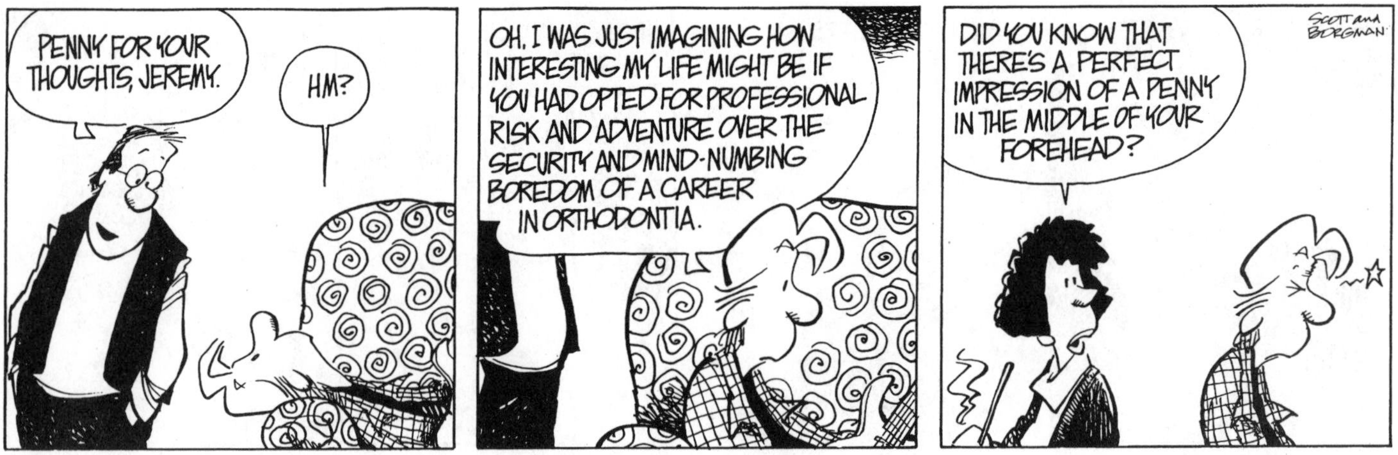
PENNY FOR YOUR THOUGHTS, JEREMY.
HM?
OH, I WAS JUST IMAGINING HOW INTERESTING MY LIFE MIGHT BE IF YOU HAD OPTED FOR PROFESSIONAL RISK AND ADVENTURE OVER THE SECURITY AND MIND-NUMBING BOREDOM OF A CAREER IN ORTHODONTIA.
SCOTT and BORGMAN
DID YOU KNOW THAT THERE'S A PERFECT IMPRESSION OF A PENNY IN THE MIDDLE OF YOUR FOREHEAD?

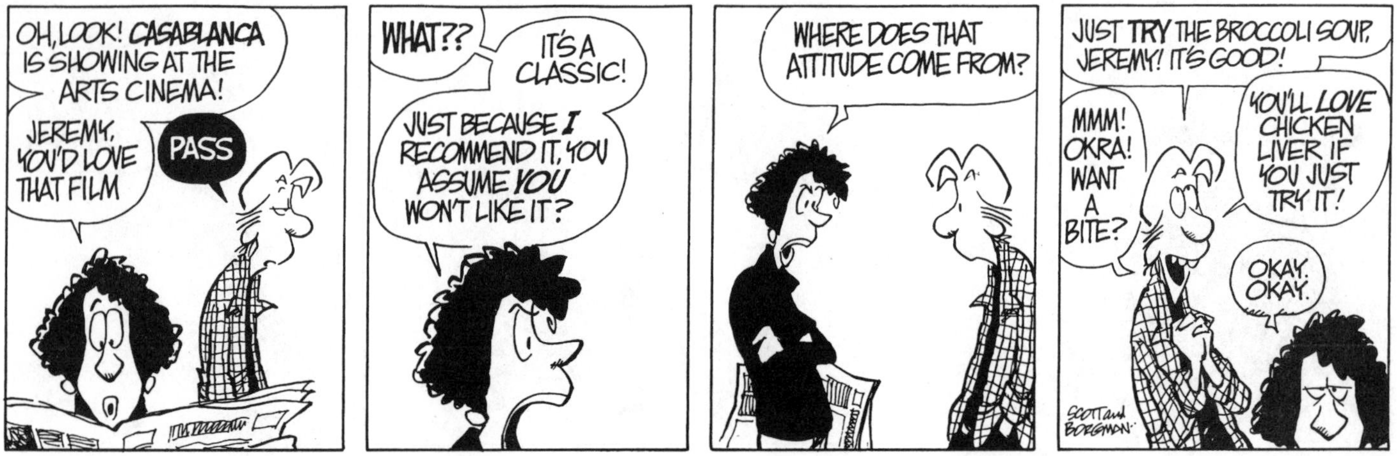
OH, LOOK! CASABLANCA IS SHOWING AT THE ARTS CINEMA!
JEREMY, YOU'D LOVE THAT FILM
PASS
WHAT??
IT'S A CLASSIC!
JUST BECAUSE I RECOMMEND IT, YOU ASSUME YOU WON'T LIKE IT?
WHERE DOES THAT ATTITUDE COME FROM?
JUST TRY THE BROCCOLI SOUP, JEREMY! IT'S GOOD!
MMM! OKRA! WANT A BITE?
YOU'LL LOVE CHICKEN LIVER IF YOU JUST TRY IT!
OKAY. OKAY.
SCOTT and BORGMAN

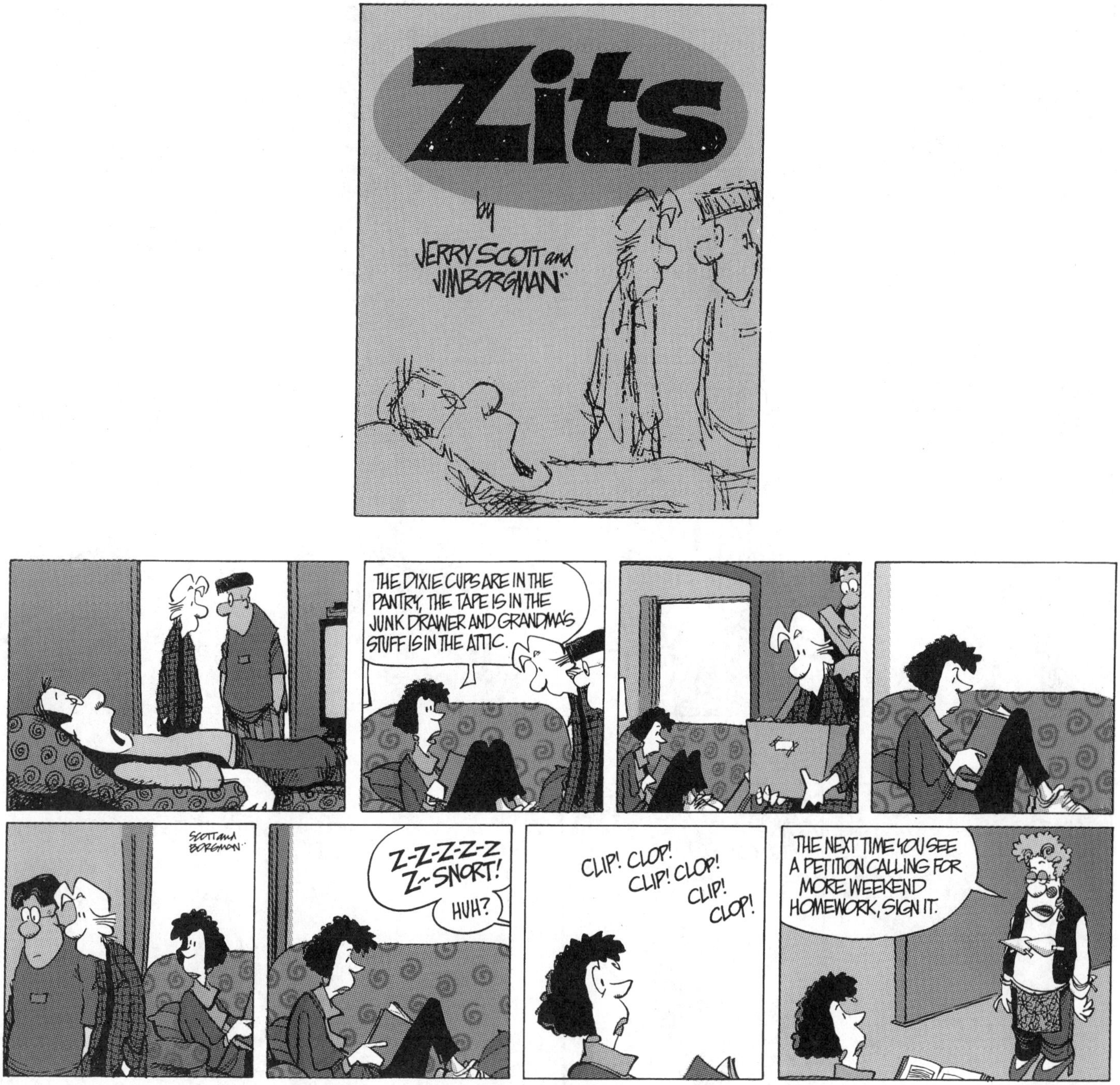
Zits
by
JERRY SCOTT and
JIM BORGMAN
THE DIXIE CUPS ARE IN THE PANTRY, THE TAPE IS IN THE JUNK DRAWER AND GRANDMA'S STUFF IS IN THE ATTIC.
SCOTT and BORGMAN
Z-Z-Z-Z-Z Z~SNORT!
HUH?
CLIP! CLOP! CLIP! CLOP! CLIP! CLOP!
THE NEXT TIME YOU SEE A PETITION CALLING FOR MORE WEEKEND HOMEWORK, SIGN IT.

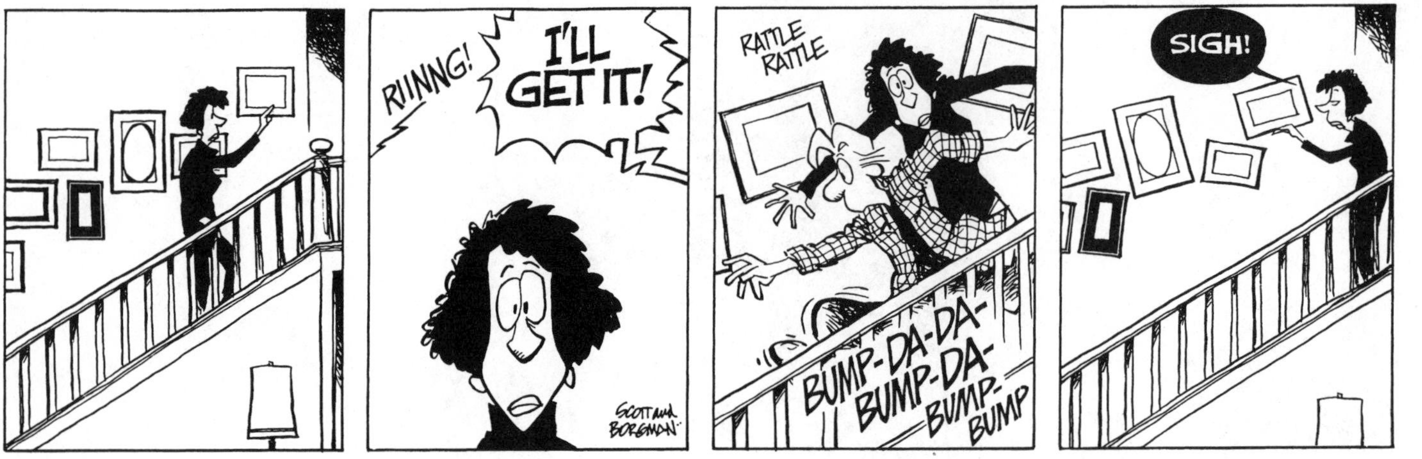
RIIING!
I'LL GET IT!
RATTLE RATTLE
BUMP-DA-DA-BUMP-DA-BUMP-BUMP
SIGH!

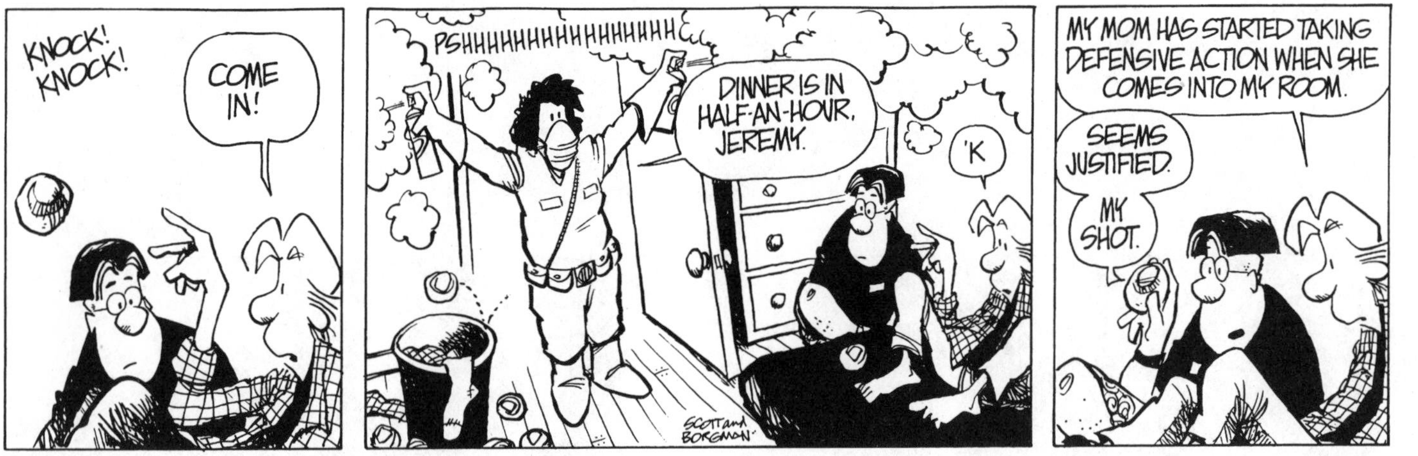
KNOCK! KNOCK!
COME IN!
PSHHHHHHHHHHHHHHHHH
DINNER IS IN HALF-AN-HOUR, JEREMY.
'K
MY MOM HAS STARTED TAKING DEFENSIVE ACTION WHEN SHE COMES INTO MY ROOM.
SEEMS JUSTIFIED.
MY SHOT.

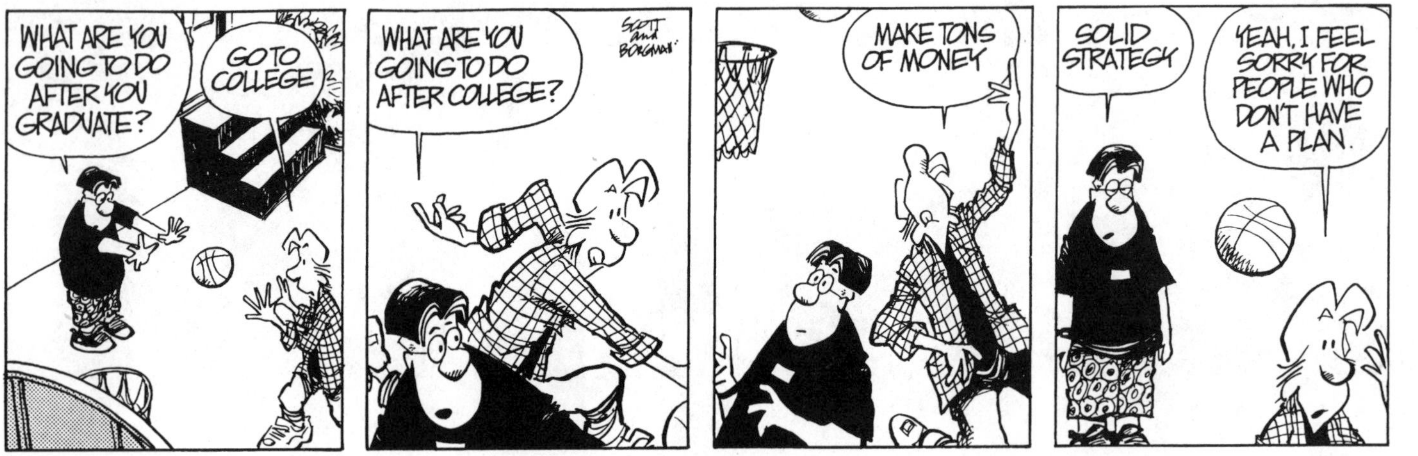
WHAT ARE YOU GOING TO DO AFTER YOU GRADUATE?
GO TO COLLEGE
WHAT ARE YOU GOING TO DO AFTER COLLEGE?
MAKE TONS OF MONEY
SOLID STRATEGY
YEAH, I FEEL SORRY FOR PEOPLE WHO DON'T HAVE A PLAN.

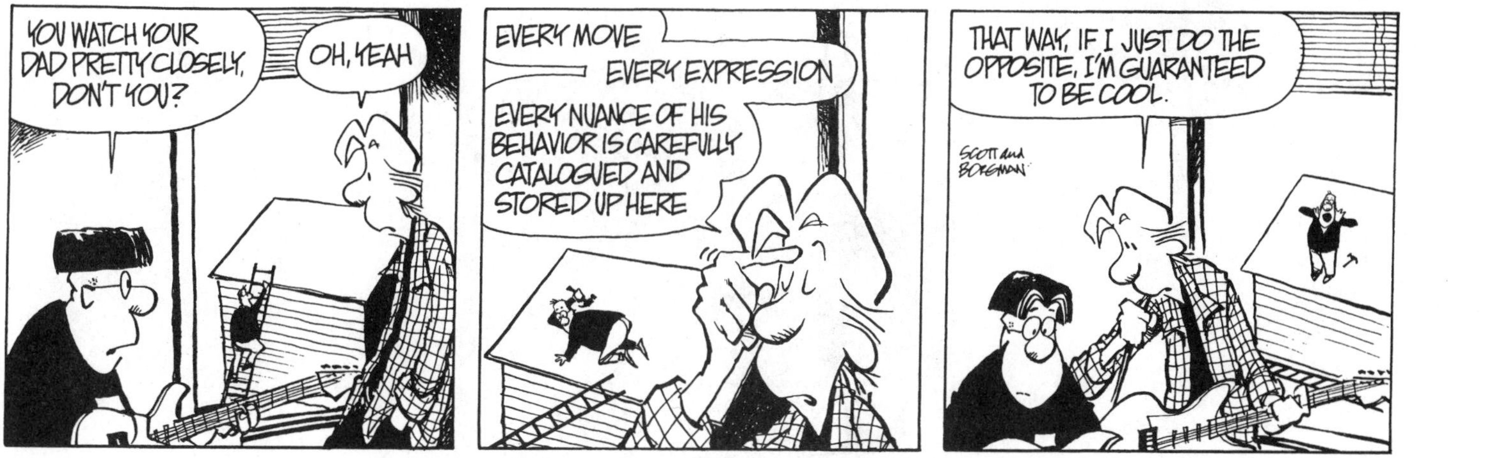
YOU WATCH YOUR DAD PRETTY CLOSELY, DON'T YOU?
OH, YEAH
EVERY MOVE
EVERY EXPRESSION
EVERY NUANCE OF HIS BEHAVIOR IS CAREFULLY CATALOGUED AND STORED UP HERE
THAT WAY, IF I JUST DO THE OPPOSITE, I'M GUARANTEED TO BE COOL.
SCOTT AND BORGMAN

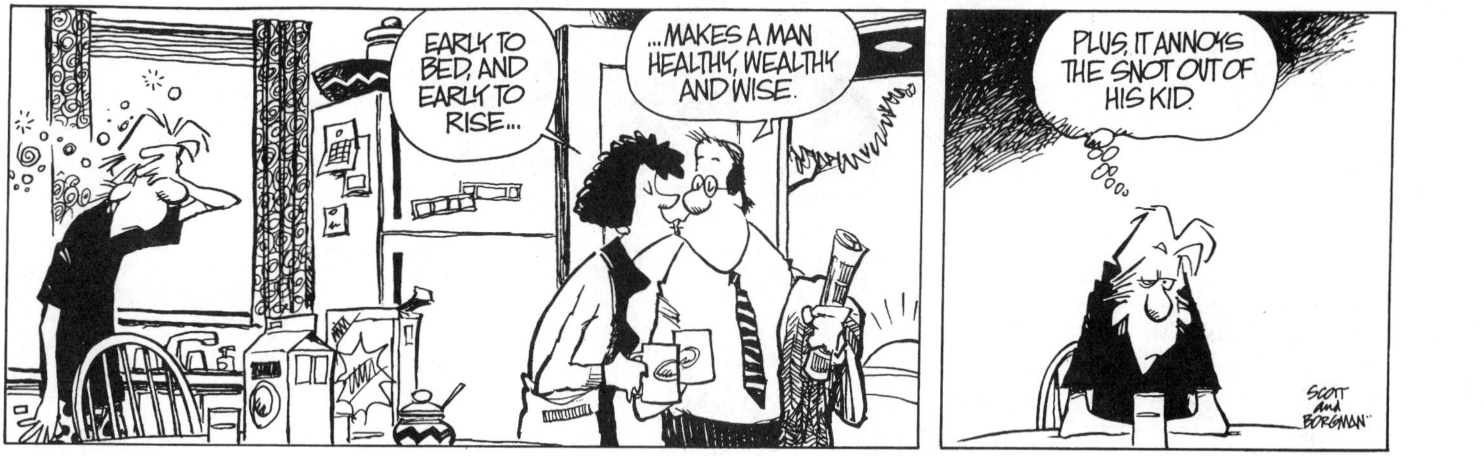
EARLY TO BED, AND EARLY TO RISE...
...MAKES A MAN HEALTHY, WEALTHY AND WISE.
PLUS, IT ANNOYS THE SNOT OUT OF HIS KID.
SCOTT AND BORGMAN

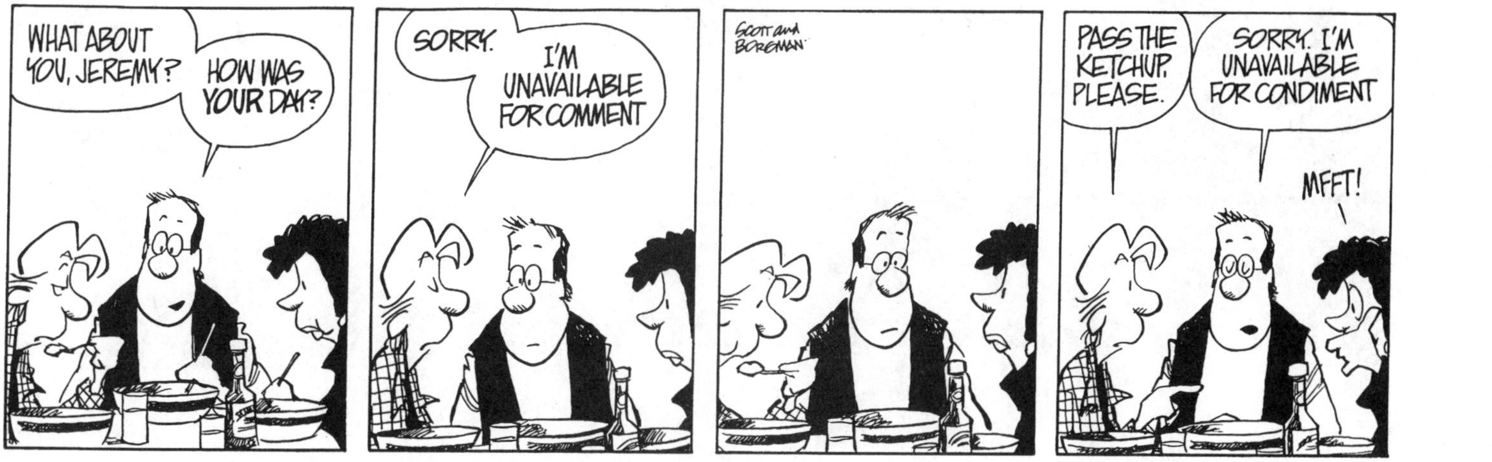
WHAT ABOUT YOU, JEREMY?
HOW WAS YOUR DAY?
SORRY.
I'M UNAVAILABLE FOR COMMENT
SCOTT AND BORGMAN
PASS THE KETCHUP, PLEASE.
SORRY. I'M UNAVAILABLE FOR CONDIMENT
MFFT!

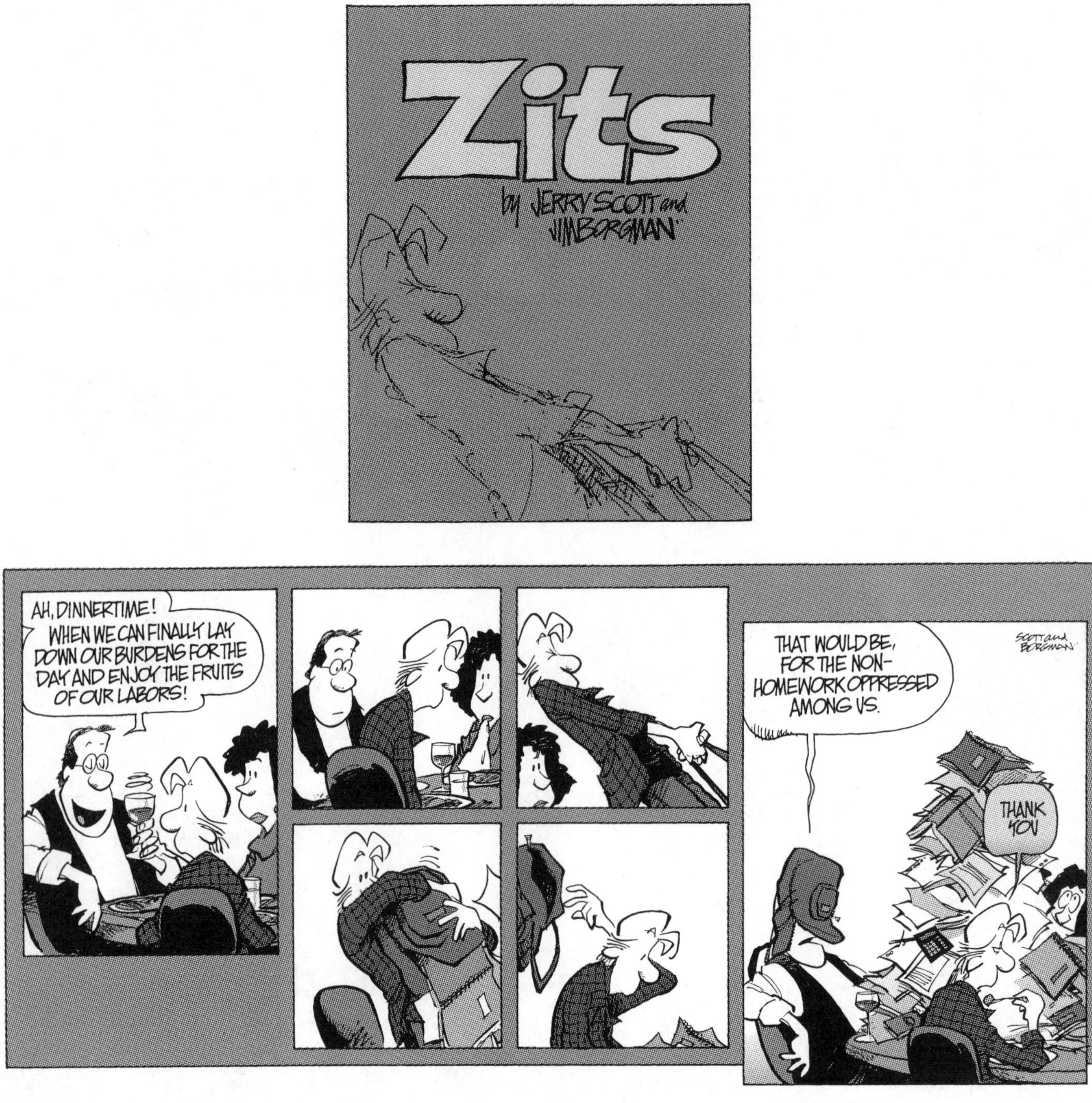
Zits
by JERRY SCOTT and JIM BORGMAN
AH, DINNERTIME! WHEN WE CAN FINALLY LAY DOWN OUR BURDENS FOR THE DAY AND ENJOY THE FRUITS OF OUR LABORS!
THAT WOULD BE, FOR THE NON-HOMEWORK OPPRESSED AMONG US.
SCOTT and BORGMAN
THANK YOU

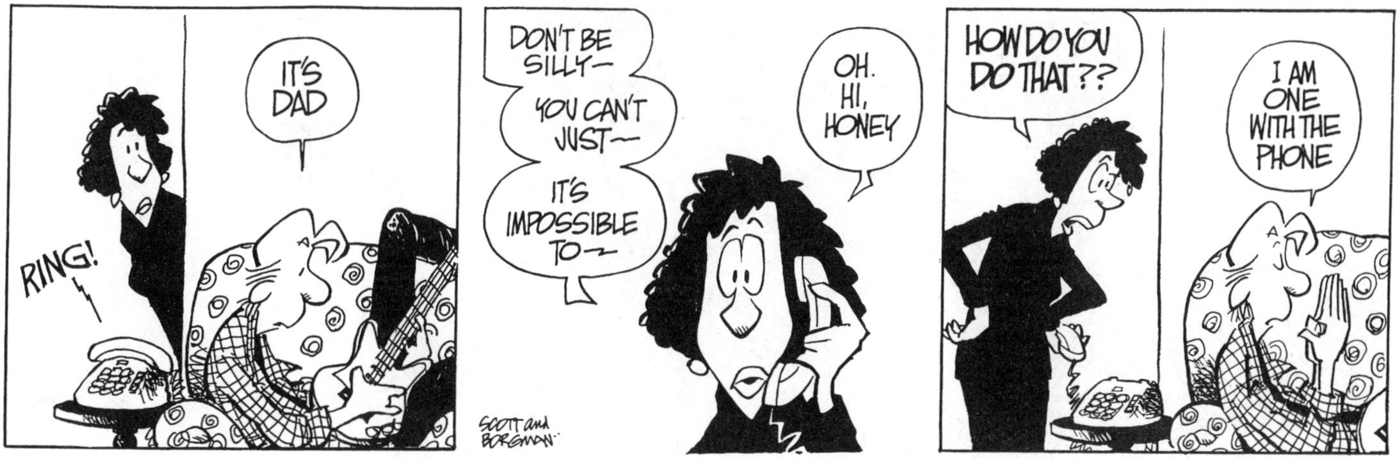
RING!
IT'S DAD
DON'T BE SILLY—
YOU CAN'T JUST—
IT'S IMPOSSIBLE TO—
OH. HI, HONEY
HOW DO YOU DO THAT??
I AM ONE WITH THE PHONE
SCOTT and BORGMAN

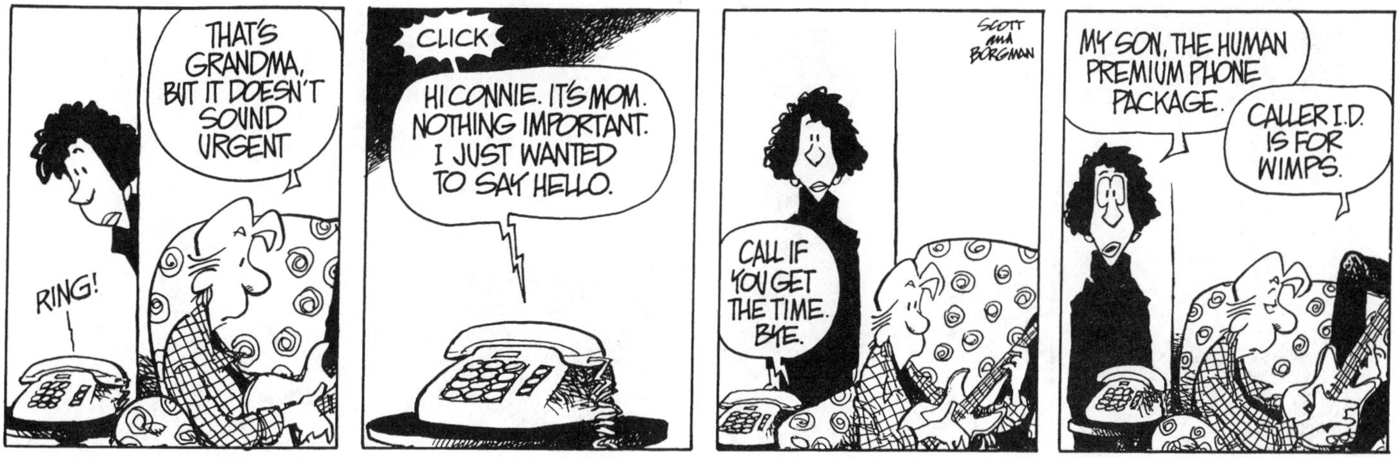
THAT'S GRANDMA, BUT IT DOESN'T SOUND URGENT
RING!
CLICK
HI CONNIE. IT'S MOM. NOTHING IMPORTANT. I JUST WANTED TO SAY HELLO.
CALL IF YOU GET THE TIME. BYE.
SCOTT and BORGMAN
MY SON, THE HUMAN PREMIUM PHONE PACKAGE.
CALLER I.D. IS FOR WIMPS.

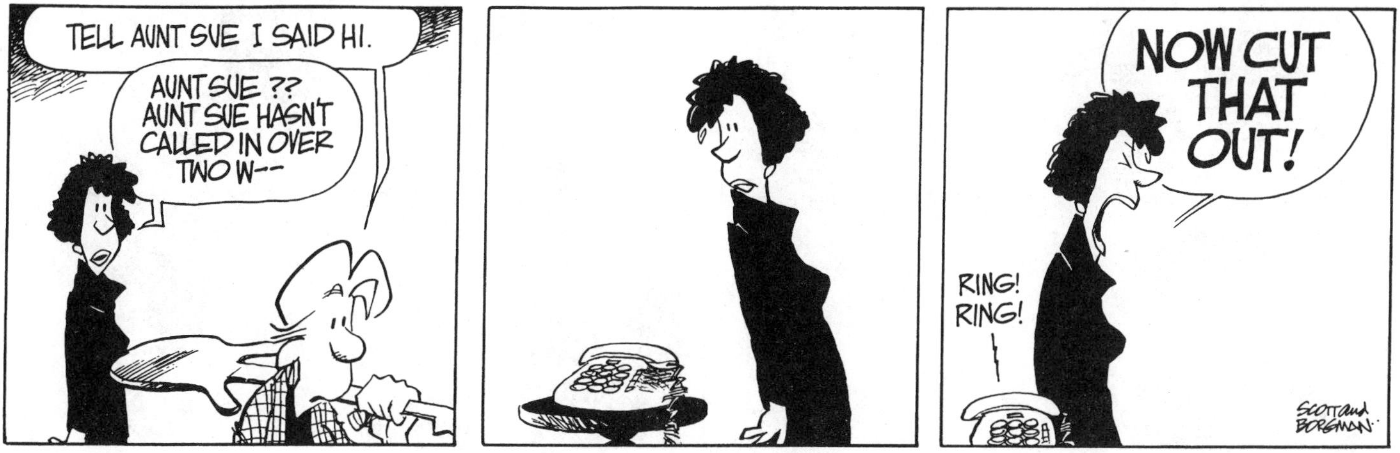
TELL AUNT SUE I SAID HI.
AUNT SUE?? AUNT SUE HASN'T CALLED IN OVER TWO W--
NOW CUT THAT OUT!
RING! RING!
SCOTT and BORGMAN

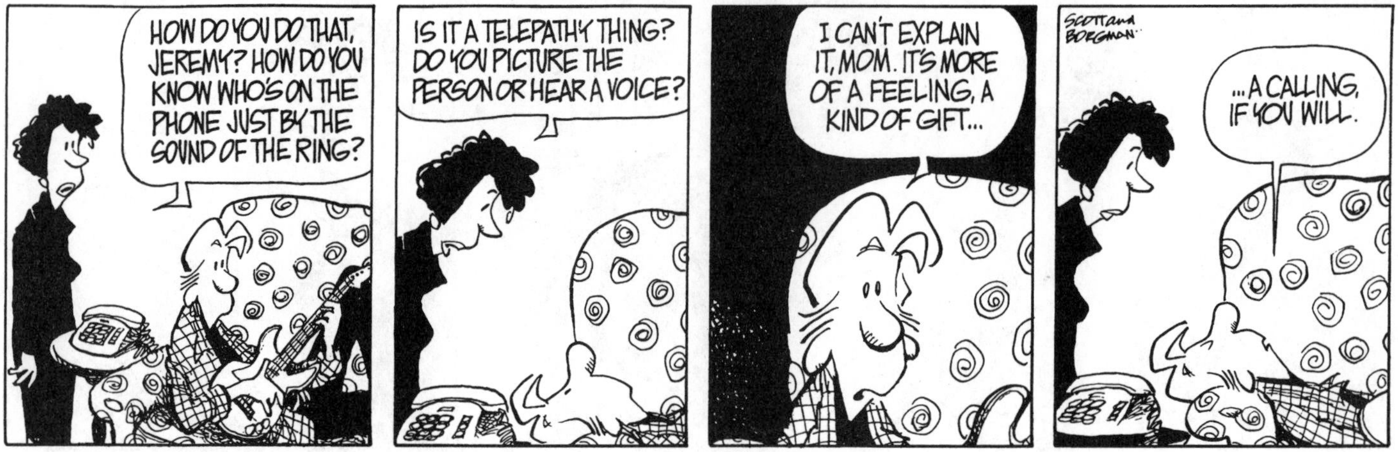
HOW DO YOU DO THAT, JEREMY? HOW DO YOU KNOW WHO'S ON THE PHONE JUST BY THE SOUND OF THE RING?
IS IT A TELEPATHY THING? DO YOU PICTURE THE PERSON OR HEAR A VOICE?
I CAN'T EXPLAIN IT, MOM. IT'S MORE OF A FEELING, A KIND OF GIFT...
...A CALLING, IF YOU WILL.

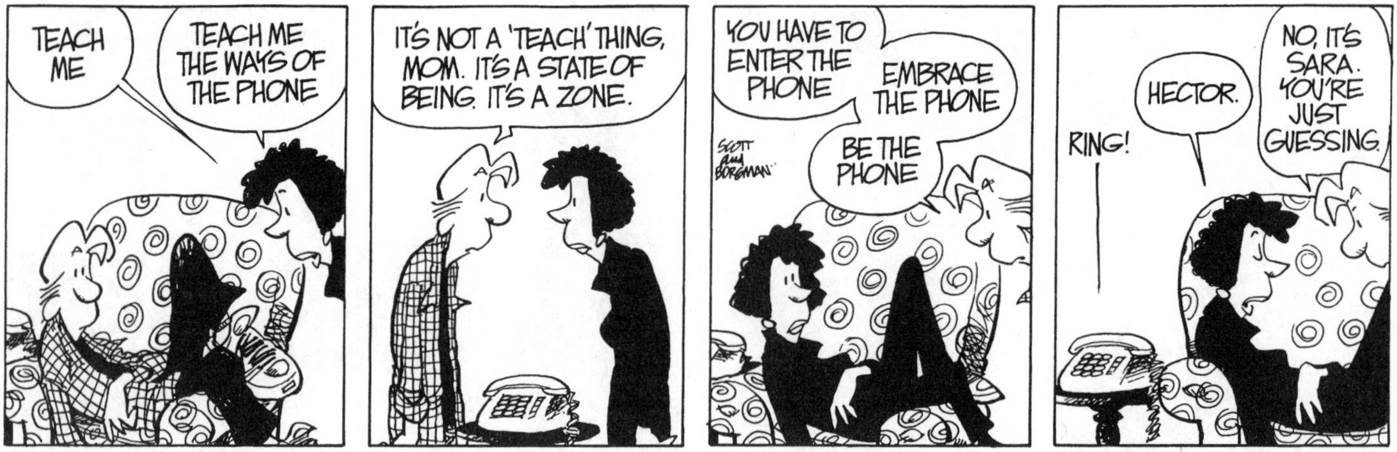
TEACH ME
TEACH ME THE WAYS OF THE PHONE
IT'S NOT A 'TEACH' THING, MOM. IT'S A STATE OF BEING. IT'S A ZONE.
YOU HAVE TO ENTER THE PHONE
EMBRACE THE PHONE
BE THE PHONE
RING!
HECTOR.
NO, IT'S SARA. YOU'RE JUST GUESSING.

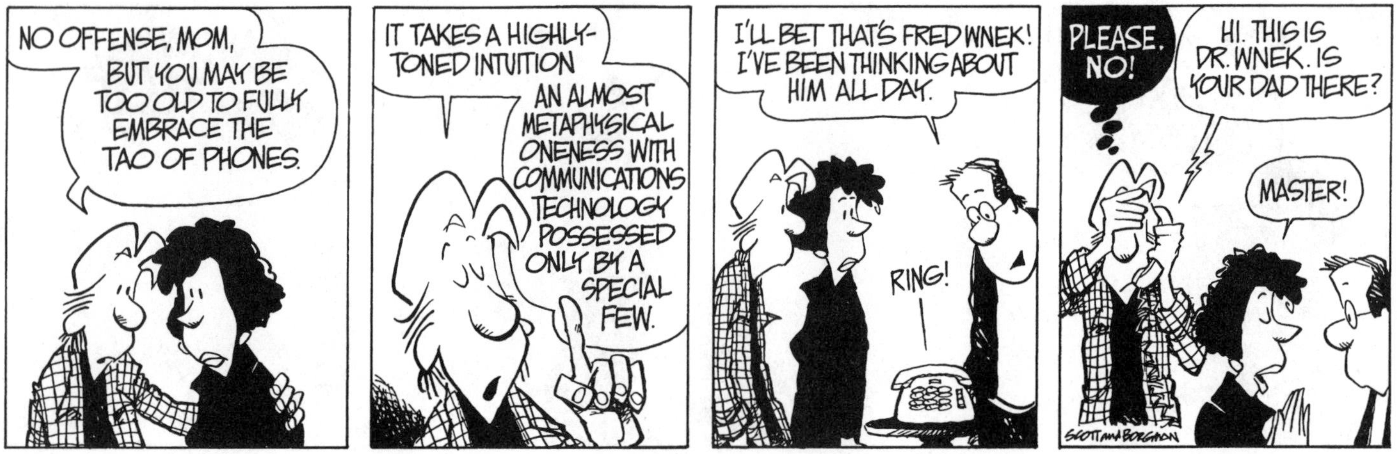
NO OFFENSE, MOM,
BUT YOU MAY BE TOO OLD TO FULLY EMBRACE THE TAO OF PHONES.
IT TAKES A HIGHLY-TONED INTUITION
AN ALMOST METAPHYSICAL ONENESS WITH COMMUNICATIONS TECHNOLOGY POSSESSED ONLY BY A SPECIAL FEW.
I'LL BET THAT'S FRED WNEK! I'VE BEEN THINKING ABOUT HIM ALL DAY.
RING!
PLEASE. NO!
HI. THIS IS DR. WNEK. IS YOUR DAD THERE?
MASTER!

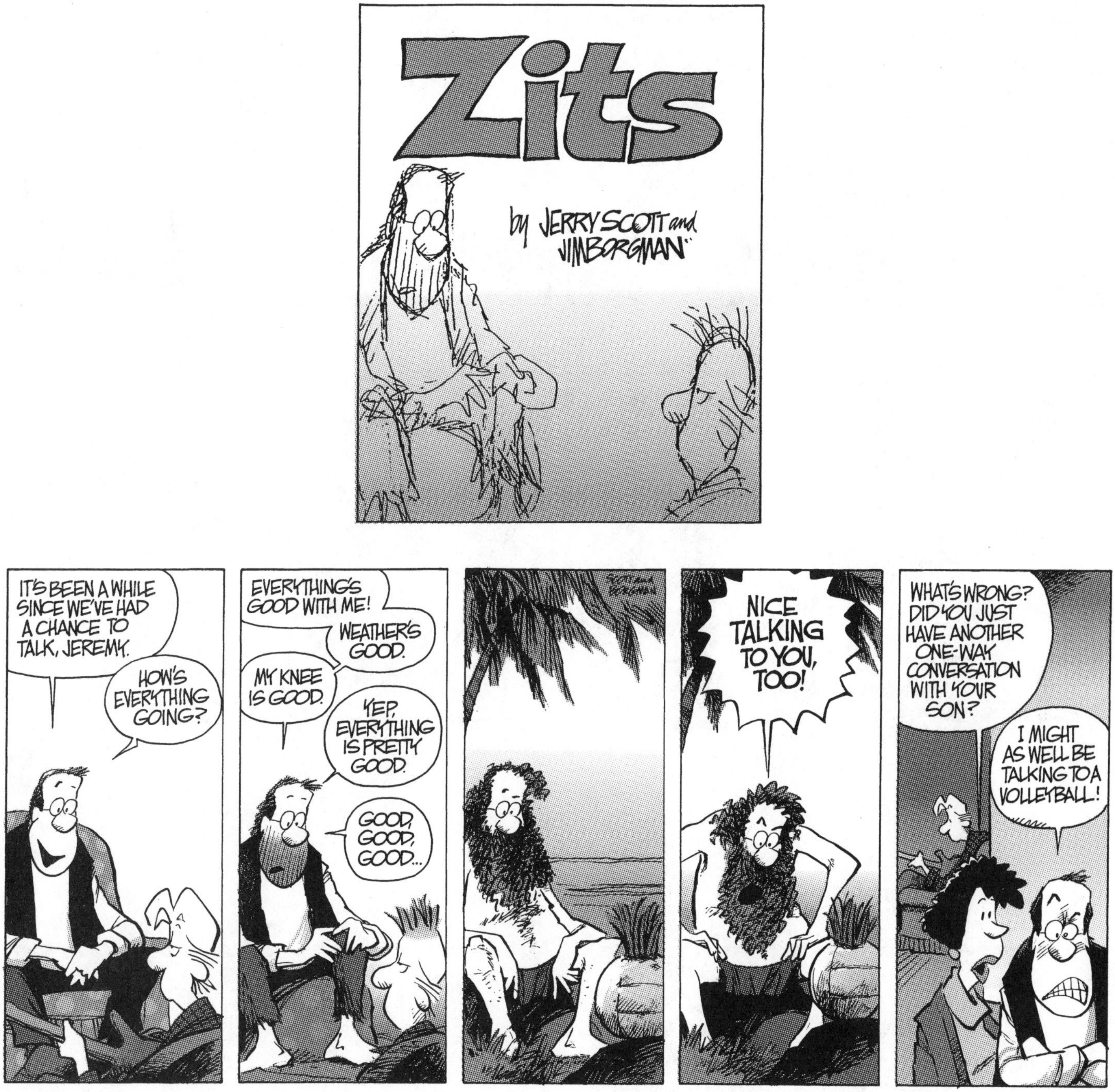
Zits
by JERRY SCOTT and JIM BORGMAN
IT'S BEEN A WHILE SINCE WE'VE HAD A CHANCE TO TALK, JEREMY.
HOW'S EVERYTHING GOING?
EVERYTHING'S GOOD WITH ME!
WEATHER'S GOOD.
MY KNEE IS GOOD.
YEP, EVERYTHING IS PRETTY GOOD.
GOOD, GOOD, GOOD...
SCOTT and BORGMAN
NICE TALKING TO YOU, TOO!
WHAT'S WRONG? DID YOU JUST HAVE ANOTHER ONE-WAY CONVERSATION WITH YOUR SON?
I MIGHT AS WELL BE TALKING TO A VOLLEYBALL!

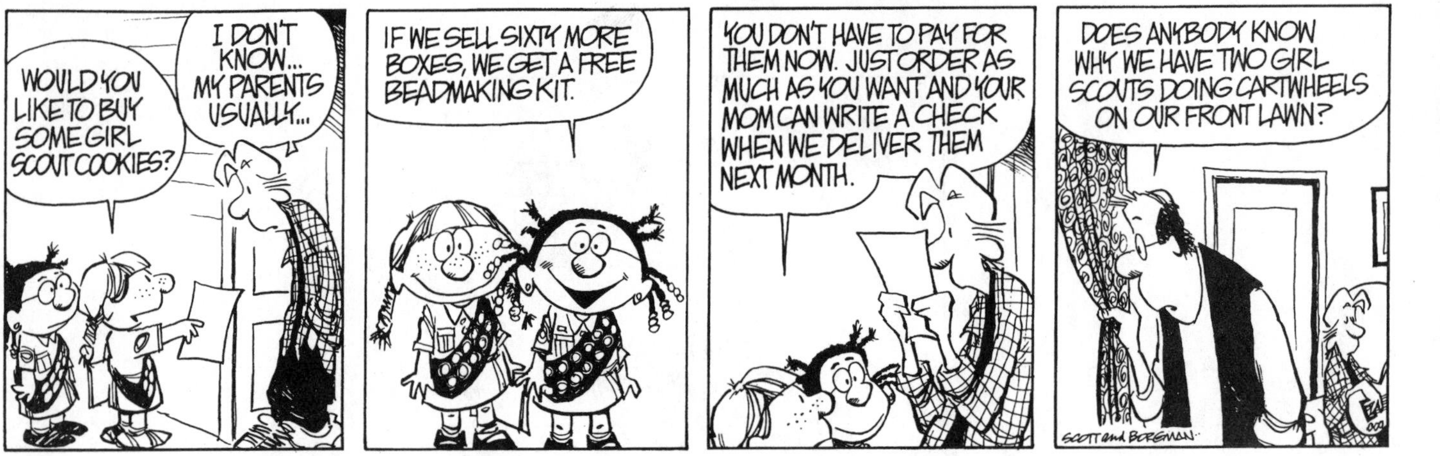
WOULD YOU LIKE TO BUY SOME GIRL SCOUT COOKIES?
I DON'T KNOW... MY PARENTS USUALLY...
IF WE SELL SIXTY MORE BOXES, WE GET A FREE BEADMAKING KIT.
YOU DON'T HAVE TO PAY FOR THEM NOW. JUST ORDER AS MUCH AS YOU WANT AND YOUR MOM CAN WRITE A CHECK WHEN WE DELIVER THEM NEXT MONTH.
DOES ANYBODY KNOW WHY WE HAVE TWO GIRL SCOUTS DOING CARTWHEELS ON OUR FRONT LAWN?
SCOTT and BORGMAN

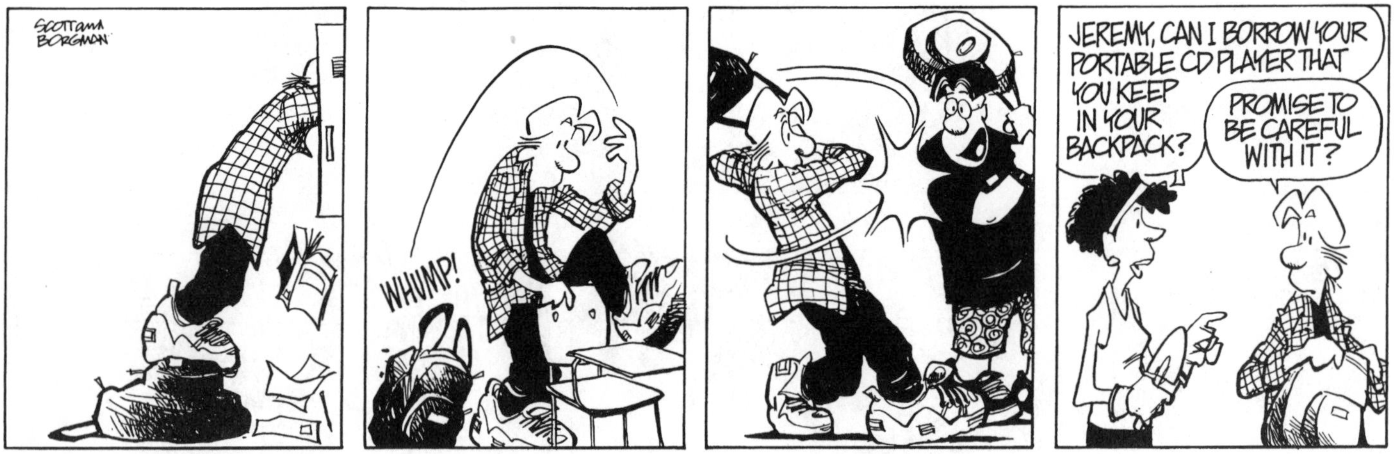
SCOTT and BORGMAN
WHUMP!
JEREMY, CAN I BORROW YOUR PORTABLE CD PLAYER THAT YOU KEEP IN YOUR BACKPACK?
PROMISE TO BE CAREFUL WITH IT?

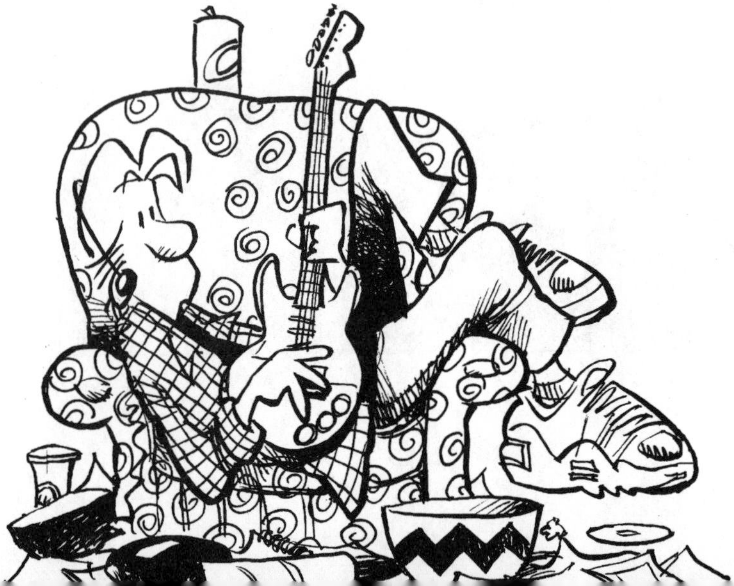

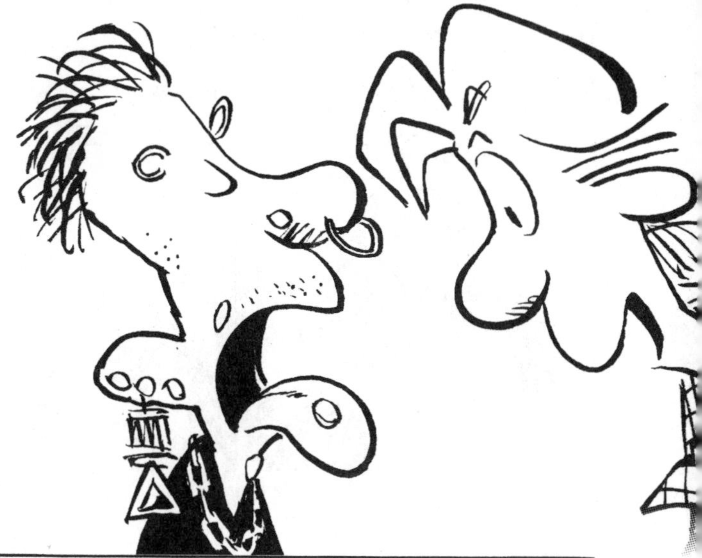

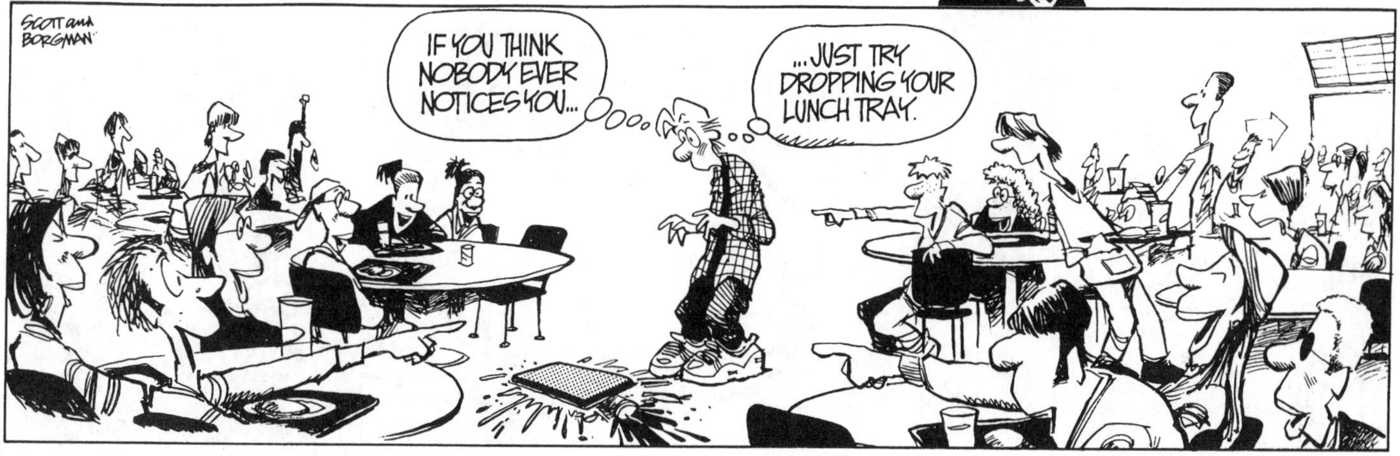
SCOTT and BORGMAN
IF YOU THINK NOBODY EVER NOTICES YOU...
...JUST TRY DROPPING YOUR LUNCH TRAY.

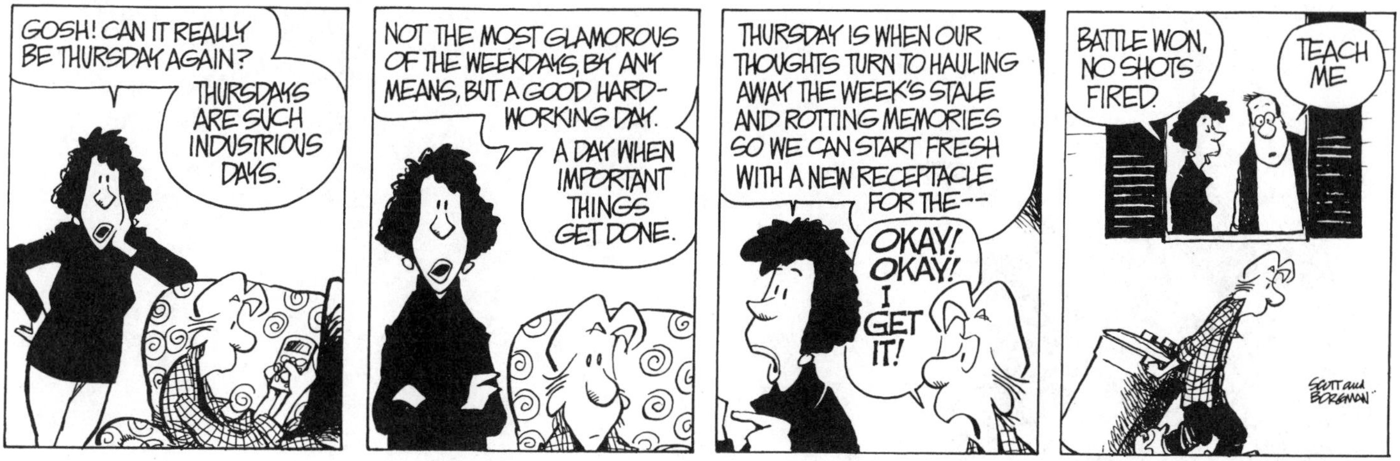
GOSH! CAN IT REALLY BE THURSDAY AGAIN?
THURSDAYS ARE SUCH INDUSTRIOUS DAYS.
NOT THE MOST GLAMOROUS OF THE WEEKDAYS, BY ANY MEANS, BUT A GOOD HARD-WORKING DAY.
A DAY WHEN IMPORTANT THINGS GET DONE.
THURSDAY IS WHEN OUR THOUGHTS TURN TO HAULING AWAY THE WEEK'S STALE AND ROTTING MEMORIES SO WE CAN START FRESH WITH A NEW RECEPTACLE FOR THE--
OKAY! OKAY! I GET IT!
BATTLE WON, NO SHOTS FIRED.
TEACH ME
SCOTT and BORGMAN

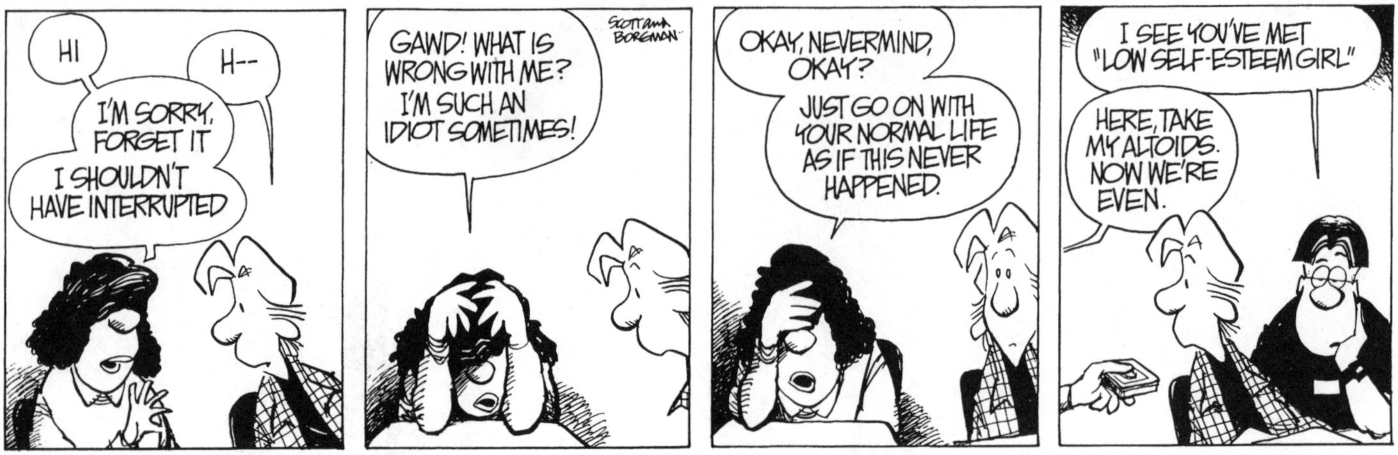
HI
H--
I'M SORRY, FORGET IT
I SHOULDN'T HAVE INTERRUPTED
GAWD! WHAT IS WRONG WITH ME? I'M SUCH AN IDIOT SOMETIMES!
OKAY, NEVERMIND, OKAY?
JUST GO ON WITH YOUR NORMAL LIFE AS IF THIS NEVER HAPPENED.
I SEE YOU'VE MET "LOW SELF-ESTEEM GIRL"
HERE, TAKE MY ALTOIDS. NOW WE'RE EVEN.

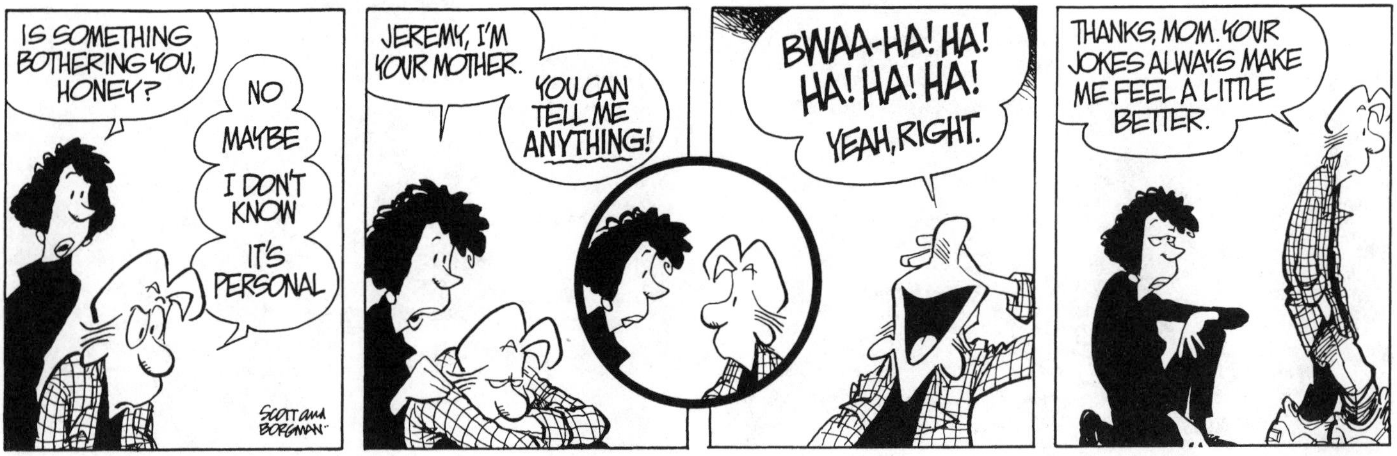
IS SOMETHING BOTHERING YOU, HONEY?
NO
MAYBE
I DON'T KNOW
IT'S PERSONAL
JEREMY, I'M YOUR MOTHER.
YOU CAN TELL ME ANYTHING!
BWAA-HA! HA! HA! HA! HA!
YEAH, RIGHT.
THANKS, MOM. YOUR JOKES ALWAYS MAKE ME FEEL A LITTLE BETTER.

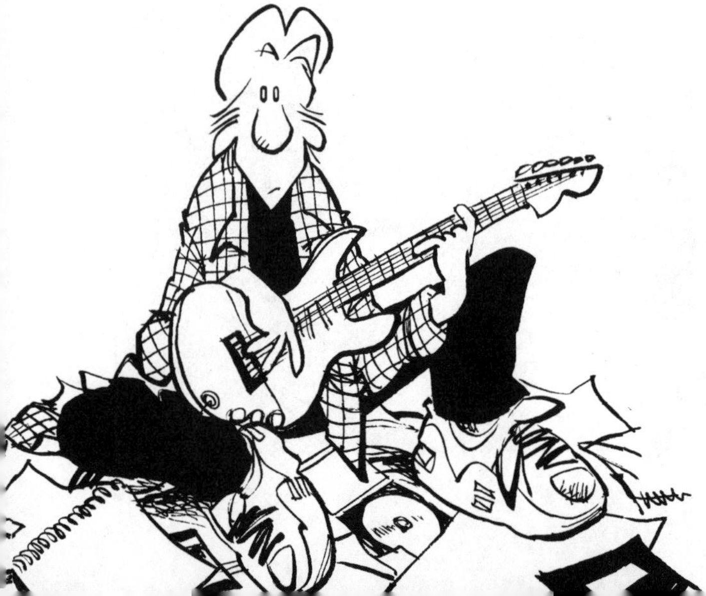

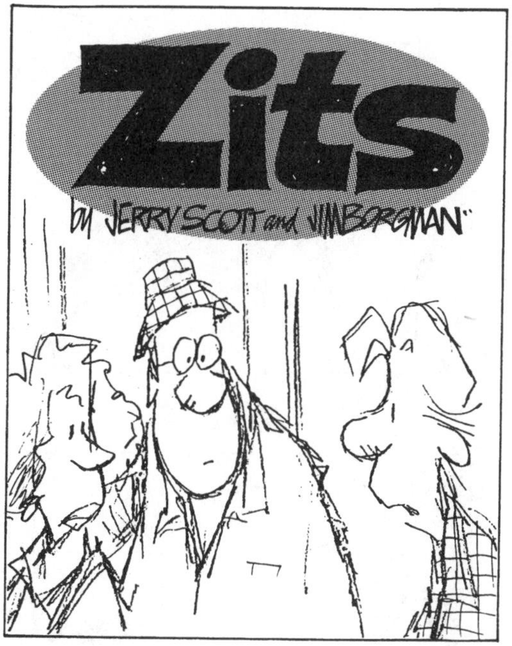
Zits
by JERRY SCOTT and JIM BORGMAN

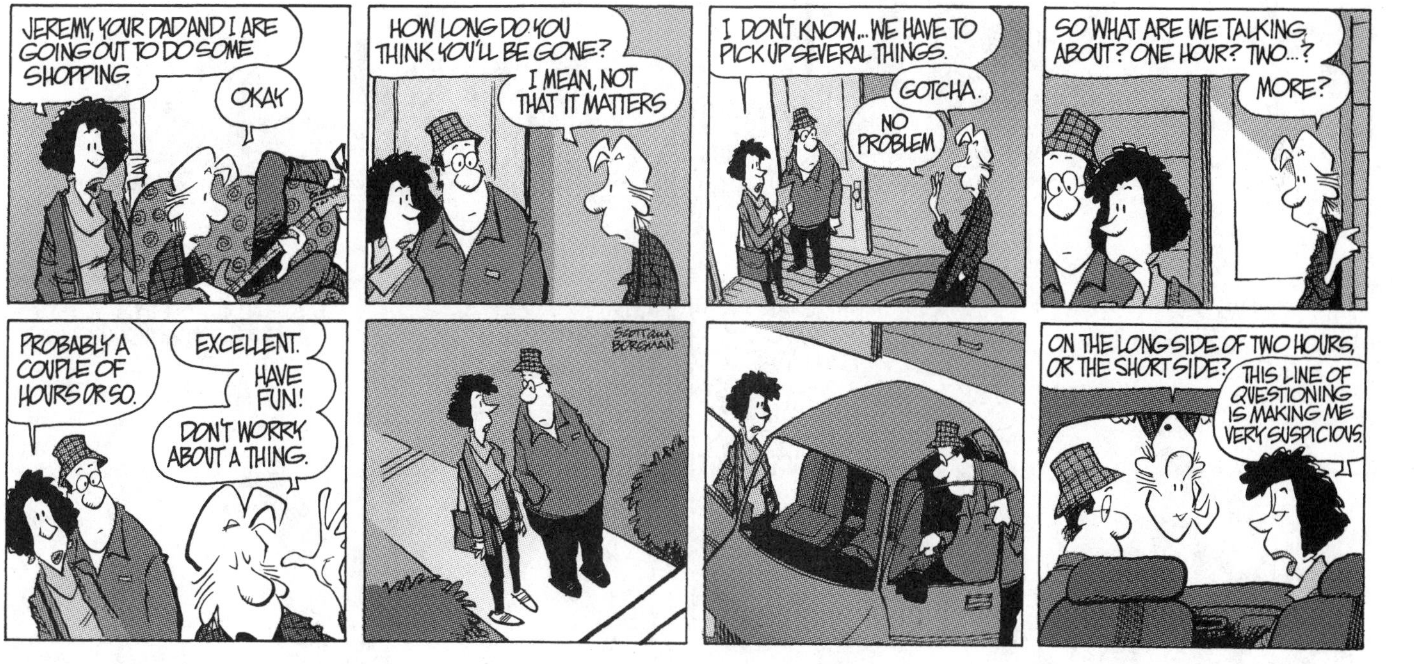
JEREMY, YOUR DAD AND I ARE GOING OUT TO DO SOME SHOPPING.
OKAY
HOW LONG DO YOU THINK YOU'LL BE GONE?
I MEAN, NOT THAT IT MATTERS
I DON'T KNOW... WE HAVE TO PICK UP SEVERAL THINGS.
GOTCHA.
NO PROBLEM
SO WHAT ARE WE TALKING ABOUT? ONE HOUR? TWO...?
MORE?
PROBABLY A COUPLE OF HOURS OR SO.
EXCELLENT.
HAVE FUN!
DON'T WORRY ABOUT A THING.
ON THE LONG SIDE OF TWO HOURS, OR THE SHORT SIDE?
THIS LINE OF QUESTIONING IS MAKING ME VERY SUSPICIOUS.

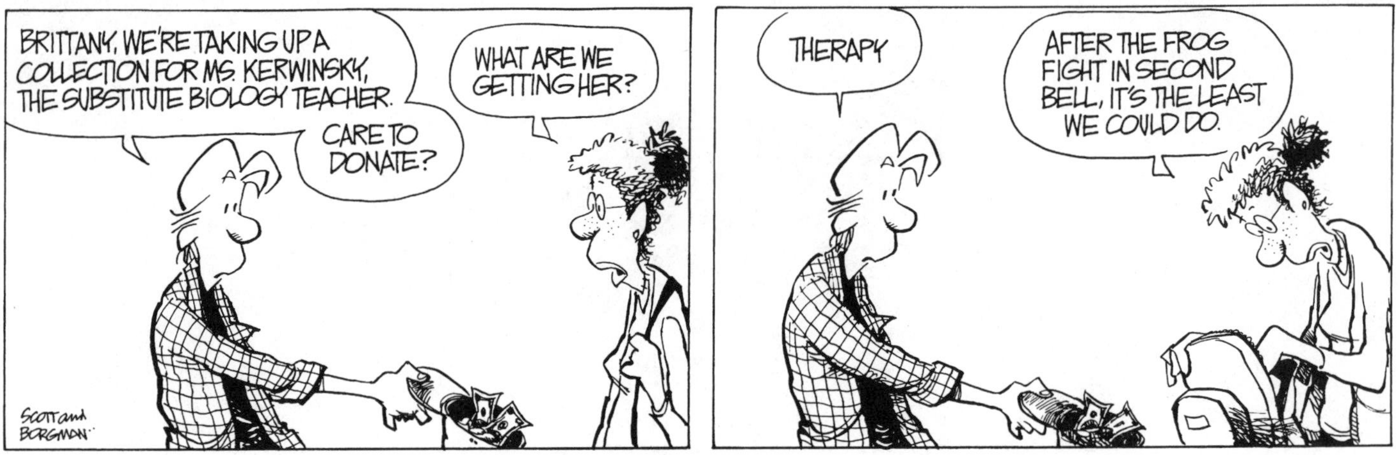
BRITTANY, WE'RE TAKING UP A COLLECTION FOR MS. KERWINSKY, THE SUBSTITUTE BIOLOGY TEACHER.
CARE TO DONATE?
WHAT ARE WE GETTING HER?
SCOTT AND BORGMAN
THERAPY
AFTER THE FROG FIGHT IN SECOND BELL, IT'S THE LEAST WE COULD DO.

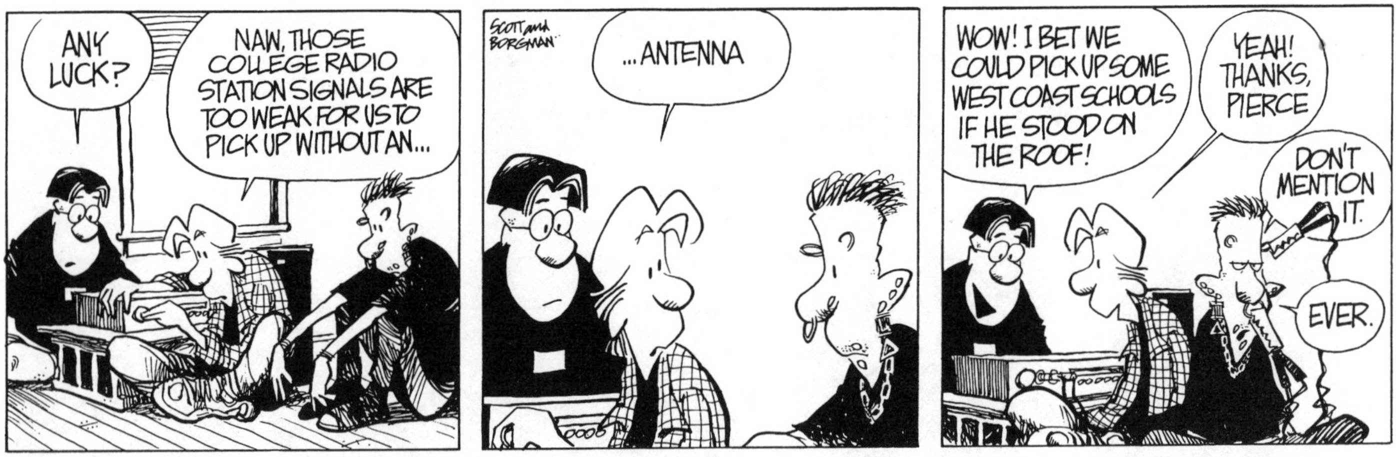
ANY LUCK?
NAW, THOSE COLLEGE RADIO STATION SIGNALS ARE TOO WEAK FOR US TO PICK UP WITHOUT AN...
SCOTT AND BORGMAN
...ANTENNA
WOW! I BET WE COULD PICK UP SOME WEST COAST SCHOOLS IF HE STOOD ON THE ROOF!
YEAH! THANKS, PIERCE
DON'T MENTION IT.
EVER.

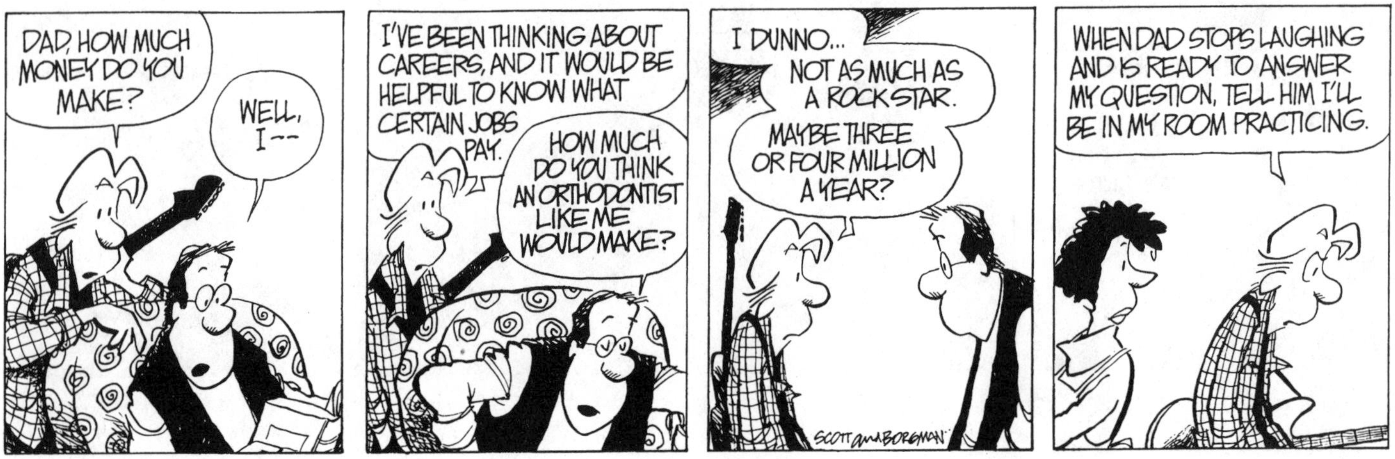
DAD, HOW MUCH MONEY DO YOU MAKE?
WELL, I--
I'VE BEEN THINKING ABOUT CAREERS, AND IT WOULD BE HELPFUL TO KNOW WHAT CERTAIN JOBS PAY.
HOW MUCH DO YOU THINK AN ORTHODONTIST LIKE ME WOULD MAKE?
I DUNNO...
NOT AS MUCH AS A ROCK STAR.
MAYBE THREE OR FOUR MILLION A YEAR?
SCOTT AND BORGMAN
WHEN DAD STOPS LAUGHING AND IS READY TO ANSWER MY QUESTION, TELL HIM I'LL BE IN MY ROOM PRACTICING.

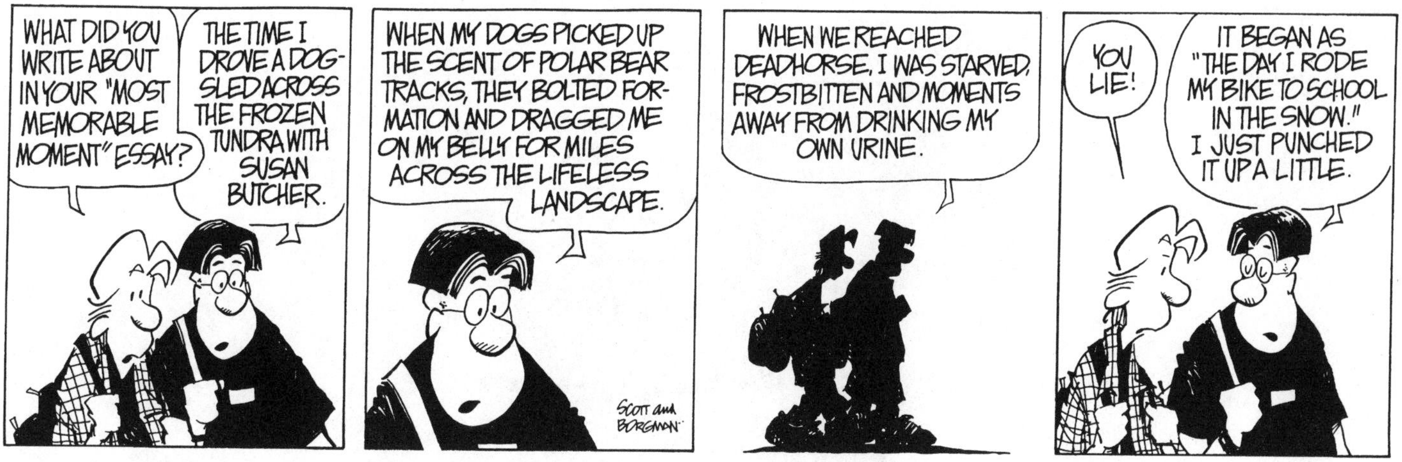
WHAT DID YOU WRITE ABOUT IN YOUR "MOST MEMORABLE MOMENT" ESSAY?
THE TIME I DROVE A DOG-SLED ACROSS THE FROZEN TUNDRA WITH SUSAN BUTCHER.
WHEN MY DOGS PICKED UP THE SCENT OF POLAR BEAR TRACKS, THEY BOLTED FORMATION AND DRAGGED ME ON MY BELLY FOR MILES ACROSS THE LIFELESS LANDSCAPE.
SCOTT AND BORGMAN
WHEN WE REACHED DEADHORSE, I WAS STARVED, FROSTBITTEN AND MOMENTS AWAY FROM DRINKING MY OWN URINE.
YOU LIE!
IT BEGAN AS "THE DAY I RODE MY BIKE TO SCHOOL IN THE SNOW." I JUST PUNCHED IT UP A LITTLE.

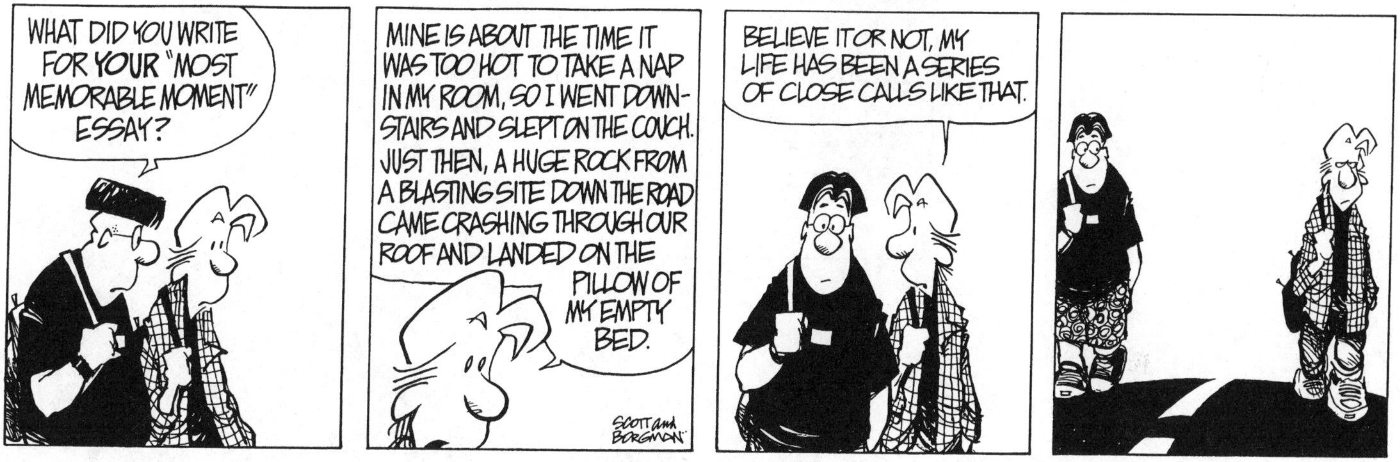
WHAT DID YOU WRITE FOR YOUR "MOST MEMORABLE MOMENT" ESSAY?
MINE IS ABOUT THE TIME IT WAS TOO HOT TO TAKE A NAP IN MY ROOM, SO I WENT DOWNSTAIRS AND SLEPT ON THE COUCH. JUST THEN, A HUGE ROCK FROM A BLASTING SITE DOWN THE ROAD CAME CRASHING THROUGH OUR ROOF AND LANDED ON THE PILLOW OF MY EMPTY BED.
SCOTT AND BORGMAN
BELIEVE IT OR NOT, MY LIFE HAS BEEN A SERIES OF CLOSE CALLS LIKE THAT.

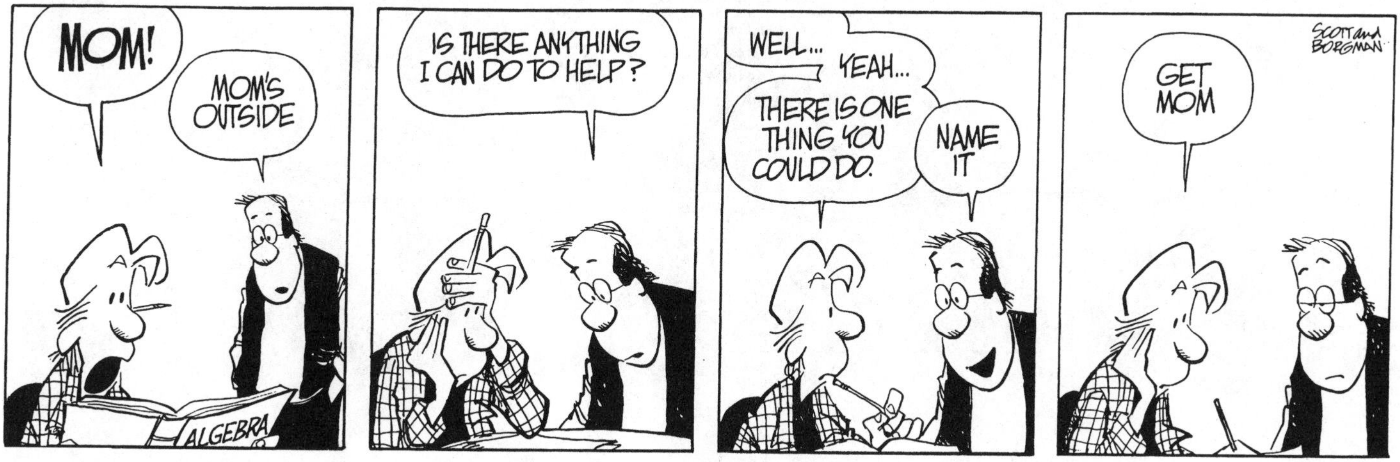
MOM!
MOM'S OUTSIDE
ALGEBRA
IS THERE ANYTHING I CAN DO TO HELP?
WELL... YEAH...
THERE IS ONE THING YOU COULD DO.
NAME IT
SCOTT AND BORGMAN
GET MOM

Zits
by JERRY SCOTT and JIM BORGMAN

JERRY SCOTT and JIM BORGMAN
200-236
GASP!
THE STAIRS IN THE "B" CONCOURSE ARE A LOT LESS CROWDED.
SOMETIMES I'M NOT SURE WHETHER I'M CHANGING CLASSES OR SPAWNING!

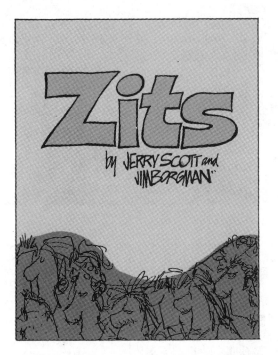

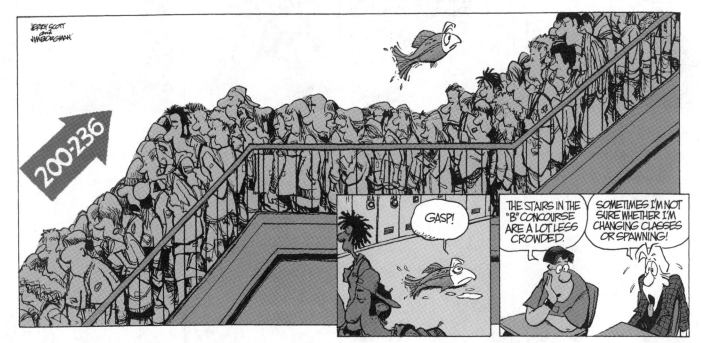

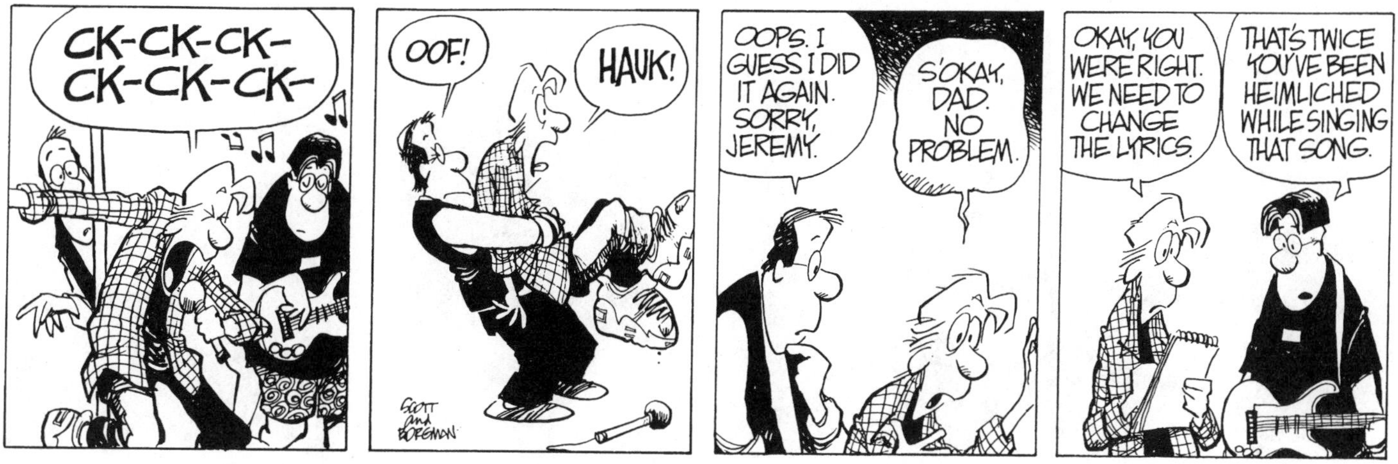
CK-CK-CK-
CK-CK-CK-
OOF!
HAUK!
SCOTT and BORGMAN
OOPS. I GUESS I DID IT AGAIN. SORRY, JEREMY.
S'OKAY, DAD. NO PROBLEM.
OKAY, YOU WERE RIGHT. WE NEED TO CHANGE THE LYRICS.
THAT'S TWICE YOU'VE BEEN HEIMLICHED WHILE SINGING THAT SONG.

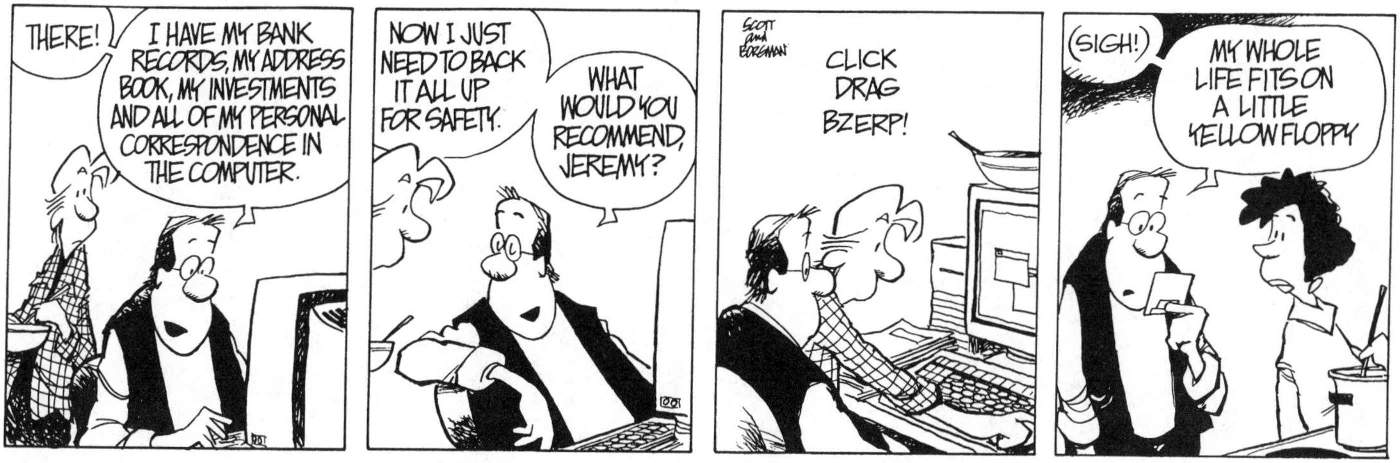
THERE!
I HAVE MY BANK RECORDS, MY ADDRESS BOOK, MY INVESTMENTS AND ALL OF MY PERSONAL CORRESPONDENCE IN THE COMPUTER.
NOW I JUST NEED TO BACK IT ALL UP FOR SAFETY.
WHAT WOULD YOU RECOMMEND, JEREMY?
SCOTT and BORGMAN
CLICK
DRAG
BZERP!
(SIGH!)
MY WHOLE LIFE FITS ON A LITTLE YELLOW FLOPPY

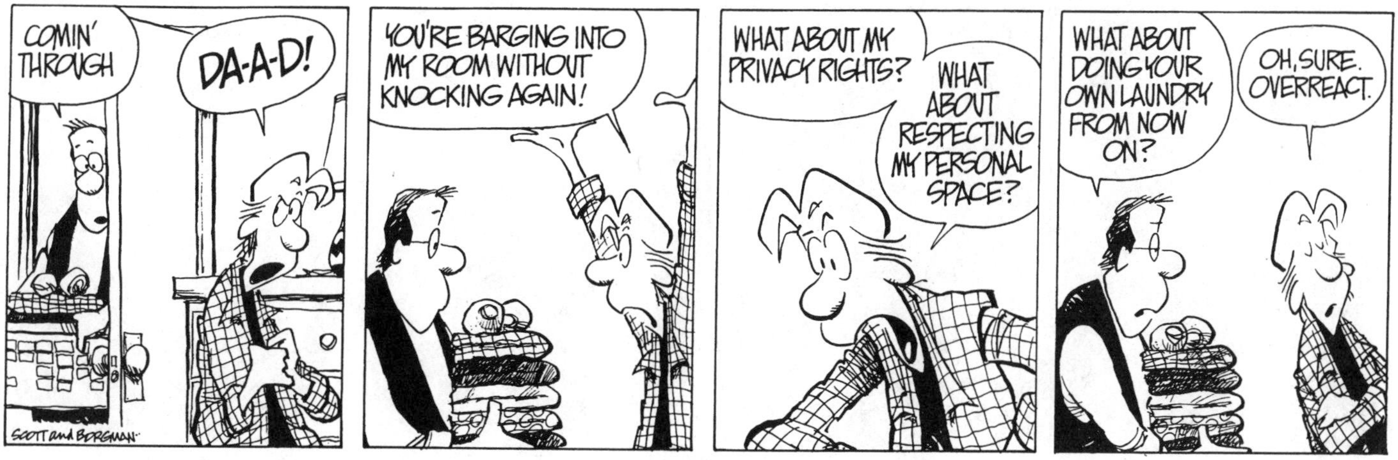
COMIN' THROUGH
DA-A-D!
SCOTT and BORGMAN
YOU'RE BARGING INTO MY ROOM WITHOUT KNOCKING AGAIN!
WHAT ABOUT MY PRIVACY RIGHTS?
WHAT ABOUT RESPECTING MY PERSONAL SPACE?
WHAT ABOUT DOING YOUR OWN LAUNDRY FROM NOW ON?
OH, SURE. OVERREACT.

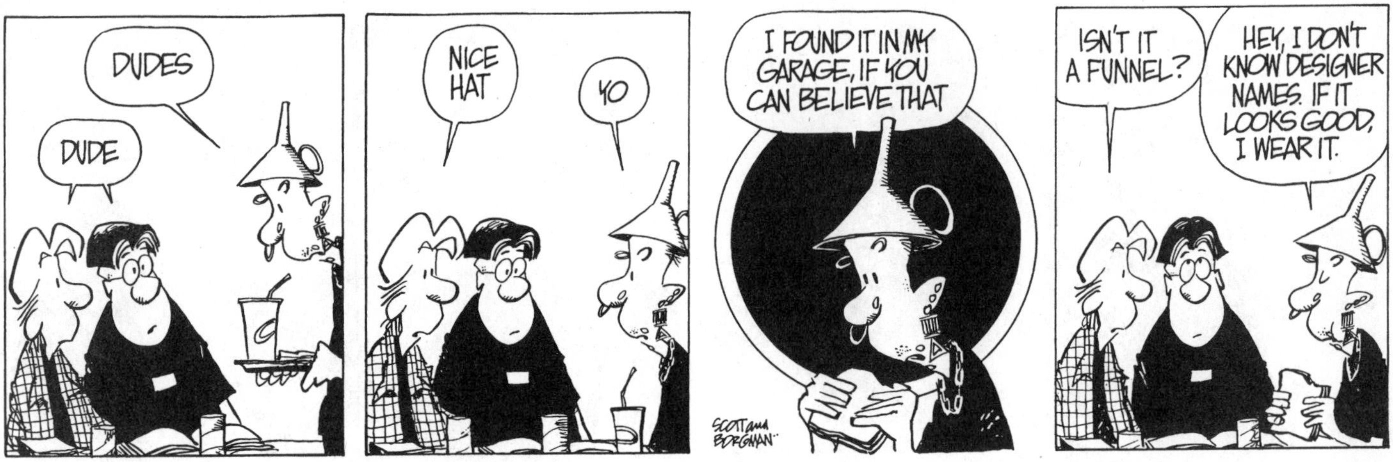
DUDE
DUDES
NICE HAT
YO
I FOUND IT IN MY GARAGE, IF YOU CAN BELIEVE THAT
SCOTT and BORGMAN
ISN'T IT A FUNNEL?
HEY, I DON'T KNOW DESIGNER NAMES. IF IT LOOKS GOOD, I WEAR IT.

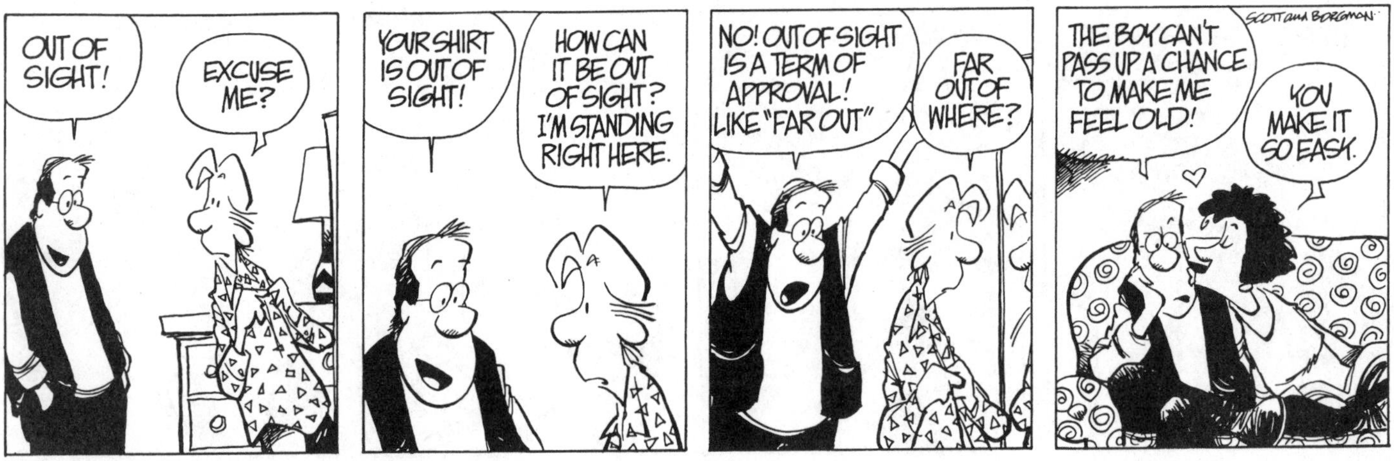
OUT OF SIGHT!
EXCUSE ME?
YOUR SHIRT IS OUT OF SIGHT!
HOW CAN IT BE OUT OF SIGHT? I'M STANDING RIGHT HERE.
NO! OUT OF SIGHT IS A TERM OF APPROVAL! LIKE "FAR OUT"
FAR OUT OF WHERE?
SCOTT and BORGMAN
THE BOY CAN'T PASS UP A CHANCE TO MAKE ME FEEL OLD!
YOU MAKE IT SO EASY.

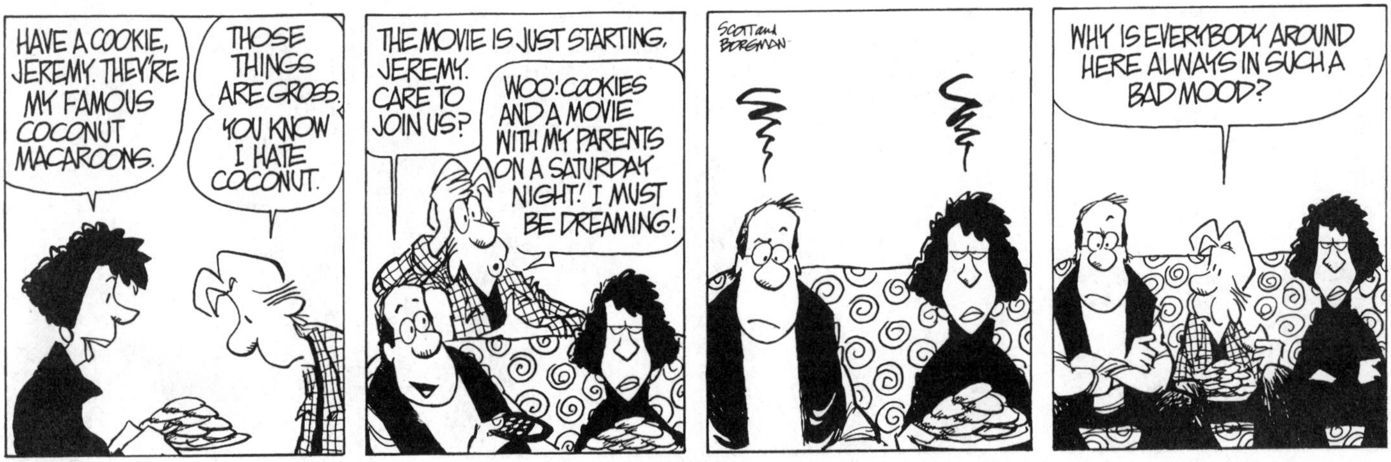
HAVE A COOKIE, JEREMY. THEY'RE MY FAMOUS COCONUT MACAROONS.
THOSE THINGS ARE GROSS. YOU KNOW I HATE COCONUT.
THE MOVIE IS JUST STARTING, JEREMY. CARE TO JOIN US?
WOO! COOKIES AND A MOVIE WITH MY PARENTS ON A SATURDAY NIGHT! I MUST BE DREAMING!
SCOTT and BORGMAN
WHY IS EVERYBODY AROUND HERE ALWAYS IN SUCH A BAD MOOD?

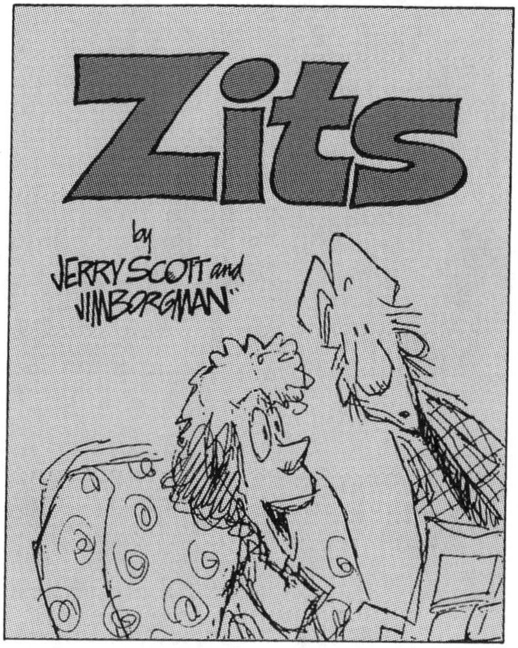
Zits
by
JERRY SCOTT and
JIM BORGMAN

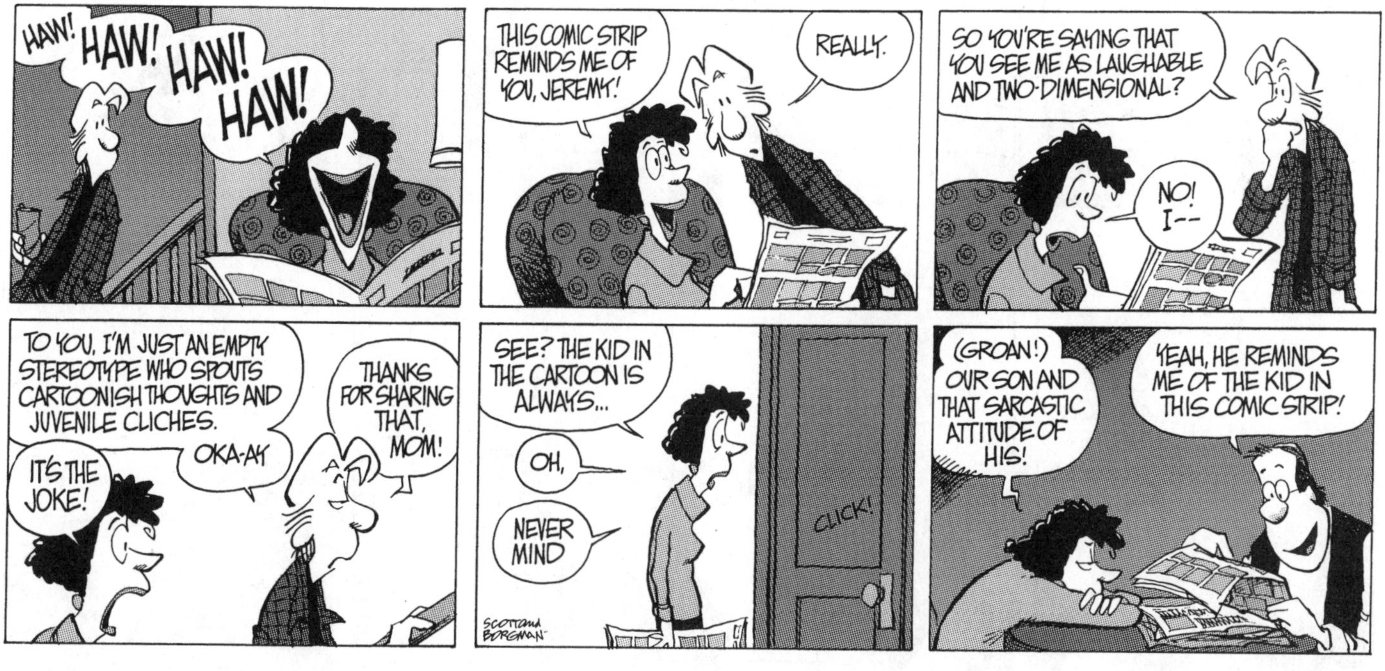
HAW! HAW! HAW! HAW!
THIS COMIC STRIP REMINDS ME OF YOU, JEREMY!
REALLY.
SO YOU'RE SAYING THAT YOU SEE ME AS LAUGHABLE AND TWO-DIMENSIONAL?
NO! I--
TO YOU, I'M JUST AN EMPTY STEREOTYPE WHO SPOUTS CARTOONISH THOUGHTS AND JUVENILE CLICHES.
IT'S THE JOKE!
OKA-AY
THANKS FOR SHARING THAT, MOM!
SEE? THE KID IN THE CARTOON IS ALWAYS...
OH,
NEVER MIND
CLICK!
SCOTT and BORGMAN
(GROAN!) OUR SON AND THAT SARCASTIC ATTITUDE OF HIS!
YEAH, HE REMINDS ME OF THE KID IN THIS COMIC STRIP!

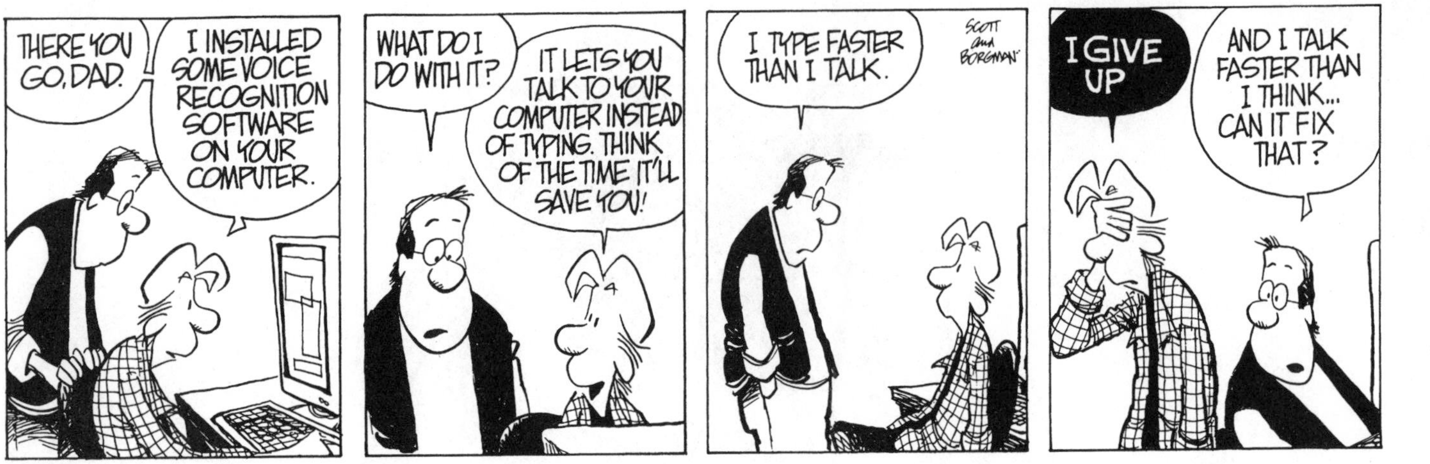
THERE YOU GO, DAD.
I INSTALLED SOME VOICE RECOGNITION SOFTWARE ON YOUR COMPUTER.
WHAT DO I DO WITH IT?
IT LETS YOU TALK TO YOUR COMPUTER INSTEAD OF TYPING. THINK OF THE TIME IT'LL SAVE YOU!
I TYPE FASTER THAN I TALK.
SCOTT and BORGMAN
AND I TALK FASTER THAN I THINK... CAN IT FIX THAT?
I GIVE UP

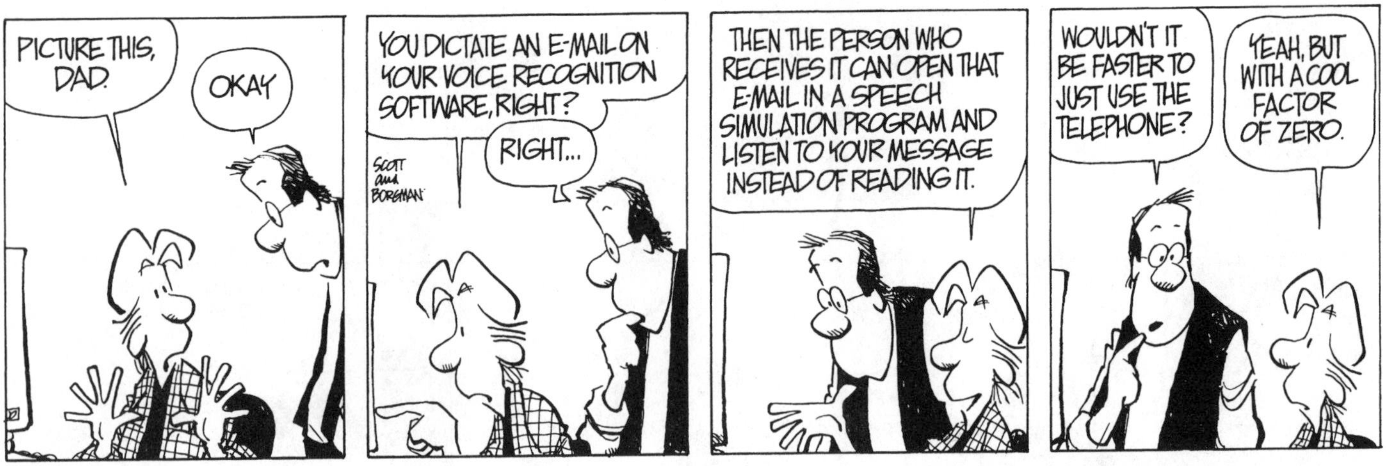
PICTURE THIS, DAD.
OKAY
YOU DICTATE AN E-MAIL ON YOUR VOICE RECOGNITION SOFTWARE, RIGHT?
RIGHT...
SCOTT and BORGMAN
THEN THE PERSON WHO RECEIVES IT CAN OPEN THAT E-MAIL IN A SPEECH SIMULATION PROGRAM AND LISTEN TO YOUR MESSAGE INSTEAD OF READING IT.
WOULDN'T IT BE FASTER TO JUST USE THE TELEPHONE?
YEAH, BUT WITH A COOL FACTOR OF ZERO.

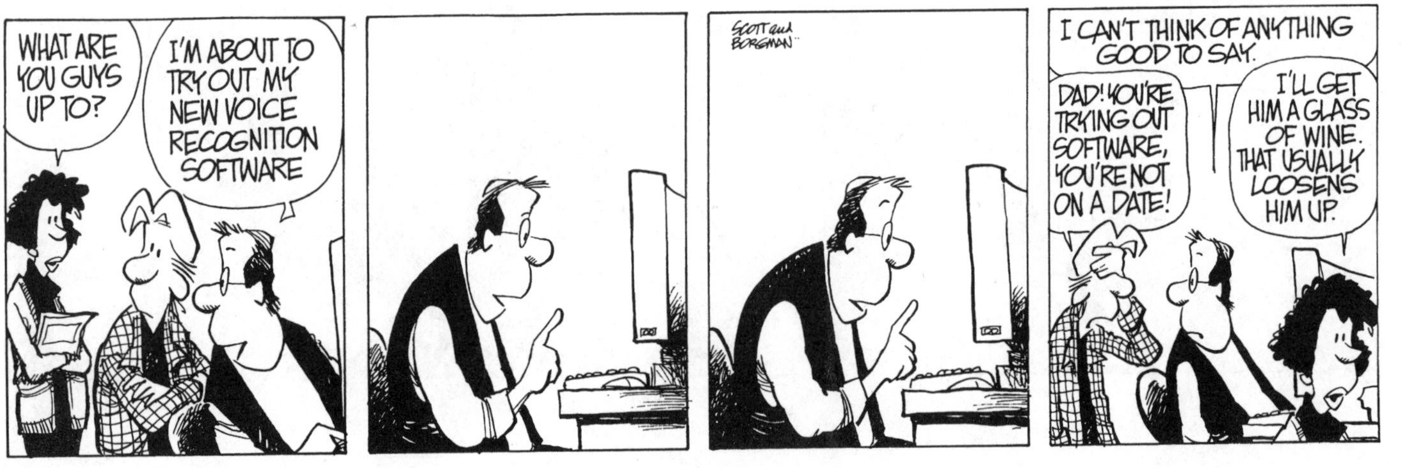
WHAT ARE YOU GUYS UP TO?
I'M ABOUT TO TRY OUT MY NEW VOICE RECOGNITION SOFTWARE
SCOTT and BORGMAN
I CAN'T THINK OF ANYTHING GOOD TO SAY.
DAD! YOU'RE TRYING OUT SOFTWARE, YOU'RE NOT ON A DATE!
I'LL GET HIM A GLASS OF WINE. THAT USUALLY LOOSENS HIM UP.

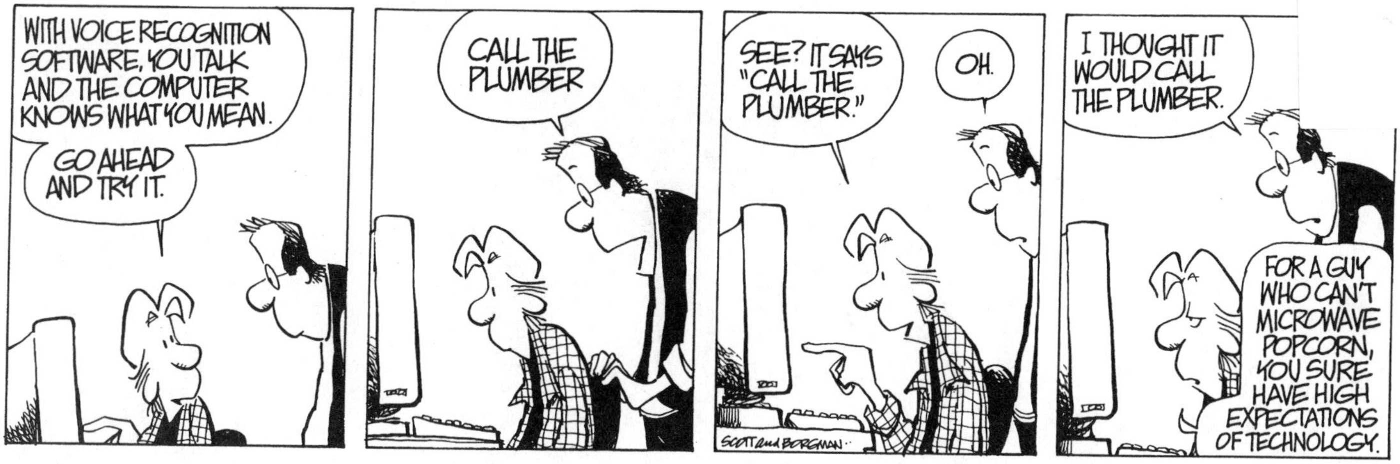
WITH VOICE RECOGNITION SOFTWARE, YOU TALK AND THE COMPUTER KNOWS WHAT YOU MEAN.
GO AHEAD AND TRY IT.
CALL THE PLUMBER
SEE? IT SAYS "CALL THE PLUMBER."
OH.
I THOUGHT IT WOULD CALL THE PLUMBER.
FOR A GUY WHO CAN'T MICROWAVE POPCORN, YOU SURE HAVE HIGH EXPECTATIONS OF TECHNOLOGY.
SCOTT and BORGMAN

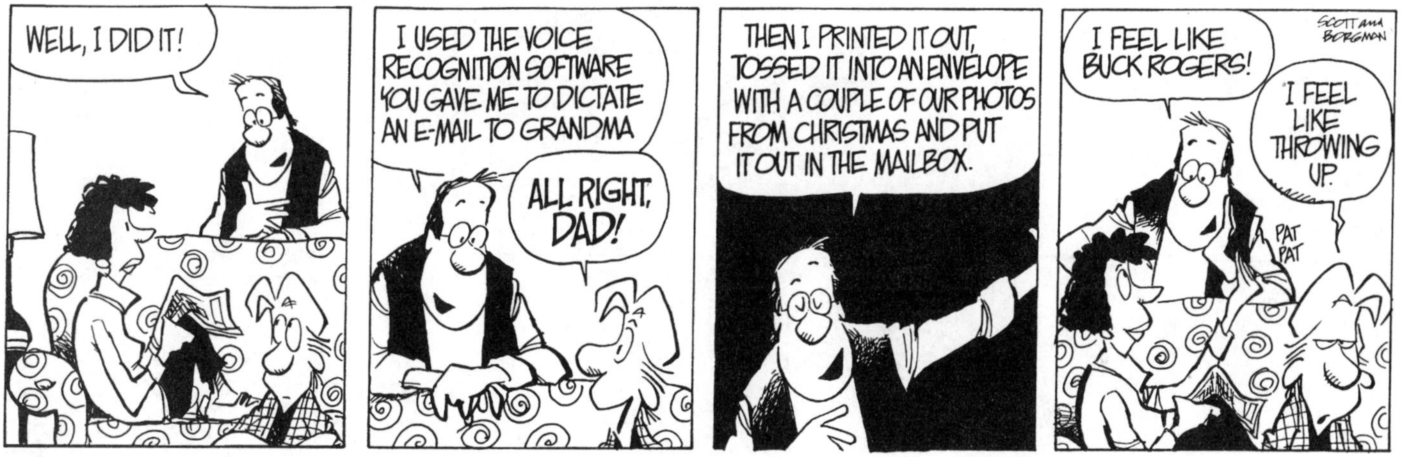
WELL, I DID IT!
I USED THE VOICE RECOGNITION SOFTWARE YOU GAVE ME TO DICTATE AN E-MAIL TO GRANDMA
ALL RIGHT, DAD!
THEN I PRINTED IT OUT, TOSSED IT INTO AN ENVELOPE WITH A COUPLE OF OUR PHOTOS FROM CHRISTMAS AND PUT IT OUT IN THE MAILBOX.
I FEEL LIKE BUCK ROGERS!
I FEEL LIKE THROWING UP.
PAT PAT
SCOTT and BORGMAN

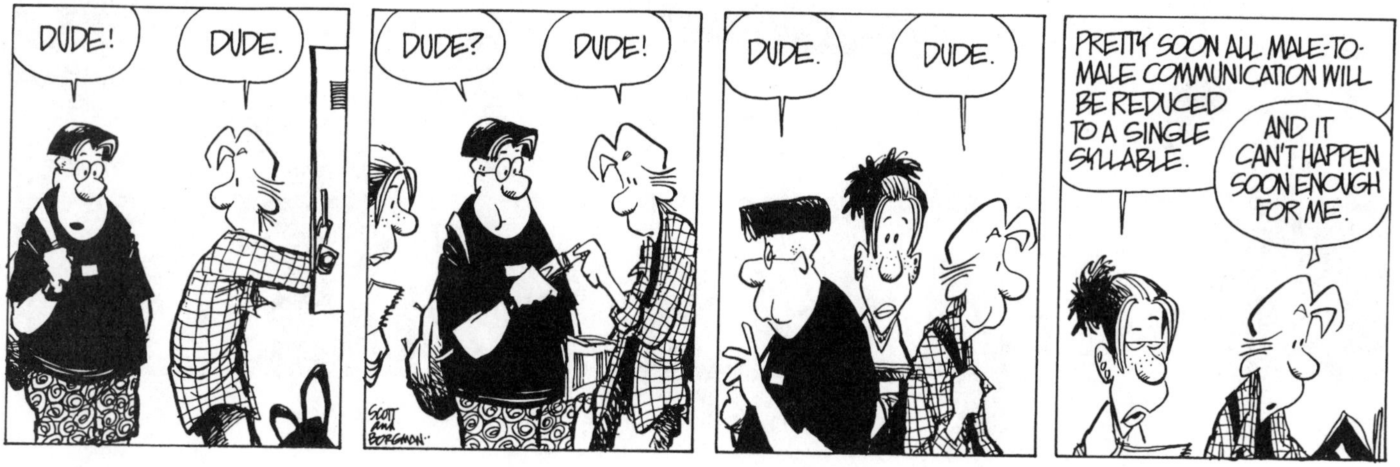
DUDE!
DUDE.
DUDE?
DUDE!
DUDE.
DUDE.
PRETTY SOON ALL MALE-TO-MALE COMMUNICATION WILL BE REDUCED TO A SINGLE SYLLABLE.
AND IT CAN'T HAPPEN SOON ENOUGH FOR ME.
SCOTT and BORGMAN

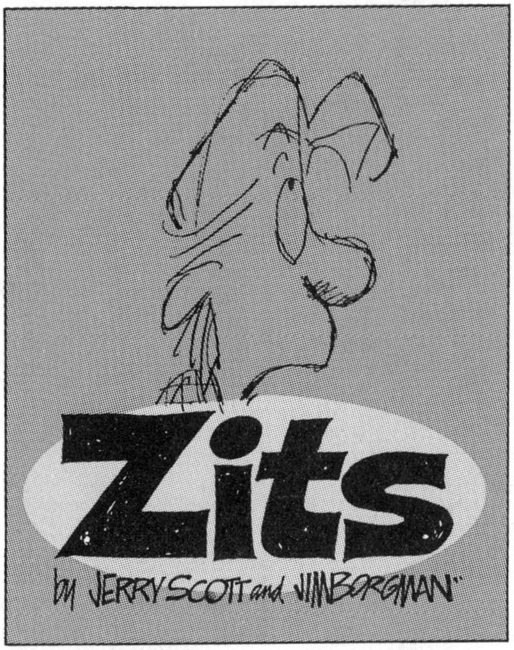
Zits
by JERRY SCOTT and JIM BORGMAN

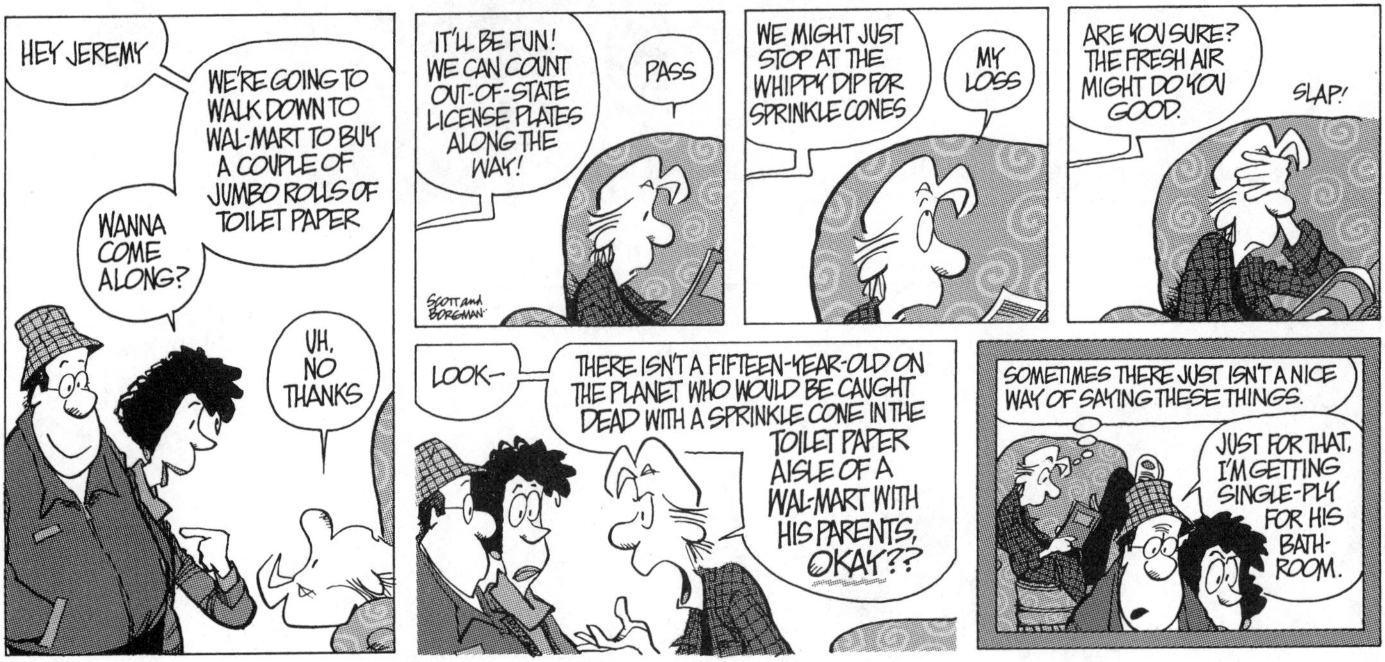
HEY JEREMY
WE'RE GOING TO WALK DOWN TO WAL-MART TO BUY A COUPLE OF JUMBO ROLLS OF TOILET PAPER
WANNA COME ALONG?
UH, NO THANKS
IT'LL BE FUN! WE CAN COUNT OUT-OF-STATE LICENSE PLATES ALONG THE WAY!
PASS
SCOTT and BORGMAN
WE MIGHT JUST STOP AT THE WHIPPY DIP FOR SPRINKLE CONES
MY LOSS
ARE YOU SURE? THE FRESH AIR MIGHT DO YOU GOOD.
SLAP!
LOOK—
THERE ISN'T A FIFTEEN-YEAR-OLD ON THE PLANET WHO WOULD BE CAUGHT DEAD WITH A SPRINKLE CONE IN THE TOILET PAPER AISLE OF A WAL-MART WITH HIS PARENTS, OKAY??
SOMETIMES THERE JUST ISN'T A NICE WAY OF SAYING THESE THINGS.
JUST FOR THAT, I'M GETTING SINGLE-PLY FOR HIS BATH-ROOM.

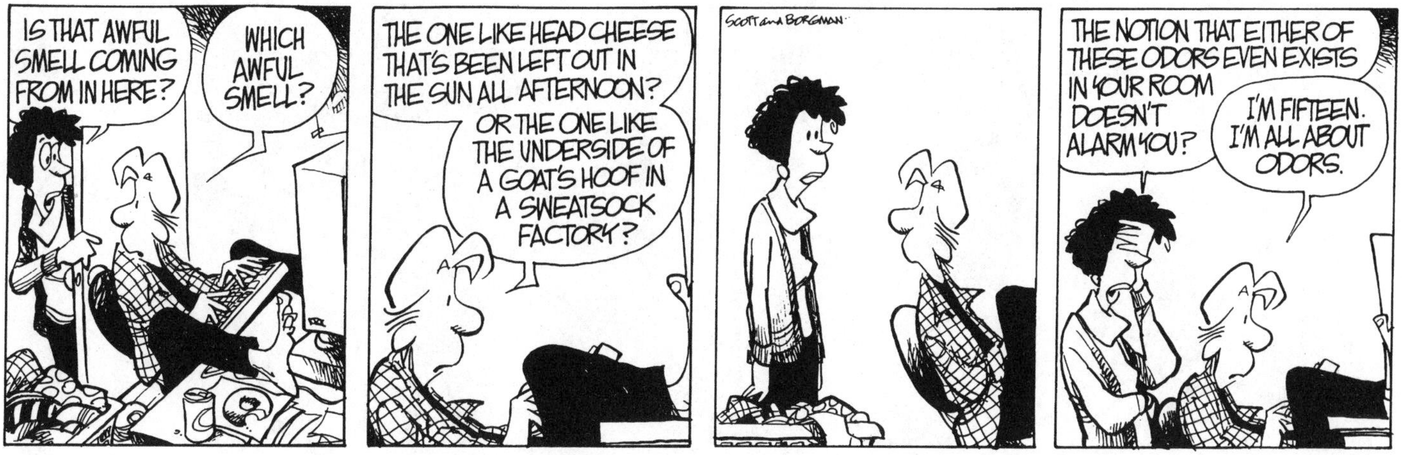
IS THAT AWFUL SMELL COMING FROM IN HERE?
WHICH AWFUL SMELL?
THE ONE LIKE HEAD CHEESE THAT'S BEEN LEFT OUT IN THE SUN ALL AFTERNOON?
OR THE ONE LIKE THE UNDERSIDE OF A GOAT'S HOOF IN A SWEATSOCK FACTORY?
SCOTT and BORGMAN
THE NOTION THAT EITHER OF THESE ODORS EVEN EXISTS IN YOUR ROOM DOESN'T ALARM YOU?
I'M FIFTEEN. I'M ALL ABOUT ODORS.

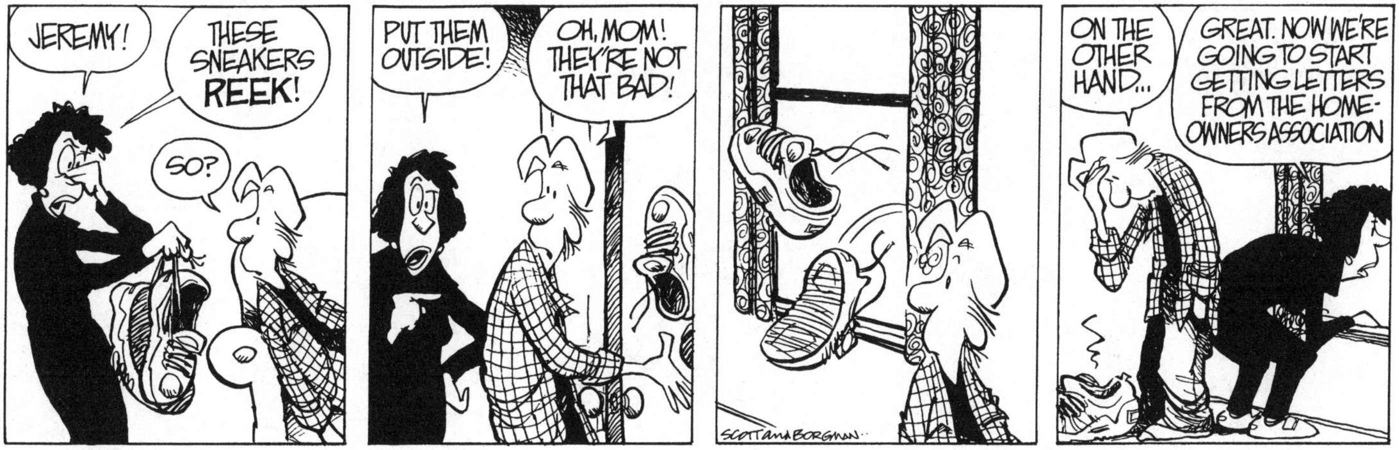
JEREMY!
THESE SNEAKERS **REEK**!
SO?
PUT THEM OUTSIDE!
OH, MOM! THEY'RE NOT THAT BAD!
SCOTT and BORGMAN
ON THE OTHER HAND...
GREAT. NOW WE'RE GOING TO START GETTING LETTERS FROM THE HOME-OWNERS ASSOCIATION

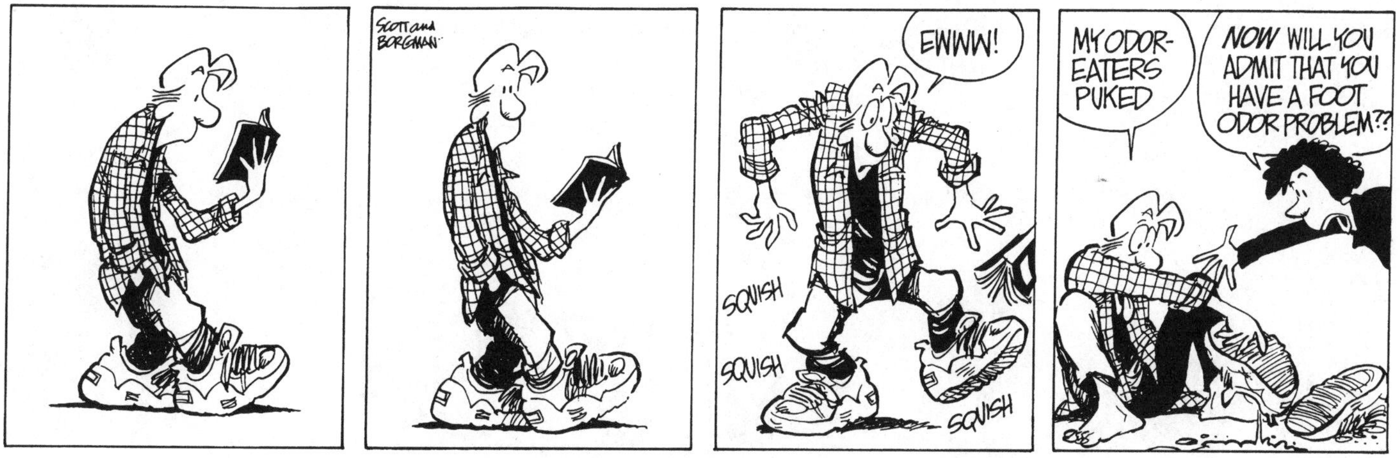
SCOTT and BORGMAN
EWWW!
SQUISH
SQUISH
SQUISH
MY ODOR-EATERS PUKED
*NOW* WILL YOU ADMIT THAT YOU HAVE A FOOT ODOR PROBLEM??

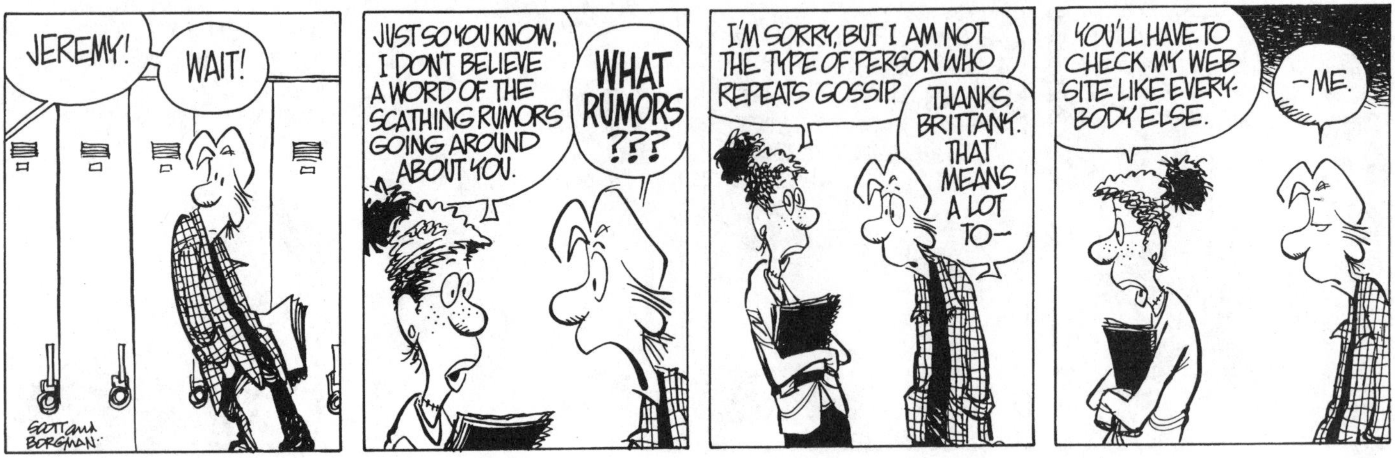
JEREMY!
WAIT!
JUST SO YOU KNOW, I DON'T BELIEVE A WORD OF THE SCATHING RUMORS GOING AROUND ABOUT YOU.
WHAT RUMORS ???
I'M SORRY, BUT I AM NOT THE TYPE OF PERSON WHO REPEATS GOSSIP.
THANKS, BRITTANY. THAT MEANS A LOT TO—
YOU'LL HAVE TO CHECK MY WEB SITE LIKE EVERYBODY ELSE.
—ME.

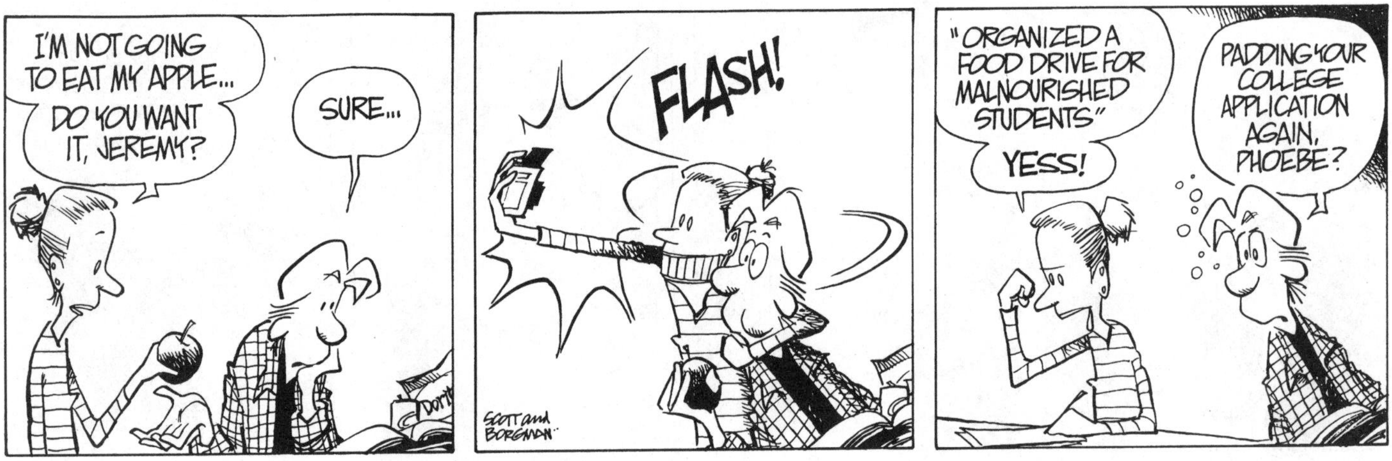
I'M NOT GOING TO EAT MY APPLE...
DO YOU WANT IT, JEREMY?
SURE...
FLASH!
"ORGANIZED A FOOD DRIVE FOR MALNOURISHED STUDENTS"
YESS!
PADDING YOUR COLLEGE APPLICATION AGAIN, PHOEBE?

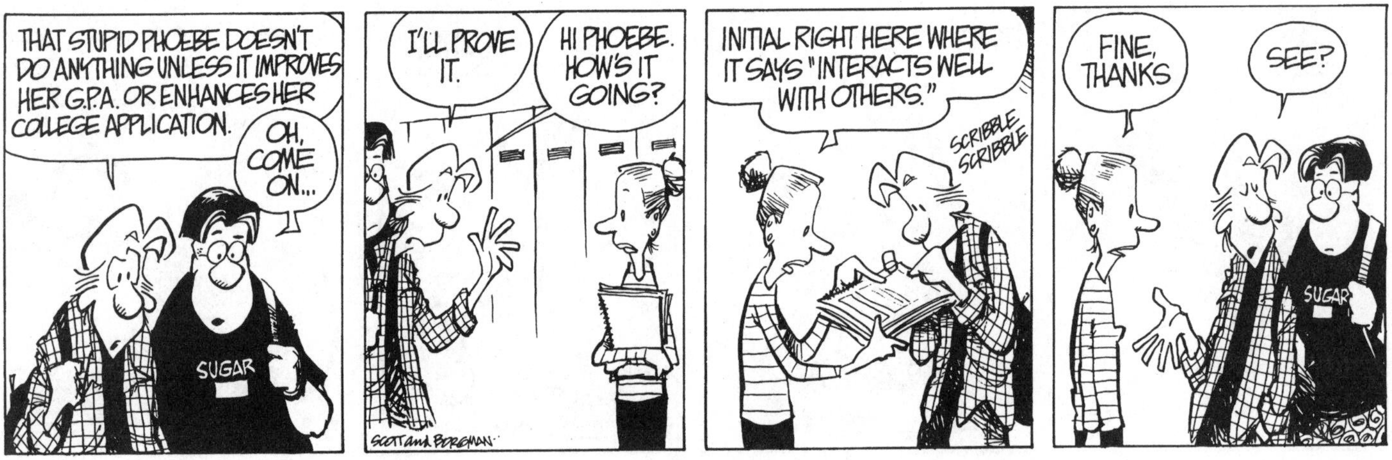
THAT STUPID PHOEBE DOESN'T DO ANYTHING UNLESS IT IMPROVES HER G.P.A. OR ENHANCES HER COLLEGE APPLICATION.
OH, COME ON...
SUGAR
I'LL PROVE IT.
HI PHOEBE. HOW'S IT GOING?
INITIAL RIGHT HERE WHERE IT SAYS "INTERACTS WELL WITH OTHERS."
SCRIBBLE SCRIBBLE
FINE, THANKS
SEE?
SUGAR

Zits
by
JERRY SCOTT and
JIM BORGMAN

A SKULL WEARING A BARBED WIRE COWBOY HAT, WITH A SNAKE CRAWLING OUT OF THE LEFT EYE SOCKET, OVER CROSSED STRATOCASTERS
ONE OR TWO COLORS OF INK... VERY TASTEFUL... TATTOOED ABOUT THIS SIZE RIGHT HERE.
SO
WHAT DO YOU THINK?
WHY DON'T WE JUST HAVE GRANDMA EMBROIDER THE WORD "LOSER" ACROSS YOUR FOREHEAD IN BRIGHT RED LETTERS INSTEAD?
I'LL GO CALL HER NOW
SO, THAT WAS A "NO"?
SCOTT and BORGMAN

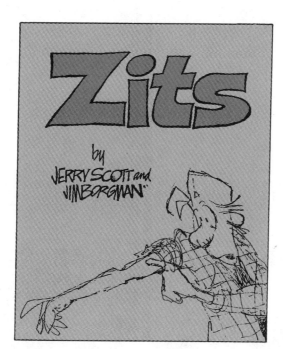

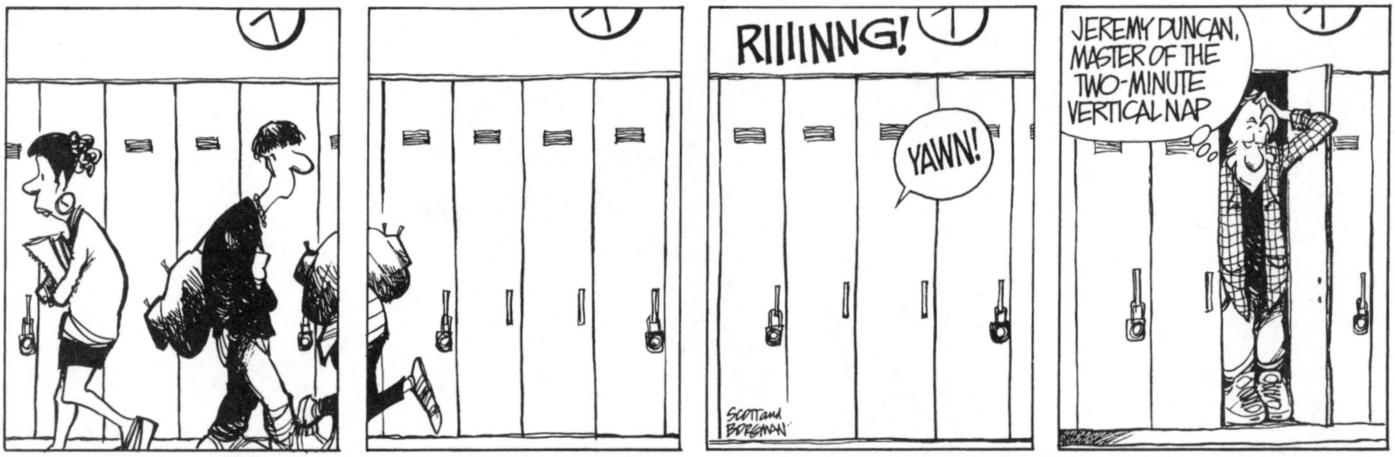
RIIIINNG!
YAWN!
JEREMY DUNCAN, MASTER OF THE TWO-MINUTE VERTICAL NAP

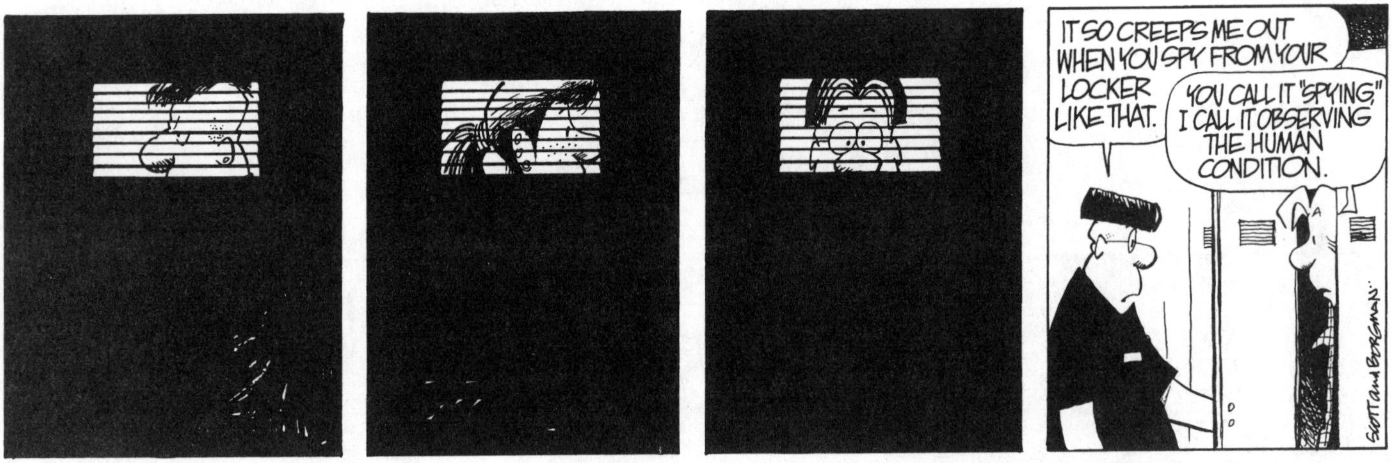
IT SO CREEPS ME OUT WHEN YOU SPY FROM YOUR LOCKER LIKE THAT.
YOU CALL IT "SPYING," I CALL IT OBSERVING THE HUMAN CONDITION.

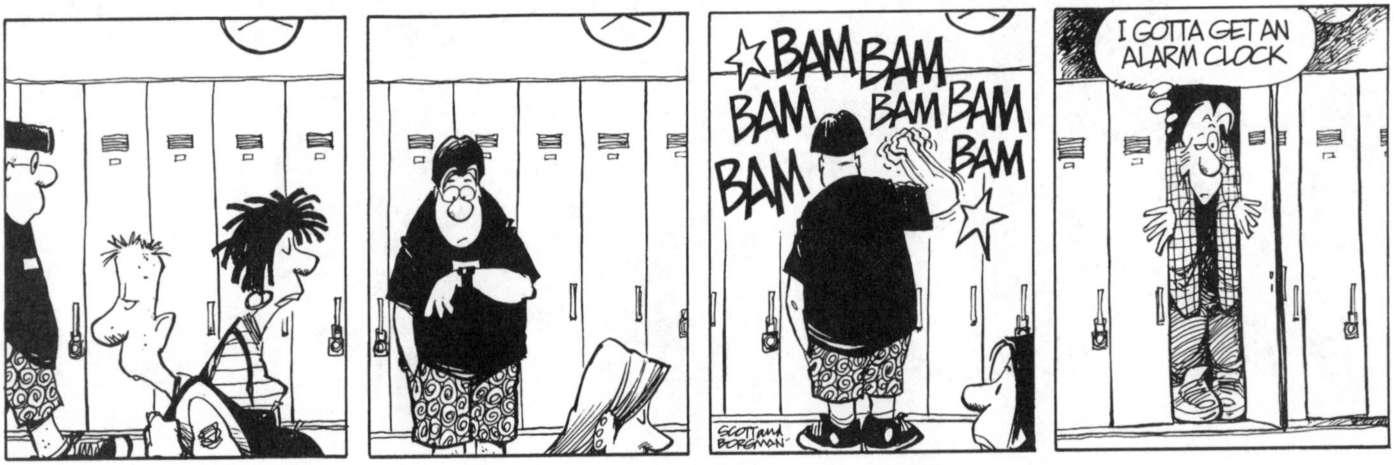
BAM BAM BAM BAM BAM BAM BAM
I GOTTA GET AN ALARM CLOCK

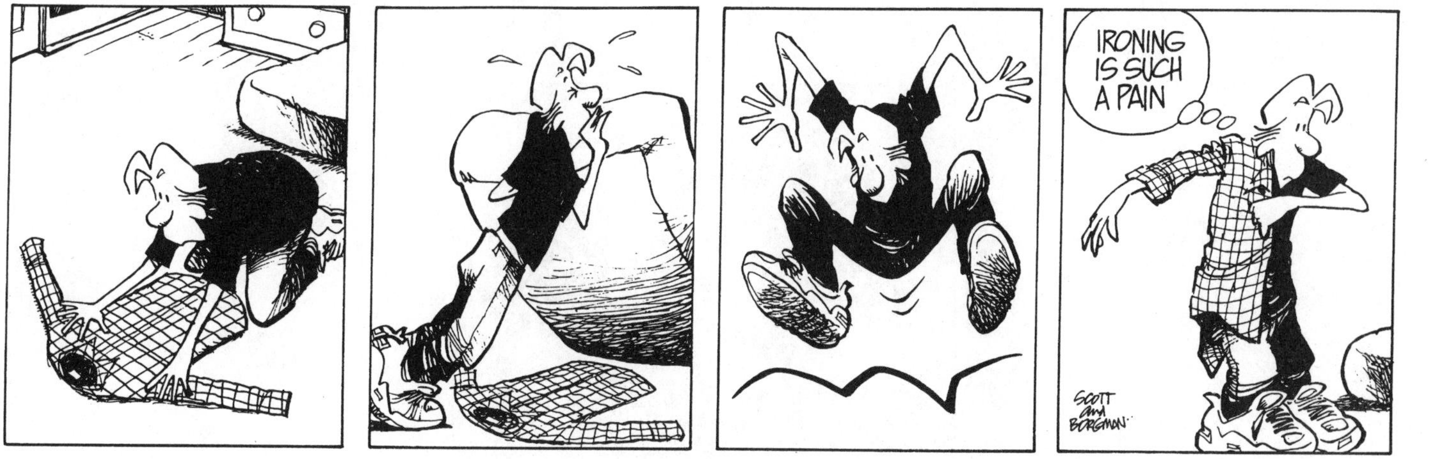
IRONING IS SUCH A PAIN
SCOTT AND BORGMAN

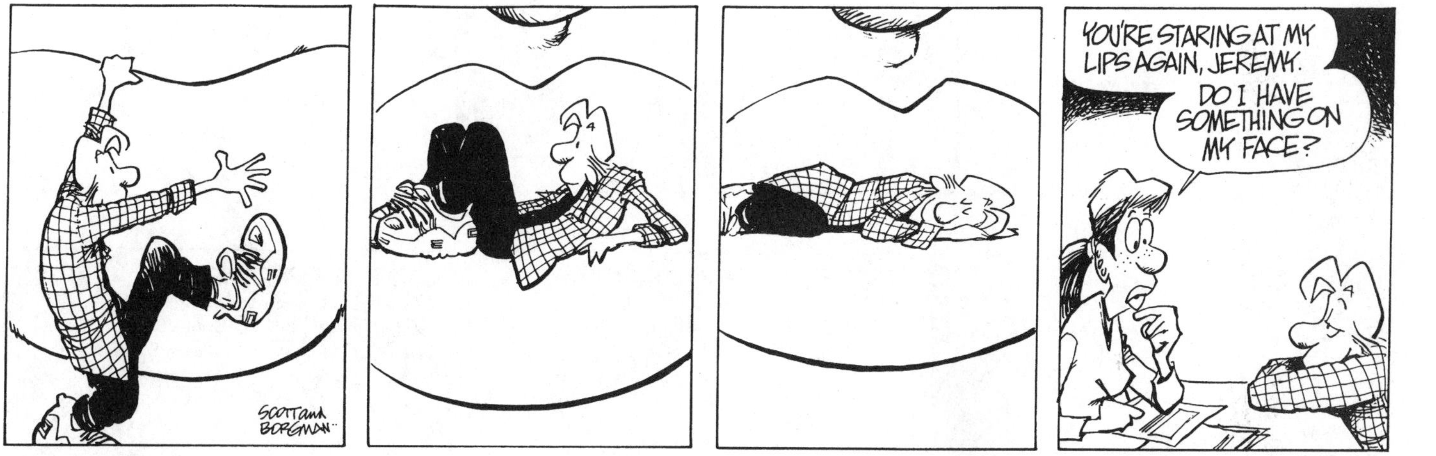
SCOTT AND BORGMAN
YOU'RE STARING AT MY LIPS AGAIN, JEREMY.
DO I HAVE SOMETHING ON MY FACE?

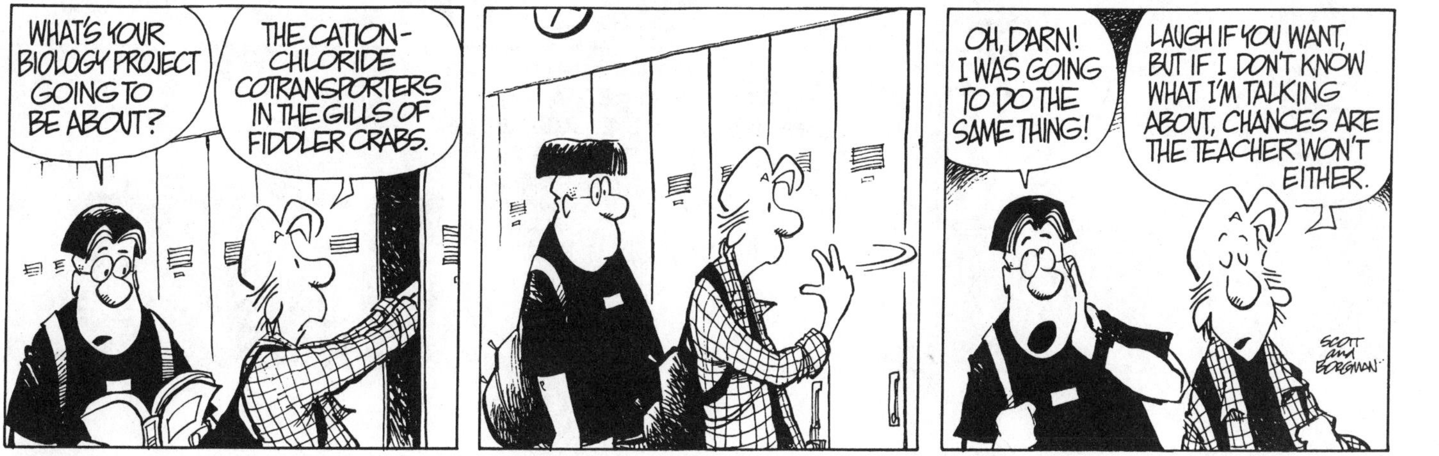
WHAT'S YOUR BIOLOGY PROJECT GOING TO BE ABOUT?
THE CATION-CHLORIDE COTRANSPORTERS IN THE GILLS OF FIDDLER CRABS.
OH, DARN! I WAS GOING TO DO THE SAME THING!
LAUGH IF YOU WANT, BUT IF I DON'T KNOW WHAT I'M TALKING ABOUT, CHANCES ARE THE TEACHER WON'T EITHER.
SCOTT AND BORGMAN

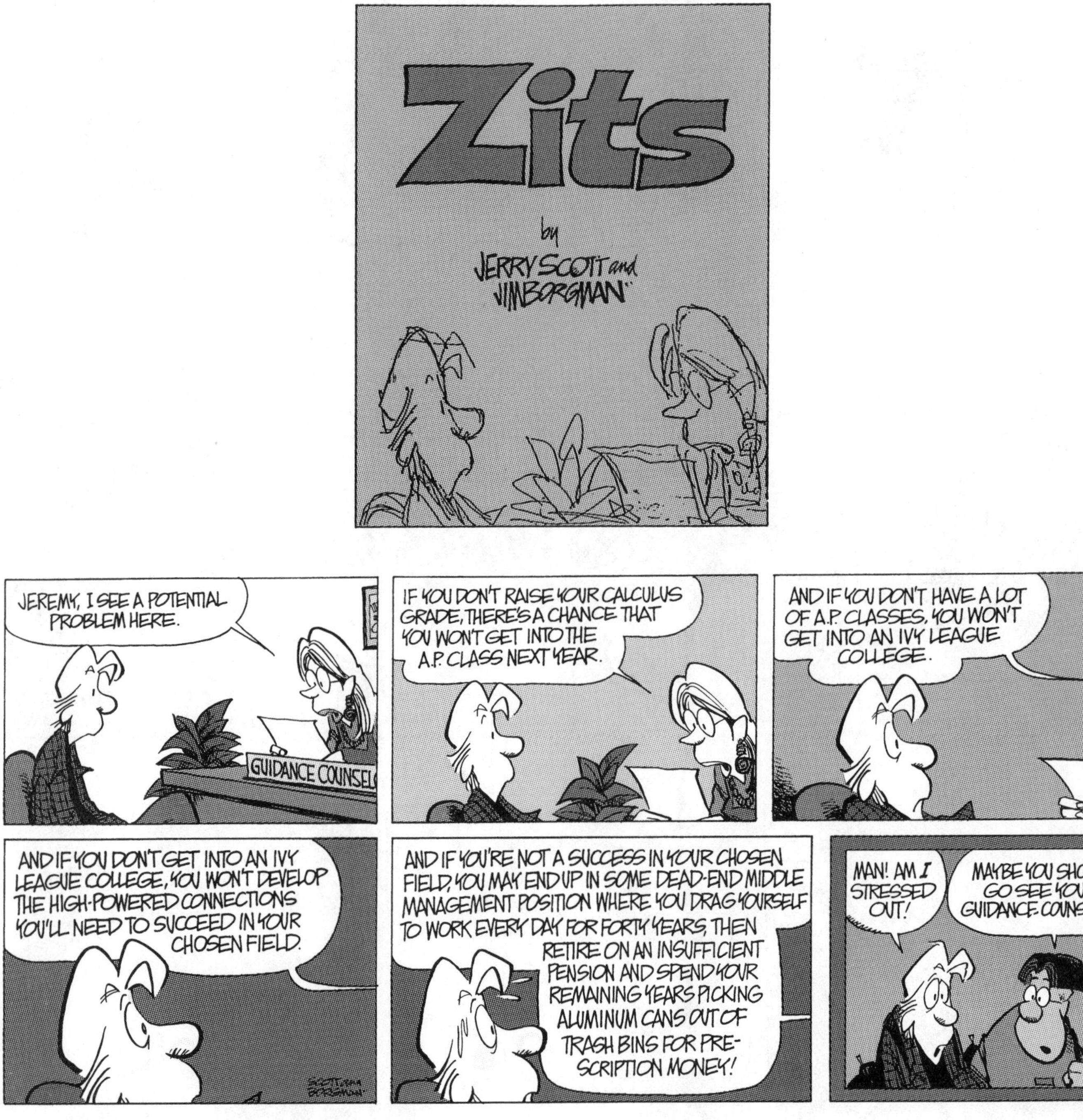
Zits
by
JERRY SCOTT and
JIM BORGMAN
JEREMY, I SEE A POTENTIAL PROBLEM HERE.
GUIDANCE COUNSEL
IF YOU DON'T RAISE YOUR CALCULUS GRADE, THERE'S A CHANCE THAT YOU WON'T GET INTO THE A.P. CLASS NEXT YEAR.
AND IF YOU DON'T HAVE A LOT OF A.P. CLASSES, YOU WON'T GET INTO AN IVY LEAGUE COLLEGE.
AND IF YOU DON'T GET INTO AN IVY LEAGUE COLLEGE, YOU WON'T DEVELOP THE HIGH-POWERED CONNECTIONS YOU'LL NEED TO SUCCEED IN YOUR CHOSEN FIELD.
AND IF YOU'RE NOT A SUCCESS IN YOUR CHOSEN FIELD, YOU MAY END UP IN SOME DEAD-END MIDDLE MANAGEMENT POSITION WHERE YOU DRAG YOURSELF TO WORK EVERY DAY FOR FORTY YEARS, THEN RETIRE ON AN INSUFFICIENT PENSION AND SPEND YOUR REMAINING YEARS PICKING ALUMINUM CANS OUT OF TRASH BINS FOR PRESCRIPTION MONEY!
MAN! AM I STRESSED OUT!
MAYBE YOU SHOULD GO SEE YOUR GUIDANCE COUNSELOR

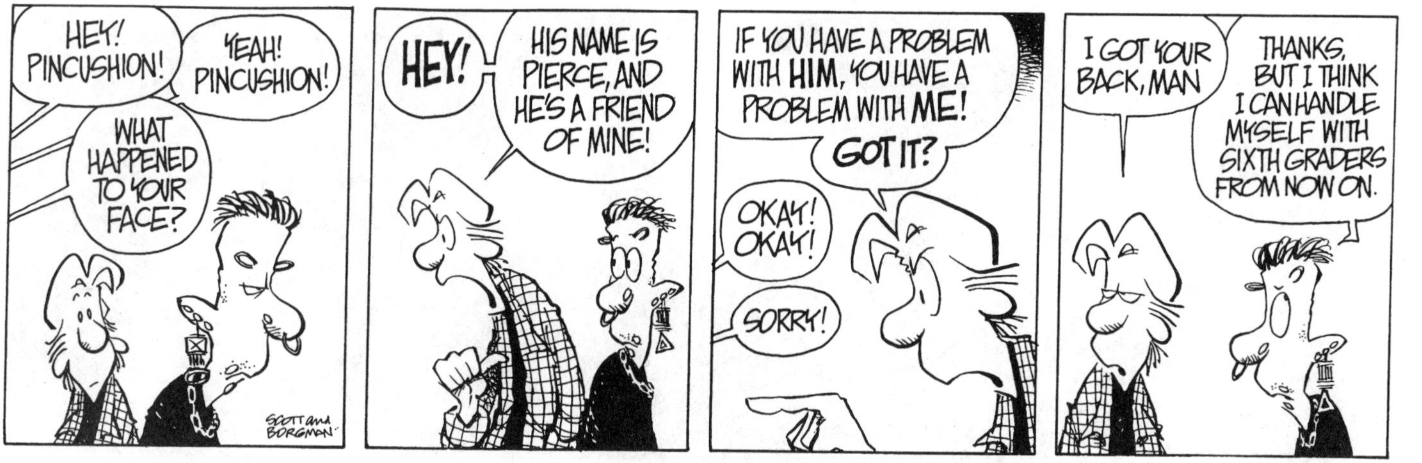
HEY! PINCUSHION!
YEAH! PINCUSHION!
WHAT HAPPENED TO YOUR FACE?
SCOTT AND BORGMAN
HEY!
HIS NAME IS PIERCE, AND HE'S A FRIEND OF MINE!
IF YOU HAVE A PROBLEM WITH HIM, YOU HAVE A PROBLEM WITH ME!
GOT IT?
OKAY! OKAY!
SORRY!
I GOT YOUR BACK, MAN
THANKS, BUT I THINK I CAN HANDLE MYSELF WITH SIXTH GRADERS FROM NOW ON.

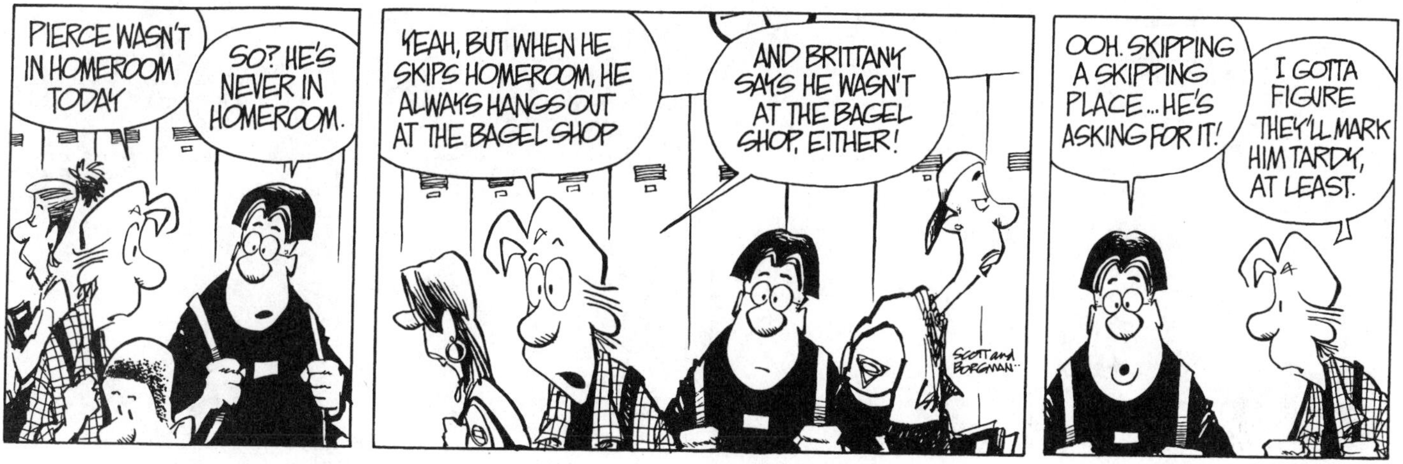
PIERCE WASN'T IN HOMEROOM TODAY
SO? HE'S NEVER IN HOMEROOM.
YEAH, BUT WHEN HE SKIPS HOMEROOM, HE ALWAYS HANGS OUT AT THE BAGEL SHOP
AND BRITTANY SAYS HE WASN'T AT THE BAGEL SHOP, EITHER!
SCOTT AND BORGMAN
OOH. SKIPPING A SKIPPING PLACE... HE'S ASKING FOR IT!
I GOTTA FIGURE THEY'LL MARK HIM TARDY, AT LEAST.

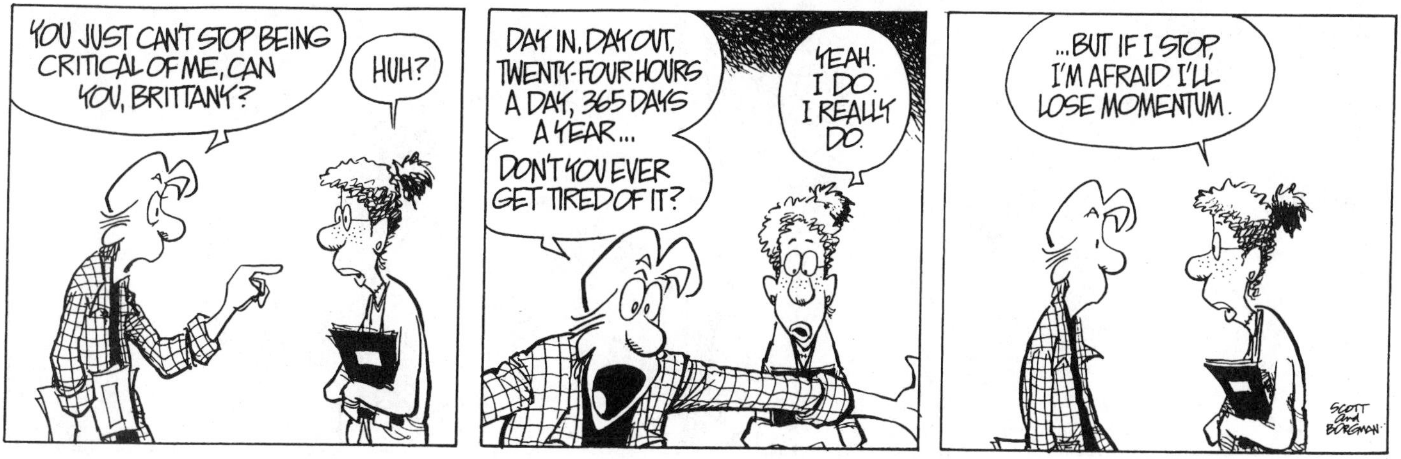
YOU JUST CAN'T STOP BEING CRITICAL OF ME, CAN YOU, BRITTANY?
HUH?
DAY IN, DAY OUT, TWENTY-FOUR HOURS A DAY, 365 DAYS A YEAR...
DON'T YOU EVER GET TIRED OF IT?
YEAH. I DO. I REALLY DO.
...BUT IF I STOP, I'M AFRAID I'LL LOSE MOMENTUM.
SCOTT AND BORGMAN

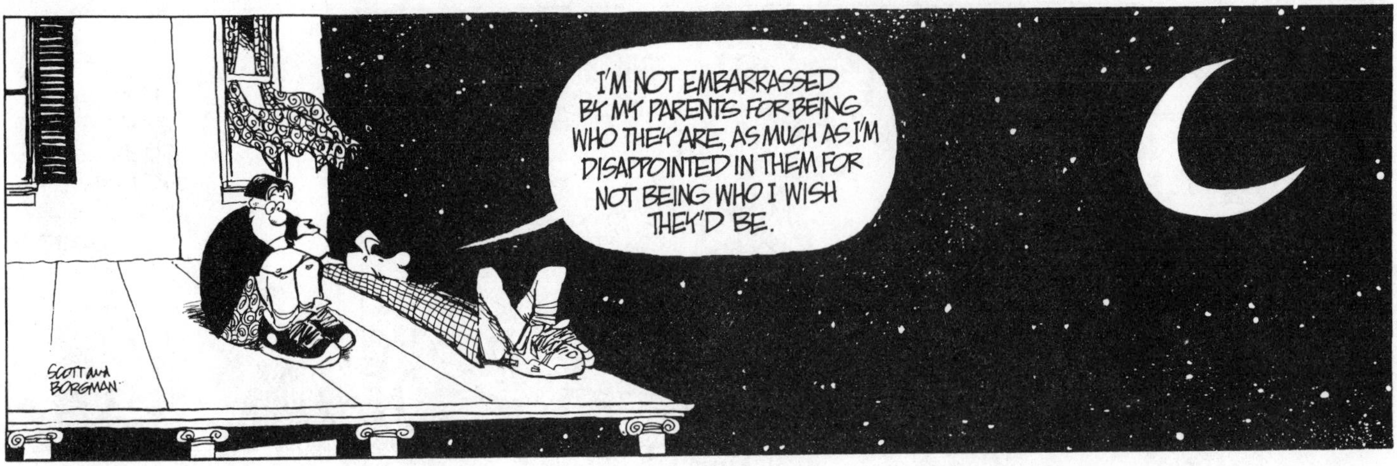
I'M NOT EMBARRASSED BY MY PARENTS FOR BEING WHO THEY ARE, AS MUCH AS I'M DISAPPOINTED IN THEM FOR NOT BEING WHO I WISH THEY'D BE.
SCOTT and BORGMAN

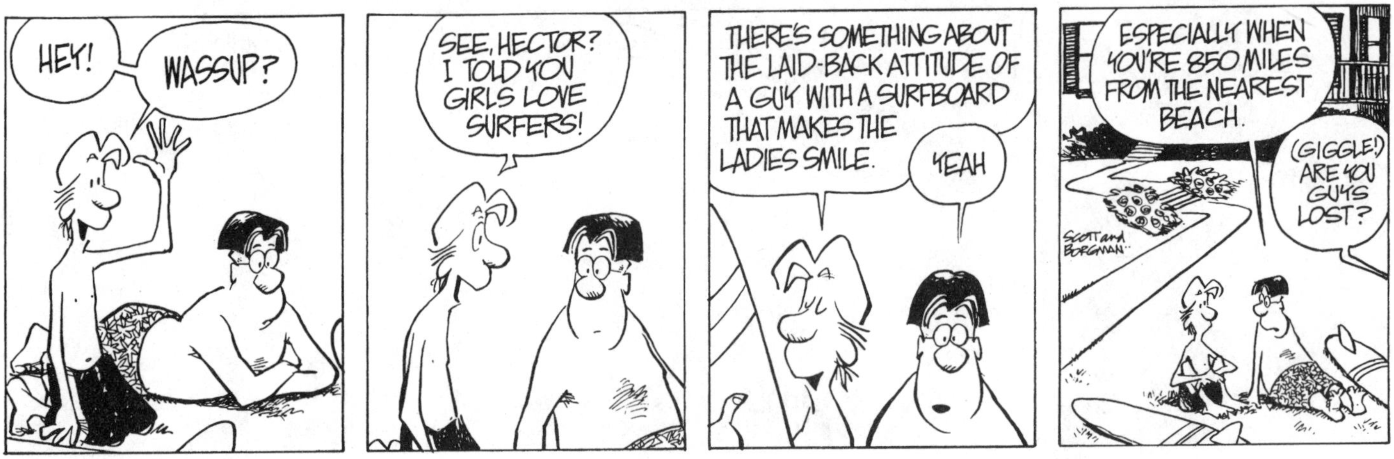
HEY!
WASSUP?
SEE, HECTOR? I TOLD YOU GIRLS LOVE SURFERS!
THERE'S SOMETHING ABOUT THE LAID-BACK ATTITUDE OF A GUY WITH A SURFBOARD THAT MAKES THE LADIES SMILE.
YEAH
ESPECIALLY WHEN YOU'RE 850 MILES FROM THE NEAREST BEACH.
(GIGGLE!) ARE YOU GUYS LOST?
SCOTT and BORGMAN

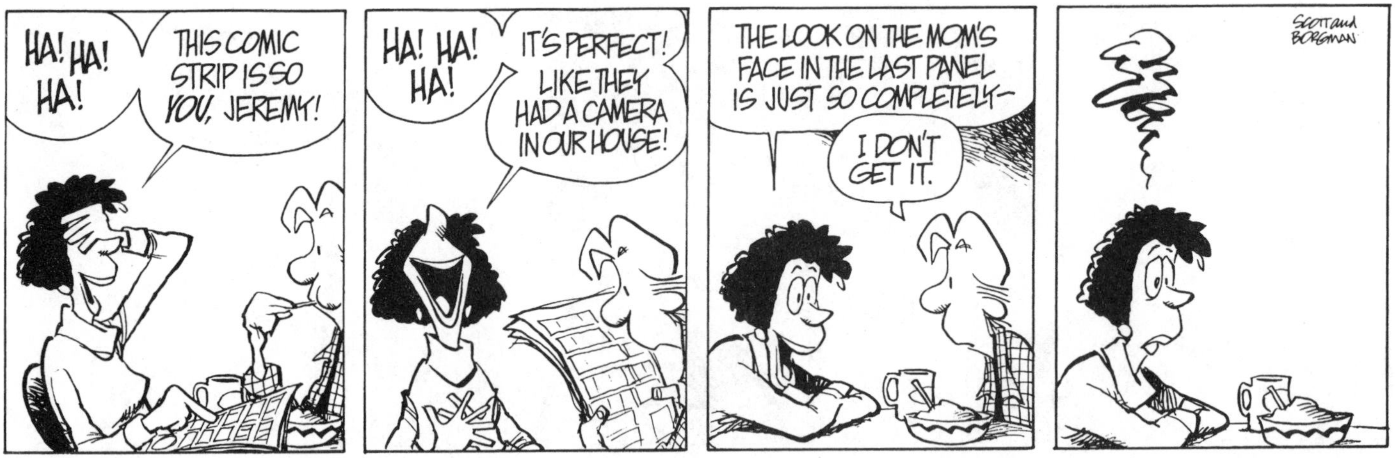
HA! HA! HA!
THIS COMIC STRIP IS SO YOU, JEREMY!
HA! HA! HA!
IT'S PERFECT! LIKE THEY HAD A CAMERA IN OUR HOUSE!
THE LOOK ON THE MOM'S FACE IN THE LAST PANEL IS JUST SO COMPLETELY—
I DON'T GET IT.
SCOTT and BORGMAN